THE MISSIONS OF JESUS AND THE DISCIPLES
ACCORDING TO THE FOURTH GOSPEL

The Missions of Jesus and the Disciples according to the Fourth Gospel

With Implications for the Fourth Gospel's Purpose and the Mission of the Contemporary Church

Andreas J. Köstenberger

WILLIAM B. EERDMANS PUBLISHING COMPANY
GRAND RAPIDS, MICHIGAN / CAMBRIDGE, U.K.

© 1998 Wm. B. Eerdmans Publishing Co.
255 Jefferson Ave. S.E., Grand Rapids, Michigan 49503 /
P.O. Box 163, Cambridge CB3 9PU U.K.

Printed in the United States of America

02 01 00 99 98   7 6 5 4 3 2 1

Library of Congress Cataloging-in-Publication Data

Köstenberger, Andreas J., 1957 —
The missions of Jesus and the disciples according to the Fourth Gospel:
with implications for the Fourth Gospel's purpose and the mission
of the contemporary church / Andreas J. Köstenberger.
p.   cm.
Includes bibliographical references and index.
ISBN 0-8028-4255-0 (pbk.: alk. paper)
1. Bible. N.T. John — Language, style.
2. Greek, Biblical — Semantics.
3. Missions — Theory.
I. Title.
BS2440.K67 1998
226.5'06 — dc21   97-35709
                                   CIP

Contents

CHAPTER 3
THE MISSION OF JESUS
ACCORDING TO THE FOURTH GOSPEL

CHAPTER 4
THE MISSION OF THE DISCIPLESR
ACCORDING TO THE FOURTH GOSPEL

CHAPTER 5
IMPLICATIONS

For my beloved wife:
cherished companion,
best friend
(Prov. 31:10-31)

Abbreviations

AnBib	Analecta Biblica
ATANT	Abhandlungen zur Theologie des Alten und Neuen Testaments
ATR	*Anglican Theological Review*
AusBR	*Australian Biblical Review*
BBB	Bonner biblische Beiträge
BBET	Beiträge zur biblischen Exegese und Theologie
BBR	*Bulletin of Biblical Research*
BECNT	Baker Exegetical Commentary on the New Testament
BETL	Bibliotheca ephemeridum theologicarum lovaniensium
BFCT	Beiträge zur Förderung christlicher Theologie
BHT	Beiträge zur historischen Theologie
Bib	*Biblica*
BibLeb	*Bibel und Leben*
BibRes	*Biblical Research*
BJRL	*Bulletin of the John Rylands University Library of Manchester*
BR	*Biblical Research*
BSRel	Biblioteca di Scienze Religiose
BTB	*Biblical Theology Bulletin*
BU	Biblische Untersuchungen
BZ	*Biblische Zeitschrift*
BZNW	Beihefte zur Zeitschrift für neutestamentliche Wissenschaft
CBQ	*Catholic Biblical Quarterly*
Chr	*Christus*
CJT	*Canadian Journal of Theology*
ConBNT	Coniectanea Biblica, New Testament
ConNT	Coniectanea neotestamentica
CQR	*Church Quarterly Review*
CrisTR	*Criswell Theological Review*
CurTM	*Currents in Theology and Mission*

EBC	Expositor's Bible Commentary
EHS	Europäische Hochschulschriften
EKKNT.V	Evangelisch-katholischer Kommentar zum Neuen Testament, Vorarbeiten
EMQ	*Evangelical Missions Quarterly*
EMZ	*Evangelische Missions-Zeitschrift*
EstBib	*Estudios bíblicos*
ETL	*Ephemerides theologicae lovanienses*
EvQ	*Evangelical Quarterly*
EvT	*Evangelische Theologie*
ExpTim	*Expository Times*
FB	Forschung zur Bibel
FRLANT	Forschungen zur Religion und Literatur des Alten und Neuen Testaments
FTS	Frankfurter Theologische Studien
FThSt	Freiburger Theologische Studien
HTKNT	Herders theologischer Kommentar zum Neuen Testament
HUT	Hermeneutische Untersuchungen zur Theologie
IDB	*Interpreter's Dictionary of the Bible*
IKZ	*Internationale Kirchliche Zeitschrift*
Int	*Interpretation*
IRT	Issues in Religion and Theology
ITQ	*Irish Theological Quarterly*
JAAR	*Journal of the American Academy of Religion*
JBL	*Journal of Biblical Literature*
JETS	*Journal of the Evangelical Theological Society*
JSNT	*Journal for the Study of the New Testament*
JSNTSup	Journal for the Study of the New Testament — Supplement Series
JTS	*Journal of Theological Studies*
KD	*Kerygma und Dogma*
MT	*Melito Theologica*
Neot	*Neotestamentica*
NICNT	New International Commentary on the New Testament
NIDNTT	*New International Dictionary of New Testament Theology*
NovT	*Novum Testamentum*
NovTSup	Novum Testamentum, Supplements
NRT	*La nouvelle revue théologique*
NTAbh	Neutestamentliche Abhandlungen
NTOA	Novum Testamentum et Orbis Antiquus
NTS	*New Testament Studies*
OBO	Orbis biblicus et Orientalis
QD	Quaestiones Disputatae

RBib	Recherches Bibliques
RevExp	*Review and Expositor*
RevistB	*Revista bíblica*
RHPR	*Revue d'histoire et de philosophie religieuses*
RivB	*Rivista biblica*
RSR	*Recherches de science religieuse*
RTR	*Reformed Theological Review*
SANT	Studien zum Alten und Neuen Testament
SBLDS	Society of Biblical Literature Dissertation Series
SBS	Stuttgarter Bibelstudien
SBT	Studies in Biblical Theology
SBT	*Studia biblica et theologica*
SE	*Studia Evangelica*
SJT	*Scottish Journal of Theology*
SNTSMS	Society for New Testament Studies Monograph Series
TBei	*Theologische Beiträge*
TDNT	*Theological Dictionary of the New Testament*
Them	*Themelios*
ThStud	Theologische Studien
TLZ	*Theologische Literaturzeitung*
TrinJ	*Trinity Journal*
TU	Texte und Untersuchungen
TynBul	*Tyndale Bulletin*
TZ	*Theologische Zeitschrift*
WBC	Word Biblical Commentary
WMANT	Wissenschaftliche Monographien zum Alten und Neuen Testament
WTJ	*Westminster Theological Journal*
WUNT	Wissenschaftliche Untersuchungen zum Neuen Testament
WW	*Word and World*
ZNW	*Zeitschrift für die neutestamentliche Wissenschaft*
ZRGG	*Zeitschrift für Religions- und Geistesgeschichte*
ZTK	*Zeitschrift für Theologie und Kirche*
ZVRW	*Zeitschrift für vergleichende Rechtswissenschaft*

Lists of Figures and Excursuses

FIGURES

EXCURSUSES

Preface

The present work represents a revision of my doctoral dissertation, completed under Prof. D. A. Carson at Trinity Evangelical Divinity School in December 1993. I want to take this opportunity to express my gratitude to Dr. Carson for his formative influence on my theological apprehension of the Fourth Gospel and my scholarly work. Thanks are also due Dr. G. R. Osborne, second reader of my dissertation, and Dr. W. J. Larkin, my first mentor at Columbia Biblical Seminary. Space fails me to acknowledge all those who have contributed to the present study in some way; they may not find their names here, but I will not forget their friendship and support along the way.

Since the present work has entered the editorial process, I have read with benefit, among other works, B. Witherington's *John's Wisdom*, P. Anderson's *The Christology of the Fourth Gospel*, G. Van Belle's *The Signs Source in the Fourth Gospel*, R. G. Maccini's *Her Testimony Is True*, and A. Obermann's *Die christologische Erfüllung der Schrift im Johannesevangelium*. I have reviewed all of these works for various scholarly journals. However, I chose not to incorporate interactions with these studies into the existing manuscript in order not to compromise the integrity of the present investigation as it was originally conceived. None of these works affects the substance of the present study.

The following articles of mine appeared in recent years disseminating the substance of some of the material published here for the first time in full: "The 'Greater Works' of the Believer According to John 14:12," *Didaskalia* 6 (1995): 36-45; "The Seventh Johannine Sign: A Study in John's Christology," *BBR* 5 (1995): 87-103; and "The Challenge of a Systematized Biblical Theology: Missiological Insights from the Gospel of John," *Missiology* 23 (1995): 445-64. "The Two Johannine Words for Sending: A Study of John's Use of Words with Reference to General Linguistic Theory" is to appear in a forthcoming collection of essays entitled *Linguistics and the New Testament: Critical Junctions*, ed. S. E. Porter and D. A. Carson, JSNTSup (Sheffield: Sheffield Academic Press). I would also like to refer the reader to my forthcoming article "Jesus as Rabbi in the Fourth Gospel"

(*BBR* 8 [1998]), which goes beyond the present work and supplements it at several points.

Finally, the vision for the comprehensive biblical teaching on mission mentioned in the closing chapter of the present work is about to become a reality, at least *in nuce,* through the forthcoming work I am coauthoring with P. T. O'Brien, tentatively titled *Salvation unto the Ends of the Earth: A Biblical Theology of Mission* (New Studies in Biblical Theology; Leicester: IVP/Grand Rapids: Wm. B. Eerdmans). May the present study benefit not merely the scholarly world but also the contemporary church, as it strives to be both biblical and relevant in its mission.

This study is dedicated to my dear wife, with gratitude and rejoicing.

Soli Deo Gloria.

ANDREAS J. KÖSTENBERGER

Introduction

The word "mission," similar to the term "discipleship," is commonplace in the contemporary church. Young people may go on a short-term mission or prospective missionaries join a mission agency. In theological writings, too, the expression "mission" is ubiquitous. Numerous studies on mission in various portions of Scripture have appeared in recent years.[1] Reference is regularly made to the "mission of Jesus" or "the mission of Paul." Clearly, however, the term "mission" does not have the same meaning in all of the above uses. One aspect of its range of meaning has to do with the cross-cultural dimension of the proclamation of the gospel. Another sense of the word roughly equates "mission" with "ministry," perhaps invoking a person's sense of call or purpose.

In the midst of this terminological diversity, it is not always easy to maintain precision and clarity in dialogue and scholarly discourse. The question also arises as to what extent the different uses of the word "mission" are tied to *biblical* words or concepts. To complicate matters, different biblical authors may vary in their mission terminology and theology. Thus it becomes important to speak of *John's* or *Matthew's* mission concept before tying the various strands of biblical teaching on mission together.

With the blooming of missiology into a full-fledged academic discipline, perhaps biblical scholars have yielded too much territory to it. Also, at times the communication between missiologists and biblical scholars itself has been disturbed, or has been absent altogether. In light of these developments, it would seem desirable to return to the various corpora of Scripture in a search for the

---

1. Cf., e.g., Mortimer Arias and Alan Johnson, *The Great Commission: Biblical Models for Evangelism* (Nashville: Abingdon, 1992); David J. Bosch, *Transforming Mission: Paradigm Shifts in Theology of Mission* (Maryknoll, N.Y.: Orbis, 1991); Z. Kato, *Die Völkermission im Markusevangelium,* EHS 23/252 (Frankfurt am Main: Peter Lang, 1986); Karl Kertelge, ed., *Mission im Neuen Testament,* QD 93 (Freiburg: Herder, 1982); R. Uro, *Sheep Among the Wolves: A Study on the Mission Instruction of Q* (Helsinki: Suomalainen Tiedeakatemia, 1987); S. G. Wilson, *The Gentiles and the Gentile Mission in Luke-Acts,* SNTSMS 23 (Cambridge: Cambridge University Press, 1973).

respective biblical theologies of mission. Out of these biblical-theological studies, a biblical theology of mission could eventually be synthesized. This biblical
theology, in turn, could then function as the basis for the mission practice of
the contemporary church.

It is the purpose of the present study to make a contribution toward such
a project by providing an investigation of the Fourth Gospel's teaching on
mission. While considerable work has been done on this subject in recent years,
it remains to integrate the findings of the respective monographs into a
balanced, comprehensive synthesis.[2] The work is conceived as a conceptual
study that seeks to locate relevant Johannine mission terminology and to explore
the relationships of its various component parts to one another. The primary
concern will be a firsthand exploration of the Fourth Gospel's teaching on
mission. Source and redaction-critical matters will be dealt with in this context
where appropriate. Moreover, while mission terminology is used in the Fourth
Gospel also with reference to John (the Baptist) and the Spirit, the focus of this
investigation will be the missions of Jesus and of the disciples. This seems
legitimate since 17:18 and 20:21 link the latter two missions explicitly, while the
former two missions are regularly presented in the Fourth Gospel in relation
to the missions of Jesus and of the disciples.

As has been noted with increasing frequency, the efforts of previous
generations of scholars have often suffered from a lack of linguistic sophistication.[3] Among such flaws are an emphasis on the diachronic rather than synchronic use of a word and a failure to distinguish between words and concepts.
To achieve greater accuracy, this monograph will use the linguistic procedure
of a semantic field study. This is the first time such an approach has been used
for the study of mission in John. As the survey of the available literature on the
subject will show, the mission concept in the Fourth Gospel has too often been
equated with the phrase "to send." As a result, studies of the sending theme in
John have not been adequate to grasp the full scope of the Fourth Gospel's
teaching on mission. In the semantic field study undergirding the present work,

---

2. Some might wish that the present work would spend more time investigating the history-of-religions background of Johannine mission teaching. The relative lack of direct exploration
of this issue does not imply that such matters are unimportant. But first things must come first;
and the first thing confronting us here is the complex and nuanced teaching on mission emerging
from the text of the Fourth Gospel as we have it. Moreover, as the following survey of scholarship
on the subject will show, helpful studies on the background of various aspects of Johannine mission
teaching have already been undertaken (one thinks, e.g., of the works by Bühner and Miranda
discussed below). Where less work has been done, however, is on the biblical-theological penetra-
tion and synthesis of mission in John. This, then, is the focus chosen for the present study. Someone
else may choose to take the findings of the present work and relate them once again to a presumed
background of the Fourth Gospel, the approximation of which must, of course, always remain
tentative.

3. Cf., e.g., Michael J. Wilkins, *The Concept of Disciple in Matthew's Gospel. As Reflected in
the Use of the Term* Μαθητής, NovTSup 59 (Leiden: E. J. Brill, 1988): 3-5.

further terminology comprising the Johannine mission concept will be identified. It will also be recognized that the notion of mission may still be present where no explicit mission word is used.

This study also attempts to make a contribution toward the answer of a theological problem. How are the missions of Jesus and of the disciples related? On the one hand, the Fourth Gospel stresses the uniqueness of Jesus' person and work. On the other hand, it patterns the sending of the disciples after that of Jesus, raising questions about degrees of continuity or discontinuity between the two missions. In the case of the Fourth Gospel's commissioning passages (i.e., 17:18 and 20:21), it is especially intriguing that there is not a clearly stated purpose for the mission of Jesus' disciples.[4] Some take this lack of a purpose statement as an indication that all of the characteristics of Jesus' mission given in the Fourth Gospel are transferable to the disciples' mission. These interpreters see 20:21 as the universal hermeneutical key for mission in the Fourth Gospel.

Others question whether it is appropriate to subsume all of the characteristics of Jesus' mission under the mission of the disciples. These writers contend that the commissioning passages should rather be seen as focusing on the kind of relationship existing between the sender and those sent. It might be more accurate to say, they argue, that 17:18 teaches that Jesus and the disciples alike are sent into the world in a certain *way*, i.e., they were chosen and called, they were set apart, and they were sent, rather than equating *every* aspect of the missions of Jesus and of the disciples.

What is at stake here is more than fine points of exegesis. The question arises whether certain views of 20:21 diminish the uniqueness accorded to Jesus in the Fourth Gospel. Entire missiological paradigms have been built around various interpretations of 20:21. The "incarnational model," for example, sees Christ as present in the church so that the church can fashion its mission after the model provided by Jesus during his earthly ministry. According to this view, the church is not just *representing* Jesus — it *is* Jesus working through his church today. The implication of this model appears to be a focus on the continuity between Jesus' mission and the church's mission.[5]

Another view, the "representational model," accentuates more keenly the discontinuity between the respective missions of Jesus and of his disciples.[6] It

---

4. Scripture references in this dissertation are to the Gospel of John unless otherwise indicated.

5. Cf. John Stott, *Christian Mission in the Modern World* (London: Church Pastoral Aid Society, 1975); "An Open Letter to David Hesselgrave," *Trinity World Forum* 16, no. 3 (1991): 1-2; and *The Contemporary Christian: Applying God's Word to Today's World* (Downers Grove, Ill.: InterVarsity, 1992).

6. Cf. David J. Hesselgrave, "Holes in 'Holistic Mission,'" *Trinity World Forum* 15, no. 3 (1990): 1-5; and "To John Stott — A Surrejoinder," *Trinity World Forum* 16, no. 3 (1991): 3-4. Hesselgrave refers also to "Alford, John Peter Lange, J. H. Bernard (in Driver, Plummer, and Briggs), Charles John Ellicott, John Calvin and many others" as holding to such a view.

acknowledges the uniqueness of Jesus' person and work while viewing the primary task of his disciples as witnessing to *Jesus*. While Jesus can be said to "give life" in a primary sense, the disciples' contribution is limited to their witness. Proponents of the "representational model" view the "incarnational model" as unduly equating the missions of Jesus and of the disciples to the extent that the uniqueness of Jesus' person and work may be compromised.

The present study of mission in the Fourth Gospel will therefore have important theological as well as missiological implications. In Chapter 1, the state of research on mission in the Fourth Gospel will be surveyed. Chapter 2 covers foundational linguistic, definitional, and literary matters. Historical and critical issues will be dealt with throughout the study as needed. The following two chapters contain the actual study of the missions of Jesus and of the disciples. Since the fourth evangelist[7] relates the disciples' mission repeatedly to the mission of Jesus (cf. 17:18 and 20:21), the latter's mission is treated first (Chapter 3).[8] In discussing the disciples' mission, special attention is given to the question of how later generations of disciples (i.e., the church) should be related to Jesus' original followers (Chapter 4). This is an important, albeit rather complex, hermeneutical issue that is rarely dealt with in studies on the subject. The present work therefore breaks new ground in attempting to provide consistent guidelines by which a transition can be made from the Fourth Gospel's disciples to believers of later generations. The monograph concludes with a chapter on the implications of the present study for the Fourth Gospel's purpose and for the mission of the contemporary church (Chapter 5). It will be asked which of the alternative views held on the Fourth Gospel's purpose appears to be supported by the findings of the present study. In an indirect manner, the study of mission in John may shed further light on the "Johannine community hypothesis" that has achieved almost paradigmatic status in Johannine studies in the last few decades. The discussion of implications for the mission of the contemporary church centers around the "incarnational model" which many writers find taught by the fourth evangelist.

7. The present monograph uses the terms "John" and "the fourth evangelist" interchangeably to refer to the final author or redactor of the Fourth Gospel (also called "John" or "John's Gospel"), i.e., the person that is substantially responsible for the Gospel in its final form. This terminology reflects the interest of this work in the theology of John's Gospel in its final formulation and does not imply or presuppose any views regarding the Gospel's authorship or the identities of the "beloved disciple" or the "fourth evangelist." This study also does not presuppose any one theory of the Fourth Gospel's redaction or its sources.

8. The procedure followed in the study closely resembles the one adopted by Rudolf Schnackenburg, "Der Missionsgedanke des Johannesevangeliums im heutigen Horizont," in *Das Johannesevangelium, Vol. IV, Ergänzende Auslegungen und Exkurse,* HTKNT (Freiburg im Breisgau: Herder, 1984), 58-72, especially 60-66, who proceeds in the following manner: 1. Die Sendung der Jünger gemäß der Sendung Jesu, a) Die Jüngersendung im Rahmen des Evangeliums, b) Das Verhältnis von Jüngersendung und Sendung Jesu, and c) Wort und Werk.

CHAPTER 1

The Subject in Recent Scholarship

The subject of mission in the Fourth Gospel began to receive increasing attention in the early 1960s. The 1970s and 1980s witnessed a growing concern with the biblical-theological dimension of mission in the Fourth Gospel. It seems therefore appropriate for the present survey to begin at the onset of this renewed interest. An attempt will be made to cover all the major monographs and articles on the subject over the last thirty years (1964-94). Proceeding chronologically, this survey will provide a basic understanding of how this Johannine concept has been treated in the past.[1] The present study will seek to build on an

---

1. The survey will cover the following works: Jean Radermakers, "Mission et Apostolat dans l'Évangile Johannique," *SE II*/1, ed. Frank L. Cross, TU 87 (Berlin: Akademie, 1964), 100-121; Ferdinand Hahn, *Mission in the New Testament*, SBT 47 (London: SCM, 1965), 152-63; Werner Bieder, *Gottes Sendung und der missionarische Auftrag nach Matthäus, Lukas, Paulus, und Johannes*, ThStud 82 (Zürich: EVZ, 1965); Josef Kuhl, *Die Sendung Jesu und der Kirche nach dem Johannes-Evangelium*, Studia Instituti Missiologica Societatis Verbi Domini 11 (St. Augustin: Steyler, 1967); James McPolin, "Mission in the Fourth Gospel," *ITQ* 36 (1969): 113-22; José Comblin, *Sent from the Father: Meditations on the Fourth Gospel*, trans. Carl Kabat (Maryknoll, N.Y.: Orbis, 1974); Albert Curry Winn, *A Sense of Mission: Guidance from the Gospel of John* (Philadelphia: Westminster, 1981); Birger Olsson, "Excursus III: Mission in Jn," in *Structure and Meaning in the Fourth Gospel: A Text-Linguistic Analysis of John 2:1-11 and 4:1-42*, ConBNT 6 (Lund: Gleerup, 1974), 241-48; Mario Veloso, *El Compromiso Cristiano: Un Estudio Sobre la Actualidad Misionera en el Evangelio de San Juan* (Buenos Aires: Zunino Ediciones, 1975); Juan Peter Miranda, *Die Sendung Jesu im vierten Evangelium: Religions- und theologiegeschichtliche Untersuchungen zu den Sendungsformeln*, SBS 87 (Stuttgart: Katholisches Bibelwerk, 1977); and *Der Vater der mich gesandt hat. Religionsgeschichtliche Untersuchungen zu den johanneischen Sendungsformeln: Zugleich ein Beitrag zur johanneischen Christologie und Ekklesiologie*, EHS 23/7 (Frankfurt am Main: Peter Lang, 1972; 2d rev. ed., 1976); Jan Adolph Bühner, *Der Gesandte und sein Weg im 4. Evangelium: Die kultur- und religionsgeschichtliche Entwicklung*, WUNT 2/2 (Tübingen: J. C. B. Mohr [Paul Siebeck], 1977); Robert Prescott-Ezickson, "The Sending Motif in the Gospel of John: Implications for Theology of Mission" (Ph.D. diss., Southern Baptist Theological Seminary, 1986); Miguel Rodriguez Ruiz, *Der Missionsgedanke des Johannesevangeliums: Ein Beitrag zur johanneischen Soteriologie und Ekklesiologie*, FB 55 (Würzburg: Echter, 1986); Teresa Okure, *The Johannine Approach to Mission: A Contextual Study of John 4:1-42*, WUNT

understanding of both the strengths and weaknesses of these works and to supply further insights or correctives where necessary.[2]

I. THE PERIOD FROM 1964 TO 1974

The studies by Radermakers, Hahn, Bieder, Kuhl, McPolin, Comblin, Winn, and Olsson fall into this period. Among these, only Kuhl's treatment is a full-fledged monograph devoted entirely to mission in John. The scope of Hahn's work is mission in the entire New Testament, while Bieder surveys mission in the four Gospels. Comblin and Winn provide primarily popular studies. Radermaker's contribution consists in a short essay on the Johannine sending terminology, while Olsson includes a brief excursus on mission in John in a text-linguistic analysis of a particular pericope in the Fourth Gospel. Following the order of publication, Radermakers's contribution will be treated first.

Radermakers (1964)[3] contends that there are not two separate missions in the Fourth Gospel but one, i.e., God's, with the missions of Jesus and of the disciples functioning in a subordinate way. The author analyzes the Johannine terminology for the sending of the Son, πέμπω and ἀποστέλλω, and concludes with a discussion of the mission and "apostolat" of Jesus and others in the Fourth Gospel. The latter term is perhaps infelicitous since the Fourth Gospel itself avoids the equivalent Greek noun. Radermakers believes that the phrase ὁ πέμψας με (πατήρ) points to the Father's initiative in sending the Son (or, in the case of 20:21, to the Son's initiative in sending the disciples), while ἀποστέλλω refers to Jesus' accomplishment of his historical work of salvation. The former expression thus is found to highlight the Son's divine origin, while the latter is taken to emphasize the Son's work. The accuracy of this differentiation in Johannine sending terminology will be subjected to a detailed evaluation in Chapter 3 below.

Hahn's study of mission in the New Testament (1965) is *religions-geschichtlich* in scope.[4] The author sets out to explore the relationship between Jews and Gentiles in the initial stages of the mission of the early church. Hahn finds evidence for the early church's adherence to the principle "to the Jew first" in the Synoptics as well as in Pauline literature. He places the Johannine writings

---

2/31 (Tübingen: J. C. B. Mohr [Paul Siebeck], 1988); and Giuseppe Ghiberti, "Missione di Gesù e di discepoli nel quarto Vangelo," *Ricerche Storico Bibliche* 2 (1990): 185-200.

2. Cf. also the *Forschungsbericht* by Okure, 7-35. She groups the available literature into these four main categories: (1) those that debate the missionary character of the Gospel, (2) those that search for the possible models that could have inspired the evangelist's portrait of Jesus as "the one sent," (3) those that focus on the theological and Christological aspects of mission in the Gospel, and (4) those that debate the missionary stance of the Johannine community. Cf. p. 8.

3. Radermakers, 100-121.

4. Hahn, especially 152-63.

as belonging to a stage of the church's mission where the major concern had shifted from evangelization to the edification of already existing communities of believers. Thus Hahn's treatment of mission in the Fourth Gospel appears already largely predetermined by his overall *religionsgeschichtlich* reconstruction. Without much direct recourse to the text of the Fourth Gospel itself, Hahn seems to rule out a priori the possibility that the Fourth Gospel was written with the intent of leading unbelievers to faith in Jesus as Messiah. The course sketched by Hahn bears a certain resemblance to the systematized biblical theology of mission to which the present study seeks to make a contribution. It seems advisable, however, to proceed inductively and to allow one's detailed study of John's teaching on mission itself to provide clues regarding the purpose of John's Gospel and its place in the mission of the early church.

Bieder's (1965) study of the church's missionary mandate in the four Gospels devotes thirteen pages to John.[5] His contribution is predominantly practical and missiological. Bieder notes that John sets the Christian community in radical contrast to the world and points out the difference between John's perspective and the contemporary tendency toward partnership or at least dialogue with the world.[6] Bieder is careful to maintain that John's point of view is not a radical dualism. Nevertheless, John sees the world as under the domination of evil and in need of salvation. The author asks, "Ist es denn nicht die bleibende Aufgabe der Kirche, gerade *weil* sie um ihre missionarische Sendung in der Welt weiß, die Trennung zur Welt sich klar zu machen, in die hinein sie mit ihrem Glauben gerufen ist?"[7] Bieder keenly observes, "Im Johannesevangelium ist die erstaunliche Tatsache offenkundig, daß gerade der Gegensatz zur Welt keine amissionarischen, sondern missionarische Folgen hat."[8]

In his discussion of 20:20-21, Bieder emphasizes the importance of the church's accurate understanding of the identity of its sender, Jesus the Messiah. The church needs to know Jesus as the Crucified and Risen One. Bieder expresses strong disagreement with John A. T. Robinson's thesis, presented in *Honest to God* (1963), that lowers Jesus to a "human being for others," as well with those who would elevate Jesus to the rank of a half-divine being. He concludes, "Die Voraussetzung für jeden missionarischen Aufbruch ist Jesus Christus als der Gekreuzigte und als der Auferstandene. Es ist der Dienst des Heiligen Geistes an der Kirche, daß er sie zu Jesus Christus zurückführt, daß er *ihn* zum Zentrum ihres Denkens und Lebens macht."[9]

Bieder sees Jesus' statements regarding his followers' peace (cf. 14:28; 20:19, 21) and unity (cf. 17:20-25) to have important implications for his disciples' mission. He understands peace as wholeness even amongst the dis-

5. Bieder, 40-52.
6. Bieder, 42.
7. Bieder, 42.
8. Bieder, 44.
9. Bieder, 46.

ciples and notes that believers need peace and unity with one another, if their mission is to be accomplished. The author also draws lessons for the church's mission from other passages in the Fourth Gospel such as 4:34-38; 12:20-22; Jesus' prayer in John 17; and 20:23.[10] Despite the limited scope of Bieder's treatment (its length, date, and primarily practical orientation), his discussion provides many helpful practical insights for the church's mission from the Fourth Gospel and ranks among the most stimulating treatments of the subject.

The work by Kuhl (1967) has been described as "the most important work" on mission in the Fourth Gospel in its time.[11] After a survey of the Old Testament and of the historical background of the sending theme, Kuhl devotes the bulk of his study to an exploration of the sending theology of the Fourth Gospel, providing many helpful insights. His exploration of the sending theme in the Fourth Gospel is doubtless the most extensive and thorough treatment up to that date. Kuhl's method, however, is flawed, since he does not adequately distinguish between a term's diachronic and synchronic uses. Moreover, Kuhl's use of the terms "Mission" and "Sendung" is imprecise, if not contradictory, a weakness that may be due at least in part to Kuhl's failure to define his terms.[12] This serious limitation exposes the need for a biblical-theological study of mission in the Fourth Gospel that is more rigorously controlled methodologically and based on a considered definition of mission in John.

McPolin (1969), following a topical approach, chooses as the major headings for his treatment "The Mission of the Baptist," "The Mission of Jesus," "The Mission of the Spirit," and "The Mission of the Disciples."[13] This author acknowledges God as the source of all mission related in the Fourth Gospel: "All other missions revolve about that of Jesus, but the Father is the 'mission centre,' the source from which all missions derive. He alone is the unsent sender."[14] It may be better still to subordinate the missions of John and of the Spirit to the missions of Jesus and of the disciples. Overall, McPolin's study provides a helpful introduction to mission in the Fourth Gospel. Although the author's treatment is basic, McPolin deserves credit for being among the first to focus his attention on a significant Johannine theme.

Comblin's (1974) less scholarly treatment[15] points out some of the basic connections between the Johannine mission theme and words such as *Father,*

10. Bieder, 50-52.
11. Cf. Kuhl. The assessment was made by Prescott-Ezickson, 29; cf. also Robert Kysar, *The Fourth Evangelist and His Gospel: An Examination of Contemporary Scholarship* (Minneapolis: Augsburg, 1975), 244.
12. See further the discussion of definitional issues in Chapter 2 with a more detailed critique of Kuhl's study.
13. Cf. McPolin, 113-22.
14. McPolin, 114. In this McPolin agrees with Radermakers, whose contribution has already been discussed above.
15. Comblin.

sent, man, world, to do, works, signs, testimony, glory, to know, disciples, to believe, truth, love, and life. Comblin espouses the view that Jesus is the model "missionary" for all Christians. When Christians accept the fact that they are sent by God on a mission, they find their true authenticity as human beings. In this contention one possibly finds a reflection of Comblin's exposure to liberation theology while serving as a professor in Latin America. Comblin's general thesis that the Fourth Gospel presents Jesus as a model "missionary" for all Christians comes close to the "incarnational model" already mentioned. A more detailed study than that conducted by Comblin would be necessary in order to determine whether the Johannine mission concept is accurately represented by such a model of the church's mission.

Comblin also sparked a more academic work by Albert Curry Winn (1981),[16] who relates the Johannine sending motif to the ideas of speaking God's words, doing God's works, doing God's will, and drawing life from the Father. Winn's primary concern is a practical one. He seeks to rekindle people's commitment to "missions" (modern evangelical use of the term) by showing that the mission theme is central to the Gospel of John. Using the sending motif as an organizing principle, Winn seeks to develop other aspects of Johannine theology around it. For the present study with its more tightly controlled methodology, Winn's treatment is of limited value.

Olsson's monograph (1974) offers a text-linguistic analysis of 2:1-11 and 4:1-42. The use of mission vocabulary such as θερίζειν, συνάγειν, and καρπός in 4:34-38 prompts Olsson to provide an excursus on "Mission in John."[17] The author begins by discussing the concept of "harvest" (θερίζειν, συνάγειν, and καρπός) in refererence to God's eschatological intervention in the world. Olsson provides numerous references to antecedent passages on the "harvest" motif in the Old Testament and intertestamental Jewish writings. He also draws attention to the fact that Jesus' death is often linked in the Fourth Gospel to statements regarding the gathering of God's children (cf. especially 6:12-13; 17:21; 19:23-24; cf. also 11:52; 12:32; and John 21).

Olsson considers the word καρπός as the keyword of mission in John. Beginning his discussion with 12:24, the author also addresses 4:36 and John 15, the only other passages in the Fourth Gospel where καρπός is used. Olsson sees in these passages a clear reference to Jesus' continued mission through his disciples.[18] He concludes, "The mission in Jn may be best described as the gathering of the people of God, who are dispersed throughout the world. . . . The mission is a result of Jesus' death, and thus possible only when Jesus is

---

16. Winn.

17. Olsson, 241-48.

18. Cf. Olsson, 247-48. Contra Rainer Borig, *Der wahre Weinstock: Untersuchungen zu Jo 15,1-10*, SANT 16 (München: Kösel, 1967), who attempts to show that the expression "to bear fruit" (καρπὸν φέρειν) cannot in any passage mean "Missionsfrucht" but only "religiös-sittliche Tat." Olsson also refers to Thüsing's monograph and the commentaries by Brown and Lindars.

glorified. Then begins the gathering in of 'God's scattered children,' the calling and uniting of Jesus' 'own sheep' into a flock. Jesus as reaper (the disciples) 'receives wages' and 'gathers fruit.'"[19] In his well-focused discussion, Olsson provides some useful observations on Johannine mission terminology. However, his treatment, which concentrates on 4:34-38, lacks integration with passages such as 17:18 and 20:21.

II. THE PERIOD FROM 1975 TO 1984

The following decade saw the publication of a monograph by Veloso, two works by Miranda, and a study by Bühner. The interests of both Miranda and Bühner lie in the identification of the most probable background for the Johannine sending concept. While this period is characterized by fewer studies on the subject, the contributions by Miranda and Bühner join Kuhl's work in providing the most significant monographs up to that date.

Veloso (1975) launches a broadly conceived study.[20] After surveying the terms ἀποστέλλειν and πέμπειν, he surveys mission in the Old Testament. He then treats the unity of the Father and the Son, followed by an investigation of the activity of the Son in revelation, salvation, and the giving of eternal life. Veloso closes with the mission of the Spirit and the incorporation of believers into Jesus' mission. Because of its broadly conceived nature, this study is superficial and unoriginal.

Miranda's first study (1972, rev. ed. 1976) lays the groundwork for his second study (1977) by investigating the Fourth Gospel's sending terminology, its sending formulae, and the concept of the eschatological prophet. His second study further develops these themes.[21] The author sets forth the following theses:

1. the sending of Jesus is prophetically understood in the Fourth Gospel as the coming of the eschatological prophet like Moses; Deuteronomic prophetic tradition influenced Johannine sending Christology via the early Semitic messenger concept and late Jewish messenger law;
2. sending is not identical with the Father-Son relationship or unity; rather, these are to be understood in the context of the juridical sending concept; in the Son title, it is not the identity of nature between the sender and the one sent that is emphasized, but the Son's identification with the Father in action;
3. sending in the Johannine sense is, in the ultimate analysis, Jesus' prophetic

19. Olsson, 248.
20. Cf. Veloso, *El Compromiso Cristiano.*
21. Cf. Miranda, *Vater der mich gesandt hat; Sendung Jesu.*

messenger role: he is the completely authorized messenger of God; sending therefore expresses the idea of authorization;

4. the restriction of the Johannine idea of sending to Jesus' descent (sending as *katabasis*) leads to the mistaken characterization of the sending of Jesus as incarnation; however, sending and *katabasis* need to be separated;

5. the historical background of the Johannine sending concept is to be found neither in the gnostic redeemer myth nor in wisdom speculation, but in the ancient Semitic messenger concept and later Jewish messenger law in a prophetic context; the view that the gnostic redeemer myth or wisdom are the background for the Johannine sending concept were largely conditioned by the presupposition that it functioned to support the (ontological) unity of Father and Son;

6. source criticism is not helpful for the distillation of a "genuinely Johannine" notion of sending (through a delimitation of the fourth evangelist from a supposed *Grundschrift* and the supposed later redactors) nor is it helpful for the sketch of a theological-historical line of development of Johannine sending Christology;

7. at the beginning of Johannine sending Christology seem to be the kerygmatically shaped sending formulae that are closely tied to the cross-death of Jesus and whose function consists of the characterization of Jesus' cross-death as the work of God; they belong to the time of mission.[22]

Miranda views the conflict between Judaism and the Johannine community (climaxing around A.D. 90) as the second stage of the development of Johannine sending Christology. In the controversy with rabbinic-pharisaic circles, the sending of Jesus was stressed in the sense of divine authorization: Jesus is the Messiah and Son of God, because he is the eschatological prophet like Moses (Miranda places at this juncture the development of the ὁ πέμψας formula). The third stage, according to Miranda, is to be found in the internal controversy of the Johannine community (cf. 1 John). In its struggle against proto-gnostic opponents, the community uses the kerygmatic sending formula that stresses the sending of Jesus into death for the sake of the salvation of humankind.

Many of Miranda's insights are very valuable, such as his distinction between sending and "descending" terminology and his understanding of the Johannine sending concept in terms of authorization. It appears unduly reductionistic, however, to limit the Fourth Gospel's sending Christology exclusively to its functional dimension and to eliminate completely the fuller personal dimension of which it is a part. Rather than erecting a dichotomy between the Fourth Gospel's Father-Son Christology and sending Christology, should one not see the latter as embedded in the former?

22. Cf. the convenient summary in Juan Miranda, *Sendung Jesu*, 90-92.

Bühner (1977) investigates the cultural and historical antecedents of the Johannine mission concept. In his search for cultural antecedents, he looks at the messenger in the ancient Orient and Jewish teaching on representatives. Under historical antecedents, Bühner treats descending and ascending messengers of God in Jewish religion and the prophet as *shaliaḥ* of God. He discerns three emphases in the Fourth Gospel's teaching on mission:

1. the Son of Man and descent/ascent: 3:13; 6:33, 38, 41, 50, 62; cf. also 3:31 (ὁ ἄνωθεν ἐρχόμενος) and 8:23 (ἐκ τῶν ἄνω εἰμί); the term ὑψωθῆναι (3:14; 8:28; 12:32, 34) also has a vertical dimension;
2. Father-Son Christology: besides ἀποστέλλειν and πέμπειν, see especially the summary by Jesus in 16:28; cf. also 8:14; 16:5, 10 as well as 13:1-3;
3. the Logos-concept in the prologue.[23]

Perhaps a fourth theme may be added: that of the authoritative rabbi who gathers around him a circle of devoted followers (1:37-43; 6:60-71; chapters 13–17; 20–21).

Bühner summarizes, "Der johanneische Jesus hat in der Terminologie des vierten Ev. als Menschensohn mit Ab- und Aufstieg zu tun, als der vom Vater gesandte Sohn kehrt er nach Beendigung seiner Sendung zu seinem himmlischen Vater und Auftraggeber zurück, und in bezug auf den Logos ist ihm eine kosmische Präexistenz zugesprochen."[24] Bühner's study is especially helpful in that it links modes of movement in Jesus' mission (such as descent/ascent or sending/return) to Christological titles (such as the Son of Man or the Son of the Father). However, while Bühner's interest is primarily in Christology, this monograph seeks to explore the Fourth Gospel's portrayal of the disciples' mission as well.

III. THE PERIOD FROM 1985 TO 1994

The last ten years saw the publication of three works that originated as doctoral dissertations. Of these, Prescott-Ezickson's is the most basic and narrowly conceived work, while Okure's study possesses the highest degree of sophistication. An essay by Ghiberti will also be reviewed.

Prescott-Ezickson's dissertation (1986) represents a study of the sending motif in the Fourth Gospel with implications for the theology of mission.[25] After surveying the state of research, the author discusses sending terminology in the Fourth Gospel (in his case, ἀποστέλλω, πέμπω, and ἔρχομαι). He then

23. Cf. Bühner, 2-3.
24. Bühner, 4.
25. Prescott-Ezickson.

briefly treats the concept of agency and "the sending language as revelation." In the main section of his work, "Sending in the Theology of the Fourth Gospel," Prescott-Ezickson investigates the sendings of Jesus, of the disciples, and of the Spirit. He follows John Stott, who sees 20:21 as presenting Jesus' mission as the "model" for the church's mission. Stott broadly defines mission as "service to humanity," including, but not limited to, "evangelism."[26]

Prescott-Ezickson takes his cue from George Peters, who apparently all but equates not just the manner of the sendings of Jesus and of the disciples but also the purpose: "Full weight is given to *kathōs* — in like manner. We are to be in all things his followers — teachers of the truth, manifesting the life and character of God, bearing the sins of others in their own persons. He sends them to be saviors in their own narrow world."[27] Prescott-Ezickson continues, "This quote of Peters refers back to 3:16-17, where Jesus says he was sent to save the world not to condemn the world. Since the disciples are sent as Jesus was sent, with no dilution or minimization of purpose of mission, then *whatever Jesus was sent by the Father to do, the disciples are sent by Jesus to do, including to save the world and not to condemn the world.*"[28] However, not only is this procedure imprecise owing to a lack of attention to the contexts of the passages cited, it also leads to doubtful theological conclusions regarding the nature of the missions of Jesus and of the disciples.[29]

Rodriguez Ruiz (1986), in a slight revision of a 1985 dissertation under Rudolf Schnackenburg, explicitly distinguishes between the primary nature of Jesus' mission and that of the disciples, tracing the concept of mission through a series of passages in the Fourth Gospel which he considers significant.[30] He gives special consideration to the call of the disciples (1:29-51), the programmatic discussion in chapter 3, the story of the Samaritan mission (4:1-42), the three allusions to the Gentile mission (7:35; 10:16; 11:51-52), its opening with the coming of the Greeks (12:20-36), the farewell discourse(s) (chapters 13–16), Jesus' final prayer (chapter 17), the commissioning of the disciples (20:21-23), and the catch of fish as a symbol for the church's post-Easter mission (21:1-14). The subtitle of Ruiz's study is "Ein Beitrag zur johanneischen Soteriologie und Ekklesiologie," since Ruiz sees a close connection between the mission concept in John and soteriology and ecclesiology.[31] Ruiz follows his

---

26. Cf. John R. W. Stott, *Christian Mission in the Modern World* (London: Church Pastoral Aid Society, 1975), 22-34.

27. Cf. Prescott-Ezickson, 128, quoting George W. Peters, *A Biblical Theology of Missions* (Chicago: Moody, 1972), 195, who in turn cites Lyman Abbot, *Illustrated Commentary on John* (New York: Barnes, 1897), 208.

28. Cf. Prescott-Ezickson, 128 (emphasis added).

29. See already the above Introduction. For a thorough critique of Stott's contentions, cf. Chapter 5.

30. Cf. Ruiz, *Missionsgedanke des Johannesevangeliums.*

31. Cf. Ruiz, 22-23: "Weil der Missionsgedanke mit der Christologie und Ekklesiologie der jeweiligen ntl. Autoren eng verbunden ist und sich das Joh-Ev von anderen ntl. Autoren bezüglich

mentor Schnackenburg in holding that the Fourth Gospel is a "Gemein-deschrift," designed to strengthen the faith of a believing community. Mission, according to Ruiz, is therefore only indirectly promoted in that a strengthening of the community will have an impact on the surrounding world.[32] However, this contention appears to be more a presupposition than the result of a detailed study of the Fourth Gospel itself and therefore must be subjected to closer scrutiny.

Okure's monograph on "The Johannine Approach to Mission" (1988) represents the most important recent treatment of mission in the Fourth Gospel. The study focuses on John 4, a passage Okure considers to have para-digmatic function for the Johannine mission concept.[33] Indeed, Okure calls the chapter "a passage universally recognized as being the most overtly concerned with mission in the Gospel."[34] Okure's method "combines rhetorical and literary analysis in the quest for theological meaning viewed from the standpoint of the Evangelist and of his intended audience."[35] Using this "contextual method," Okure focuses on the final text as a whole and claims to interpret every passage in light of the whole Gospel. Making use of categories employed by the Roman rhetorician Quintilian, she labels 4:1-26/27 as *narratio*, 31-38 as *expositio*, and 28-30 and 39-42 as *demonstratio*.

Perhaps the weakest point of Okure's highly suggestive work is the specula-tive nature of her conclusions regarding the significance of the Johannine mission concept for a reconstruction of the Fourth Gospel's life-setting. Okure asserts,

> The Gospel evidence taken by itself suggests that the basic missionary prob-lems in the Johannine community lay in the tendency on the part of some, at least, of the missionary disciples to set themselves against Jesus by claiming for themselves the glory of the missionary enterprise, thus forgetting that they were sent, which means dependent. This Christ-rivalry, it would seem, went hand in hand with a lack of love and fellowship within the community, which lack of fellowship threatened the very significance of the community as an eschatological group of believers who witness to the reality of Jesus' life-giving mission from the Father.[36]

---

dieser beiden Fragen stark unterscheidet, möchten wir in dieser Untersuchung nach der Besonderheit und Eigenart des joh Missionsgedankens und nach seiner Verankerung in dem christlichen Gesamt-kontext fragen." Ruiz adds, "Demnach soll nach dem Zusammenhang der zur selben Konstellation gehörenden joh theologischen Begriffe 'Sendung,' 'Heilsgeschehen' und 'Missionswerk' gefragt wer-den" (23). But it is unclear what Ruiz means by "zur selben Konstellation gehörend." Cf. the approach taken in the present study, especially the semantic field survey and semantic clustering.

32. Cf. Ruiz, 24-38.

33. Cf. Okure, 56, where she calls John 4:1-42 "a miniature of the whole Gospel."

34. Okure, 285.

35. Okure, 50.

36. Cf. Okure, 232. Okure herself had predicted that "the interpretation given concerning the situation of the Johannine community is likely to emerge as the most controverted of the study" (xvii).

Okure's contention that "an attitude of boasting, a tendency to behave as if they owned the mission, and pride in a variety of forms must have constituted a special weakness of the Johannine audience" is almost impossible to verify.[37] Here the observation rings true that "[t]he hesitant suggestions of earlier scholars have now become the 'givens' of this generation of scholars, who feel free to build fresh, hesitant suggestions on top of them."[38] Despite these limitations, Okure's study remains the best study available on the subject to date in its thoroughgoing interaction with the relevant literature and its original methodological and biblical-theological contribution.

Finally, Giuseppe Ghiberti (1990) contributes a fifteen-page article with the title "Missione di Gesù e di discepoli nel quarto Vangelo." He shows an awareness of most (if not all) of the important works discussed above.[39] Ghiberti discusses the following subjects: the uniqueness of the Johannine perspective on mission; the mission of Jesus in relation to Johannine Christology, soteriology, and the Spirit; and the mission of the disciples. Ghiberti's study of the disciples' mission breaks down into three further elements: its transmission, its relation to the will of Jesus, and the "missionary tension" *(tensione missionaria)* in the "Johannine community." The brevity of this contribution prevents it from being more than a survey of the relevant literature with a few added reflections by the author himself. Ghiberti does, however, refer to many issues relevant for the present work.

IV. SUMMARY

The contributions surveyed above provide a wealth of insights regarding the background and content of John's teaching on mission. None of these works, however, is completely free from limitations. Of the most valuable monographs exclusively devoted to the subject at hand, Miranda and Bühner approach the Fourth Gospel with an interest in locating the conceptual background for the Johannine sending concept. While providing suggestive treatments on background issues, however, these writers do not fill the need for a thorough conceptual study of mission in the Fourth Gospel. Moreover, their interest is primarily in Christology, while the present study seeks to explore also the mission of the disciples. Kuhl's study comes closer to the goal of providing a conceptual study of mission in John. In his case, however, it is the lack of linguistic sophistication that renders his work too imprecise to be fully adequate. Okure's

37. Okure, 287.

38. Cf. D. A. Carson, review of *Overcoming the World: Politics and Community in the Gospel of John* by David Rensberger, *Themelios* 17 (1991): 28.

39. Ghiberti also refers to Lucien Legrand, *Il Dio che viene: La missione nella Bibbia* (Rome, 1989); and Virgilio Pasquetto, *Incarnazione e comunione con Dio: La venuta di Gesù nel mondo e il suo ritorno al luogo d'origine secondo il IV vangelo* (Rome: Edizioni del Teresianum, 1982).

monograph, finally, focuses on John 4 rather than surveying mission in the entire Gospel. As will be developed in greater detail below, Okure's approach also is not free from difficulties with regard to linguistic methodology and historical reconstruction. The present monograph sets out to supplement these studies and to correct the observed limitations.

CHAPTER 2

Foundations

A study of mission in the Fourth Gospel needs to be built upon proper linguistic, definitional, and literary foundations. How can one avoid reading one's own conception of mission into John's Gospel? How can one be sure to have grasped the entire scope of John's teaching on mission? What is the relationship between John's mission *teaching* and mission *terminology*? These are some of the most important questions that must be addressed in the present chapter before embarking on the actual study of the missions of Jesus and of the disciples in the following chapters.

In the discussion of this monograph's linguistic foundations, it will be necessary to deal at some length with questions such as: What is the difference between words and concepts? What is a concept? How can one study a concept in a given book of Scripture? In the past, scholars have occasionally failed to distinguish between words and concepts, with the result that they claim to explicate the meaning of a word while in fact providing a history of the use of a particular concept. This lack of methodological precision needs to be avoided, since it renders such treatments inaccurate or ambiguous, at least in part.

Rather than focusing on the study of words, this monograph will therefore utilize a semantic field approach. Such a study recognizes that words with similar meanings sustain a relationship with one another as part of a semantic field. It is argued that a biblical concept may best be accessed by the determination and study of the various terms comprising such a semantic domain. Provision will also be made for the possibility that not all aspects of a biblical concept find expression in a given terminology. This will be facilitated by a further screening of the Fourth Gospel in order to determine any additional passages where mission is involved. On the basis of a semantic field survey and the identification of semantic clusters of mission in John (i.e., the concatenation of mission terms in close proximity to one another), a working definition of mission will be developed. A section on the literary approach taken to the Fourth Gospel in the present study will conclude this chapter.

I. LINGUISTIC FOUNDATIONS

The discussion of this monograph's linguistic foundations will begin with a detailed rationale for a semantic field approach. Following this rationale, a semantic field survey of mission in the Fourth Gospel will be conducted and semantic clusters will be identified.

A. Rationale for a Semantic Field Approach

1. The Role of Terminology

What is the proper role of terminology in understanding a biblical concept? Some studies give the appearance that words are the only way by which biblical concepts may be communicated. Other approaches, by seeking to grasp the nonverbal dimension of a concept, neglect words used in Scripture. The present monograph attempts to strike a balance between these extremes by acknowledging the role played by words in the communication of concepts while not confining the expression of concepts exclusively to verbal means.

Older studies are frequently tied too closely to a given biblical word or words.[1] In recent years, the pendulum appears to have swung in the other direction. An example of this is the treatment by Okure.[2] When considering criteria for the selection of texts, Okure begins her discussion with sending terminology, i.e., ἀποστέλλειν, πέμπειν, and ἔρχεσθαι.[3] She proceeds to suggest a more complete list of the Johannine terminology of mission organized by "perspective": (1) of the Father: διδόναι, ζητεῖν, ἑλκύειν, ἐργάζομαι, ζωοποιεῖν, δοξάζειν, ἔργον, γεωργός; (2) of the Son: καταβαίνειν, λαλεῖν, κοπιᾶν, κρίνειν, ἀκούειν, ζωοποιεῖν, τιμᾶν, ποιεῖν, τελεῖν; (3) of the audience: πιστεύειν, ἀκούειν, ἔρχεσθαι, τιμᾶν, λαμβάνειν, θερίζειν. Noting that even this more extensive list is by no means exhaustive, Okure concludes "that terminology itself is just as expansive as the Gospel material," subsequently setting aside terminology as a criterion for the selection of texts altogether. Asserting that "[t]o use terminology . . . as the basic criterion . . . would be to confine the study to the realm of ideas and abstractions," Okure chooses instead to study one specific pericope where mission *occurs,* regardless of whether certain "mission words" are found in this passage or not, in order to capture a "context of living interaction."

---

1. Cf. the assessment by Teresa Okure, *The Johannine Approach to Mission*, WUNT 2/31 (Tübingen: J. C. B. Mohr [Paul Siebeck], 1988), 52-53.

2. Okure, 53.

3. Okure rightly chides those writers who tend to focus exclusively on the "sending/coming" of Jesus (naming "Kuhl, Miranda, Rademarkers [sic], Moule and others") for overlooking the importance of other mission terminology in John.

Indeed, terminology is not the only way by which a concept may be communicated. The concern to give adequate attention to the Fourth Gospel's narrative context is certainly valid. Okure appears to react too strongly, however, against the fallacy she perceives in many of the studies preceding her, i.e., an exclusive focus on words. As will be argued, the answer to the problems exposed by a number of earlier studies is not the setting aside of the study of biblical words altogether, but the recognition of the proper limitations of word studies and greater linguistic sophistication in the exploration of biblical concepts. One important element in such a pursuit is the distinction between words and context, and the differentiation between words and concepts. These two subjects will treated next.

2. Words and Context

What is the proper relationship between words and context in the study of biblical concepts? Many older treatments tend to detect meanings in biblical words that are actually supplied by the context in which those words are used.[4] However, it is important to distinguish between information supplied by the context in which a word occurs and the component of meaning contributed by the word itself. As one authority in the field comments, "Meaning is determined on the basis of the congruence of two factors, semantic field . . . and context."[5]

Among these two factors, context must have priority. Silva writes, "[A]mong the divers meanings a word possesses, the only one that will emerge into consciousness is the one determined by the context."[6] Thiselton points to the principle of "situation," quoting Lyons: "Any meaningful linguistic unit . . . has meaning in context. The context of the utterance is the situation in which it occurs. . . . The concept of 'situation' is fundamental for semantic statement. . . . Situation must be given equal weight with linguistic form in semantic theory."[7] Louw and Nida make reference to the basic principle of semantic analysis "that differences in meaning are marked by context, either textual or

---

4. Cf. James Barr, *The Semantics of Biblical Literature* (Oxford: Oxford University Press, 1961); Moisés Silva, *Biblical Words and Their Meanings: An Introduction to Lexical Semantics* (Grand Rapids: Zondervan, 1983). See also the comments on "the inhibiting effects of traditional assumptions about language" by Anthony C. Thiselton, "Semantics and New Testament Interpretation," in *New Testament Interpretation,* ed. I. Howard Marshall (Grand Rapids: Wm. B. Eerdmans, 1977), 76-78; Grant R. Osborne's comments on "semantic fallacies" in *The Hermeneutical Spiral. A Comprehensive Introduction to Biblical Interpretation* (Downers Grove, Ill.: InterVarsity, 1991), 65-75; D. A. Carson, *Exegetical Fallacies* (Grand Rapids: Baker, 1984), especially 25-66 where Carson discusses common word study fallacies; and Peter Cotterell and Max Turner, *Linguistics and Biblical Interpretation* (Downers Grove, Ill.: InterVarsity, 1989), 106-28. See also the critique of Kuhl's work above and below.

5. Osborne, 414.

6. Silva, *Biblical Words,* 139. The reference is to J. Vendryes, *A Linguistic Introduction to History* (New York: Alfred A. Knopf, 1925), 177.

7. Cf. Thiselton, 75. The reference is to John Lyons, *Structural Semantics: An Analysis of Part of the Vocabulary of Plato* (Oxford: Oxford University Press, 1963), 23-24.

extratextual. . . . Since any differences of meaning are marked by context, it follows that the correct meaning of any term is that which fits the context best."[8]

Nevertheless, the fact that context must be given priority[9] does not warrant the neglect of the other factor relevant for determining a term's meaning, i.e., semantic field. Three lessons for the present study emerge therefore from these insights: first, semantic field (i.e., terminology) and context are *both* important for the study of a biblical concept; second, context has priority over semantic field; third, if the second point is kept in mind, semantic field seems to be a very appropriate starting point to guide one to at least some of the most relevant contexts which need to be considered in one's study of a concept. Terminology must not function as a straitjacket but should rather serve as a guide to relevant contexts which subsequently need to be studied inductively.

3. Words and Concepts

How can a narrow focus on words in the study of biblical themes be avoided? Part of the solution to this kind of reductionism is an expansion of one's focus beyond *words* to *concepts.* Thus Osborne cautions against "the failure to consider the concept as well as the word, that is, the other ways the biblical writers could say the same thing."[10] Silva argues that one's grouping of semantically related terms needs to evince sensitivity to linguistic theory, rather than merely being a matter of convenience.[11]

A proper approach involves the exploration of entire biblical concepts in the place of mere studies of biblical words: "We dare never study only occurrences of the particular term if our purpose is to trace the theology behind a word or phrase. . . . None of us ever uses the exact same words to describe our thoughts. Rather, we use synonyms and other phrases to depict our ideas. Therefore a truly complete picture must cluster semantically related terms and phrases."[12]

These general considerations can be illustrated by different procedures followed by treatments of mission or sending in the Fourth Gospel. The methodological discussion in such studies has largely centered around the question whether such investigations should only consider Johannine references to "sending" or whether one should conceive of "sending" as part of a broader conceptuality that may conveniently be termed "mission."

---

8. Cf. Johannes P. Louw and Eugene A. Nida, *Greek-English Lexicon of the New Testament Based on Semantic Domains,* 2 vols. (New York: United Bible Societies, 1988, 1989), 1:xvi.

9. This is Okure's main contention; hence her "contextual method" (cf. Okure, 50-51). Okure also utilizes insights from rhetorical criticism.

10. Osborne, 74.

11. Cf. Silva, *Biblical Words,* 21, referring to his review of the *New International Dictionary of New Testament Theology* in *WTJ* 43 (1980-81): 395-99; quoted by Osborne, 74.

12. Cf. Osborne, 74.

Senior opts for a narrow view of mission in the Fourth Gospel when he asserts that "we can limit ourselves to explicit 'sending passages.' "[13] Mercer, too, does not mention coming, going, or other mission terminology.[14] He deals exclusively with sending terminology in the Fourth Gospel, arguing that " 'Sending' . . . is a major motif in the fourth gospel and one that has been seriously neglected and somewhat misunderstood by Johannine scholars."[15]

Bultmann, on the other hand, understands mission in John more broadly.[16] Besides "sending," he considers related Johannine terms such as "coming into the world" and "being consecrated and sent." He notes that "the counterpart of his [Jesus'] sending is his 'coming' or 'having come,' " and observes important parallel uses of "sending" and "coming" in the Fourth Gospel (7:28; 8:42; 17:8). Bultmann also points to the correspondence of Jesus' departure and his coming (cf., e.g., 8:14: "I came from the Father and have come into the world; again, I am leaving the world and I am going to the Father").[17] He concludes that "His [Jesus'] coming and going belong together as a unit," and notes further John's occasional use of "ascending/descending" terminology for Jesus' "coming" and "going."[18]

As a screening of the relevant literature indicates, these two approaches

13. Cf. Donald Senior and Carroll Stuhlmueller, *The Biblical Foundations for Mission* (Maryknoll, N.Y.: Orbis, 1983), 289-90.

14. Cf. Calvin Mercer, "Jesus the Apostle: 'Sending' and the Theology of John," *JETS* 35 (1992): 457-62. While Mercer does not consider mission terminology other than "sending" in the Fourth Gospel, he uses the term "mission," as on p. 457: "The theme of God's sending Jesus on a special mission occurs throughout the fourth gospel and in various ways."

15. Cf. Mercer, 456. This verdict may be a bit harsh, since there is a significant body of specialized literature on the subject (which Mercer only mentions cursorily in a few footnotes; but see the survey of the state of research in Chap. 1 of the present study). Especially in regard to sending, it should be noted that most commentators recognize the importance of this terminology in the Fourth Gospel. However, the concept of *mission*, understood more broadly than sending, has yet to be given the prominence due it in treatments of Johannine theology.

16. Cf. Rudolf Bultmann, *Theology of the New Testament,* trans. Kendrick Grobel, 2 vols. (New York: Charles Scribner's Sons, 1955), 2:33-40. Cf. also H. R. Lemmer, "A possible understanding by the implied reader, of some of the *coming-going-being sent* pronouncements, in the Johannine farewell discourses," *Neot* 25 (1992): 289-310.

17. Bultmann, *Theology of the New Testament,* 2:34.

18. Bultmann, *Theology of the New Testament,* 2:35. Cf. also John R. W. Stott, "Open Letter to David Hesselgrave," *Trinity World Forum* 16, no.3 (1991): 2, who argues for a definition of "mission" that exceeds narrow verbal boundaries and proceeds rather along conceptual lines. Juan Miranda, too, considers various sets of mission terminology in the Fourth Gospel. His interest, however, similar to Bühner's, is in history-of-religions and cultural-theological dimensions. Cf. Juan Peter Miranda, *Der Vater der mich gesandt hat. Religionsgeschichtliche Untersuchungen zu den johanneischen Sendungsformeln: Zugleich ein Beitrag zur johanneischen Christologie und Ekklesiologie,* EHS 23/7 (Frankfurt am Main: Peter Lang, 1972); and *Die Sendung Jesu im vierten Evangelium: Religions- und theologiegeschichtliche Untersuchungen zu den Sendungsformeln,* SBS 87 (Stuttgart: Katholisches Bibelwerk, 1977). Cf. also Jan Adolph Bühner, *Der Gesandte und sein Weg im 4. Evangelium: Die kultur- und religionsgeschichtliche Entwicklung,* WUNT 2/2 (Tübingen: J. C. B. Mohr [Paul Siebeck], 1977).

are not always mutually exclusive. This is at times due to the fact that a given author's procedure is not clearly articulated or executed. Kuhl, for example, treats largely the same material under "sending" that the present study treats under "mission." He considers the words parallel to sending, studies the relevant contexts, and achieves results that are similar to those obtained by scholars who study mission terminology more broadly. However, the term "sending" no longer adequately describes the subject of Kuhl's study. "Mission" is a better term, since it has a conceptual dimension and does not link one's subject exclusively to one word, as does "sending." Kuhl's study is an instance of a writer's claim to study words when really studying concepts, including those concepts' diachronic backgrounds.[19]

In light of the above considerations, it is apparent that the study of Johannine teaching on mission needs to be more comprehensive than a mere consideration of sending terminology. While no Greek noun for "mission" is found, Stott is surely right when he writes, "Although 'mission' is not, of course, a biblical word (any more than 'trinity' and 'sacrament' are), yet the concept is biblical."[20] Indeed, as Stott contends, the term "mission" is "a useful piece of shorthand for a biblical concept."[21] As already mentioned, the term "send," while providing a fitting starting point in studying mission ter-minology, is at times used in conjunction with similar terminology, such as "coming [into the world]" (cf. 7:28; 8:42; 17:8). One should therefore include this term, as well as other related phrases, in the semantic field of mission in John's Gospel.

4. Definition of Concept

Granted that one's study needs to transcend biblical words to include concepts, the question remains, what is meant by "concept"? Regarding the definition of the term "concept," Cotterell and Turner note the difference between *lexical concepts* (i.e., "a minimal set of salient features which allow individual examples to be identified as belonging to the semantic class") and *a broader notion of concept* which transcends a term's lexical dimension to include also its relation to associated ideas and its theological significance.[22]

Cotterell and Turner further point out that concepts should not be viewed

---

19. Cf. Barr's 1961 critique in *Semantics of Biblical Language.* Kuhl's study dates from 1967.

20. Cf. John R. W. Stott, "Open Letter to David Hesselgrave," 1. Stott goes on to say that "the word remains a useful shorthand for what Christ sends his people into the world to do." Whether Stott is correct in defining mission as broadly as "everything the church is sent into the world to do," is another question. Cf. David J. Hesselgrave, "To John Stott — A Surrejoinder," *Trinity World Forum* 16, no. 3 (1991), 3; and the extensive discussion in Chapter 5.

21. Cf. John R. W. Stott, *The Contemporary Christian: Applying God's Word to Today's World* (Downers Gove, Ill.: InterVarsity, 1992), 342.

22. Cf. Cotterell and Turner, 125.

as static entities but rather in their dynamic relationships with other concepts. They distinguish between a static concept-oriented and a dynamic field-oriented approach in determining the meaning of words.[23] Regarding the concept-oriented approach, the following objections can be raised:

1. there is the danger of an "illegitimate totality transfer" (i.e., the assumption that every time a given word is used, the whole range of meaning of the term is brought along);
2. different definitions of a given concept may be operative for different language users (hence the futility of referring to "the concept of mission" in general terms; the question remains: *Whose* concept of mission is at work?);
3. concepts, because they are mental objects, are not accessible to objective analysis, and so theories of meaning should not be based on them.[24]

In light of these objections, a field-oriented approach is to be preferred.[25] Rather than seeking to study abstract general concepts, this approach gives greater room to the actual phenomena in the text under consideration. Thus attention is paid to the different possible meanings of a given word in different contexts, to the different uses of one and the same word by different language users, and to the various occurrences of a set of terms as "a verbal description of a set of related elements of meaning that together form a coherent and discrete abstraction."[26]

This field-oriented approach thus provides an adequate answer to the concerns by Okure discussed earlier. Okure fears that using terminology as a criterion for the selection of mission texts in the Fourth Gospel will inevitably lead to a static approach that loses sight of the "context of living interaction" in John's Gospel. In light of the distinction just made between a static concept-oriented approach and a dynamic field-oriented model, it is apparent that Okure discards the former without considering the possible viability of the latter. While Okure properly objects to an approach to lexical sense which understands a concept as linguistically associated inextricably with a lexical form, the distinction between lexical and discourse concepts helps alleviate the reductionism Okure perceives.[27]

23. Cf. Cotterell and Turner on a concept-oriented approach to word sense, 146-54; on a field-oriented approach to word sense, 154-55.

24. Cf. Cotterell and Turner, 147-54.

25. See the discussion of the semantic field approach below.

26. Cotterell and Turner, 149.

27. Cf. Cotterell and Turner, 152 and 180; on the distinction between lexical and discourse concepts, see further the discussion below. Cf. John Beekman, John Callow, and Michael Kopesec, *The Semantic Structure of Written Communication*, 5th ed. (Dallas: Summer Institute of Linguistics, 1981), 41-51.

5. Lexical and Discourse Concepts

The distinction between a static concept-oriented approach and a dynamic field-oriented approach hinges largely on the distinction between lexical and discourse concepts. Here the fundamental insight applies that a given word in context may resonate with connotations it acquired by its previous associations in earlier discourse contexts. This is illustrated by Cotterell and Turner, who refer to the problem of confusing a concept which essentially amounts to the lexical sense of a word with some broader concept present in a given context.[28] The example is given of "Uncle George's old red bike" which later in a story may be referred to simply as "the bike." In that case the term "the bike" viewed as a discourse concept should be understood as "Uncle George's old red bike" with all the connotations previously linked to it.

Cotterell and Turner consider lexical sense as a special type of concept, defining concept as "a cognitive construct, a discrete bundle of meanings composing an independent unit of meaning with a central, or prominent element, further defined by other delimiting elements."[29] Discourse concepts are said to "denote not only the lexical sense of the expression involved, but also germane elements of meaning contributed by the context."[30] For the purposes of the present study, it is the cumulative total of discourse concepts of mission in the Fourth Gospel that reflects most accurately "the Johannine approach to mission." This Johannine teaching on mission can be understood as the mental construct associated with mission in the mind of the fourth evangelist which finds concrete expression in terms of clusters of discourse concepts. These discourse concepts, in turn, are best accessed by way of a semantic field survey and the identification of semantic clusters. Finally, each of the relevant references needs to be analyzed by means of contextual exegesis.[31]

6. A Recent Study Supporting the Approach Taken Here

One recent study provides particular support for the methodology chosen in this monograph, i.e., a technical linguistic essay entitled "Πέμπω: per una ricerca del 'campo semantico' nel NT" by Angelico-Salvatore Di Marco. This writer argues for a semantic field approach while choosing πέμπω, one of the two Johannine words for "sending," as his paradigm word. Di Marco argues independently for an approach similar to the one taken here and expresses the following concerns:

28. Cotterell and Turner, 151.
29. Cf. Cotterell and Turner, 151.
30. Cotterell and Turner, 152.
31. Regarding the issue of coherence in the Fourth Gospel's teaching on mission, see the discussion of literary foundations later in this chapter.

1. in studying a given motif in Scripture, it is useful to think in terms of entire concepts rather than mere words or sets of words (in the present scenario, "mission" rather than the Johannine words of "sending," i.e., ἀποστέλλω and πέμπω);

2. however, it is important to recognize that the term "mission" is a contemporary one — though that does not mean that the term could not be useful for discussing a biblical concept nor that the biblical writers may not have had a concept of "mission" in mind as they wrote;

3. the interpreter should be sensitive to the fact that his or her own understanding of "mission" may reflect contemporary rather than biblical usage; one should find out what biblical *words* may be included as well as identify other components of the biblical (here Johannine) concept of "mission";

4. one should not seek to justify one's concept of mission in the Bible; rather, the Bible should be used to clarify or reconfigure it; perhaps one could put together a "Begriffslexikon";

5. a semantic field should be more than a word field; it should be a "significance field" or a "concept field"; concepts may be expressed in different terms, phrases, and texts: "the concept of mission can be found where the term 'mission'-πέμπω is not present."[32]

Corroborating the approach taken in this study, Di Marco arrives at similar conclusions as the present writer regarding: (1) the need for a study of a biblical concept rather than a study of (a set of) biblical words; (2) the importance of retaining links between the definition of such a concept with the biblical text; (3) the necessity of acknowledging one's contemporary presuppositions and conceptualities in order not to import into the biblical text one's own conceptual notions; and (4) his recommendation of a semantic field approach. Di Marco's contention that the concept of mission can be found where the term "mission"-πέμπω is not present is fully supported by the approach chosen in this monograph.

7. The Advantages of a Semantic Field Approach: Conclusion

The contention that semantic field surveys provide the best access for the study of a particular concept is amply supported by the most respected authorities in the field of linguistics. Nida has urged years ago that more use should be made of the methods of field semantics in biblical lexicology, contending, "Critical

---

32. Cf. Angelico-Salvatore Di Marco, "Πέμπω: per una ricerca del 'campo semantico' nel NT," *RivB* 40 (1992): 385-419, especially 409-10. Di Marco's major contribution is in terms of analysis; his article is primarily devoted to theoretical reflections on semantic fields in general; πέμπω is only chosen as an example. Thus Di Marco's implementation of his own insights is only rudimentary. Essentially, he seeks to identify an "archilexeme," an overarching term, under which subgroups, "classemes," can be subsumed.

studies of meaning must be based primarily upon the analysis of related meanings of different words, not upon the the different meanings of single words."[33] A pioneer of field semantics, Trier, has maintained that a word has meaning "only as part of a whole . . . it yields a meaning only within a field."[34] Following de Saussure, Trier perceived the task of the semanticist as setting up lexical systems or subsystems *(Wortfelder)* describing the following semantic relations: sameness or similarity of meaning (synonymity); oppositions or incompatibility of meaning (antonymy or complementarity); and a special kind of inclusiveness of meaning (hyponymy) where one word expresses a class to which a given item belongs. This construction of semantic fields (Trier's *Wortfelder;* de Saussure's "associative fields" or systems of paradigmatic relations) constitutes the programme of field semantics.

Lyons sums up the advantages of a semantic field approach as follows:

> People often think of the meanings of words as if each of them had an independent and separate existence. But . . . no word can be fully understood independently of other words that are related to it and delimit its sense. Looked at from a semantic point of view, the lexical structure of a language — the structure of its vocabulary — is best regarded as a large and intricate network of sense-relations; it is like a huge, multidimensional, spider's web, in which each strand is one such relation and each knot in the web is a different lexeme.[35]

In light of these observations, it is therefore possible to summarize the rationale for the adoption of a semantic field approach in the present monograph. The following considerations apply:

1. The place of terminology in the study of a biblical concept, while to be subordinated to the role a word plays in its literary context, is nevertheless significant. Terminology is therefore a fitting starting point for one's study of a biblical concept.
2. Concepts need to be seen as more than collocations of words. Transcending their lexical dimension, concepts function as discourse concepts and must be studied in relation to the associations attached to them in their contexts.
3. The exploration of Johannine mission teaching on a conceptual rather than merely verbal level is all the more important since the fourth evan-

33. Eugene A. Nida, "The Implications of Contemporary Linguistics for Biblical Scholarship," *JBL* 91 (1972): 85.

34. J. Trier, *Der deutsche Wortschatz im Sinnbezirk des Verstandes* (Heidelberg, 1931), 6, quoted by Thiselton, "Semantics and the New Testament," 90.

35. John Lyons, *Language, Meaning and Context* (London: Fontana [Collins], 1981), 75; quoted in Cotterell and Turner, 155.

gelist frequently uses synonyms and stylistic variation. A study of "send-ing" alone therefore would run the risk of missing certain aspects of the mission concept.

4. A semantic field approach is therefore best suited to study the concept of mission in the Fourth Gospel. A semantic field survey will yield relevant mission terminology which can serve as a guide to mission texts in the Fourth Gospel. A screening of these texts will in turn make it possible to formulate a working definition of mission in the Fourth Gospel.

B. Implementation of the Chosen Methodology

1. Semantic Field Survey of Mission in the Fourth Gospel

The semantic field survey of mission in the Fourth Gospel presented below is based on a number of detailed readings of John's Gospel itself with special attention to terms that may merit inclusion in the category of Johannine mission terminology. On an implicit level, of course, everything the fourth evangelist portrays Jesus as doing can in one sense be considered as part of Jesus' carrying out his mission. This observation applies, for example, to Jesus' conversations with Nicodemus and the Samaritan woman (chaps. 3 and 4) or to the various healings Jesus performs. A close reading of the text of the Fourth Gospel indi-cates, however, that in virtually every case there are verbal reinforcements pro-vided that make Jesus' (or the disciples') actions more explicit. This may be accomplished by comments added by the fourth evangelist or by words at-tributed to Jesus himself. Perhaps the most striking example of such a procedure is the discussion of Jesus' "works," called "signs" by the fourth evangelist, which pervades the first part of the Fourth Gospel (chapters 1–12). Jesus' conversation with Nicodemus includes a discussion of the descending and ascending Son of Man as well as references to the sending of the Son (cf. 3:13-15, 16-17). The encounter with the Samaritan woman is framed by references to Jesus' mission and implications for the mission of the disciples (see especially 4:34-38). While the concern is therefore legitimate that no expression of the concept of mission in the Fourth Gospel be missed by a focus on terminology, an actual reading of John's Gospel indicates that explicit language regularly accompanies implicit cues. Nevertheless, the broader dimensions of the mission concept in John will consistently be kept in mind during the actual study of mission in Chapters 3 and 4 below.

Repeated readings of the Fourth Gospel have yielded the observation that John's teaching on mission appears to be centered primarily around two seman-tic fields. The first semantic field of mission terminology comprises a variety of terms which denote an activity involving movement from one place to another: "send" (ἀποστέλλω, πέμπω); "come" (ἔρχομαι and derivatives), "go" (πορεύομαι, ὑπάγω), "(be)come" (γίνομαι); "descend" (καταβαίνω), "ascend" (ἀναβαίνω), "leave" (μεταβαίνω); "follow" (ἀκολουθέω); "bring," "lead" (ἄγω), and "gather" (συνάγω).[36]

The second semantic field of mission in the Fourth Gospel appears to include terms for the task, or the work, that one is sent (or has come) to carry out. Frequently used in conjunction with words of the semantic field delineated above (cf. 4:34, 38; 5:36; 6:29, 38; 7:31; 8:29; 9:4; 10:36-38; 17:3-4), these terms denote the completion of a work (ἔργον, ἐργάζομαι, κόπος, κοπιάω, ποιέω), which, in the Fourth Gospel's terminology, may be explicated in terms of the working of "signs" (σημεῖον). Other task terminology includes the expressions "harvest" (θερίζω) and "bear fruit" (φέρω καρπόν, συνάγω καρπόν).

The following semantic fields, with their component elements, should therefore be considered.[37]

I. Activity Involving Movement from One Place to Another[38]
   A. Send
      1. ἀποστέλλω
      2. πέμπω

36. Note that not all instances of these terms in the Fourth Gospel will necessarily be relevant. Examples of this are references to "going," "departing," "coming," or other terminology which describes a mere physical movement from one geographical location to another. Ultimately, the meaning of a given term in context is determinative.

37. Since the terms included in these two semantic fields are to function primarily as an entry point to some of the relevant mission passages in the Fourth Gospel, we need not fear that any important terms may have been omitted. Ultimately it is exegesis in context, not isolated word meanings, that are determinative. The semantic field survey is not meant to be taken as an exclusive grid but rather as a help for exegesis. To this exegesis Chapters 3 and 4 will be devoted. A word should also be said about the noninclusion (or only partial inclusion) of certain terms. It is important to realize that just because a word is occasionally used in conjunction with, or even parallel to, an included term does not mean that the word should be included in the two semantic fields. This is why words such as δίδωμι or θέλημα were not accepted. Of course, where these two terms are used in conjunction with mission vocabulary, exegesis will still consider them. For example, θέλημα is in a number of passages used parallel with ἔργον (cf., e.g., 4:34). The notion of "will" is also found in δεῖ expressions which will be discussed under the heading "Other Terminology Related to 'Sending' in the Fourth Gospel" together with the relevant uses of θέλημα, τελειόω, and purpose statements in connection with terms of sending or coming below. Examples of words besides θέλημα that are set in relation to mission terminology in the Fourth Gospel by way of parallel usage include: λαλέω (in 8:29 parallel to ποιέω); δίδωμι (in 3:16-17 parallel to ἀποστέλλω); ῥήματα (in 14:10-11 parallel to ἔργα); perhaps even ὑψόω (used in conjunction with Son of Man terminology which is in turn linked with descending/ascending; cf. 3:13; 8:28; 12:32).

38. Cf. Louw and Nida, who group all of the terms in the first semantic field under the subdomain "linear movement" (#15). They distinguish between "come" as denoting no reference point in space in and of itself (subdomain A, 1-17), and "send" as well as "descend/ascend" which have such a point of reference (D, 66-67; J, K, 101-117). The term cluster "bring/lead/gather" involves multiple movement toward or away from a particular point (M, 123-134), and "follow" indicates the movement of one or a number of persons after (and in the same direction as) one or a number of other persons (T, 156-157).

B. Come, Go, Become
 1. ἔρχομαι
 2. εἰσέρχομαι
 3. ἀπέρχομαι
 4. ἐξέρχομαι
 5. πορεύομαι
 6. ὑπάγω
 7. γίνομαι
 8. ἥκω

C. Descend, Ascend, Leave
 1. ἀναβαίνω
 2. καταβαίνω
 3. μεταβαίνω

D. Follow: ἀκολουθέω

E. Bring, Lead, Gather
 1. συνάγω
 2. ἄγω

II. The Accomplishment of a Task[39]
 A. Work [noun or verb], Do
  1. ἔργον
  2. ἐργάζομαι
  3. κόπος
  4. κοπιάω
  5. ποιέω

 B. Sign: σημεῖον

 C. Harvest, Bear Fruit
  1. θερίζω
  2. φέρω καρπόν
  3. συνάγω καρπόν

39. Cf. Louw and Nida. The terms in the second semantic field are grouped by Louw and Nida under the subdomain #42 "perform, do." The exception is σημεῖον, which is included in this semantic subdomain since the term is used in Johannine theology in close connection with ἔργον (sometimes synonymously or at least pointing to the same referent: cf., e.g., John 9:3-4 and 9:16; note that 10:38 and 14:11 use ἔργον with reference to Jesus' miracles which are at other places in the Fourth Gospel called "signs"). Generally, it should be noted that it seems appropriate in one's grouping of terms in linguistic subdomains to leave room for stylistic peculiarities of a given author. Louw and Nida themselves, though grouping σημεῖον under "non-verbal communication" (443), note that σημεῖον is "an event" which in John "in a number of contexts may be rendered as 'miracle'" (443). This is exactly John's point — Jesus' works are revelation, i.e., vehicles of communication, "signs" that speak. Therefore, in John's conceptual framework, ἔργον and σημεῖον share at least partially a certain semantic field. Indeed, within certain limits, semantic fields can be configured differently according to an author's usage of terms. Cf. in this regard Moisés Silva's perceptive review of Louw and Nida in *WTJ* 51 (1989): 163-67. Silva notes the principle of collocation, i.e., the tendency for a given word to occur in association with another word, and the significance of this phenomenon for the word's meaning (166-67).

These terms are used with reference to Jesus and/or the disciples in the Fourth Gospel.[40] The following chart lists the relevant passages under the respective semantic domain:

I. Activity Involving Movement from One Place to Another
   A. Send
      1. Jesus:
         3:17, 34; 4:34; 5:23, 24, 30, 36, 37, 38; 6:29, 38, 39, 44, 57; 7:16, 18, 28, 29, 33; 8:16, 18, 26, 29, 42; 9:4, 7; 10:36; 11:42; 12:44, 45, 49; 14:24; 15:21; 16:5; 17:3, 8, 18, 21, 23, 25; 20:21 (17:18 and 20:21 are in the active voice)
      2. Disciples:
         4:38; 17:18; 20:21 (always in the passive voice)
      3. General:
         13:16, 20
   B. Come, Go, Become
      1. Jesus:
         1:9, 14, 17; 3:2, 19, 31; 4:25; 5:40, 43; 6:14; 7:27, 28, 31, 33, 41, 42; 8:14, 21, 22, 42; 9:39; 10:10; 11:27; 12:13, 15, 46, 47; 13:3; 14:2, 3, 4, 5, 12, 18, 28; 16:5, 7, 10, 17, 27, 28, 30; 17:8, 11, 13; 18:37; 21:22
      2. [Potential] Disciples:
         1:12, 39, 46, 47; 4:38; 5:40; 6:35, 37, 44, 45, 65; 7:37; 14:6; 15:16
   C. Descend, Ascend, Leave
      1. Jesus:
         3:13; 6:33, 38, 41, 42, 50, 51, 58, 62; 13:1; 20:17
      2. Disciples:
         not used
   D. Follow
      1. Jesus:
         not used
      2. Disciples:
         1:37, 38, 40, 43; 8:12; 10:4, 5, 27; 12:26; 13:33, 36, 37; 18:15; 20:6; 21:19, 20, 23
   E. Bring, Lead, Gather
      1. Jesus:
         10:16; 11:52
      2. Disciples:
         1:42; 6:12-13
II. The Accomplishment of a Task

---

40. Occasionally in the Fourth Gospel, these terms may occur with reference to someone other than Jesus or the disciples, as in the case of "sending" verbs, which are also used in connection with John the Baptist or the Spirit. But see already the comments in the Introduction above.

A. Work [noun or verb], Do
   1. Jesus:
      2:11, 18, 23; 3:2; 4:6, 34, 45, 46, 48, 54 (twice); 5:11, 15, 16, 17,
      19, 20, 27, 30, 36 (twice); 6:2, 6, 14, 30, 38, 39, 40; 7:3 (twice), 4,
      21 (twice), 23, 31; 8:28, 29; 9:3, 4, 16, 33; 10:25 (twice), 32, 33, 37
      (twice), 38 (twice); 11:37, 45, 46; 12:18, 24, 37; 13:7, 12, 15;
      14:10, 11, 12 (twice), 13, 14, 31; 15:24; 17:4 (twice); 20:30; 21:25
   2. Disciples:
      6:28-29 (?); 14:12 (works); 15:5, 8, 16
B. Sign
   1. Jesus:
      2:11, 18, 23; 3:2; 4:48, 54; 6:2, 14, 26, 30; 7:31; 9:16; 11:47; 12:18,
      37; 20:30
   2. Disciples:
      not used
C. Harvest, Bear Fruit
   1. Jesus: 4:36 (?), 38; 12:24
   2. Disciples:
      4:38; 6:28 (?); 13:15, 17; 14:12

While a detailed exploration of these data must await Chapters 3 and 4, a few preliminary observations may be made. It is already evident that Jesus' mission is presented in more comprehensive terms than that of the disciples. Specifically, the scope of terms used with reference to Jesus' mission includes: being sent or send; come, go, and become; descend, ascend, and leave; bring, lead, gather; work [noun or verb]; do; sign; harvest, and bear fruit. By contrast, the range of terms used for the disciples' mission is much smaller, as is the total number of occurrences of these expressions: being sent (but not send); go; follow; lead, gather; work [pl. noun and verb], do; and harvest. Notably, the largest body of mission data for the disciples' mission is found in the word group "to follow," a term that is not used for Jesus' mission at all. The term "sign," on the other hand, is used exclusively with reference to Jesus. The sheer quantity of mission terminology used with regard to Jesus and the comparatively small number of passages addressing the disciples' mission make it clear that the focus of the Fourth Gospel's mission teaching is on Jesus.

2. Identification of Semantic Clusters

After a semantic field survey has helped identify potentially relevant mission terms in the Fourth Gospel, and before a comprehensive working definition of mission will be given, there remains one further methodological step, i.e., the identification of semantic clusters. Semantic clusters may be defined as portions of text where a certain kind of terminology (in the case of the present study, mission terminology) is used with high frequency. This applies both to pericopae that include multiple occurrences of one mission term and to those which contain a variety of expressions related to mission. While only the immediate context of such passages is given below, the discussion of the missions of Jesus and of the disciples in Chapters 3 and 4 will consider the broader contexts of each pericope. Mission terminology identified in the preceding semantic field survey is highlighted. The following semantic clusters of mission in the Fourth Gospel can be identified:

Cluster #1: Jesus is coming into the world (1:9, 11, 14, 17)

ᵀΗν τὸ φῶς τὸ ἀληθινόν, ὃ φωτίζει πάντα ἄνθρωπον, ἐρχόμενον εἰς τὸν κόσμον. . . . εἰς τὰ ἴδια ἦλθεν, καὶ οἱ ἴδιοι αὐτὸν οὐ παρέλαβον. . . . Καὶ ὁ λόγος σὰρξ ἐγένετο καὶ ἐσκήνωσεν ἐν ἡμῖν. . . . ἡ χάρις καὶ ἡ ἀλήθεια διὰ Ἰησοῦ Χριστοῦ ἐγένετο.

Cluster #2: Jesus calls others to follow; Andrew brings brother to Jesus (1:37-43)

καὶ ἤκουσαν οἱ δύο μαθηταὶ αὐτοῦ λαλοῦντος καὶ ἠκολούθησαν τῷ Ἰησοῦ. στραφεὶς δὲ ὁ Ἰησοῦς καὶ θεασάμενος αὐτοὺς ἀκολουθοῦντας λέγει αὐτοῖς . . . ᵀΗν Ἀνδρέας ὁ ἀδελφὸς Σίμωνος Πέτρου εἷς ἐκ τῶν ἀκουσάντων παρὰ Ἰωάννου καὶ ἀκολουθησάντων αὐτῷ. . . . ἤγαγεν αὐτὸν πρὸς τὸν Ἰησοῦν. . . . καὶ λέγει αὐτῷ ὁ Ἰησοῦς, Ἀκολούθει μοι.

Cluster #3: Jesus descends, ascends, is sent, comes (3:2, 13-19, 31-34)

ῥαββί, οἴδαμεν ὅτι ἀπὸ θεοῦ ἐλήλυθας διδάσκαλος· οὐδεὶς γὰρ δύναται ταῦτα τὰ σημεῖα ποιεῖν ἃ σὺ ποιεῖς, ἐὰν μὴ ᾖ ὁ θεὸς μετ' αὐτοῦ. . . . καὶ οὐδεὶς ἀναβέβηκεν εἰς τὸν οὐρανὸν εἰ μὴ ὁ ἐκ τοῦ οὐρανοῦ καταβάς, ὁ υἱὸς τοῦ ἀνθρώπου. καὶ καθὼς Μωϋσῆς ὕψωσεν τὸν ὄφιν ἐν τῇ ἐρήμῳ, οὕτως ὑψωθῆναι δεῖ τὸν υἱὸν τοῦ ἀνθρώπου, ἵνα πᾶς ὁ πιστεύων ἐν αὐτῷ ἔχῃ ζωὴν αἰώνιον. Οὕτως γὰρ ἠγάπησεν ὁ θεὸς τὸν κόσμον, ὥστε τὸν υἱὸν τὸν μονογενῆ ἔδωκεν, ἵνα πᾶς ὁ πιστεύων εἰς αὐτὸν μὴ ἀπόληται ἀλλ' ἔχῃ ζωὴν αἰώνιον. οὐ γὰρ ἀπέστειλεν ὁ θεὸς τὸν υἱὸν εἰς τὸν κόσμον ἵνα κρίνῃ τὸν κόσμον, ἀλλ' ἵνα σωθῇ ὁ κόσμος δι' αὐτοῦ. . . . αὕτη δέ ἐστιν ἡ κρίσις, ὅτι τὸ φῶς ἐλήλυθεν εἰς τὸν κόσμον. . . . ὁ ἐκ τοῦ οὐρανοῦ ἐρχόμενος [ἐπάνω πάντων ἐστίν]. . . . ὃν γὰρ ἀπέστειλεν ὁ θεὸς τὰ ῥήματα τοῦ θεοῦ λαλεῖ.

Cluster #4: Jesus sends disciples to harvest; they enter into others' labor (4:34-38)

Ἐμὸν βρῶμά ἐστιν ἵνα ποιήσω τὸ θέλημα τοῦ πέμψαντός με καὶ τελειώσω αὐτοῦ τὸ ἔργον. . . . ὁ θερίζων μισθὸν λαμβάνει καὶ συνάγει καρπὸν εἰς ζωὴν αἰώνιον. . . . ἐγὼ <u>ἀπέστειλα</u> ὑμᾶς <u>θερίζειν</u> ὃ οὐχ ὑμεῖς <u>κεκοπιάκατε·</u> ἄλλοι <u>κεκοπιάκατε</u> καὶ ὑμεῖς εἰς τὸν <u>κόπον</u> αὐτῶν <u>εἰσεληλύθατε</u>.

Cluster #5: Jesus is working like the Father, is sent, comes (5:16-43)

καὶ διὰ τοῦτο ἐδίωκον οἱ Ἰουδαῖοι τὸν Ἰησοῦν, ὅτι ταῦτα ἐποίει ἐν σαββάτῳ. . . . Ὁ πατήρ μου ἕως ἄρτι <u>ἐργάζεται</u>, κἀγὼ <u>ἐργάζομαι</u>. . . . οὐ δύναται ὁ υἱὸς <u>ποιεῖν</u> ἀφ' ἑαυτοῦ οὐδὲν ἐὰν μή τι βλέπῃ τὸν πατέρα <u>ποιοῦντα</u>. ἃ γὰρ ἂν ἐκεῖνος <u>ποιῇ</u>, ταῦτα καὶ ὁ υἱὸς ὁμοίως <u>ποιεῖ</u>. ὁ γὰρ πατὴρ φιλεῖ τὸν υἱὸν καὶ πάντα δείκνυσιν αὐτῷ ἃ αὐτὸς <u>ποιεῖ</u>, καὶ μείζονα τούτων δείξει αὐτῷ <u>ἔργα</u>, ἵνα ὑμεῖς θαυμάζητε. . . . ὁ μὴ τιμῶν τὸν υἱὸν οὐ τιμᾷ τὸν πατέρα τὸν <u>πέμψαντα</u> αὐτόν. . . . ὁ τὸν λόγον μου ἀκούων καὶ πιστεύων τῷ <u>πέμψαντί</u> με ἔχει ζωὴν αἰώνιον. . . . καὶ ἐξουσίαν ἔδωκεν αὐτῷ κρίσιν ποιεῖν, ὅτι υἱὸς ἀνθρώπου ἐστίν. . . . οὐ δύναμαι ἐγὼ <u>ποιεῖν</u> ἀπ' ἐμαυτοῦ οὐδέν. . . . οὐ ζητῶ τὸ θέλημα τὸ ἐμὸν ἀλλὰ τὸ θέλημα τοῦ <u>πέμψαντός</u> με. . . . τὰ γὰρ <u>ἔργα</u> ἃ δέδωκέν μοι ὁ πατὴρ ἵνα τελειώσω αὐτά, αὐτὰ τὰ <u>ἔργα</u> ἃ <u>ποιῶ</u> μαρτυρεῖ περὶ ἐμοῦ ὅτι ὁ πατήρ με <u>ἀπέσταλκεν</u>. καὶ ὁ <u>πέμψας</u> με πατὴρ ἐκεῖνος μεμαρτύρηκεν περὶ ἐμοῦ. . . . καὶ τὸν λόγον αὐτοῦ οὐκ ἔχετε ἐν ὑμῖν μένοντα, ὅτι ὃν <u>ἀπέστειλεν</u> ἐκεῖνος, τούτῳ ὑμεῖς οὐ πιστεύετε. . . . ἐγὼ <u>ἐλήλυθα</u> ἐν τῷ ὀνόματι τοῦ πατρός μου, καὶ οὐ λαμβάνετέ με·

Cluster #6: The issue of signs; Jesus is sent, descends, ascends (6:2, 14, 26, 29-62)

ἠκολούθει δὲ αὐτῷ ὄχλος πολύς, ὅτι ἐθεώρουν τὰ σημεῖα ἃ ἐποίει ἐπὶ τῶν ἀσθενούντων. . . . Οἱ οὖν ἄνθρωποι ἰδόντες ὃ ἐποίησεν σημεῖον. . . . ζητεῖτέ με οὐχ ὅτι εἴδετε σημεῖα. . . . <u>ἐργάζεσθε</u> μὴ τὴν βρῶσιν τὴν ἀπολλυμένην ἀλλὰ τὴν βρῶσιν τὴν μένουσαν εἰς ζωὴν αἰώνιον, ἣν ὁ υἱὸς τοῦ ἀνθρώπου ὑμῖν δώσει. . . . Τί ποιῶμεν ἵνα <u>ἐργαζώμεθα</u> τὰ <u>ἔργα</u> τοῦ θεοῦ; . . . Τοῦτό ἐστιν τὸ <u>ἔργον</u> τοῦ θεοῦ, ἵνα πιστεύητε εἰς ὃν <u>ἀπέστειλεν</u> ἐκεῖνος. . . . Τί οὖν <u>ποιεῖς</u> σὺ σημεῖον, ἵνα ἴδωμεν καὶ πιστεύσωμέν σοι; τί <u>ἐργάζῃ</u>; . . . ὁ γὰρ ἄρτος τοῦ θεοῦ ἐστιν ὁ <u>καταβαίνων</u> ἐκ τοῦ οὐρανοῦ καὶ ζωὴν διδοὺς τῷ κόσμῳ. . . . ὅτι <u>καταβέβηκα</u> <u>ἀπὸ τοῦ οὐρανοῦ</u> οὐχ ἵνα <u>ποιῶ</u> τὸ θέλημα τὸ ἐμὸν ἀλλὰ τὸ θέλημα τοῦ <u>πέμψαντός</u> με. τοῦτο δέ ἐστιν τὸ θέλημα τοῦ <u>πέμψαντός</u> με, ἵνα πᾶν ὃ δέδωκέν μοι μὴ ἀπολέσω. . . . τοῦτο γάρ ἐστιν τὸ θέλημα τοῦ πατρός μου, ἵνα πᾶς ὁ θεωρῶν τὸν υἱὸν καὶ πιστεύων εἰς αὐτὸν ἔχῃ ζωὴν αἰώνιον. . . . ἐγώ εἰμι ὁ ἄρτος ὁ <u>καταβὰς ἐκ τοῦ οὐρανοῦ</u>. . . . πῶς νῦν λέγει ὅτι ἐκ τοῦ οὐρανοῦ <u>καταβέβηκα</u>; . . . οὐδεὶς δύναται <u>ἐλθεῖν</u> πρός με, ἐὰν μὴ ὁ πατὴρ ὁ <u>πέμψας</u> με ἑλκύσῃ αὐτόν, κἀγὼ ἀναστήσω αὐτὸν ἐν τῇ ἐσχάτῃ ἡμέρᾳ. . . . οὗτός ἐστιν ὁ ἄρτος ὁ ἐκ τοῦ οὐρανοῦ <u>καταβαίνων</u>, ἵνα τις ἐξ αὐτοῦ φάγῃ καὶ μὴ ἀποθάνῃ. . . . ἐγώ εἰμι ὁ ἄρτος ὁ ζῶν ὁ ἐκ τοῦ οὐρανοῦ <u>καταβάς</u>. . . . καθὼς <u>ἀπέστειλέν</u> με ὁ ζῶν πατὴρ κἀγὼ ζῶ διὰ τὸν πατέρα. . . . οὗτός ἐστιν ὁ ἄρτος ὁ ἐξ οὐρανοῦ <u>καταβάς</u>, οὐ καθὼς ἔφαγον οἱ πατέρες καὶ ἀπέθανον. . . . ἐὰν οὖν θεωρῆτε τὸν υἱὸν τοῦ ἀνθρώπου <u>ἀναβαίνοντα</u> ὅπου ἦν τὸ πρότερον;

Cluster #7: Jesus is sent, comes, will depart (7:16-18, 27-42; 8:12-29, 42)

Ἡ ἐμὴ διδαχὴ οὐκ ἔστιν ἐμὴ ἀλλὰ τοῦ <u>πέμψαντός</u> με. ἐάν τις θέλῃ τὸ θέλημα αὐτοῦ <u>ποιεῖν</u>, γνώσεται περὶ τῆς διδαχῆς πότερον ἐκ τοῦ θεοῦ ἐστιν ἢ ἐγὼ ἀπ' ἐμαυτοῦ λαλῶ. . . . ὁ δὲ ζητῶν τὴν δόξαν τοῦ <u>πέμψαντος</u> αὐτὸν οὗτος ἀληθής ἐστιν. . . . ὁ δὲ χριστὸς ὅταν <u>ἔρχηται</u> οὐδεὶς γινώσκει πόθεν ἐστίν. . . . καὶ ἀπ' ἐμαυτοῦ οὐκ <u>ἐλήλυθα</u>, ἀλλ' ἔστιν ἀληθινὸς ὁ <u>πέμψας</u> με, ὃν ὑμεῖς οὐκ οἴδατε. ἐγὼ οἶδα αὐτόν, ὅτι παρ' αὐτοῦ εἰμι κἀκεῖνός με <u>ἀπέστειλεν</u>. . . . ὁ χριστὸς ὅταν <u>ἔλθῃ</u> μὴ πλείονα <u>σημεῖα</u> ποιήσει ὧν οὗτος ἐποίησεν; . . . Ἔτι χρόνον μικρὸν μεθ' ὑμῶν εἰμι καὶ <u>ὑπάγω</u> πρὸς τὸν <u>πέμψαντά</u> με. . . . Μὴ γὰρ ἐκ τῆς Γαλιλαίας ὁ χριστὸς <u>ἔρχεται</u>; οὐχ ἡ γραφὴ εἶπεν ὅτι ἐκ . . . τῆς κώμης ὅπου ἦν Δαυὶδ <u>ἔρχεται</u> ὁ χριστός; . . . ὁ <u>ἀκολουθῶν</u> ἐμοὶ οὐ μὴ περιπατήσῃ ἐν τῇ σκοτίᾳ, ἀλλ' ἕξει τὸ φῶς τῆς ζωῆς. . . . οἶδα πόθεν <u>ἦλθον</u> καὶ ποῦ <u>ὑπάγω</u>. ὑμεῖς δὲ οὐκ οἴδατε πόθεν <u>ἔρχομαι</u> ἢ ποῦ <u>ὑπάγω</u>. . . . ὅτι μόνος οὐκ εἰμί, ἀλλ' ἐγὼ καὶ ὁ <u>πέμψας</u> με πατήρ. . . . καὶ μαρτυρεῖ περὶ ἐμοῦ ὁ <u>πέμψας</u> με πατήρ. . . . Ἐγὼ <u>ὑπάγω</u> καὶ ζητήσετέ με, καὶ ἐν τῇ ἁμαρτίᾳ ὑμῶν ἀποθανεῖσθε. . . . ὅπου ἐγὼ <u>ὑπάγω</u> ὑμεῖς οὐ δύνασθε ἐλθεῖν. . . . πολλὰ ἔχω περὶ ὑμῶν λαλεῖν καὶ κρίνειν, ἀλλ' ὁ <u>πέμψας</u> με ἀληθής ἐστιν. . . . Ὅταν ὑψώσητε τὸν υἱὸν τοῦ ἀνθρώπου, τότε γνώσεσθε ὅτι ἐγώ εἰμι, καὶ ἀπ' ἐμαυτοῦ ποιῶ οὐδέν, ἀλλὰ καθὼς ἐδίδαξέν με ὁ πατὴρ ταῦτα λαλῶ. καὶ ὁ <u>πέμψας</u> με μετ' <u>ἐμοῦ</u> ἐστιν· οὐκ <u>ἀφῆκέν</u> με μόνον, ὅτι ἐγὼ τὰ ἀρεστὰ αὐτῷ <u>ποιῶ</u> πάντοτε. . . . ἐγὼ γὰρ ἐκ τοῦ θεοῦ <u>ἐξῆλθον</u> καὶ <u>ἥκω</u>· οὐδὲ γὰρ ἀπ' ἐμαυτοῦ <u>ἐλήλυθα</u>, ἀλλ' ἐκεῖνός με <u>ἀπέστειλεν</u>.

Cluster #8: Jesus is sent, comes (9:3-4, 7, 16, 31, 33, 39)

. . . ἵνα φανερωθῇ τὰ ἔργα τοῦ θεοῦ ἐν αὐτῷ. ἡμᾶς δεῖ ἐργάζεσθαι τὰ ἔργα τοῦ <u>πέμψαντός</u> με ἕως ἡμέρα ἐστίν· <u>ἔρχεται</u> νὺξ ὅτε οὐδεὶς δύναται <u>ἐργάζε-</u><u>σθαι</u>. . . . Ὕπαγε νίψαι εἰς τὴν κολυμβήθραν τοῦ Σιλωάμ (ὃ ἑρμηνεύεται <u>ἀπεσταλμένος</u>). . . . Πῶς δύναται ἄνθρωπος ἁμαρτωλὸς τοιαῦτα <u>σημεῖα</u> <u>ποιεῖν</u>; . . . ἐάν τις θεοσεβὴς ᾖ καὶ τὸ θέλημα αὐτοῦ <u>ποιῇ</u> τούτου ἀκούει. . . . εἰ μὴ ἦν οὗτος παρὰ θεοῦ οὐκ ἠδύνατο <u>ποιεῖν</u> οὐδέν. . . . Εἰς κρίμα ἐγὼ εἰς τὸν κόσμον τοῦτον <u>ἦλθον</u>, ἵνα οἱ μὴ βλέποντες βλέπωσιν. . . .

Cluster #9: Disciples follow; Jesus is sent, comes, will bring others also, offers works as witness (10:4-10, 16, 25, 27, 32, 36-38)

. . . ἔμπροσθεν αὐτῶν πορεύεται, καὶ τὰ πρόβατα αὐτῷ <u>ἀκολουθεῖ</u>, ὅτι οἴδασιν τὴν φωνὴν αὐτοῦ· ἀλλοτρίῳ δὲ οὐ μὴ <u>ἀκολουθήσουσιν</u>, ἀλλὰ φεύξον- ται ἀπ' αὐτοῦ. . . . ἐγὼ <u>ἦλθον</u> ἵνα ζωὴν ἔχωσιν καὶ περισσὸν ἔχωσιν. . . . κἀκεῖνα δεῖ με <u>ἀγαγεῖν</u> καὶ τῆς φωνῆς μου ἀκούσουσιν, καὶ γενήσονται μία ποίμνη, εἷς ποιμήν. . . . τὰ <u>ἔργα</u> ἃ ἐγὼ <u>ποιῶ</u> ἐν τῷ ὀνόματι τοῦ πατρός μου ταῦτα μαρτυρεῖ περὶ ἐμοῦ. . . . κἀγὼ γινώσκω αὐτὰ καὶ <u>ἀκολουθοῦσίν</u> μοι, κἀγὼ δίδωμι αὐτοῖς ζωὴν αἰώνιον. . . . Πολλὰ <u>ἔργα</u> καλὰ ἔδειξα ὑμῖν ἐκ τοῦ πατρός· διὰ ποῖον αὐτῶν <u>ἔργον</u> ἐμὲ λιθάζετε; . . . ὃν ὁ πατὴρ ἡγίασεν καὶ <u>ἀπέστειλεν</u> εἰς τὸν κόσμον ὑμεῖς λέγετε ὅτι Βλασφημεῖς, ὅτι εἶπον, Υἱὸς τοῦ θεοῦ εἰμι; εἰ οὐ <u>ποιῶ τὰ ἔργα</u> τοῦ πατρός μου, μὴ πιστεύετέ μοι· εἰ δὲ <u>ποιῶ</u>, κἂν ἐμοὶ μὴ πιστεύητε, τοῖς <u>ἔργοις</u> πιστεύετε.

Cluster #10: Jesus is sent, comes, does signs, gathers (11:27, 42, 47, 52)

ἐγὼ πεπίστευκα ὅτι σὺ εἶ ὁ Χριστὸς ὁ υἱὸς τοῦ θεοῦ ὁ εἰς τὸν κόσμον <u>ἐρχόμενος</u>. . . . ἵνα πιστεύσωσιν ὅτι σύ με <u>ἀπέστειλας</u>. . . . οὗτος ὁ ἄνθρωπος πολλὰ <u>ποιεῖ σημεῖα</u>. . . . τέκνα τοῦ θεοῦ τὰ διεσκορπισμένα <u>συναγάγῃ</u> εἰς ἕν.

Cluster #11: Jesus is sent, comes; the disciples are to follow; unbelief despite signs (12:13-15, 18, 24, 26, 37, 44-49)

εὐλογημένος ὁ <u>ἐρχόμενος</u> ἐν ὀνόματι κυρίου. . . . ἰδοὺ ὁ βασιλεύς σου <u>ἔρχεται</u>. . . . διὰ τοῦτο ὑπήντησεν αὐτῷ ὁ ὄχλος ὅτι ἤκουσαν τοῦτο αὐτὸν <u>πεποιηκέναι τὸ σημεῖον</u>. . . . ἐὰν μὴ ὁ κόκκος τοῦ σίτου πεσὼν εἰς τὴν γῆν ἀποθάνῃ, αὐτὸς μόνος μένει· ἐὰν δὲ ἀποθάνῃ, πολὺν καρπὸν φέρει. . . . ἐὰν ἐμοί τις διακονῇ, ἐμοὶ <u>ἀκολουθείτω</u>, καὶ ὅπου εἰμὶ ἐγὼ ἐκεῖ καὶ ὁ διάκονος. . . . Τοσαῦτα δὲ αὐτοῦ <u>σημεῖα πεποιηκότος</u> ἔμπροσθεν αὐτῶν οὐκ ἐπίστευον εἰς αὐτόν. . . . Ὁ πιστεύων εἰς ἐμὲ οὐ πιστεύει εἰς ἐμὲ ἀλλὰ εἰς τὸν <u>πέμψαντά</u> με, καὶ ὁ θεωρῶν ἐμὲ θεωρεῖ τὸν <u>πέμψαντά</u> με. ἐγὼ φῶς εἰς τὸν κόσμον <u>ἐλήλυθα</u>, ἵνα πᾶς ὁ πιστεύων εἰς ἐμὲ ἐν τῇ σκοτίᾳ μὴ μείνῃ. . . . οὐ γὰρ <u>ἦλθον</u> ἵνα κρίνω τὸν κόσμον, ἀλλ' ἵνα σώσω τὸν κόσμον. . . . ὅτι ἐγὼ ἐξ ἐμαυτοῦ οὐκ ἐλάλησα, ἀλλ' ὁ <u>πέμψας</u> με πατὴρ αὐτός μοι ἐντολὴν δέδωκεν.

Cluster #12: Jesus descended, was sent, came from, will depart; disciples cannot follow now, will do greater works, are to go (13:1-3, 15-17, 20, 36-37; 14:2-5, 10-14, 18, 23-24, 28, 31; 15:5, 8, 14-16, 21-22, 24; 16:5-7, 10, 17, 27-30)

ἦλθεν αὐτοῦ ἡ ὥρα ἵνα <u>μεταβῇ</u> ἐκ τοῦ κόσμου τούτου πρὸς τὸν πατέρα. . . . ἀπὸ θεοῦ <u>ἐξῆλθεν</u> καὶ πρὸς τὸν θεὸν <u>ὑπάγει</u>. . . . ὑπόδειγμα γὰρ δέδωκα ὑμῖν ἵνα καθὼς ἐγὼ ἐποίησα ὑμῖν καὶ ὑμεῖς <u>ποιῆτε</u>. . . . οὐκ ἔστιν δοῦλος μείζων τοῦ κυρίου αὐτοῦ οὐδὲ ἀπόστολος μείζων τοῦ <u>πέμψαντος</u> αὐτόν. εἰ ταῦτα οἴδατε, μακάριοί ἐστε ἐὰν <u>ποιῆτε</u> αὐτά. . . . ὁ λαμβάνων ἄν τινα <u>πέμψω</u> ἐμὲ λαμβάνει, ὁ δὲ ἐμὲ λαμβάνων λαμβάνει τὸν <u>πέμψαντά</u> με. . . . κύριε, ποῦ <u>ὑπάγεις</u>; ἀπεκρίθη [αὐτῷ] Ἰησοῦς, Ὅπου <u>ὑπάγω</u> οὐ δύνασαί μοι νῦν <u>ἀκολουθῆσαι</u>, <u>ἀκολουθήσεις</u> δὲ ὕστερον. . . . διὰ τί οὐ δύναμαί σοι <u>ἀκολουθῆσαι</u> ἄρτι; . . . εἰ δὲ μή, εἶπον ἂν ὑμῖν ὅτι <u>πορεύομαι</u> ἑτοιμάσαι τόπον ὑμῖν; καὶ ἐὰν <u>πορευθῶ</u> καὶ ἑτοιμάσω τόπον ὑμῖν, πάλιν <u>ἔρχομαι</u> καὶ παραλήμψομαι ὑμᾶς πρὸς ἐμαυτόν. . . . καὶ ὅπου [ἐγὼ] <u>ὑπάγω</u> οἴδατε τὴν ὁδόν. κύριε, οὐκ οἴδαμεν ποῦ <u>ὑπάγεις</u>. . . . ὁ δὲ πατὴρ ἐν ἐμοὶ μένων <u>ποιεῖ τὰ ἔργα</u> αὐτοῦ. πιστεύετέ μοι. . . . εἰ δὲ μή, διὰ τὰ <u>ἔργα</u> αὐτὰ πιστεύετε. . . . ὁ πιστεύων εἰς ἐμὲ τὰ ἔργα ἃ ἐγὼ ποιῶ κἀκεῖνος ποιήσει, καὶ μείζονα τούτων ποιήσει, ὅτι ἐγὼ πρὸς τὸν πατέρα πορεύομαι· καὶ ὅ τι ἂν αἰτήσητε ἐν τῷ ὀνόματί μου τοῦτο ποιήσω. . . . ἐγὼ ποιήσω. . . . Οὐκ ἀφήσω ὑμᾶς ὀρφανούς, ἔρχομαι πρὸς ὑμᾶς. . . . ὁ πατήρ μου ἀγαπήσει αὐτὸν καὶ πρὸς αὐτὸν ἐλευσόμεθα καὶ μονὴν παρ' αὐτῷ ποιησόμεθα. καὶ ὁ λόγος ὃν ἀκούετε οὐκ ἔστιν ἐμὸς ἀλλὰ τοῦ πέμψαντός με πατρός. . . . ὑπάγω καὶ ἔρχομαι πρὸς ὑμᾶς. εἰ ἠγαπᾶτέ με ἐχάρητε ἂν ὅτι πορεύομαι πρὸς τὸν πατέρα. . . . ἀλλ' ἵνα γνῷ ὁ κόσμος ὅτι ἀγαπῶ τὸν πατέρα, καὶ καθὼς ἐνετείλατο μοι ὁ πατήρ, οὕτως ποιῶ. . . . ὁ μένων ἐν ἐμοὶ κἀγὼ ἐν αὐτῷ οὗτος φέρει καρπὸν πολύν, ὅτι χωρὶς ἐμοῦ οὐ δύνασθε ποιεῖν οὐδέν. . . . ἐν τούτῳ ἐδοξάσθη ὁ πατήρ μου, ἵνα καρπὸν πολὺν φέρητε καὶ γένησθε ἐμοὶ μαθηταί. . . . ὑμεῖς φίλοι μού ἐστε ἐὰν ποιῆτε ἃ ἐγὼ ἐντέλλομαι ὑμῖν. οὐκέτι λέγω ὑμᾶς δούλους, ὅτι ὁ δοῦλος οὐκ οἶδεν τί ποιεῖ αὐτοῦ ὁ κύριος. . . . οὐχ ὑμεῖς με ἐξελέξασθε, ἀλλ' ἐγὼ ὑμᾶς ἐξελεξάμην καὶ ἔθηκα ὑμᾶς ἵνα ὑμεῖς ὑπάγητε καὶ καρπὸν φέρητε. . . . ἀλλὰ ταῦτα πάντα ποιήσουσιν εἰς ὑμᾶς διὰ τὸ ὄνομά μου, ὅτι οὐκ οἴδασιν τὸν πέμψαντά με. εἰ μὴ ἦλθον καὶ ἐλάλησα αὐτοῖς, ἁμαρτίαν οὐκ εἴχοσαν. . . . εἰ τὰ ἔργα μὴ ἐποίησα ἐν αὐτοῖς ἃ οὐδεὶς ἄλλος ἐποίησεν, ἁμαρτίαν οὐκ εἴχοσαν. . . . Νῦν δὲ ὑπάγω πρὸς τὸν πέμψαντά με, καὶ οὐδεὶς ἐξ ὑμῶν ἐρωτᾷ με, ποῦ ὑπάγεις; . . . συμφέρει ὑμῖν ἵνα ἐγὼ ἀπέλθω. ἐὰν γὰρ μὴ ἀπέλθω, ὁ παράκλητος οὐκ ἐλεύσεται πρὸς ὑμᾶς· ἐὰν δὲ πορευθῶ, πέμψω αὐτὸν πρὸς ὑμᾶς. . . . περὶ δικαιοσύνης δέ, ὅτι πρὸς τὸν πατέρα ὑπάγω καὶ οὐκέτι θεωρεῖτέ με. . . . ὅτι ὑπάγω πρὸς τὸν πατέρα; . . . ὅτι ἐγὼ παρὰ [τοῦ] θεοῦ ἐξῆλθον. ἐξῆλθον παρὰ τοῦ πατρὸς καὶ ἐλήλυθα εἰς τὸν κόσμον· πάλιν ἀφίημι τὸν κόσμον καὶ πορεύομαι πρὸς τὸν πατέρα. . . . ἐν τούτῳ πιστεύομεν ὅτι ἀπὸ θεοῦ ἐξῆλθες.

Cluster #13: Jesus was sent, is coming to Father; disciples are sent (chap. 17)

ἵνα γινώσκωσιν σὲ τὸν μόνον ἀληθινὸν θεὸν καὶ ὃν ἀπέστειλας Ἰησοῦν Χριστόν. ἐγώ σε ἐδόξασα ἐπὶ τῆς γῆς τὸ ἔργον τελειώσας ὃ δέδωκάς μοι ἵνα ποιήσω. . . . ἔγνωσαν ἀληθῶς ὅτι παρὰ σοῦ ἐξῆλθον, καὶ ἐπίστευσαν ὅτι σύ με ἀπέστειλας. . . . καὶ αὐτοὶ ἐν τῷ κόσμῳ εἰσίν, κἀγὼ πρὸς σὲ ἔρχομαι· . . . νῦν δὲ πρὸς σὲ ἔρχομαι καὶ ταῦτα λαλῶ ἐν τῷ κόσμῳ. . . . καθὼς ἐμὲ ἀπέστειλας εἰς τὸν κόσμον, κἀγὼ ἀπέστειλα αὐτοὺς εἰς τὸν κόσμον. . . . ἵνα καὶ αὐτοὶ ἐν ἡμῖν ὦσιν, ἵνα ὁ κόσμος πιστεύῃ ὅτι σύ με ἀπέστειλας. . . . ἵνα ὦσιν τετελειωμένοι εἰς ἕν, ἵνα γινώσκῃ ὁ κόσμος ὅτι σύ με ἀπέστειλας καὶ ἠγάπησας αὐτοὺς καθὼς ἐμὲ ἠγάπησας. . . . ὁ κόσμος σε οὐκ ἔγνω, ἐγὼ δέ σε ἔγνων, καὶ οὗτοι ἔγνωσαν ὅτι σύ με ἀπέστειλας.

Cluster #14: Disciples attempt to follow; Jesus came into world (18:15, 37)

Ἠκολούθει δὲ τῷ Ἰησοῦ Σίμων Πέτρος καὶ ἄλλος μαθητής. . . . ἐγὼ εἰς τοῦτο γεγέννημαι καὶ εἰς τοῦτο ἐλήλυθα εἰς τὸν κόσμον, ἵνα μαρτυρήσω τῇ ἀληθείᾳ.

Cluster #15: Jesus about to ascend; sends disciples (20:17, 21)

μή μου ἅπτου, οὔπω γὰρ <u>ἀναβέβηκα</u> πρὸς τὸν πατέρα· . . . <u>Ἀναβαίνω</u> πρὸς τὸν πατέρα μου καὶ πατέρα ὑμῶν. . . . καθὼς <u>ἀπέσταλκέν</u> με ὁ πατήρ, κἀγὼ <u>πέμπω</u> ὑμᾶς.

Cluster #16: Disciples are to follow until Jesus comes (21:19-23)

<u>Ἀκολούθει</u> μοι. . . . ὁ Πέτρος βλέπει τὸν μαθητὴν ὃν ἠγάπα ὁ Ἰησοῦς <u>ἀκολουθοῦντα</u>, ὃς καὶ ἀνέπεσεν. . . . ἐὰν αὐτὸν θέλω μένειν ἕως <u>ἔρχομαι</u>, τί πρὸς σέ; σύ μοι <u>ἀκολούθει</u>. . . . ἐὰν αὐτὸν θέλω μένειν ἕως <u>ἔρχομαι</u> [τί πρὸς σέ];

These sixteen semantic clusters of mission in the Fourth Gospel attest to the pervasiveness of mission in John's thought. At the beginning of the Gospel, reference is made to Jesus' coming into the world. The first part of John is characterized by discussions of the works or "signs" of Jesus, the "Son of the Father." The second part of the Gospel focuses on Jesus' return and on the future mission of the disciples. Since there are comparatively few references to the disciples' mission in the Fourth Gospel, much of John's teaching on it must be gleaned from the places where it is linked explicitly with the mission of Jesus (cf. especially 14:12; 17:18; and 20:21).

The semantic clusters identified above make possible a study of mission in the Fourth Gospel that is both methodologically rigorous and empirically verifiable. They provide a basic backdrop against which John's teaching on mission can be traced, showing compositional developments and emphases and giving a perspective regarding the material available on the missions of Jesus and of the disciples. It also becomes apparent that John's teaching on mission may function as an integrative principle connecting various strands of Johannine theology. It remains for the study of the missions of Jesus and of the disciples in the following chapters to explore these relationships. The semantic field survey and the identification of semantic clusters have merely laid a groundwork, taking inventory, as it were, of John's teaching on mission.

II. DEFINITIONAL FOUNDATIONS

It is now possible and necessary to develop a tentative definition of the term "mission" according to the Fourth Gospel. After screening the available literature for the kinds of definitions discussed there, a working definition will be given. This definition will function as a heuristic guide throughout the study of the missions of Jesus and of the disciples in John's Gospel. The issue will be revisited in the final chapter in order to determine whether or not the tentative definition should be modified.

A. Lessons from the Relevant Literature

Some of the differences in scope and actual findings that emerge when the various studies of mission in the Fourth Gospel are compared, may be accounted for by the variety of ways in which the term "mission" has been understood. DuBose assesses the situation as follows:

> Despite the excellent studies on the subject, most writers who in some way deal with the meaning of "mission" reflect the following weaknesses: 1) some assume rather than give a definition; 2) some give or imply definitions but do not employ them consistently in the development of their material; 3) some imply more than one working definition without clearly demonstrating their conceptual relationship; 4) some state a definition but do not give any biblical basis for it; 5) some use biblical words but define them in terms of concepts of traditional North Atlantic mission administration.[41]

A screening of the relevant literature confirms the validity of DuBose's observations. One of the most common deficiences is the practice of providing general definitions of "mission" that tend to level the distinctions made by individual biblical writers. Hahn (1965), for example, defines it as "the Church's service, made possible by the coming of Christ and the dawning of the eschatological event of salvation, and founded in Jesus' commission."[42] Not only is Hahn's terminology vague ("service"), but it also spans mission in the entire New Testament, a practice that appears to give inadequate consideration to the different ways in which the various biblical writers conceive of mission. DuBose himself, too, fails to distinguish clearly between the different conceptions of mission by the various biblical writers. He understands mission simply as sending, maintaining, "No matter how it is used, the word send *always has* a threefold idea: 1) an intelligent sending source, 2) a sending medium or agent, either personal or impersonal, 3) a sending purpose. . . . The language and idea of the sending convey exactly what the language and idea of mission convey. A mission always has a source, a medium, and a purpose."[43] However, DuBose's quest for a commonly agreed upon basis for a definition of mission neglects individual distinctions in the term's usage.

Other writers imply definitions but do not employ them consistently, or they imply more than one working definition without clearly demonstrating their relationship. Kuhl, for example, who never defines his terms explicitly, appears to equate "mission" and "sending" for the most part of his study.[44]

---

41. Cf. Francis M. DuBose, *God Who Sends: A Fresh Quest for Biblical Mission* (Nashville: Broadman, 1983), 15.

42. Ferdinand Hahn, *Mission in the New Testament,* SBT 47 (London: SCM, 1965), 173.

43. DuBose, 37.

44. Cf. Josef Kuhl, *Die Sendung Jesu und der Kirche nach dem Johannes-Evangelium,* Studia

Toward the end of his investigation, however, he introduces the term "Mission," apparently using it in terms of cross-cultural ministry.[45] From this point on, Kuhl uses the term "Mission" to describe what throughout his study was referred to as "Sendung," thus subsuming all of his findings of the Fourth Gospel's sending terminology under "Mission."[46] But not everything Kuhl has said throughout his study regarding "sending" in John's Gospel should be equated with the modern understanding of cross-cultural ministry.

Finally, some are reluctant to provide any definitions at all in an effort to remain neutral at the inception of their study. While it is clearly not possible to start one's exploration without presuppositions, the openness to the thought- world of the biblical writers desired by such scholars is certainly commendable. Nevertheless, it is beneficial to make explicit a working definition in the early stages of a study for the following reasons. First, whether one articulates such a definition or not, the fact remains that every scholar operates with some kind of working definition in collecting his data and in evaluating them. To refrain from stating it does not mean that one does not have such a definition, it only obscures the fact that one does and makes it harder for others to follow and test a given writer's work. Second, stating a working definition in the early stages of a work does not remove the need to return to definitional matters toward the end of the study in order to determine whether or not one's initial "heuristic guess" was, in fact, accurate. Third, while the hesitation to substitute one's own definition for that of a given biblical author is appropriate, it seems unobjectionable to develop a working definition of a term after a careful screening of the work under consideration. In this "hermeneutical spiral," one's own presuppositions should be expected to be challenged and, if necessary, modified so that a working definition based on one's reading of the biblical text can truly be said to reflect biblical, not merely contemporary, terminology.

The reluctance to define mission is characteristic of Okure's work, who refrains from defining mission at the beginning of her study, maintaining that "[t]o attempt to give a definition of mission at this point of the research would be tantamount to furnishing conclusions before the enquiry is even undertaken. For the whole point of the research is precisely to discover what the Evangelist himself understands by mission."[47] Despite these reservations, Okure provides some clues regarding her own understanding of mission in the Fourth Gospel.

Instituti Missiologica Societatis Verbi Domini 11 (St. Augustin: Steyler, 1967), 1: "Was läßt sich aus dem vierten Ev entnehmen über die *Mission,* d.h. über die *Sendung* der Jüngergemeinschaft in der Zeit des Heiligen Geistes?"

45. Cf. Kuhl, 220.

46. Cf. Kuhl, 226ff. Note, for example, the statement, "Die missionarische Tätigkeit ist die wichtigste und heiligste Aufgabe der Kirche" where "missionarisch" is used in the (contemporary) sense of cross-cultural evangelization (p. 227, n. 260).

47. Okure, 37-38.

Positively, she claims that "[t]he Johannine conception of mission thus embraces the whole spectrum of activity which results from Jesus' 'sending/coming' into the world."[48] Negatively, she asserts that mission in John does not carry the primary meaning of "outreach to non-believers."[49] These excerpts gleaned from the introductory chapter of Okure's study illustrate the fact that, despite her reluctance to provide an explicit definition, she has certain presuppositions of what mission in the Fourth Gospel is or is not.

Ruiz likewise rejects the idea of providing a working definition in the early stages of his work.[50] To develop such a definition, according to Ruiz, is the task of missiology, not exegesis.[51] However, if the goal of exegesis transcends the interpretation of individual passages and includes one's apprehension of a biblical writer's conception of a given subject, seeking to define this concept is not only helpful but necessary. It is certainly correct that one should avoid superimposing one's own definition on the biblical text. It seems, however, desirable to approach a biblical book *on its own terms* and to develop an increasingly accurate understanding of a given biblical writer's conceptual framework, i.e., his "definition," of a given subject. Since the title of Ruiz's study is "Der Missionsgedanke *des Johannesevangeliums*," it seems reasonable to expect his treatment to be concerned about this issue.[52]

Every effort should be made to avoid these deficiencies. Since one's definition, explicit or implicit, will influence one's choice of methodology, determine one's data base, and help shape one's conclusions, it is imperative to indicate clearly the sense in which mission is to be understood in one's treatment. To be sure, in working toward a definition of mission in the Fourth Gospel, one must carefully consider what, in the conceptual world of the fourth evangelist, comprises mission terminology. Admittedly, this is a difficult task,

---

48. Okure, 38-39.

49. Okure, 38.

50. Miguel Rodriguez Ruiz, *Der Missionsgedanke des Johannesevangeliums: Ein Beitrag zur johanneischen Soteriologie und Ekklesiologie*, FB 55 (Würzburg: Echter, 1986), 18: "Es kann dabei zu Beginn keine Definition von 'Mission' dargeboten werden, da dies bereits eine unzulässige Vorwegnahme oder gar Präjudizierung der Ergebnisse der folgenden exegetischen Untersuchung bedeuten würde."

51. Ruiz: "Eigentlich brauchen wir keine theologische Definition von 'Mission' und streben auch nicht nach der Herausarbeitung einer solchen. Dies ist die Aufgabe der Missionswissenschaft, nicht der Exegese. Uns genügen die Grundlinien des allgemeinen Begriffs von 'Mission' und 'Sendung.'"

52. When Ruiz avails himself of the "Grundlinien des allgemeinen Begriffs von 'Mission' und 'Sendung,'" he indirectly acknowledges a need for at least a working definition of the concept he seeks to study. In fact, Ruiz resorts to a missiological, not a biblical-theological definition to fill this need: "Es darf hier demnach nur auf einige Grundsätze hingewiesen werden, denen wohl die meisten Missiologen folgen dürften und die dem allgemeinen Sprachgebrauch entsprechen. . . . Das Wort 'Mission' bezieht sich *im deutschen Sprachgebrauch* auf die 'Verbreitung einer religiösen Lehre unter Andersgläubigen, bes. der christlichen Lehre unter Heiden.'" This definition is taken from the 1793 edition of the German dictionary "Duden"!

since, as argued, one should not tie the occurrence of a concept exclusively to word usage. Nevertheless, a delineation of Johannine mission terminology should be attempted, not in order to limit the Fourth Gospel's teaching on mission to passages where such terminology occurs, but to provide a general framework within which one can begin to study mission in John's Gospel.

B. Working Definition of Mission in the Fourth Gospel

The following observations emerge from the perusal of the relevant literature on the subject: first, it is not only appropriate but indeed necessary to provide a working definition of mission in John during the early stages of one's study of this concept; second, the attempt should be made to define mission *in the Fourth Gospel*, not mission *in general*; third, the broader concept of "mission," not merely the word "sending," should be considered.

The semantic field survey conducted above has indicated two essential components of mission in the Fourth Gospel. The first component is an effort to accomplish a purpose or a charge by *a sender* or by *sent ones*. This semantic field comprises terms denoting various modes of movement, i.e., besides "sending" also "coming (into the world)," "ascending" or "descending," and a number of other terms. The second component of mission terminology in the Fourth Gospel appears to be a *task*, i.e., a certain kind of work that a given individual or group is seeking to accomplish. For example, much space is given in the Fourth Gospel to the discussion of Jesus' work or works. The fourth evangelist develops the symbolism inherent in some selected works of Jesus while labelling them as "signs."

On the basis of these observations, the following working definition of mission in the Fourth Gospel can be set forth: "Mission is the specific *task* or purpose which a person or group seeks to accomplish, *involving various modes of movement,* be it sending or being sent, coming and going, ascending and descending, gathering by calling others to follow, or following."[53] This definition will serve as a heuristic guide for the study of the missions of Jesus and of the disciples in the following two chapters. The definitional issue will be revisited in the final chapter in order to determine whether the definition just given is adequate or if it needs to be corrected or further expanded.

---

53. According to this definition, it is meaningful to speak also of a mission *of God* according to the Fourth Gospel, since God sends his Son (cf. 3:16) and works through him (cf. 5:17; 14:10). However, the Fourth Gospel's focus is not on God's mission *per se*, but on his mission *through Jesus* and on Jesus' mission through his followers (see especially 17:18 and 20:21).

III. LITERARY FOUNDATIONS

Contemporary Johannine research largely operates on the basis of one of two basic literary theories. Some follow a modified version of Bultmann's two-source theory, others hold to various stages of revision of a "Grundschrift" underlying the Gospel. Bultmann's theory of "signs" and "discourse" sources for the Gospel has not commended unqualified support.[54] The hypothesis of a more comprehensive Johannine redaction of a "Grundschrift" likewise awaits a more definitive formulation.[55] Both theories must, moreover, account for the Fourth Gospel's aporiae (seams).[56] Even there, however, firm solutions remain elusive. In a recent survey of New Testament scholarship, Martin Hengel asks,

> Who among us can claim to know what kinds of authorial breaks and dialectic contrasts should be expected from an ancient author whom we do not know and who lives in a different world? Who is right regarding the aporiae of the Fourth Gospel? The "seamless garment" of a D. F. Strauß or the countless source and redaction theories — notably regarding a work whose almost monomaniac stylistic unity (and theological dialectic) is scarcely surpassed by any other piece of ancient literature?[57]

In the light of these caveats, it seems appropriate to adopt in the present monograph a stance of cautious agnosticism regarding possible sources or redac-

54. But see the work of Robert Fortna, *The Gospel of Signs: A Reconstruction of the Narrative Source Underlying the Fourth Gospel* (Cambridge: Cambridge University Press, 1970); and *The Fourth Gospel and Its Predecessors: From Narrative Source to Present Gospel* (Philadelphia: Fortress, 1988). Cf. also D. Moody Smith, *The Composition and Order of the Fourth Gospel: Bultmann's Literary Theory* (New Haven: Yale University Press, 1965).

55. Cf. Raymond E. Brown, "'Other Sheep Not of This Fold': The Johannine Perspective on Christian Diversity in the Late First Century," *JBL* 97 (1978): 5-22; and *The Community of the Beloved Disciple* (New York: Paulist, 1979). Cf. also the helpful discussions by Andreas Lindemann, "Gemeinde und Welt im Johannesevangelium," in *Kirche: Festschrift für Günther Bornkamm*, ed. Dieter Lührmann and Georg Strecker (Tübingen: J. C. B. Mohr [Paul Siebeck], 1980), 135-38; and Georg Richter, "Zum gemeindebildenden Element in den johanneischen Schriften," in *Studien zum Johannesevangelium*, BU 13 (Regensburg: Friedrich Pustet, 1977), 383-414.

56. These literary "seams" include the following: the transition from 1:18 to 1:19; the numbering of signs in 2:11 and 4:54 that appears oblivious of signs mentioned in 2:23 and 3:2 and is subsequently dropped; the mention of Judea in 3:22 in comparison to 2:23–3:21; the sequence of chapters 5 and 6; the challenge of 7:3-5 compared with 2:23 and chapter 5; the insertion of 7:53–8:11; the reference to the anointing in 11:2 even though the event does not occur until chapter 12; the abrupt ending in 14:31; the apparent contradiction between 16:5 and 13:36 as well as 14:5; lack of clarity in 19:5, 9, 13; the "ending" of 20:30-31 followed by chapter 21; and the relationship between chapter 21 and the rest of the Gospel. Cf. Gary Burge, "The Literary Seams in the Fourth Gospel," *Covenant Quarterly* 48 (1990): 15-23.

57. Hengel also refers to Karl Barth's characterization of John's Gospel as "anstößig durch Beharrlichkeit des *einen* Tones." Cf. Martin Hengel, "Aufgaben der neutestamentlichen Wissenschaft," *NTS* 40 (1994): 335. Translations from the German in this monograph are the present author's unless otherwise indicated.

tions of the Fourth Gospel.[58] Owing to the Gospel's uniformity of style, it is difficult to isolate sources from the text of the Fourth Gospel on merely stylistic or ideological grounds.[59] While there are discernible units of discourses and narrative portions in the Fourth Gospel, the lines between these are not always clear. Moreover, even if John's Gospel were to reflect a number of sources, the possibility would remain that their author should be identified with the final redactor.

Indeed, recent literary as well as thematic studies have shown the Fourth Gospel's overarching literary unity and its delicate construction.[60] Many scholars have also detected a remarkable coherence in theological perspective.[61] The semantic field survey and the identification of semantic clusters of mission in John conducted above, too, seem to suggest that the mission concept is a pervasive feature of the entire Gospel. It is therefore reasonable to allow for the following possibilities: (1) the final redactor's use of sources other than his own, with the result that his Gospel incorporates diverse strands of mission teaching according to his various sources, or (2) the possibility that John's Gospel presents coherent teaching on mission, indicating that the final redactor (author) appropriated whatever sources he used (if any) to the extent that it is very difficult to identify them.

Neither of these views is without difficulties. If John's teaching on mission were found to reflect diverse perspectives, perhaps indicating different stages of redaction, the question would still remain which of these stages should be made the basis of one's interpretation.[62] The issue would arise whether the interpreta-

---

58. Cf. Oscar Cullmann, *The Johannine Circle* (London: SCM, 1976) who rejects complicated redactional theories as well as identifiable sources. Raymond E. Brown, *Community*, 20, purports to base his conclusions on the existing Gospel rather than on any reconstructed sources. Cf. also John Ashton, *Understanding the Fourth Gospel* (Oxford: Oxford University Press, 1990), 246: "It is obviously impossible to produce a totally convincing reconstruction, and the graveyards of New Testament scholarship are littered with discarded skeletons."

59. Cf. most recently, Eugen Ruckstuhl, *Die literarische Einheit des Johannesevangeliums*, NTOA 5 (Göttingen: Vandenhoeck & Ruprecht, 1987 [1951]); and Eugen Ruckstuhl and Peter Dschulnigg, *Stilkritik und Verfasserfrage im Johannesevangelium*, NTOA (Göttingen: Vandenhoeck & Ruprecht, 1991). Cf. also Burge, "Literary Seams,"17-18.

60. Cf. especially R. Alan Culpepper, *The Anatomy of the Fourth Gospel: A Study in Literary Design* (Philadelphia: Fortress, 1983). The Gospel's literary unity, of course, may be due to the redaction of the fourth evangelist or of a later "Johannine redactor." It appears that it can be accounted for most plausibly if the fourth evangelist is both the author of possible sources and the final redactor of the Fourth Gospel.

61. Cf., e.g., Severino Pancaro, *The Law in the Fourth Gospel: The Torah and the Gospel, Moses and Jesus, Judaism and Christianity According to John*, NovTSup 42 (Leiden: E. J. Brill, 1975), 2: "The Johannine 'theology' of the Law . . . is well defined and consistently worked out, even though the Gospel was no doubt the end-result of a long process of evolution . . . we found that, whatever the history of the Fourth Gospel, it presents a view which is neither contradictory nor inconsistent. Consequently, the questions of 'Traditionsgeschichte' and 'Redaktionsgeschichte' do not occupy a significant place in our investigation."

62. Cf. Burge, 23, warning against the danger of replacing the final text of the Fourth Gospel with a supposed earlier, more pristine message from John.

tion of the Fourth Gospel should consist of a mere descriptive exposition of the various redactional stages, or whether one should rule out from consideration those texts that are believed to have been added during later stages of revision.[63] On the other hand, one may choose to make the final text of John's Gospel the basis of interpretation, a trend that has become increasingly common in recent canon-critical, narrative-critical, or other literary approaches.[64] Nevertheless, even if theological and terminological coherence should be judged more likely, it would still be necessary to account for the literary seams found in the Gospel.

For the purposes of the present study, it seems best to approach the text on its own terms, i.e., as a literary whole, and to trace the development of the Fourth Gospel's teaching on mission in its various narrative contexts.[65] In the effort to determine the Johannine approach to mission, one should allow for the possibility that there is a unified authorial perspective reflected in the final text of the Fourth Gospel that is consistent as well as coherent.[66] However, it will still be necessary to consider the implications of various source and redaction-critical proposals for John's teaching on mission throughout the following study (Chapters 3 and 4).[67] Once the various components of John's mission teaching have been identified, the function of this teaching in its original setting can be discussed, including possible ramifications for the church's mission today (Chapter 5).

63. Cf. Lindemann, 137-38.

64. Cf., e.g., Eugene E. Lemcio, "Father and Son in the Synoptics and John: A Canonical Reading," in Robert W. Wall and Eugene E. Lemcio, *The New Testament as Canon: A Reader in Canonical Criticism*, JSNTSup 76 (Sheffield: JSOT, 1992), 78-108; Mark W. G. Stibbe, *John as Storyteller: Narrative Criticism and the Fourth Gospel*, SNTSMS 73 (Cambridge: Cambridge University Press, 1992); J. Eugene Botha, *Jesus and the Samaritan Woman: A Speech Act Reading of John 4:1-42*, NovTSup 65 (Leiden: E. J. Brill, 1991).

65. Cf., e.g., Francis J. Moloney, *The Johannine Son of Man*, BSRel 14, 2d ed. (Rome: Libreria Ateneo Salesiano, 1978), who adopts a similar approach, citing also C. H. Dodd, *The Interpretation of the Forth Gospel* (Cambridge: Cambridge University Press, 1953). Moloney maintains that, whatever the sources behind the Fourth Gospel, the text as we have it must have made sense to somebody at some time, or it would not be the way it is.

66. On authorial intention, see Osborne, 366-415; Anthony C. Thiselton, *The Two Horizons: New Testament Hermeneutics and Philosophical Description* (Grand Rapids: Wm. B. Eerdmans, 1980); *New Horizons in Hermeneutics* (Grand Rapids: Zondervan, 1992); and William W. Klein, Craig L. Blomberg, and Robert L. Hubbard, Jr., *Introduction to Biblical Interpretation* (Dallas: Word, 1993), 5-12 and 87-151. Note that without authorial intention, one ultimately ends in solipsism. Also, coherence of a text is secured only by the assumption of authorial intent.

67. One may advocate a healthy scepticism toward the claim of some to be able to read off from the Gospel the history of the community who produced it. One should certainly not assume the identity of the *originating* and the *recipient* community as appears to be done by Brown, *Community*, 55: "The reconstruction of Johannine community history thus far has involved an *originating* group of Jewish Christians (including disciples of JBap) and a later group of Jewish Christians of anti-Temple persuasion with their Samaritan converts . . . but there are clear signs of a Gentile component among the *recipients* of the Gospel." It also seems precarious to *presuppose* that the Gospel is addressed to a Christian community. Cf. Brown, *Community*, 17.

CHAPTER 3

The Mission of Jesus
according to the Fourth Gospel

What is the mission of Jesus according to the Fourth Gospel? Different answers have been given to this question. Some studies of mission in the Fourth Gospel have focused on the sending of the Son.[1] Others have emphasized the coming and returning, descending and ascending figure or the eschatological shepherd-teacher.[2] Yet others have found the Johannine signs central to John's portrayal of Jesus as Messiah.[3] It is the purpose of this monograph to provide a comprehensive treatment of the Fourth Gospel's teaching on mission that explores the interrelationships between its various components. While there are monographs on certain aspects of John's teaching on mission, there is to date no available study on the entire Johannine approach to mission that does full justice to its richness and complexity.

Also, while the fourth evangelist may have drawn on a variety of sources, and while the Gospel may have undergone various stages of redaction, the fact remains that the final text of John combines the various strands of Christology

---

1. Cf., e.g., the statement by Jaak Seynaeve, "Les verbes ἀποστέλλω et πέμπω dans le vocabulaire théologique de Saint Jean," in *L'Évangile de Jean. Sources, Rédaction, Théologie*, BETL 44, ed. Marinus de Jonge (Leuven: Gombleux, 1977), 389: "Dans le vocabulaire de la mission, les verbes ἀποστέλλω et πέμπω occupent une place de choix." Cf. also the studies by Juan Miranda and J. A. Bühner. But cf. Ernst Käsemann, *The Testament of Jesus: A Study of the Gospel of John in the Light of Chapter 17*, trans. Gerhard Krodel (Philadephia: Fortress, 1968), 11: "The formula 'the Father who sent me' is . . . neither the only nor the most typical Christological formula in the Gospel."

2. On the Johannine descent-ascent motif, cf. Godfrey C. Nicholson, *Death as Departure. The Johannine Descent-Ascent Scheme*, SBLDS 63 (Chico, Calif.: Scholars Press, 1983). On Jesus as the eschatological shepherd-teacher, cf. R. T. France, *Jesus and the Old Testament: His Application of Old Testament Passages to Himself and His Mission* (London: Tyndale, 1971).

3. Cf., e.g., Robert T. Fortna, *The Gospel of Signs: A Reconstruction of the Narrative Source Underlying the Fourth Gospel* (Cambridge: Cambridge University Press, 1970).

and teaching on mission to form one complex construct. While it will therefore be helpful to inquire as to the historical antecedents of certain terms, and worthwhile to consider the possibility that a given aspect may have been contributed by the fourth evangelist himself or may have been taken over by him from earlier sources or stages of redaction, the focus will be on an exploration of the Fourth Gospel's textual phenomena themselves, in an effort to delineate as precisely as possible John's mission concept and his view of the relationship between the missions of Jesus and of his followers.

In the present chapter, the mission of Jesus will be discussed along the lines of continuity or discontinuity with the mission of the disciples. The working definition at the end of the previous chapter will function as a heuristic guide. The semantic clusters will be used as entrance points to some of the most relevant mission texts. While the task and the charge of a given person or group appear to be the abiding features of John's mission concept, the semantic clusters of mission in the Fourth Gospel also lead us to passages where Jesus is characterized in various ways. The following study will therefore begin with a section on the person of Jesus before discussing his task and charge.

I. THE PERSON OF JESUS[4]

Jesus is shown in the Fourth Gospel to possess divine as well as human attributes, characteristics[5] that qualify him for a unique mission.[6]

A. The Divinity and Uniqueness of Jesus

1. Claims of Jesus' Pre-existence

References to Jesus' divinity frame the entire Gospel, spanning from the prologue to the closing statement. Starting with a reference to Jesus' divine nature and origin, the fourth evangelist maintains that the Word that "became flesh" (cf. 1:14) was more than a mere human being, since in the beginning, "the Word

---

4. John's portrayal of the mission of Jesus links various modes of movement with certain characterizations of Jesus. The present discussion is merely designed to lay the foundation for a more detailed treatment in the section on *Modes of Movement in Jesus' Mission* below.

5. Robert T. Fortna, *The Fourth Gospel and Its Predecessors: From Narrative Source to Present Gospel* (Philadelphia: Fortress, 1988), links the narratives taken from the "signs" source with a this-worldly Jesus and the speeches with an other-worldly Jesus. There is doubtless substantial evidence for such a claim. At any rate, however, the fact remains that both strands are ultimately combined in the final text of the Fourth Gospel.

6. It is neither possible nor necessary to give a full-fledged account of Johannine Christology here. Bibliographic references are provided to the relevant literature while detailed interaction is limited to issues where the subject of this monograph is materially affected.

was God" (1:1).[7] Apart from explicit assertions of Jesus' pre-existence (cf. 1:15, 30; 8:58; 17:5, 24),[8] this claim is implied in many references to Jesus' "having come" in the Fourth Gospel (cf., e.g., 5:43; 6:14; 7:28; 9:39; 10:10; 11:27; 12:46; 15:22; 18:37), in references to Jesus' "being from God" (cf. 6:46; 7:29; 9:33; 16:27, 28; 17:8) or his "having been sent" (cf. 3:17; 4:34; 5:23, 24, 30, 36, 37, 38; passim), in certain "I am" sayings (cf., e.g., 8:58), and in the claim that Isaiah saw Jesus' glory (cf. 12:41).[9] The Word is also said to have been "with God" (1:1-2), a fact that would render Jesus uniquely qualified to "narrate the Father" to human beings: "No one has ever seen God, but God the only Son, who is at the Father's side, has made him known" (1:18).[10]

2. Acknowledgment and Worship of Jesus as Lord (and God)

Jesus is shown to be acknowledged as "Lord" (cf. 6:68; 11:3, 12, 21, 27, 32; 13:6, 9, 25, 36; 14:5, 8, 22; 21:16, 17, 20, 21) and worshiped as "Lord" (cf. 9:38) and even "Lord and God" (cf. 20:28).[11]

3. Jesus' Appropriation of the Divine Name and Other Explicit and Implicit Claims of Divinity

Jesus is also presented in John's Gospel as appropriating the divine title "I am," in probable allusion to Isaiah (cf. the LXX's rendering of the Hebrew אני יהיה with ἐγώ εἰμι in Isa 43:10-13, 25; 45:18; 48:12; 51:12; 52:6), which in turn may

---

7. Cf. Murray J. Harris, *Jesus as God: The New Testament Use of* Theos *in Reference to Jesus* (Grand Rapids: Baker, 1992), 51-71. Cf. also Brian A. Mastin, "A Neglected Feature of the Christology of the Fourth Gospel," *NTS* 22 (October 1975): 32-51; Kikuo Matsunaga, "The 'Theos' Christology as the Ultimate Confession of the Fourth Gospel," in *Annual of the Japanese Biblical Institute* VII, ed. Masao Sekine and Akira Satake (Tokyo: Yamamoto Shoten, 1981), 124-45; Günter Reim, "Jesus as God in the Fourth Gospel: The Old Testament Background," *NTS* 30 (1984): 158-60.

8. On Jesus' pre-existence, cf. Robert G. Hamerton-Kelly, *Pre-Existence, Wisdom and the Son of Man*, SNTSMS 21 (Cambridge: Cambridge University Press, 1973); Gerhard Schneider, "Präexistenz Christi: Der Ursprung einer neutestamentlichen Vorstellung und das Problem ihrer Auslegung," in *Neues Testament und Kirche: Festschrift für Rudolf Schnackenburg*, ed. Joachim Gnilka (Freiburg im Breisgau: Herder, 1974), 399-412.

9. Cf. T. E. Pollard, *Johannine Christology and the Early Church* (Cambridge: Cambridge University Press, 1970), 16-17.

10. "To narrate" is the meaning of ἐξηγεῖσθαι in the Lucan writings, the only other corpus in the NT where the term occurs; cf. Luke 24:35; Acts 10:8; 15:12, 14; 21:19. Cf. also Harris, 73-103; Otto Hofius, " 'Der in des Vaters Schoß ist.' Joh 1,18," *ZNW* 80 (1989): 163-71; Johannes P. Louw, "Narrator of the Father — ἐξηγεῖσθαι and related terms in Johannine Christology," *Neot* 2 (1968): 32-40.

11. Regarding the historicity of 20:28, cf. Harris, 111-19; Cf. also the highly suggestive *religionsgeschichtlich* treatment by Larry W. Hurtado, *One God, One Lord: Early Christian Devotion and Ancient Jewish Monotheism* (Philadelphia: Fortress, 1988); and his convenient summary in "The Origins of the Worship of Christ," *Them* 19, no. 2 (1994): 4-8.

represent a development of Exodus 3:14.[12] The phrase ἐγώ εἰμι is used absolutely in 8:24, 28, 58; 13:19 (cf. also 6:20; and 18:5).[13] It also occurs in the predicate nominative in the "I am" sayings: 6:35, 51; 8:12 (cf. 9:5); 10:7, 9, 11, 14; 11:25; 14:6; and 15:1, 5. This self-designation of Jesus is frequently in the Fourth Gospel linked with Jesus' performance of signs (cf., e.g., 6:35; 11:25).[14]

Besides appropriating the divine self-reference "I am," Jesus in the Fourth Gospel is repeatedly said to have claimed equality with God. In 5:17-18, Jesus' activity is linked with the activity of God in creation (cf. already 1:3). In 8:58, Jesus apparently claims pre-existence (cf. also 1:1-2; 17:5, 24). In 10:30, Jesus explicitly states, "I and the Father are one" (cf. 10:31-39).[15] Jesus' unique relationship with the Father is also affirmed in 14:9-11, 20, and 23. Jesus is presented as possessing supernatural knowledge in 1:48 (Nathanael under the fig tree); 2:19 (the nature of Jesus' death; cf. also 12:24); 11:14 (Lazarus' death); 13:38 (Peter's denials); and 21:18-19 (Peter's manner of death).

4. Jesus' Uniqueness and Unique Sonship

The fourth evangelist uses the term μονογενής to point to Jesus' uniqueness (cf. 1:14, 18; 3:16, 18).[16] But even where μονογενής is not used, the Fourth Gospel portrays Jesus, and Jesus alone, as "the Son," i.e., the Son of the Father (cf. 3:17, 35, 36; 5:19, 20, 21, 22, 23, 25, 26; 6:40; 8:35, 36; 14:13; 17:1), the Son of God (cf. 1:34, 49; 3:18; 5:25; 10:36; 11:4, 27; 19:7; 20:31).[17] The designation "Son" has

12. Representatives of this view include C. K. Barrett, *The Gospel According to St. John,* 2d ed. (Philadelphia: Westminster, 1978), 291-92; C. H. Dodd, *The Interpretation of the Fourth Gospel* (Cambridge: Cambridge University Press, 1953), 93-96; and Philip B. Harner, *The "I Am" of the Fourth Gospel* (Philadelphia: Fortress, 1970), 60. On the "I am" sayings in the Fourth Gospel, cf. also Leon L. Morris, *Jesus Is the Christ: Studies in the Theology of John* (Grand Rapids: Wm. B. Eerdmans, 1989), 107-25; Raymond E. Brown, "Appendix IV: EGO EIMI — 'I AM,'" in *The Gospel According to John* (New York: Doubleday, 1966), 1:533-38; and Rudolf Schnackenburg, "Excursus 8: The Origin and Meaning of the ἐγώ εἰμι Formula," in *The Gospel According to St. John* (New York: Crossroad, 1990), 2:79-89.

13. Cf. especially Heinrich Zimmermann, "Das absolute ἐγώ εἰμι als neutestamentliche Offenbarungsformel," *BZ* 4 (1960): 54-69, 266-76. Note that 8:28-29 and 18:8-9 refer to Jesus' oneness with the Father as well as to Jesus' obedience and subordination to the Father (cf. Harner, "I Am," 55).

14. Cf. Otto Betz, *Jesus. Der Messias Israels: Aufsätze zur biblischen Theologie,* WUNT 42 (Tübingen: J. C. B. Mohr [Paul Siebeck], 1967), 413.

15. Cf. David Allen Fennema, "Jesus and God According to John: An Analysis of the Fourth Gospel's Father/Son Christology" (Ph.D. diss., Duke University, 1979), Chapter 5, who argues that the fourth evangelist expands the Jewish concept of God while steering clear of ditheism.

16. The exact meaning of the term μονογενής is disputed. Cf. especially P. Winter, "Μονογενής παρὰ πατρός," *ZRGG* 5 (1953): 335-65; John V. Dahms, "John's Use of μονογενής reconsidered," *NTS* 29 (1983): 222-32.

17. Cf. John Ashton, *Understanding the Fourth Gospel* (Oxford: Oxford University Press, 1990), 292-329; Marinus de Jonge, *Jesus, Stranger from Heaven and Son of God: Jesus Christ and the Christians in Johannine Perspective,* SBL Sources for Biblical Study 11, ed. and trans. John E. Steely (Missoula, Mont.: Scholars Press, 1977); Dodd, *Interpretation of Fourth Gospel,* 250-53;

important Old Testament precedents already in the Messianic passages of Psalm 2:7 and 2 Samuel 7:14. Moreover, in 20:17, Jesus, when talking about his return to the Father, does not group himself with his disciples in relation to the Father but maintains a distinction between his and their relationship with God, referring to "my Father and your Father, my God and your God."[18]

5. Jesus' Messiahship

The term Χριστός is used in the Fourth Gospel for Jesus, and for Jesus alone (cf. 1:41; 4:25, 29; 7:26, 27, 31, 41, 42; 9:22; 10:24; 11:27; 12:34; and 20:31; in 1:41 and 4:29 the term occurs in conjunction with Μεσσίας; the expression Ἰησοῦς Χριστός is found in 1:17 and 17:3).[19] The designation Χριστός is often linked in the Fourth Gospel with Jewish Messianic expectations.[20] The fourth evangelist endeavors to dissociate Jesus' Messiahship from political overtones (cf., e.g., 6:15; 18:36-37), an effort some interpret as a Johannine defense and further development of the σημεῖα-source's Christology.[21]

6. Strategic Placement of References to Jesus' Divinity

The importance given by the fourth evangelist to the divine nature and origin of Jesus is also seen in his strategic placement of references. Jesus' divine nature

---

Fennema, "Jesus and God"; Martin Hengel, *Der Sohn Gottes: Die Entstehung der Christologie und die jüdisch-hellenistische Religionsgeschichte* (Tübingen: J. C. B. Mohr [Paul Siebeck], 1975); Dom John Howton, " 'Son of God' in the Fourth Gospel," *NTS* 10 (1963/64): 227-37; George Mlakuzhyil, "The Son of God, the Son, the Father, and the Son of Man," in *The Christocentric Literary Structure of the Fourth Gospel*, AnBib 117 (Rome: Pontifical Bible Institute, 1987), 256-64; Morris, "Son of God," in *Jesus Is the Christ*, 89-106; Franz Mußner, "Ursprünge und Entfaltung der neutestamentlichen Sohneschristologie: Versuch einer Rekonstruktion," in *Grundfragen der Christologie heute*, QD 72, ed. Leo Scheffczyk (Freiburg im Breisgau: Herder, 1975), 77-113; A. T. Robertson, *The Divinity of Christ in the Gospel of John* (New York: Fleming H. Revell, 1916).

18. Cf. Robert Beauvery, " 'Mon Père et votre Père,' " *Lumière et vie* 20 (1971): 75-87.

19. Cf. Mlakuzhyil, 245-56; Ashton, 238-79.

20. Some believe that at an early stage of Johannine tradition (i.e., the "signs source") there were no high Christological affirmations but rather stories portraying Jesus as a wonder-worker fulfilling the traditional Jewish expectations of a Messiah. Cf. Fortna, *Fourth Gospel and Its Predecessor*, passim; Ashton, 246. Later on, it is alleged these traditions were fused with ascriptions of deity to Jesus, especially by way of the designation "Son of God." Whatever the case may be, these traditions are found side by side in the final text of the Gospel and function as an appeal to John's readers to believe in Jesus (cf., e.g., 20:30-31). Cf. also Jacob Neusner, William Scott Green, and Ernest S. Frerichs, eds., *Judaisms and Their Messiahs at the Turn of the Christian Era* (Cambridge: Cambridge University Press, 1987), who point to the diversity of Jewish Messianic expectations at the time of Jesus. While one should place the evidence from the Fourth Gospel itself in the larger context of one's understanding of Jewish Messianic expectations, there appears to be no good reason why the passages indicating such expectations in John's Gospel should be ruled out *a priori* as potential sources similar to other intertestamental and New Testament literature.

21. Cf., e.g., Fortna, *Fourth Gospel and Its Predecessor*, 228-29.

and origin are highlighted in the introductions to both parts of his Gospel (1:1-4 and 13:1-3), as well as near its conclusion (20:28).[22] It may be inferred that, for the fourth evangelist, Jesus' unique identity functions as the foundation for his unique mission.

B. The Humanity of Jesus

At the same time, Jesus is portrayed in the Fourth Gospel as combining within himself attributes of humanity with those of divinity.[23]

1. Various Human Attributes

Thus the fourth evangelist shows Jesus as attending a wedding with his mother and his disciples (2:1-2; cf. 2:12). Jesus is cast as worn out, thirsty, and asking for a drink (4:6-7; cf. 19:28). He appears weeping at the tomb of a friend (11:35). He dies (19:30) and is buried (19:38-42).[24]

2. Human Designations

Jesus' "human" name, Ἰησοῦς, occurs 244 times in the Fourth Gospel. Twice in the Gospel Jesus is identified as "Joseph's son" (cf. 1:45; 6:42). He is also frequently addressed as a "teacher" (ῥαββί: 1:38, 49; 3:2; 4:31; 6:25; 9:2; 11:8; 13:13-14; ῥαββουνί: 20:16; διδάσκαλος: 1:38; [8:4;] 20:16; in both cases as translations of ῥαββί or ῥαββουνί) and "sir" (κύριος; 4:11, 15, 49; 5:7; 11:34, 39).[25] The designation ὁ ἄνθρωπος is applied to Jesus in 4:29; 5:12; 7:46; 8:40; 9:11, 16, 24; 10:33; 11:47, 50; 14:5; and 18:14, 17, 29.

3. The Title "Son of Man"

There is also a conflation of human and divine elements in the title "Son of Man" (ὁ υἱὸς τοῦ ἀνθρώπου), a term found in 1:51; 3:13, 14; 5:27; 6:27, 53, 62; 8:28; 9:35; 12:23, 24; and 13:31.[26] The term is frequently associated in John with

22. Cf. Harris, 105-29.

23. Cf. Stephen S. Smalley, *John: Evangelist and Interpreter: History and Interpretation in the Fourth Gospel* (Greenwood, S.C.: Attic), 219.

24. For a defense of the Fourth Gospel's presentation of the humanity as well as the divinity of Jesus, cf. Marianne Meye Thompson, *The Humanity of Jesus in the Fourth Gospel* (Philadelphia: Fortress, 1988). Cf. now also idem, "The Historical Jesus and the Johannine Christ," in *Exploring the Gospel of John: In Honor of R. Moody Smith*, ed. R. Alan Culpepper and C. Clifton Black (Louisville, Ky.: Westminster/John Knox, 1996), 21-42.

25. Cf. Andreas J. Köstenberger, "Jesus as Rabbi in the Fourth Gospel," *BBR* 8 (1998).

26. On the Johannine "Son of Man," cf. Ashton, 337-73; Delbert Burkett, *The Son of Man*

Jesus' exaltation and glorification (cf. 3:14; 8:28; 12:23, 34; 13:31) and is also linked with the descent/ascent motif (cf. 1:51; 3:13). Its roots are very likely in the Danielic figure of 7:13-14 (כבר אנש).[27]

C. Implications for the Study of John's Teaching on Mission

What are the implications of the Fourth Gospel's portrayal of Jesus for an understanding of John's teaching on mission? The most important finding of the above survey is that the fourth evangelist accentuates in a variety of ways the uniqueness of Jesus. This is done, amongst other things, by his use of numerous Christological designations as well as by his application of the term μονογενής to Jesus. Notably, this expression is linked by John with both Jesus' incarnation (cf. 1:14, 18) and his saving cross-death (cf. 3:16, 18). The fourth

in the Gospel of John, JSNTSup 56 (Sheffield: JSOT, 1991); Chrys C. Caragounis, The Son of Man, WUNT 38 (Tübingen: J. C. B. Mohr [Paul Siebeck], 1986); Joseph Coppens, "Le fils de l'homme dans l'évangile johannique," ETL 52 (1976): 28-81; Edwin D. Freed, "The Son of Man in the Fourth Gospel," JBL 86 (1967): 402-9; Barnabas Lindars, "The Son of Man in the Johannine Christology," in Christ and Spirit: In Honour of C. F. D. Moule, ed. Barnabas Lindars and Stephen S. Smalley (London: SCM, 1973), 43-60; Barnabas Lindars, Jesus Son of Man: A Fresh Examination of the Son of Man Sayings in the Gospels in the Light of Recent Research (Grand Rapids: Wm. B. Eerdmans, 1983), 145-57; and "The Son of Man in the Johannine Christology," in Christ and Spirit: In Honour of C. F. D. Moule, ed. Barnabas Lindars and Stephen S. Smalley (London: SCM, 1973), 43-60; Randy L. Maddox, "The Function of the Son of Man in the Gospel of John," in Reconciliation and Hope: New Testament Essays on Atonement and Eschatology Presented to L. L. Morris on His 60th Birthday, ed. Robert J. Banks (Exeter: Paternoster; Grand Rapids: Wm. B. Eerdmans, 1974), 186-204; I. Howard Marshall, "Who Is This Son of Man?" in The Origins of New Testament Christology (Downers Grove, Ill.: InterVarsity, 1976), 63-82; I. Howard Marshall, "The Son of Man in Contemporary Debate," in Jesus the Saviour: Studies in New Testament Theology (Downers Grove, Ill.: InterVarsity, 1990), 100-120; Francis J. Moloney, The Johannine Son of Man; and "The Johannine Son of Man," BTB 6 (1976), 177-89; Charles Francis Digby Moule, "Neglected Features in the Problem of 'the Son of Man,'" in Neues Testament und Kirche: Festschrift für Rudolf Schnackenburg, ed. Joachim Gnilka (Freiburg im Breisgau: Herder, 1974), 413-28; John Painter, "The Enigmatic Johannine Son of Man," in The Four Gospels: 1992 Festschrift Frans Neirynck, BETL C, ed. F. van Segbroeck, C. M. Tuckett, G. van Belle, and J. Verheyden, vol. 3 (Leuven: University Press, 1992), 1869-87; Margaret Pamment, "The Son of Man in the Fourth Gospel," JTS 36 (1985): 56-66; Robert Rhea, The Johannine Son of Man, ATANT 76 (Zürich: Theologischer, 1990); Eugen Ruckstuhl, "Die johanneische Menschensohnforschung 1957-1969," in Theologische Berichte 1, ed. Josef Pfammatter and Franz Furger (Zürich: Benziger, 1972), 171-284, and "Abstieg und Erhöhung des johanneischen Menschensohnes," in Jesus und der Menschensohn: Für Anton Vögtle, ed. Rudolf Pesch and Rudolf Schnackenburg (Freiburg im Breisgau: Herder, 1975), 314-41; Rudolf Schnackenburg, "Der Menschensohn im Johannesevangelium," NTS 11 (1964/65): 123-37; Siegfried Schulz, Untersuchungen zur Menschensohn-Christologie im Johannesevangelium: Zugleich ein Beitrag zur Methodengeschichte der Auslegung des 4. Evangeliums (Göttingen: Vandenhoeck & Ruprecht, 1957); and Stephen S. Smalley, "The Johannine Son of Man Sayings," NTS 15 (1979): 278-301.

27. See further the discussion of the instances in the Fourth Gospel where Son of Man terminology is linked with descent-ascent language.

evangelist thus is found to link these aspects of Jesus' mission explicitly with Jesus' unique personal characteristics. Whatever role therefore remains for Jesus' followers, it appears that a line should be drawn between the unique aspects of Jesus' mission and the disciples' participation in that mission. The following discussion of the task of Jesus will continue to investigate the Fourth Gospel's portrayal of the mission of Jesus with a view toward elements of continuity and discontinuity with the mission of the disciples.

II. THE TASK OF JESUS

What is the Fourth Gospel's description of the task of Jesus, especially with a view toward its relationship to the disciples' task? The link in 14:12 suggests a certain degree of continuity between the two. On the other hand, the fact that the working of signs is in the Fourth Gospel reserved for Jesus may suggest that the fourth evangelist differentiates between the tasks to be accomplished by Jesus and those to be fulfilled by Jesus' followers. The present discussion is designed to lay the groundwork for the comparison between the tasks of Jesus and of the disciples which will be attempted in Chapter 4 below.

Mission has been defined above as "the specific *task* or purpose which a person or group seeks to accomplish." In Jesus' case, the Fourth Gospel delineates this task by using the nouns ἔργον, σημεῖον, and κόπος, as well as the verbs ἐργάζομαι, ποιέω, and κοπιάω.[28] These terms often occur in conjunction with one another.[29] While κόπος and κοπιάω are limited to chapter 4,[30] the terms ἔργον and σημεῖον, often in the plural and complemented by the verbs ἐργάζομαι or ποιέω, occur frequently and need therefore be given thorough consideration. This is especially important since the designations "works" and "signs" sustain a relationship in the Fourth Gospel that is difficult to determine.

A. Compositional Flow

At the beginning of the study of Jesus' work, i.e., his signs and works, it will be helpful to trace the various references by following the compositional flow of

---

28. Cf. also "harvest terminology" such as θερίζω, φέρω/συνάγω καρπόν. See semantic field II in Chapter 2 above.

29. Cf., e.g., 6:30: τί ποιεῖς σὺ σημεῖα; τί ἐργάζῃ;

30. Cf. Adolf von Harnack, "κόπος (Κοπιᾶν, Οἱ Κοπιῶντες) im frühchristlichen Sprachgebrauch," ZNW 27 (1928): 1-10, who argues that the κόπος word group generally carried the connotation of slave labor and that for this reason the word gradually faded out of usage in the early church. This would account for the scarcity of the term in the Fourth Gospel. It would also provide indirect support for the authenticity of the logia in 4:34-38.

the entire Gospel. In the first section of the Gospel (chapters 2–4, marked by the *inclusio* of 2:11 and 4:54), Jesus' task is described primarily in terms of his signs (cf. 2:11, 18, 23; 3:2; 4:45, 46, 48, 54). Jesus' first two signs in Galilee are explicitly linked by the evangelist in 4:46a. The pericope of John 4:34-38 (note the *inclusio* of κεκοπιακώς in 4:6 with κεκοπιάκατε, κεκοπιάκασιν, and κόπον in v. 38) includes repeated references to Jesus' work, using a variety of mission terminology (ποιέω, ἔργον, and πέμπω in 4:34; κοπιάω, κόπος, and ἀποστέλλω in 4:38). The reader begins to get to know Jesus as one who performs signs, especially in his native Galilee (cf. 2:11; 4:54; but note 2:23; 3:2).

The next section (5–12) begins with another sign (cf. 7:31). This sign occasions a discussion of the relation of Jesus' work to God the Father's work (cf. 5:16-20, 36; cf. 7:21, 23, 31).[31] John stitches the preceding two healing signs with the nature sign in 6:2 (σημεῖον is also used in 6:14, 26, and 30). Again, Jesus' signs provide the backdrop for a more general discussion of the Father's will (cf. 6:38-40). Another sign follows (9:16), cast in terms of Jesus' doing of God's work (cf. 9:3-4). Jesus' works (ἔργα) are again the focus of controversy in 10:25, 31, and 38. John 11:37 links the two healings of John 9 and 11 (cf. also 12:18). Both 2:11 and 11:4, 40 also refer to the signs' revelation of "glory." In 12:37, Jesus' ministry is summarized in terms of his performance of signs (cf. also 20:30 and 21:25).

The Farewell Discourse (13–17) begins with Jesus' work of service to his disciples (ποιέω; cf. 13:7, 12, 15). Later Jesus discusses the general nature of his works, referring also to "greater works" to be done by his followers after Jesus' return to the Father (14:10-12). For the first time Jesus also speaks of things he will do once with the Father (cf. 14:13-14). In his final prayer, Jesus reports the completion of his work (17:4). This reference and 4:34 are the only uses of ἔργον in the singular with reference to Jesus in John. The two passages should therefore probably be seen as forming an *inclusio*, enveloping all the references to Jesus' ἔργα. The signs references embrace an even larger portion of the Gospel, extending from 2:11 to 20:30.

A few general conclusions emerge from this brief survey of "task terminology" in the Fourth Gospel. First, Jesus' performance of signs pervades John's presentation of Jesus' mission in the first part of the Gospel (1–12). Second, repeatedly these signs give occasion to a more general discussion of Jesus' work in terms of Jesus' doing of works (ἔργα) or of doing God's will (θέλημα).[32] The

---

31. The suggestion has been made, originally by Bultmann, that the order of chapters 5 and 6 should be reversed to facilitate a smoother flow of the passage, both in terms of content and with regard to geographical references. The complete lack of manuscript evidence, however, renders this unlikely. But the point is moot concerning the present study.

32. Cf. Wilhelm Wilkens, *Zeichen und Werke: Ein Beitrag zur Theologie des 4. Evangeliums in Erzählungs- und Redestoff*, ATANT 55 (Zürich: Zwingli, 1969), who tries to explain the differences between signs and works by a two-stage compositional theory of the Fourth Gospel. Wilkens conjectures that a signs gospel was expanded with discourse material and redacted, and that it was

oscillating nature of signs and works terminology in the Fourth Gospel can be illustrated as follows.

Fig. 1. Jesus' Signs and Works

Signs	Work(s)
2:11, 18, 23; 3:2	4:34 (sg.)
4:48, 54	5:20, 36
6:2, 14, 26, 30	7:3, 21
7:31	9:3, 4
9:16	10:25, 32, 33, 37, 38
11:47; 12:18, 37 (summary)	14:10, 11, 12; 15:24; 17:4 (sg.)
20:30 (summary)[33]	

Third, Jesus' task is discussed primarily in 1–12, with the important exception of 14:10-14, there however in relation to the future work of his followers. Fourth, the signs seem to constitute the undergirding structure of the Fourth Gospel's presentation of Jesus' work, while the more general discussions of Jesus' work form a bridge between Jesus' own works and the future works of his disciples (cf. especially 14:12). John depicts the missions of Jesus and of the disciples therefore both in terms of dissimilarity (cf. the exclusive use of σημεῖον for Jesus) and in terms of commonality (cf. the shared usage of ἔργα).

Signs and Works

1. Signs

The expression "signs" is not used in relation to the disciples' mission in the Fourth Gospel.[34] Since it is their mission that is the ultimate reference point

---

at this stage that the word "works" was added. But as the following chart shows, the oscillating nature of signs and works terminology makes such a theory rather implausible. For a similar theory to Wilkens's, cf. Willem Nicol, *The Semeia in the Fourth Gospel: Tradition and Redaction,* NovTSup 32 (Leiden: E. J. Brill, 1972).

33. Note also the reference to "signs" in the summary passage in 10:41 (referring to John the Baptist).

34. Fortna, *Fourth Gospel and Its Predecessor,* 223, maintains that the "signs" concept is the work of the pre-Johannine author of a σημεῖα-source. One problem with this view, and one that is rarely mentioned in this regard, is the fact that it appears implausible for such an author to have developed such a concept at roughly the same time that the Synoptic Gospels, from which such a concept is entirely absent, were composed. It seems more plausible that the fourth evangelist, working toward the end of the first century, developed such a concept, transforming the Synoptic tradition (with which he may have been familiar) at this point.

in the present monograph, it may be asked why a further exploration of Jesus' signs is even necessary. Should one not conclude from the exclusive application of σημεῖον to Jesus in John's Gospel that this term constitutes an element of dissimilarity between the missions of Jesus and his followers and refrain from further study? While not entirely implausible, such a conclusion would be premature. The sole use of σημεῖον with reference to Jesus may indeed create a presumption along the lines just stated, but it would be possible for Jesus' working of signs to be subsumed under the reference to the disciples' greater works in 14:12. For this reason it is important to explore exactly what, for the fourth evangelist, constitutes a "sign."[35] If it were observed, for example, that in John's thought the working of signs is limited to the public phase of Jesus' ministry prior to his crucifixion and resurrection, this would suggest that Jesus' followers are not called to perform signs in the Johannine sense of the term, since they were not commissioned until after Jesus' resurrection (cf. 20:21-23). If, on the other hand, the signs concept should be found to be more open-ended in its connection with "works" terminology, the lines between the missions of Jesus and of his followers should not be drawn so rigidly.

No consensus has been reached to date regarding the exact number and identity of the Johannine signs. In order to determine the nature and purpose of these signs, however, it is important to establish as precisely as possible which events are presented as signs in the Fourth Gospel. As this issue is discussed, a clearer understanding of the nature of a Johannine sign will emerge that, in turn, can be used to inform the discussion of the issues raised in the introduction to this section regarding the relationship between the missions of Jesus and of his followers, here with reference to the working of signs.

a. The Number and Identity of the Johannine Signs

As noted, the study of Jesus' signs provides an important vantage point from which to view the mission of the disciples according to the Fourth Gospel.[36] A

---

35. It seems important at the outset to distinguish between a Johannine sign and Johannine symbolism. Clearly there are elements of symbolism in the Fourth Gospel beside the events designated as σημεῖα, such as metaphoric language, symbolic discourses, double meanings, and many more. Our present concern, however, is more narrowly focused and relates only to that component of Johannine symbolism that is concentrated on events explicitly referred to as "signs" by the fourth evangelist. On Johannine symbolism in general, see Dodd, 133-43; and the helpful discussion including further bibliography in R. Alan Culpepper, *The Anatomy of the Fourth Gospel* (Philadelphia: Fortress, 1983), 180-202.

36. While there are numerous studies on the Fourth Gospel's signs, there appears to be no treatment devoted to an exact delineation of the number and identity of the Johannine signs. Helpful studies on various other aspects on signs in John include Jürgen Becker, "Wunder und Christologie: Zum literarkritischen und christologischen Problem der Wunder im Johannes-

more extensive investigation of this issue is also called for on account of the following reasons.

First, while six Johannine signs are commonly acknowledged, there is no agreement regarding possible other signs in the Fourth Gospel. Indeed, some even question whether one should look for further signs in John at all. By a thorough exploration of the alternative proposals, perhaps greater clarity, if not consensus, could be achieved. Second, if a seventh or even other signs could be identified with a significant degree of plausibility, a closer investigation may aid in the apprehension of the characteristics of the Johannine signs in general. Third, such a study would be important since the signs occupy a central place in John's Christology (cf. 20:30). Clarity regarding the number and identity of the Johannine signs would therefore result in a refined understanding of the Christological presentation of the Fourth Gospel as a whole. Fourth, since the Johannine signs function as an important structural component, a precise delineation of the signs may also help clarify the structure of the Gospel.

---

evangelium," *NTS* 16 (1969/70): 130-48; Otto Betz, "Das Problem des Wunders bei Flavius Josephus im Vergleich zum Wunderproblem bei den Rabbinen und im Johannesevangelium," in *Jesus*, 409-19; Wolfgang J. Bittner, *Jesu Zeichen im Johannesevangelium: Die Messias-Erkenntnis im Johannesevangelium vor ihrem jüdischen Hintergrund*, WUNT 2/26 (Tübingen: J. C. B. Mohr [Paul Siebeck], 1987); Raymond E. Brown, "Appendix III: Signs and Works," in *The Gospel According to John* (New York: Doubleday, 1966), 1:525-32; D. A. Carson, "The Purpose of Signs and Wonders in the New Testament," in *Power Religion*, ed. Michael S. Horton (Chicago: Moody, 1992), 89-118; W. D. Davies, "The Johannine 'Signs' of Jesus," in *A Companion to John: Readings in Johannine Theology*, ed. Michael J. Taylor (New York: Alba, 1977), 91-115; Robert T. Fortna, *The Gospel of Signs* (Cambridge: Cambridge University Press, 1970), 100-101; Donald Guthrie, "The Importance of Signs in the Fourth Gospel," *Vox Evangelica* V (1967), 72-83; Loren L. Johns and Douglas B. Miller, "The Signs as Witnesses in the Fourth Gospel: Reexamining the Evidence," *CBQ* 56 (1994): 519-35; Marinus de Jonge, "Signs and Works in the Fourth Gospel," in *Miscellanea Neotestamentica*, vol. 2, ed. T. Baarda, A. F. J. Klijn, and W. C. van Unnik, NovTSup 48 (Leiden: E. J. Brill, 1978), 107-25; Mark Kiley, "The Exegesis of God: Jesus' Signs in John 1–11," in *SBL Seminar Papers* 27 (Atlanta, Ga.: Scholars Press, 1988), 555-69; Eduard Lohse, "Miracles in the Fourth Gospel," in *What about the New Testament? In Honour of Christopher Evans*, ed. Morna D. Hooker and Colin J. A. Hickling (London: SCM, 1975), 64-75; Morris, 20-42; Willem Nicol, *Semeia in the Fourth Gospel*; Peter J. Riga, "Signs of Glory: The Use of Semeion in John's Gospel," *Int* 17 (1963): 402-10; Rudolf Schnackenburg, *Gospel According to St. John* 1:515-28; Udo Schnelle, *Antidocetic Christology in the Gospel of John: An Investigation of the Place of the Fourth Gospel in the Johannine School*, trans. Linda M. Maloney (Minneapolis: Fortress, 1992), 74-175; Marianne Meye Thompson, "Signs and Faith in the Fourth Gospel," *BBR* 1 (1991): 89-108; and "Signs, Seeing, and Faith," in *Humanity of Jesus*, 53-86; and Wilhelm Wilkens, *Zeichen und Werke*. Cf. also the bibliography in Brown, *Gospel According to John*, 1:531-32, with reference to some helpful older treatments on signs in the Fourth Gospel.

b. The Six Explicitly Identified Signs in the Fourth Gospel

How many signs are there in the Fourth Gospel, and what are they? The Fourth Gospel explicitly identifies,[37] and commentators generally acknowledge, the following six signs:[38]

(1) the changing of water into wine (2:1-11);
(2) the healing of the nobleman's son (4:46-54);
(3) the healing of the lame man (5:1-15);
(4) the feeding of the multitude (6:1-15);
(5) the healing of the blind man (chap. 9); and
(6) the raising of Lazarus (chap. 11).[39]

Whether any *other* work of Jesus is referred to as a "sign," however, is disputed.

Why should one look further? Should one not rest content with six Johannine signs, regarding the *number* of signs in John merely incidental and irrelevant or possibly finding in the number six evidence for John's view that Jesus' signs are of necessity imperfect and incomplete, thus accentuating the uniqueness and significance of Jesus' resurrection?[40] Indeed, care should be taken not to press one's search for a seventh (or *other)* Johannine sign unduly. On the other hand, the number seven appears to have some importance for John in the case of the

37. There are 17 occurrences of the term σημεῖον in John's Gospel: 2:11, 18, 23; 3:2; 4:48, 54; 6:2, 14, 26, 30; 7:31; 9:16; 10:41; 11:47; 12:18, 37; and 20:30. John 2:11 refers to Jesus' changing of water into wine; 2:18 to the temple cleansing; 2:23 and 3:2 make general reference to "the signs" Jesus is performing; in 4:48, Jesus chastises people for their insistence on "signs and wonders" in order to believe; 4:54 refers to Jesus' healing of the nobleman's son; 6:2 talks about signs Jesus is doing upon the sick; 6:14 relates to Jesus' feeding of the multitudes; 6:30 records the Jews' request for yet another sign; 7:31 asks, in the context of discussion over Jesus' healing of a lame man (cf. 5:1-15), whether the Christ will do more signs than Jesus; 9:16 makes reference to Jesus' opening the eyes of a blind man; 10:41 says that John the Baptist did not do any signs; 11:47 and 12:18 refer to Jesus' raising of Lazarus; 12:37 concludes that even though Jesus did all these signs, the Jews still did not believe in him; and 20:30 notes that Jesus did many other signs, but that the evangelist selected certain signs to lead his readers to faith in Jesus.

38. Some commentators, while acknowledging the six signs listed below, may also include additional signs. These will be treated as possible signs below. See also the chart below.

39. Cf. Morris, 21; Smalley, *John: Evangelist and Interpreter,* 86-87; and Dodd, 438. Some have organized these σημεῖα in various ways, such as two groupings of three, each incorporating a nature and two healing miracles (cf. John N. Sanders, *A Commentary on the Gospel According to St. John* [London: Adam & Charles Black, 1968], 5) or as three signs occurring in Galilee and three in Jerusalem and district (cf. John H. Bernard, *A Critical and Exegetical Commentary on the Gospel According to St. John* [Edinburgh: T & T Clark, 1928], 1:clxxvi; note, however, that the sequence is broken with miracles ##1, 2, and 4 occurring in Galilee and ##3, 5, and 6 in Jerusalem and vicinity). It should be noted that until the issue of possible further signs in John is settled, such classifications remain preliminary. Since it is possible to group the Johannine signs in a number of plausible ways, the question remains which, if any, of these classifications reflects Johannine intent.

40. Cf. Sanders, 5, who holds that John has six signs, not seven, and that the number six, being one less than the perfect number, points to the great sign of the resurrection.

seven "I am" sayings of Jesus (cf. 6:35, 51; 8:12 = 9:5; 10:7, 9; 10:11, 14; 11:25; 14:6; and 15:1, 5).[41] But *regardless* of whether the number seven is significant for John or not, and whether or not any symbolism is attached to the numbers six *or* seven, it is important to identify properly all the signs in John's Gospel. They are too crucial a part of John's Christological presentation and, indeed, of the purpose of his entire Gospel that ambiguity regarding the number and identity of the Johannine signs should be allowed to prevail.

Before seeking to identify the characteristics of a Johannine sign, it seems advisable to investigate briefly the conceptual background. John did not operate in a vacuum in formulating his theology. While there is no consensus regarding the most likely general background for John's thought or that of his various sources, it is apparent that John is deeply rooted in Old Testament symbolism.[42] The case cannot be fully argued here, nor is it necessary to do so for the purpose of the issue at hand. It will suffice to take a brief look at some relevant Old Testament passages in an effort to trace the development of the signs concept there. This survey will serve as a general backdrop for the study of the Johannine signs.

c. "Signs" in the Old Testament

Of the roughly 120 references to "signs" in the Old Testament and Apocrypha, the vast majority are clustered around two events or types of ministries: the exodus, where frequent reference is made to the "signs *and wonders*" performed by God through Moses, and the "signs" forming part of the activity of the Old Testament prophets.[43] The common element between these two clusters of references is that in both cases the signs function to authenticate the divine messengers, be it Moses

---

41. Regarding the importance of the number seven in John's Gospel, see Fortna, *Gospel of Signs*, 100-101; Ernst Lohmeyer, "Über Aufbau und Gliederung des vierten Evangeliums," *ZNW* 27 (1928): 11-36; Hans Windisch, "Der johanneische Erzählungsstil," in ΕΥΧΑΡΙΣΤΗΡΙΟΝ, ed. H. Schmidt, FRLANT n.s. 19 (Göttingen: Vandenhoeck & Ruprecht, 1923), 2:174-213. Cf. also John J. Davis, *Biblical Numerology* (Grand Rapids: Baker, 1968), 115-19; E. W. Bullinger, *Number in Scripture* (Grand Rapids: Kregel, 1967), 176.

42. Regarding the Old Testament background to John in general, see especially John W. Pryor, *John: Evangelist of the Covenant People: The Narrative and Themes of the Fourth Gospel* (Downers Grove, Ill.: InterVarsity, 1992). Cf. also D. A. Carson, "John and the Johannine Epistles," in *It Is Written: Scripture Citing Scripture*, ed. D. A. Carson and H. G. M. Williamson (Cambridge: Cambridge University Press, 1988), 245-64.

43. In the vast majority of instances, σημεῖον translates the Hebrew אוֹת. For references to signs (and wonders) during the exodus, cf. Exod. 4:8, 9, 17, 28, 30; 7:3, 8-9; 8:23; 10:1-2; 11:9, 10; 12:13; 13:9, 16; Num. 14:22; 21:8 (bronze serpent; נס); Deut. 4:34; 6:22; 7:19; 11:3; 13:1-2; 26:8; 29:2, 3; 34:10-12; Josh. 24:5; Neh. 9:10; Ps. 78:43; 105:27; 135:9; Jer. 32:20, 21; Bar. 2:11. For signs in the ministry of the OT prophets, cf. 1 Sam. 2:34; 2 Kgs. 19:29; 20:8, 9; 2 Chr. 32:24; Ps. 74:9; Isa. 7:11, 14; 20:3; 38:7, 22; 44:24-25; 66:18-19; Ezek. 4:3; 9:4, 6; 20:12, 20; Sir. 36:6. Almost all of the remaining references can be grouped under either general category. For example, Esth. 10:3 (LXX) refers to God's working of "signs and wonders" in the events commemorated in the feast of Purim. Occasionally, the term "sign" is applied to the sun, moon, and stars in the heavens (e.g., Gen. 1:14).

during the exodus or later Old Testament prophets.[44] While the emphasis regarding the signs performed during the exodus, however, is usually on their miraculous nature, this miraculous element later retreats into the background.[45]

There is little that is "miraculous," for example, in Isaiah's walking stripped and barefoot for three years as a sign of judgment against Egypt and Cush (cf. Isa. 20:3). The emphasis rather lies on the authentication of Isaiah's prophecy, and ultimately of God's sovereign power. While such prophecies were usually given on a merely verbal level, occasionally God chose to communicate by way of a visual aid, i.e., a "sign." In the case of prophetic signs, there are thus two important elements: the prophetic component, and the inherent symbolism. Both aspects combine to provide a way of revelation that, once the sign has been realized, proves the prophet to be authentic and brings glory to God.

A look at the explicitly identified Johannine signs reveals that John's "signs" concept fits well within the general development from an emphasis on the miraculous to a focus on the prophetic-symbolic dimension of a "sign."[46] The "miraculous" element is certainly not missing in the signs of John's Gospel. It appears, however, that this is not where John's emphasis lies. This seems to be suggested by the fact that the phrase "signs and wonders," which is characteristic for the types of signs performed during the exodus, occurs only once in the Fourth Gospel, and there on the lips of Jesus with a strongly negative connotation (cf. 4:48). In all the other cases, the thrust of a σημεῖον reference appears to be prophetic-symbolic: the sign's symbolism is developed, and the prophetic component is emphasized — in the case of John's Gospel the authentication of Jesus' Messianic claims.[47]

44. Cf. Davies, 92, who refers to the turning of a rod into a serpent in Exod. 4:1-9: "but it is not only called a wonder, but a sign *(ôth)*, because it points beyond itself to the power of Moses' God."

45. Cf. Bittner, 24-27, who also points to the scholarly neglect of the question of why the term "sign" gains central importance for John's Christology while it is avoided by the Synoptics. Cf. also Fritz Stolz, "Zeichen und Wunder: Die prophetische Legitimation und ihre Geschichte," *ZTK* 69 (1972): 125-44.

46. This is inadequately recognized by Karl-Heinz Rengstorf, "σημεῖον, et al.," in *TDNT*, 7:256, who claims that the Johannine signs are "theologically and fundamentally the same kind as the classical σημεῖα of the OT, the signs in Egypt in the time of Moses." Cf. also Brown, *Gospel According to John*, 1:528-29, who considers the exodus narrative to be the primary background for both signs and works terminology in the Fourth Gospel; and Robert Houston Smith, "Exodus Typology in the Fourth Gospel," *JBL* 81 (1962): 329-42.

47. As Barrett, 76, maintains, "The אוֹת-σημεῖον [is] a special part of the prophetic activity; no mere illustration, but a symbolic anticipation or showing forth of a greater reality of which the σημεῖον is nevertheless itself a part." He contends that, seen against their most probable background, the Johannine signs are therefore "σημεῖα in the Old Testament sense, special demonstrations of the character and power of God, and partial but effective realizations of his salvation." Cf. also Schnackenburg, *Gospel According to St. John*, 1:527, who refers to the symbolic actions of the prophets where the symbol was "a creative prefiguration of the future" and a "revelatory sign." Schnackenburg believes that John developed his notion of signs "in the course of his meditation on the Gospel tradition" while Barrett thinks that John the evangelist himself chose the term σημεῖον. Others, such

Whether one agrees with every detail of this reconstruction or not, the most significant insight for the purposes of the present study is that not all of the events called "signs" in the Old Testament actually were miraculous. If John can be shown to fall within this general conceptual framework, one should therefore not require an event to be miraculous for it to qualify as a Johannine sign. On the other hand, one may expect a possible sign to display a combination of prophetic and symbolic elements. The event thus points to the future when the symbol will become a reality, at which time God's messenger will be proved authentic and God will receive glory.

d. "Signs" in John's Gospel

As one surveys the six explicitly identified and commonly acknowledged Johannine signs in an effort to identify their common characteristics, the following observations can be made.

Fig. 2. The Six Explicitly Identified Signs in the Fourth Gospel

Sign	Scripture Reference	Public Event	Identified as Sign	God's Glory in Jesus
1. Changing water into wine	2:1-11	Yes	2:11	2:11 (cf. 4:48)
2. Healing nobleman's son	4:46-54	Yes	4:54	cf. 4:48; 6:2
3. Healing of lame man	5:1-15	Yes	7:21, 31	5:17-47; 7:14-24
4. Feeding of multitude	6:1-15	Yes	6:14, 26, 30	6:25-59
5. Healing of blind man	chap. 9	Yes	9:16 (cf. 11:37)	9:3-5, 35-41
6. Raising of Lazarus	chap. 11	Yes	11:47 (cf. 12:18)	11:25-27, 40
Summary	12:37			

(1) *Signs are public works of Jesus.* In each case, the term σημεῖον in the Fourth Gospel is linked with the term ποιεῖν ("do"; cf. 2:11, 23; 3:2; 4:54; 6:2, 14, 30; 7:31; 9:16; 10:41; 11:47; 12:18; 12:37; 20:30), ἰδεῖν ("see"; 4:48; 6:26), or δείκνυμι ("show"; 2:18); the verb ἀκουεῖν ("hear") is never used. This pattern of usage indicates that a "sign" is something Jesus *does* (or, in the case of 10:41, John the Baptizer has not done), not merely something he says, and something people can *see*, nor merely hear. "Signs" in John are therefore *works* of Jesus, not mere words. They are events, not mere utterances.[48]

---

as Bultmann or Fortna, conjecture that John's signs terminology stems from his use of a σημεῖα-source. However, the answer to this question does not materially affect the thesis of this paper.

48. It is improper to equate completely Jesus' works and words in the Fourth Gospel, as Bultmann does when he asserts, "The works of Jesus are his words." Cf. Rudolf Bultmann, *Theology of the New Testament,* 2 vols., trans. Kendrick Grobel (New York: Charles Scribner's Sons, 1955), 2:60; and the critique by de Jonge, "Signs and Works in the Fourth Gospel," 125. Note also that Jesus habitually refers to things he does in the Fourth Gospel as mere "works" (the only —

Moreover, all six commonly recognized Johannine signs are works done by Jesus not merely before his disciples but before an unbelieving world.[49] The changing of water into wine, the feeding of the multitude, and the various healings including the raising of Lazarus from the dead all share in common that they have as their audience people other than merely Jesus' followers. All these signs are collectively referred to by John's summary statement at the end of part one of his Gospel: "Even though Jesus had done all these signs *before them,* they [i.e., 'the Jews'] did not believe in him." The Fourth Gospel's signs are therefore confined to the period of Jesus' public ministry (i.e., chapters 1–12).

(2) *Signs are explicitly identified as such in the Fourth Gospel.* All six commonly acknowledged Johannine signs are called "signs": the changing of water into wine (cf. 2:1-11) in 2:11; the healing of the nobleman's son (cf. 4:46-54) in 4:54; the healing of the lame man (cf. 5:1-15) is included in the reference to πλεῖονα σημεῖα ("more signs") in 7:31 (cf. 7:21); the feeding of the multitude (cf. 6:1-15) is called a "sign" in 6:14, 26, 30; the healing of the blind man (cf. chapter 9) in 9:16; and the raising of Lazarus (cf. chapter 11) in 11:47 (cf. 12:18). Ultimately, the only way a "sign" can be identified as such in the Fourth Gospel is by explicit reference to an event in Jesus' public ministry as a "sign."[50]

(3) *Signs, with their concomitant symbolism, point to God's glory displayed in Jesus, thus revealing Jesus as God's authentic representative (i.e., the Messiah).*[51] The prominence of the signs in the two major summary sections of the Fourth Gospel underscores their centrality in John's Christology. Within the framework of this sending Christology, the signs are shown to authenticate Jesus as the true representative of God, revealing God's glory in Jesus.[52] Thus people's acceptance

---

disparaging — references made to "signs" by Jesus are found in 4:48 and 6:26) while it is John or other characters in the Gospel that use the terms "sign" or "signs" (John 2:11, 23; 4:54; 6:14; 12:18, 37; 20:30; Nicodemus, the Jews, or people in the crowds: 2:18; 3:2; 6:30; 7:31; 9:16; 11:47). Cf. Guthrie, "Importance of Signs in the Fourth Gospel," 79: "what Jesus meant by works was identical with what John meant by signs." Thus it appears that the term "sign" in the Fourth Gospel reflects the perspective of the audience of Jesus' works, pointing to the perceived attesting function or symbolic content of the deeds done by Jesus.

49. Cf. 12:37: "even though Jesus had done all these signs *before them*" (ἔμπροσθεν αὐτῶν), i.e., "the Jews." In 20:30, reference is made to "many other signs Jesus did *before his disciples*" (ἐνώπιον τῶν μαθητῶν). The latter passage probably points to the disciples as the primary witnesses of Jesus' signs in relation to the Fourth Gospel's readers and should not be taken to negate the fact that Jesus' signs had a wider audience than merely the disciples. Cf. Barrett, 575: "The stress on signs done by Jesus and beheld by his disciples is important and illuminates the structure and method of the gospel as a whole; there is no disparagement of the role of eye-witnesses."

50. Of course, this does not mean that there may not be some ambiguity regarding the referent of a given σημεῖον passage in the Fourth Gospel. See the discussion below.

51. Cf. Fortna, *Fourth Gospel and Its Predecessor,* 223, n. 1.

52. Fortna, *Fourth Gospel and Its Predecessor,* 233, n. 17, believes that the term δόξα is supplied by the fourth evangelist.

of the genuineness of Jesus' signs should lead to their acceptance of Jesus' Messianic mission. This is true both for Jesus' original audience and for the readers of the Fourth Gospel to whom testimony regarding Jesus' signs is supplied.

That the signs are works of Jesus that reflect God's glory can already be seen in John's account of the first sign: "This, the first of his signs, Jesus performed in Cana of Galilee. He thus revealed his glory, and his disciples put their faith in him" (2:11). The reader of the Fourth Gospel is almost certainly expected to draw the connection between this statement and the earlier assertion found in the Prologue, "The Word became flesh and made his dwelling among us. We have seen his glory, the glory of the One and Only, who came from the Father, full of grace and truth" (1:14). John thus presents Jesus' signs as the vehicles through which God's glory is revealed in Jesus. While the word "glory" is not always used in conjunction with Jesus' working of signs, all of Jesus' signs are presented as evidence that Jesus is God's authentic representative (cf. 5:17-47; 7:14-24; 6:25-59; 9:3-5, 35-41; 11:25-27, 40). The Fourth Gospel also reflects Jewish expectations that both the coming prophet and the Messiah would perform signs to prove their divine commission (cf. 6:14; 7:31).[53]

According to John, what kind of works are Jesus' signs? Great care must be taken not to import an understanding of the term "miracle" into the Fourth Gospel that is foreign to it.[54] As argued above, the most likely background for the Johannine signs are the signs of the Old Testament prophets where the symbolic-prophetic element generally predominated over the miraculous. Arguably, "to the evangelist a σημεῖον is not, in essence, a miraculous act, but a significant act, one which, for the seeing eye and the understanding mind, symbolizes eternal realities."[55] Indeed,

---

53. See the discussion of the Old Testament background of the Johannine signs above. Adolf Schlatter, *Der Evangelist Johannes: Wie er spricht, denkt und glaubt,* 2d ed. (Stuttgart: Calwer, 1948), 197, describes the Jewish sentiment as follows: "Je mehr Wunder, desto mehr Grund zum Glauben." Paul wrote in 1 Cor. 1:22, "For Jews demand signs. . . ." See also Strack-Billerbeck 1:593-96; and, Bittner, "Exkurs 1: Messias und Wunder," in *Jesu Zeichen im Johannesevangelium,* 136-50, who, convincingly, demonstrates that Old Testament prophecy raised the expectation that the Messiah would perform signs, referring primarily to passages in Isaiah, such as 11:2; 42:1, 6-7; and 61:1-2 (cf. Luke 4:14; cf. also Ps. 74:9; Sir. 36:6, 14-16; Matt. 5–7 with 8–10; Matt. 11:2-6, referring to a conglomerate of Isaianic texts, and Luke 7:18-23). Whether these expectations were actually held at the time of Jesus, however, and if so, how widely, is another question. Cf. Schnackenburg, *Gospel According to St. John,* 2:148-49, who contends, "Miracles played hardly any part in Messianic expectations in Judaism. . . . What we have here is not Jewish but Christian Messianic dogma"; and Neusner, Green, and Frerichs, whose book title speaks for itself.

54. Contra translations such as the NIV that render σημεῖον in the Fourth Gospel regularly as "miraculous sign."

55. Cf. Dodd, 90. Contra Schnackenburg, *Gospel According to St. John,* 1:515, who understands the Fourth Gospel's "signs" as Jesus' major miracles: "The signs are important works of Jesus, performed in the sight of his disciples, miracles, in fact, which of their nature should lead to faith in 'Jesus the Messiah, the Son of God' "; and Morris, 22, who defines a sign simply as "a miraculous happening that points to some spiritual truth."

the signs in John "are not mere displays of power but are symbol-laden events rich in meaning for those with eyes to see."[56]

In light of these observations, a tentative definition of a "sign" in John's Gospel can be construed as follows: "A sign is a symbol-laden, but not necessarily 'miraculous,' public work of Jesus selected and explicitly identified as such by John for the reason that it displays God's glory in Jesus, who is thus shown to be God's true representative, even the Messiah (cf. 20:30-31)."[57]

In screening the options suggested for additional signs in the Fourth Gospel, the following criteria may therefore be used:

(1) Is a given work performed by Jesus as part of his public ministry?
(2) Is an event explicitly identified as a "sign" in the Fourth Gospel?
(3) Does the event, with its concomitant symbolism, point to God's glory displayed in Jesus, thus revealing Jesus as God's true representative?

If it can be shown that one or more events in John's Gospel fit these criteria, these should take their proper place alongside the commonly recognized six signs.

e. The Suggestions for Additional Signs in John's Gospel

The suggestions for additional signs in John's Gospel include the following:[58]

(1) Jesus' cleansing of the temple (2:14-17);[59]
(2) Jesus' word regarding the serpent in the wilderness (3:14-15);[60]

---

56. Cf. Carson, "Purpose of Signs and Wonders," 93.

57. This definition is not unlike that by Thompson, "Signs and Faith in the Fourth Gospel," 93-94, who describes a Johannine sign as "a manifestation, through the person of Jesus, of God's work in the world." Cf. also George R. Beasley-Murray, *John*, WBC 36 (Waco, Tex.: Word, 1987), 387: "The 'signs' of the first twelve chapters are specifically actions of Jesus, generally miraculous, which find their exposition in discourses."

58. While not exhaustive, the following alternatives represent the most frequently made suggestions. It should be noted that some writers define the concept of a Johannine "sign" so broadly as to include virtually everything Jesus did or said in the Fourth Gospel. Davies, 95-112, for example, also includes the signs of "new birth" (John 3), "new worship" (John 4), the "light of the world" (John 7–8), and "signs that Jesus brings life through death" (11:55–12:36), including the anointing, the triumphal entry, and the grain of wheat saying. However, this terminology demonstrably departs from Johannine usage. Dodd's concept of "signs" in John, too, is unduly broad when he writes, "The works of Christ are all 'signs' of his finished work" (383). On one level, that may be true; but clearly John selects certain events in Jesus' ministry by designating them as "signs" and by exposing their symbolic significance. All signs contain symbolic elements, but not every symbolic element in the Fourth Gospel is therefore a sign. To subsume various allusions to the OT as well as instances of Johannine irony and double meaning under the category of "Johannine sign" fails to observe this distinction between symbolism and "signs."

59. Cf. Beasley-Murray, 42; D. A. Carson, *The Gospel According to John* (Grand Rapids: Wm. B. Eerdmans, 1991), 181; Dodd, 300-303, 370.

60. Cf. Brown, *Gospel According to John*, 1:528.

(3) Jesus' walking on the water (6:16-21);[61]
(4) the anointing of Jesus (12:1-8);[62]
(5) the triumphal entry (12:12-16);[63]
(6) Jesus' crucifixion and resurrection (chaps. 18–19);[64]
(7) his resurrection appearances (chaps. 20–21);[65] and
(8) the miraculous catch of fish (21:1-14).[66]

Which of the above alternatives, if any, fits the general characteristics outlined in the above definition?[67]

(1) Is a given work performed by Jesus as part of his public ministry? All six commonly recognized Johannine signs occur during the course of Jesus' public ministry (1–12). Of the suggested additional signs, only three fall into this category: the temple cleansing, the anointing of Jesus, and the triumphal entry. Jesus' word regarding the serpent in the wilderness is not an event at all but merely a word of Jesus and should therefore be ruled out from consideration.[68] The walking on the water, while being something Jesus *does,* is not a part of Jesus' *public* ministry but occurs privately before Jesus' disciples so that it, too, should be excluded.[69] The remaining alternatives, i.e., Jesus' crucifixion and resurrection, his resurrection appearances, and the miraculous catch of fish, are not a part of Jesus' public ministry narrated in 1–12 and therefore cannot be

61. Cf. Morris, 21; Fortna, *Gospel of Signs,* 64. Cf. also Davies, 93, calling this the traditional view.

62. Cf. Dodd, 438.

63. Dodd.

64. Cf. Betz, 412-13; Carson, *Gospel According to John,* 661: "the greatest sign of them all is the death, resurrection and exaltation of the incarnate Word"; Dodd, 379: "The death of Christ by crucifixion . . . is a σημεῖον of the reality which is the exaltation and the glory of Christ" (cf. also 438-40); J. Terence Forestell, *The Word of the Cross: Salvation as Revelation in the Fourth Gospel,* AnBib 57 (Rome: Biblical Institute Press, 1974), 71, who refers to "the supreme sign of the entire gospel, the exaltation and glorification of the Son of Man"; Bruce H. Grigsby, "The Cross as an Expiatory Sacrifice in the Fourth Gospel," *JSNT* 15 (1982): 64, n. 6: "it does not seem to be speculative to discuss the Johannine cross as a 'sign'"; Lucius Nereparampil, *Destroy This Temple: An Exegetico-Theological Study on the Meaning of Jesus' Temple-Logion in Jn 2:19* (Bangalore: Dharmaram Publications, 1978), 92-97; Nicol, 115: "John never directly says the resurrection is also a *semeion,* but it is significant that when the Jews ask Jesus for a *semeion* in 2:18, he answers by referring to his resurrection"; and Wilhelm Thüsing, *Die Erhöhung und Verherrlichung Jesu im Johannesevangelium,* NTAbh 21, 1/2 (Münster: W. Aschendorff, 1979), who repeatedly refers to Jesus' exaltation at the cross as a "Glaubenszeichen" (cf., e.g., 289, passim).

65. Cf. Bultmann, *Theology of the New Testament,* 2:56; Beasley-Murray, 387.

66. Cf. Smalley, *John: Evangelist and Interpreter,* 87; and "The Sign in John XXI," *NTS* 20 (1974): 275-88; Fortna, *Gospel of Signs,* 87-89.

67. For the following discussion, see the survey chart below.

68. Cf. Dodd, 300: "for John a 'sign' is something that actually happens."

69. This conclusion is drawn on internal conceptual and theological grounds. Regarding source-critical considerations, see the following note.

considered a "sign" in the Johannine sense of the word. These considerations are further clarified by dealing with the second characteristic of a Johannine "sign."

(2) Is an event explicitly identified as a "sign" in the Fourth Gospel? Of the three events identified above that fit the first criterion, i.e., being works performed by Jesus as part of his public ministry, only the temple cleansing also meets the second qualification, since neither the anointing of Jesus nor the triumphal entry are called a "sign" in the Fourth Gospel.[70] Even in the case of the temple cleansing, the designation is somewhat indirect. Immediately after cleansing the temple when Jesus is asked to perform a sign, he explains the significance of what he had just done, thus apparently inferring that the temple cleansing itself already constituted the sign people were asking for.[71] As one commentator has it, "Indeed, if the authorities had eyes to see, the cleansing of the temple was already a 'sign' they should have thought through and deciphered in terms of Old Testament Scripture."[72] That this is a legitimate inference is suggested by the parallel in 6:30 where, after Jesus' feeding of the multitude, the Jews similarly demand a sign, yet where in response Jesus offers an interpretation of what had already happened, inviting his questioners to see in the actual occurrence of the feeding of the multitude the σημεῖον they desired.[73]

Apart from the fact that the other suggested possibilities were already found to fail to meet the first criterion, they also fall short of standing the second test. None of these alternatives is called a "sign" in the Fourth Gospel. It may be objected that Jesus' crucifixion and resurrection, and perhaps even the resurrection appearances, should be seen as included in the purview of the Johan-

---

70. Neither the walking on the water nor the catch of fish are explicitly identified as signs in John. Contra Fortna, *Gospel of Signs,* 64, 87-89, who believes that John preserved the former event merely out of respect for his ("signs") source while the latter pericope was displaced from its original setting by the fourth evangelist. It is possible that the final author took over the narration of these two events from a source which had identified these as σημεῖα. However, it appears that the fourth evangelist did not preserve these stories as *signs stories* since such terminology is absent from these accounts in the final text of the Fourth Gospel.

71. Nereparampil, 92-97, objects to an inclusion of the temple cleansing under the Johannine signs by arguing that the temple cleansing cannot be a sign since it is not "miraculous." He sees the resurrection as the sign and the temple logion as the promise of a sign, maintaining that the resurrection represents "the supreme 'sign' in the full sense of the Johannine concept of *semeion.*" But Nereparampil's objection loses its force in the light of the fact that a "miraculous" element is not a necessary component of the Johannine conception of a "sign." Moreover, as has been argued, Jesus' resurrection is not a part of Jesus' public work and corresponds to the Johannine signs as reality does to symbol rather than functioning as the ultimate symbol.

72. Cf. Carson, *Gospel According to John,* 181.

73. Cf. Dodd, 301, who also notes the implication of the quote of Ps 69:10 in John 2:17, i.e., "that, just as the Righteous Sufferer of the Psalm paid the price of his loyalty to the temple, so the action of Jesus in cleansing the temple will bring him to grief."

nine "signs" by virtue of being covered by the statement in 20:30.[74] This suggestion, however, while possible, should probably be ruled out due to the following reasons.

First, Jesus' crucifixion and resurrection are the reality to which the signs point. Rather than symbolizing anything, they are significant in and of themselves. As Schnackenburg asserts, "An extension of the concept of 'sign' to take in the cross of Jesus cannot be justified."[75] The reason for this is, according to Barrett, that "in the death and resurrection of Jesus, sign and its meaning coincide."[76] Davies agrees, "The sign is not essential to the truth to which it points, but only illustrative. But the death of Jesus is not simply an illustration or a sign; it is an actual death. . . . The cross — not as a symbol or an idea — but as an actual act of self-giving is, for John, the point where God's glory is actually seen. Not the sign, not the intent, but the deed is the manifestation of the glory."[77]

Second, the Fourth Gospel's "signs" are preliminary in nature. This temporary function is intrinsic to John's conception of a "sign." Once the reality to which Jesus' "signs" point has come, no further signs are needed, nor can the crucifixion and resurrection that accomplish that reality *themselves* be called "signs." As de Jonge notes, Jesus' "death and resurrection . . . are *not* explicitly called signs. . . . This may be because, from the evangelist's post-resurrectional viewpoint, the signs bear a preliminary character, whereas death and resurrection mark the beginning of a new period."[78] Brown writes, "Thus, the miracle is a sign, not only qualitatively (a material action pointing toward a spiritual reality), but also temporally (what happens before *the hour* prophesying what will happen after the hour has come). That is why, as we have explained, the signs of Jesus are found only in the first half of the Gospel (chs. i–xii)."[79]

Third, while the "signs" reference in 20:30 allows for the possible inference that Jesus' crucifixion and resurrection should be numbered among the Johannine "signs," this inference falls short of making the connection explicit. Other explanations are possible. As passages such as 2:22 (cf. also 12:16) indicate, even the disciples' understanding of events in Jesus' ministry was predicated upon the actual occurrences of Jesus' crucifixion and resurrection. Their reception of the Holy Spirit and their commissioning by Jesus were not possible until *after* these events. Thus the fourth evangelist may choose to mention Jesus' "signs"

---

74. Cf., e.g., Carson, *Gospel According to John,* 661, who comments, somewhat tentatively, "It is possible that *miraculous signs* refers only to the miracles reported in chs. 2–12. . . . But to place this conclusion here suggests that the greatest sign of them all is the death, resurrection and exaltation of the incarnate Word. . . . But however far *miraculous signs* extends. . . ."

75. Cf. Schnackenburg, *Gospel According to St. John,* 1:520, n. 7.

76. Cf. Barrett, 78.

77. Cf. Davies, 113-14.

78. Cf. de Jonge, "Signs and Works in the Fourth Gospel," 111 and 117, n. 24.

79. Cf. Brown, *Gospel According to John,* 1:530.

once more, not because he wants to include Jesus' crucifixion and resurrection in their purview, but because the disciples are now fit to witness to the true significance of the "signs" Jesus had performed during his public ministry. It had been necessary for Jesus' crucifixion and resurrection, the reality to which those "signs" pointed, to occur in order for the disciples to be able to function as witnesses in the power of the Spirit (cf. 15:26-27). Indeed, what the Farewell Discourse expounds is not so much the significance of Jesus' death (which had already been foreshadowed by word and deed in 1–12) as the *implications* of Jesus' death for the mission of his followers.[80]

For these reasons Jesus' crucifixion, resurrection, and appearances should not be considered Johannine "signs." They do not fit the criteria laid out above in that they are neither a "public work" of Jesus nor called "signs" in John. In line with the Old Testament background sketched earlier in this essay, the Johannine "signs" point symbolically to God's future intervention. Jesus' crucifixion and resurrection, however, represent the very reality to which the earlier signs had referred. If the raising of Lazarus is a "sign," it may be asked, and if its symbolic significance is that Jesus is "the resurrection and the life," how can Jesus' resurrection *itself* also be a sign? This seems to be logically inconsistent.

Finally, the miraculous catch of fish in chapter 21, too, should be ruled out from consideration, since it is neither a part of Jesus' public ministry nor explicitly identified as a "sign" in John.[81]

(3) Does the event, with its concomitant symbolism, point to God's glory displayed in Jesus, thus revealing Jesus as God's true representative? To some extent, this criterion is met not merely by the six commonly acknowledged Johannine "signs" but also by the various suggestions for additional "signs." In a sense, everything Jesus does and says points to God's glory and reveals Jesus as God's true representative. Not everything Jesus does or says, however, is selected by the fourth evangelist as a "sign." Since it has already been shown that the temple cleansing alone meets the first two criteria, all that remains to

---

80. Contra Carson, *Gospel According to John,* 661: "But to place this conclusion here suggests that the greatest sign of them all is the death, resurrection and exaltation of the incarnate Word, the *sig*nificance of which has been carefully set forth in the farewell discourse."

81. Cf. Marie-Émile Boismard, *Moses or Jesus: An Essay in Johannine Christology,* trans. B. T. Viviano (Minneapolis: Fortress, 1993), 53, who believes that this pericope occurred originally as the third Johannine sign after 2:11 and 4:54 and that it was displaced by the final redactor to make room for the temple cleansing as the seventh sign in John's Gospel. This displacement theory remains speculative, especially since it seems to take its cues from surface similarities in wording ("first," "second," "third") while giving insufficient attention to contextual and material differences (e.g., 2:11 and 4:54 refer to the first and second signs, 21:14 to "the third time *Jesus appeared to his disciples*"). Moreover, the miraculous catch of fish is never explicitly identified as a σημεῖον in the Fourth Gospel. Nevertheless, apart from the speculative nature of his displacement theory, Boismard provides indirect support for the thesis of the present work by acknowledging the temple cleansing as a Johannine sign and by identifying the exact same seven events as signs in the Fourth Gospel.

be done is to discuss whether this event is presented in the Fourth Gospel as an incident that reveals God's glory in Jesus and that reveals Jesus as God's authentic representative.

It has already been argued that Jesus' response to the Jews' demand for a "sign" consisted in his explication of the significance of the temple cleansing he had just performed so that the temple cleansing itself is presented as a Johannine "sign" (cf. 2:18-21).[82] It is not necessary here to discuss in detail all the implications of Jesus' temple *logion* in 2:19.[83] Suffice it to say that Jesus' words were uttered in explicit response to the Jews' challenge of his authority (cf. 2:18). In Jesus' eyes, the temple cleansing was symbolic of the crucifixion and resurrection of his body, which, in turn, would replace the temple's significance in the life and worship of the Jewish nation (cf. 4:21-24). Indeed, Jesus had the authority to lay down his life and to take it up again (cf. 10:18). In this, Jesus is confirmed to be God's authentic representative.

If the temple cleansing is indeed the seventh sign of John's Gospel, the question arises why interpreters have generally failed to identify it as such. A few possible reasons come to mind. Scholarship on the temple cleansing in John has frequently focused on its placement at the beginning of Jesus' public ministry in John's Gospel in contrast with the Synoptic placement at the end of Jesus' work. Moreover, the temple cleansing is not a healing miracle as are four of the other Johannine signs, nor is it a nature miracle as are two other signs in John. Therefore the temple cleansing does not seem to fit the common stereotype of a Johannine sign. Indeed, signs in John have often been understood in terms of the miraculous

---

82. Note also the connection between the changing of water into wine and the temple cleansing. What the first sign indicates, i.e., that Jesus replaces Judaism in its various features, is applied in the case of the temple cleansing to the Jewish temple. Cf. Dodd, 303, "it seems clear that both the Miracle of Cana and the Cleansing of the Temple are σημεῖα which signify the same foundational truth: that Christ has come to inaugurate a new order in religion." Cf. also Nereparampil, 89; and Pryor, 17, who likewise emphasizes the close connection between Jesus' first sign at the wedding in Cana and the temple cleansing: "the two pericopae form an impressive and united introduction to the ministry of Jesus. Both point to the passing away of the old religion (signified by water and temple), and its replacement by the newness and superiority of Christ. He is the wine of the new age, he is its temple, the focus of worship and devotion." On the Johannine replacement motif, cf. especially Carson, "John and the Johannine Epistles," 254-56.

83. Cf. the important discussions by E. P. Sanders, *Jesus and Judaism* (Philadelphia: Fortress, 1985), 61-76; and James D. G. Dunn, *The Partings of the Ways Between Christianity and Judaism and Their Significance for the Character of Christianity* (London: SCM, 1991), 37-56. Sanders' main argument centers around the contention that not the "cleansing" of the temple stands in the foreground in John (as if Jesus' concern had been the temple's defilement or impurity) but rather its destruction and replacement (75). Dunn disputes this and identifies the temple cleansing as a symbolic action similar to those of Old Testament prophets (cf. 1 Kgs. 11:29ff; 22:11; Isa. 20:1ff; Hos. 1:3). Dunn also points to a possible reference to the temple's sanctification for its eschatological function (cf. Isa. 4:4; Ezek. 40–48; Mal. 3:1-4; Jub. 4:26; PssSol. 17:30; 1 En. 90:28-29; 11QT 29.8-10; cf. Isa. 56:7), perhaps with overtones of a new eschatological community (51). The findings of the present study appear to confirm Dunn's conclusions, but the point is immaterial for the major thesis argued here.

Fig. 3. The Major Suggested Alternatives for a Seventh or Further Johannine Signs

Possible Sign	Scripture Reference	Public Event	Identified as Sign	God's Glory in Jesus
1. Temple cleansing	2:14-17	Yes	2:18	2:22 (cf. 1:14)
2. Word regarding serpent	3:14-15	No	No	3:12-21
3. Jesus' walking on water	6:16-21	No	No	6:20?
4. Anointing of Jesus	12:1-8	Yes	No	12:7?
5. Triumphal entry	12:12-16	Yes	No	12:16?
6. Crucifixion/resurrection	chaps. 18–19	No	20:30?	chap. 17
7. Resurrection appearances	chaps. 20–21	No	No	20:20, 27-28
8. Miraculous catch of fish	21:1-14	No	No	21:14

in line with the Synoptic portraits of Jesus' miracles. The six commonly acknowledged Johannine signs appear to fit the stereotype of a Synoptic-style miracle very well: they are amazing feats, displays of Jesus' power over nature, indeed, even over sickness and death. The temple cleansing, on the other hand, if measured by those characteristics, seems to fall short. Finally, it appears that the numbering of the signs performed in Cana of Galilee (cf. 2:11; 4:54) has been taken by some to exclude the possibility of any intervening signs (but cf. 2:23 and 3:2, both referring to signs of Jesus performed in Jerusalem).

While providing a number of possible explanations for the failure of some to identify the temple cleansing as the seventh Johannine sign, however, none of these obstacles is insurmountable.[84] Regarding the contention that the numbering of signs in 2:11 and 4:54 excludes any intervening signs, it should be noted that the numbering may merely refer to signs performed *in Cana of Galilee*. Another explanation may be the use of a "signs" source by the fourth evangelist who left the numbering unchanged but who may nevertheless have incorporated further signs of his own.[85] Regarding the more substantial objection that the "non-miraculous" nature of the temple cleansing disqualifies it from consideration as a Johannine sign, it may be responded that, while the temple cleansing was not "miraculous" in a narrow sense of the term, it is clearly presented by the fourth evangelist as an event that amazed and puzzled Jesus' audience to the extent that an explanation of its significance was required. Moreover, once one substitutes the Johannine concept of "signs" for the Synoptic framework of "miracles," the temple cleansing fits the category of "Johannine sign" very well indeed. As has been argued, what John considers a "sign"

---

84. Note also that there has been a significant minority of scholars, including Dodd, Carson, or Beasley-Murray, who have identified the temple cleansing as a Johannine sign.

85. Cf. especially Boismard, 53, who maintains that the "signs source" contained seven events so designated, but that the fourth evangelist considered the temple cleansing the "sign" par excellence, wherefore he transferred the catch of fish to the end of his Gospel.

is not primarily an amazing feat of power but events in Jesus' public ministry that have special symbolic significance in attesting to Jesus as God's authentic representative. Not the so-called miraculous element but the Christological symbolism is significant for John. Ultimately, all signs point to *Jesus* as the true messenger of God, the giver of life, a reality that finds its fullest expression in Jesus' resurrection from the dead, but a reality that is already given preliminary expression in the signs performed during Jesus' public ministry. According to John, the "signs," including the temple cleansing, are revelatory pictures of Jesus' true identity: he is the Christ, the Son of God (cf. 20:30).

EXCURSUS #1:
IMPLICATIONS FROM THE IDENTIFICATION
OF THE TEMPLE CLEANSING AS A JOHANNINE SIGN
FOR THE STRUCTURE OF THE FOURTH GOSPEL

The identification of the temple cleansing as an additional Johannine sign has significant implications for one's understanding of the structure of the Fourth Gospel. As can be seen in the chart below, the inclusion of the temple cleansing has two important effects on the structure of the Fourth Gospel: (1) it makes the raising of Lazarus the seventh climactic sign, providing the ultimate sign of Jesus' own resurrection; (2) it reveals the probable division of the first six Johannine signs into two categories, i.e., the three inaugural signs, and three further signs that are characterized by mounting controversy.

Jesus' raising of Lazarus, of course, is linked with Jesus' saying, "I am the resurrection and the life," and shortly thereafter with the conclusion of the fourth evangelist that "even though Jesus had done all these signs, they would not believe." It appears that, after Jesus' raising of Lazarus, no greater sign could be given. The Jews' unbelief in the face of such evidence for Jesus' Messianic identity made it clear that they would not believe Jesus' own resurrection either. The number seven, indicating completeness and perfection, shows that Jesus' performance of a resurrection provides a climax in the number of the Johannine signs.

John himself gives some clues that signs ##1 and 3, and then signs ##4 and 6, form the outer parameters of two groupings of three signs each. In the case of signs ##1 and 3, John numbers them as having both been performed in Cana of Galilee (4:54). The two healings in chapters 5 and 9 appear to be almost mirror images of each other and contain numerous textual connections.[86] The sequence of locations for the six signs reflects Jesus' continued movement from Galilee to Judea and back

---

86. Cf. J. Louis Martyn, *History and Theology in the Fourth Gospel,* 2d ed. (Nashville: Abingdon, 1979), 68-73.

again in the Fourth Gospel. The progression is as follows: Galilee/Judea/Galilee; Judea/Galilee/Judea. The climactic sign, finally, occurs in Judea.

With all seven signs taking place during Jesus' public ministry in 1–12, the references to Jesus' signs in the concluding sections of parts one and two of the Fourth Gospel appear to relate to one another in the following way. The conclusion in 12:37 shows that Jesus' Messianic signs had been rejected by the old covenant community. The conclusion in 20:30 indicates that Jesus' Messianic signs would be witnessed to by the new covenant community. Between these two conclusions, one finds sections on the implications of Jesus' exaltation for the new covenant community (13–17); on the reality to which the signs point, i.e., Jesus' crucifixion and resurrection (18–19); and on the resurrection appearances and commissioning of the new covenant community (20–21).

The following chart illustrates the resulting structure:

Fig. 4. The Seven Johannine Signs and the Structure of the Fourth Gospel

Prologue (1:1-18)
  I. THE BOOK OF SIGNS (1:19–12:50): The Signs of the Messiah
    A. The inaugural signs (Galilee/Judea/Galilee)
      1. Changing water into wine (2:1-11)
      2. Temple cleansing (2:14-17)
      3. Healing of nobleman's son (4:46-54)
    B. Controversial signs (Judea/Galilee/Judea)
      4. Healing of lame man (5:1-15)
      5. Feeding of multitude (6:1-15)
      6. Healing of blind man (9)
    C. The climactic sign (Judea)
      7. Raising of Lazarus (11)
    D. Conclusion: Jesus' Messianic signs rejected by the old covenant community (12:37)
  II. THE BOOK OF GLORY (13–20): The Reality to which the Signs Point
    A. Implications of Jesus' exaltation for the new covenant community (chaps. 13–17)
    B. The reality to which the signs point: Jesus' crucifixion and resurrection (chaps. 18–19)
    C. Resurrection appearances, commissioning of new covenant community (chaps. 20–21)
    D. Conclusion: Jesus' Messianic signs witnessed to by the new covenant community (20:30-31)
Epilogue (21)

f. Conclusion

It appears that the temple cleansing, and it alone, meets all the criteria for inclusion in the Johannine signs. It is a work performed by Jesus as part of his public ministry, it is identified as a "sign" in the Fourth Gospel, and it symbolically points to God's glory displayed in Jesus, thus revealing Jesus as God's true representative.[87] Jesus' crucifixion and resurrection, on the other hand, should not be considered as signs, since they relate to the seven signs featured in 1–12 as does reality to symbol.

The major implication of these observations regarding the mission of Jesus' followers is that the disciples are not called to perform signs in the Johannine sense of the term. This is true for the following reasons: (1) the Fourth Gospel's signs are limited to Jesus' public ministry narrated in chapters 1–12; (2) the signs' symbolism is realized in Jesus' crucifixion and resurrection so that further signs become unnecessary; and (3) the disciples' mission does not begin until after Jesus' resurrection (cf. 20:21-23).

2. Works

Attention has already been drawn to the fact that there is an important, albeit rare, terminological overlap between the works of Jesus and the works of his followers in 14:12. A study of "works" terminology with reference to Jesus will therefore be helpful for the analysis of the "greater works" passage in 14:12 in the subsequent chapter.

With very few exceptions (of which 14:12 is the most notable; cf. also 3:19-21; 6:27-30; 8:39-41), the term ἔργον is always used in the Fourth Gospel by Jesus and regarding Jesus.[88] There is a significant overlap between works and signs terminology (cf. 6:30; 9:3-4, 16). Often others, including the fourth evangelist, speak of Jesus' works as "signs," while Jesus himself refers to the same events simply as his "works" (cf., e.g., 7:21).[89] Generally, the word "sign" appears to be narrower than "work," since it alone involves an element of symbolism. Both expressions are used for specific deeds done by Jesus as well as for his entire ministry (cf. 4:34; 17:4; but cf. 12:37; 20:30-31).[90]

Reference is frequently made in the context of the discussion of Jesus'

---

87. If the temple cleansing is a Johannine sign, this would also provide an antecedent sign, notably in Jerusalem, for references to "the signs" Jesus was doing shortly thereafter in the Gospel narrative (cf. 2:23; 3:2). It is possible that the reference to "the second sign" in 4:54 merely pertains to Jesus' working of signs *in Galilee*, although this is disputed.

88. On works in the Fourth Gospel, cf. Johannes Riedl, *Das Heilswerk Jesu nach Johannes*, FThSt 93 (Freiburg im Breisgau: Herder, 1973).

89. Cf. Brown, *Gospel According to John*, 1:526.

90. Brown, *Gospel According to John*, 1:528. For a treatment on the distinction between Jesus' work and works, cf. Thüsing, 58-64.

works in the Fourth Gospel to the unity in intention and action between Jesus the Son and God the Father given expression in Jesus' works. "Jesus' works are God's works performed by and through Jesus."[91] The dependence theme is thus closely linked with works terminology, a fact that has important implications for the mission of Jesus' followers as well. Jesus' works are also marshaled as important evidence regarding Jesus' relationship with God (cf. especially 10:38 and 14:11; cf. also 5:36; 10:25; and 15:24).[92]

Moreover, John presents Jesus as viewing his works and words as equally part of his mission, often using these terms interchangeably (cf. 14:10-12; 15:22-24).[93] Thus Jesus' works include his words and are broader than his "signs": "All Jesus did *and said* on earth is summed up in the word ἔργον, and in the instances ἔργα is used, the word refers, in all likelihood, not only to the σημεῖα proper, but also to a wide range of activities, just because God is active in the Son, and the Son completely obedient to the Father."[94] Finally, "the σημεῖα are limited to Jesus' public activity, but there are also ἔργα of the exalted Lord."[95]

3. Conclusion

The signs are public works of Jesus with symbolic significance designed to lead others to faith in Jesus as the true representative of God. Jesus' performance of signs is tied to the Old Testament work of God both in the exodus but primarily in the symbolic actions and words of the prophets. The Fourth Gospel maintains that the signs are uniquely Jesus'. The disciples do not have a part in the "signs" portion of Jesus' mission (cf. 1–12).

Seven Johannine signs of Jesus were identified. The number seven may point to Jesus' complete and perfect revelation of God (cf. 1:18). Jesus' death and resurrection should not be considered as Johannine signs but rather as the realities to which the signs point. Thus there is, in Johannine thought, no need

---

91. Cf. de Jonge, "Signs and Works in the Fourth Gospel," 121.

92. Cf. de Jonge, "Signs and Works in the Fourth Gospel," 123, who notes that Jesus' works function as vehicles of legitimation: "Once one accepts that Jesus has the right to claim that his works are those of the Father, one should believe in his unique mission; no other reaction is possible"; or Schnackenburg, *Gospel According to St. John*, 1:519: "[T]hey [i.e., Jesus' works] often have the function of bearing testimony to Jesus as the envoy of God (5:36; 10:25, 37f.; 14:11; 15:24)." Cf. also Johannes Beutler, *Martyria: Traditionsgeschichtliche Untersuchungen zum Zeugnisthema bei Johannes*, FTS 10 (Frankfurt am Main: Josef Knecht, 1972).

93. However, Bultmann goes to an improper extreme when he equates Jesus' works and words in the Fourth Gospel completely: "Die Werke Jesu . . . sind seine Worte" (*Theologie des Neuen Testaments* [Tübingen, 1953, 407], quoted in de Jonge, "Signs and Works in the Fourth Gospel," 124). As de Jonge contends, "Jesus' words are effective, and his ἔργα give a reliable testimony. For those who are able to believe in it, there is a surprising unity of event and proclamation in all that God works in and through Jesus but no identity" (125).

94. Cf. de Jonge, "Signs and Works in the Fourth Gospel," 125.

95. Cf. Schnelle, 150. See the discussion of signs above.

for any more signs after Jesus' resurrection. Witness to the seven signs of Jesus, however, is still needed so that others, too, may believe in the Messiah (cf. 20:29-31).

The "works" in the Fourth Gospel refer to deeds, with no special emphasis regarding their "miraculous" nature, or words, usually done or spoken by Jesus in dependence on God the Father. The exalted Jesus will continue to do his works through the disciples (cf. 14:12).

C. The Nature of Jesus' Work according to the Fourth Gospel

The question regarding the nature of Jesus' work according to the Fourth Gospel becomes significant in the light of the link between the works of Jesus and of his followers established in 14:12. The first important issue is whether the work of Jesus according to John includes both revelatory and redemptive aspects. The second matter requiring clarification is whether this aspect (or these aspects) is tied to unique Christological characterizations or tasks in the Fourth Gospel, such as the working of signs or the incarnation for Jesus' work of revelation or his life-giving cross-death for Jesus' redemptive work. If the elements of Jesus' work are indeed tied to unique Christological designations, the contribution of the disciples should be seen not as participation in Jesus' revelatory and redemptive work in a primary sense of the term, but rather as a witness to the work already accomplished by Jesus. Thus the task of the disciples would have been perceived humbly, and a line would be drawn between the original contribution of Jesus and the subordinate function of the disciples.

In other words, the question needs to be answered whether the fourth evangelist is concerned to reserve for Jesus an ontological uniqueness or not. If so, it may still be said in a *secondary* sense that the disciples participate in Jesus' revelatory and redemptive work, but they should be considered as doing so only on the basis of Jesus' unique and complete work and mission. The relation between the missions of Jesus and of his followers, while involving elements of continuity, would then have to be seen in the light of this fundamental dissimilarity in person, role, and function. Once again, however, it is possible that the line between Jesus' work and the disciples' works is not drawn so absolutely. The following discussion will first address the issue of whether Jesus' work in John's Gospel is comprised of elements of both revelation *and* redemption or if it is solely revelatory in nature. Then the question will be asked whether these aspects of Jesus' work are in the Fourth Gospel tied to certain Christological formulations. The present treatment is designed to constitute the foundation for the investigation of the disciples' "greater works" in Chapter 4.

1. Compositional Flow

The subject of the nature of Jesus' work is directly addressed in 3:16-17: "For God did not send his Son into the world to condemn the world, but to save the world through him" (cf. also 12:47: "For I did not come to judge the world, but to save it"). It probably is the evangelist himself who describes the purpose of Jesus' mission as follows: "that whoever believes in him shall not perish but have eternal life" (3:16).

The giving of life by Jesus may be the most consistently stated purpose of Jesus' mission in the Fourth Gospel.[96] This terminology is also found in 6:57; 10:10; and 17:2 (cf. also 5:24). In different settings, i.e., in the bread of life discourse (6:57-58), the good shepherd discourse (10:7-10), and the farewell discourse (17:2-3), the purpose for Jesus' mission is equally said to be the giving of life.

It is remarkable that in all these passages (3:16-17; 6:57-58; 10:7-10; and 17:2-3), reference is made in the immediate context to Jesus' giving of his own life for the salvation of others (cf. also 14:6). The "giving" of God's Son in 3:16, a possible allusion to the *Akedah* of Genesis 22, follows hard on Jesus' reference to the serpent in the wilderness: "Just as Moses lifted up the snake in the desert, so the Son of Man must be lifted up, that everyone who believes in him may have eternal life" (3:14-15). This "lifting up" of the Son of Man, while still somewhat enigmatic in chapter 3, is later made more explicit: it refers to Jesus' death on the cross (cf. 12:32-33). The statement in 6:57-58 regarding the "bread of life" that came down from heaven is preceded by a reference to the flesh and blood of the Son of Man (6:53-56). Both of these passages, 3:13-17 and 6:53-58, feature descending/ascending terminology. Both passages are also developing Old Testament themes regarding Israel's wilderness wanderings and God's gracious provision. One thinks of the prologue, where the grace given through God by Moses is related to the grace given through God by Jesus (cf. 1:17). One also is reminded of the prologue's logos Christology and one of its possible theological antecedents, Isaiah 55:11.[97] The third passage speaking of Jesus' giving of his life, John 10:7-10, speaks of Jesus' giving of his own life for others in terms of the "good shepherd" who lays down his life for the sheep (10:11-18; cf. Ezek. 34; Zech. 9–14; and Isa. 53; cf. also 15:13).[98] Finally, Jesus' farewell

---

96. Cf. James McPolin, "Mission in the Fourth Gospel," *ITQ* 36 (1969): 118: "the primary purpose, to which all others are subordinated, is to confer life" (cf. 3:16-17 and 10:9-10: salvation; 8:12: light; 14:6: truth).

97. Note further Wis. 16:20: "Instead of these things you gave your people the food of angels, and without their toil you supplied them from heaven with bread ready to eat, providing every pleasure and suited to every taste."

98. Cf. France, building on Paul Lamarche, *Zacharie IX–XIV: Structure litteraire et messianisme* (Paris: J. Gabalda, 1961). Cf. also Johannes Beutler, "Der alttestamentlich-jüdische Hintergrund der Hirtenrede in Johannes 10," in *The Shepherd Discourse of John 10 and Its Context*, ed. Johannes Beutler and Robert T. Fortna, SNTSMS 67 (Cambridge: Cambridge University Press, 1991), 18-32.

prayer is preceded by Jesus' prediction, "a time is coming, and has come, when you will be scattered, each to his own home. You will leave me all alone. Yet I am not alone, for my Father is with me" (16:32).

The glorification of the Son mentioned in 17:1-5 harks back to statements made in 12:23-33. There the "lifting up" of the Son of Man, mentioned before in 3:14 and 8:28, is finally explicitly identified with the kind of death Jesus was going to die. The pericope's introductory statement, 12:23, also bears a resemblance to the language of 17:1-5: "The hour has come for the Son of Man to be glorified." The passage is immediately followed by Jesus' prediction: "I tell you the truth, unless a kernel of wheat falls to the ground and dies, it remains alone. But if it dies, it bears much fruit" (12:24).[99]

Overall, Jesus' mission is presented in the Fourth Gospel as one of "giving life" by giving his own life for others. Mission terminology is found prominently in all four passages: "descending and ascending" in 3:13; "sending" in 3:17 and "coming into the world" in 3:19; "sending," "descending and ascending" in 6:29-62; "coming" in 10:10; and "sending" in 17:3. The larger contexts of chapters 10 and 17 reveal further instances of mission terminology, i.e., in the case of chapter 10, "bringing" (10:16) and "following," in the case of chapter 17 "coming" and further instances of "sending."

2. Revelation and/or Salvation?

One's assessment of the Fourth Gospel's portrayal of Jesus' work seems to depend to a significant extent on one's view of the Fourth Gospel's presentation of the person of Jesus.[100] If one finds that in John's perspective of Jesus, Jesus' *divinity* predominates, one will likely conclude that Jesus' work of *revelation* is

---

99. On Jesus' death on the cross in the Fourth Gospel, cf. especially Theophil Müller, *Das Heilsgeschehen im Johannes-Evangelium: Eine exegetische Studie, zugleich der Versuch einer Antwort an Rudolf Bultmann* (Zürich-Frankfurt am Main: Gotthelf, 1961); Ulrich B. Müller, "Die Bedeutung des Kreuzestodes Jesu im Johannesevangelium: Erwägungen zur Kreuzestheologie im Neuen Testament," *KD* 21 (1975): 49-71; Peter von der Osten-Sacken, "Leistung und Grenze der johanneischen Kreuzestheologie," *EvT* 36 (1976): 154-76; Riedl, *Heilswerk Jesu nach Johannes.*

100. Cf. the discussion of *The Person of Jesus* above. On the nature of Jesus' work in the Fourth Gospel, cf. Max Turner, "Atonement and the Death of Jesus in John: Some Questions to Bultmann and Forestell," *EvQ* 62 (1990): 99-122. Cf. also the relevant contributions by Rudolf Schnackenburg, "Ist der Gedanke des Sühnetodes Jesu der einzige Zugang zum Verständnis unserer Erlösung durch Jesus Christus?" in *Der Tod Jesu: Deutungen im Neuen Testament,* QD 74, ed. Karl Kartelge (Freiburg im Breisgau: Herder, 1978), 205-30; Johannes Beutler, "Die Heilsbedeutung des Todes Jesu im Johannesevangelium nach Joh 13:1-20," in *Der Tod Jesu: Deutungen im Neuen Testament,* QD 74 (Freiburg im Breisgau: Herder, 1976), 188-205; Grigsby, 51-80; Leon Morris, "The Atonement in John's Gospel," *CrisTR* 3 (1988): 49-64; Ulrich B. Müller, "Bedeutung des Kreuzestodes Jesu im Johannesevangelium"; Georg Richter, "Die Deutung des Kreuzestodes Jesu in der Leidensgeschichte des Johannesevangeliums (Jo 13–19)," *BibLeb* 9 (1968): 21-36; and Jean Zumstein, "L'interprétation johannique de la mort du Christ," in *The Four Gospels 1992: Festschrift Frans Neirynck,* BETL C, ed. van Segbroeck et al., 3:2119-38.

tantamount. If one notes in John a significant strand of casting Jesus as human as well as divine, one is more likely to detect also references to Jesus' work of *salvation.*[101]

Bultmann contends, "The thought of Jesus' death as an atonement for sin has no place in John."[102] He argues that for John, the plight of human beings is alienation from God and existence in unbelief, darkness, and ignorance of God. Humanity does not need an appeasing sacrifice but a revealer, light, and the knowledge of God. Jesus provides for these needs, not through the cross, but through a ministry ranging from incarnation to glorification. The cross is simply a transition to glory. The one "work" Jesus has come to do is to *reveal.*[103] This work is accomplished by signs and discourses that interpret them. The Johannine sin, according to Bultmann, is ignorance — the Johannine salvation, revelation of the knowledge of God.

Forestell, seeking to modify Bultmann's thesis, states the aim of his work plainly, viz., "to show that the properly Johannine theology of salvation does not consider the death of Jesus to be a vicarious and expiatory sacrifice for sin."[104] He begins by attempting to establish the Bultmannian thesis that redemptive revelation is the central theme of Johannine theology. But while Bultmann claims that Jesus effectively only revealed that he is the revealer, Forestell understands revelation as the apocalyptic disclosure of salvation in Jesus.[105] What is more important, while Bultmann sees the cross in the Fourth Gospel simply as a stepping-stone on Jesus' way to glory, Forestell views it as the focal point of the revelation of God's love for humankind. He points to the three Johannine references to the "lifting up" of Jesus (cf. 3:14-15; 8:28-29; 12:32) and to the movement of the Johannine narrative toward the "hour" of Jesus' glorification.

---

101. Bultmann, further developed by Forestell, viewing the Johannine Jesus as Revealer, and Käsemann, who sees in John a docetic Jesus, both deny that the fourth evangelist considers Jesus' work also as redemptive. Cf. Rudolf Bultmann, *The Gospel of John,* trans. George R. Beasley-Murray (Oxford: Blackwell, 1971); *Theology of the New Testament,* 2:49-69; and "Die Bedeutung der neuerschlossenen mandäischen und manichäischen Quellen für das Verständnis des Johannesevangeliums," in *Johannes und sein Evangelium,* Wege der Forschung 82, ed. Karl Heinrich Rengstorf (Darmstadt: Wissenschaftliche Buchgesellschaft, 1973 [1925]), 402-64; J. Terence Forestell; and Ernst Käsemann. For a critique of Bultmann and Käsemann, cf. Thompson, *The Humanity of Jesus;* Leon Morris, "The Jesus of Saint John," in *Unity and Diversity in New Testament Theology: Essays in Honor of George E. Ladd,* ed. Robert A. Guelich (Grand Rapids: Wm. B. Eerdmans, 1978), 37-53.

102. Cf. Bultmann, *Theology of the New Testament,* 2:54.

103. Note, however, that revelation does not appear to be as major a theme in the Fourth Gospel as is Jesus' "giving of life." The words φωτίζω (1:9), φαίνω (1:5), ἀποκαλύπτω (12:38), and even the rather mundane word δείκνυμι (2:18; 5:20; 10:32; 14:8, 9; 20:20) are used rather infrequently. The word ὁράω occurs more often (1:18, 34, 39, 50; 3:11, 32, 36; 4:45; 5:37; 6:2, 36, 46; 8:38, 57; 9:37; 11:40; 14:7, 9; 15:24; 16:16, 17, 19, 22; 19:35, 37; 20:18, 25, 29).

104. Cf. Forestell, 2; cf. also Fortna, *Fourth Gospel and Its Predecessor,* 227, who maintains that the soteriological dimension of Jesus' death is entirely missing from the Fourth Gospel.

105. Cf. Forestell, 42.

Forestell denies that Jesus' cross-death is presented as sacrificial in passages such as 6:51 or 10:15, arguing that "Jesus' death is a revelation to men that God loves them with the self-devotion of the good shepherd."[106] In sum, for Forestell, the cross is central to John as revelation, not as an objective event of atonement. Forestell considers the reference to forgiveness in 20:23 as a later addition, and the assertion in 1:29 that Jesus is "the Lamb of God" to be a mere cultic metaphor.[107] For these reasons Forestell concludes that T. Müller was right in criticizing Bultmann's view that the death of Jesus has no salvific meaning for John, but wrong to give it the character of a vicarious expiation for sin. Rather, according to Forestell, "the evangelist understands the cross as the culminating act of a revelatory process in which God manifests himself to men and bestows upon them his own divine life."[108]

On the other side of the issue, Grigsby contends, "Through the use of 'Akedah' [1:29; 3:16; 19:17], Paschal [1:29; 19:14, 29, 36], and 'living water' [19:34; cf. 4:10-15; 7:37; 13:10] themes, the Evangelist has clearly endorsed the cultic rationale wherein sin is cleansed by either the outpoured blood of the sacrificial victim or the cultic washing with 'living water.'"[109] Grigsby argues,

> However, alongside the obvious revelatory themes just noted, the casual reader of the Fourth Gospel must also recognize that the Evangelist conceived of an expiatory rationale, however "johannized," behind Christ's death. Salvation in the Fourth Gospel is presented not only as the bestowal of eternal life, but also as a state of existence wherein sin is eliminated and judgment is escaped; and though an expiatory rationale between Christ's death and sin's removal is not as explicitly spelled out as in the Pauline literature, there are sufficient hints throughout the Gospel to suppose that the Evangelist endorsed such a rationale.[110]

Carey, too, argues that, far from being an isolated statement, 1:29 introduces a theme that recurs frequently in the Fourth Gospel (i.e., in chapters 3, 4, 6, 10, and in 12:24).[111] Jesus is the Lamb of God, God's Son sent to accomplish his Father's will and to redeem mankind, the expiation of the sins of the whole

---

106. Forestell, 76.

107. Cf. Forestell, 149, 161-62, 165-66, and 194-95. Cf. the assessment by William Loader, *The Christology of the Fourth Gospel*, BBET 23 (Frankfurt am Main: Peter Lang, 1992), 13 and 93-146; and Nicholson, 2-9.

108. Cf. Forestell, 191.

109. Cf. Grigsby, 62.

110. Cf. Grigsby, 52. Reference is made to Ulrich Müller, "Bedeutung des Kreuzestodes Jesu"; Beutler, "Heilsbedeutung," 188-205; and Siegfried Schulz, *Das Evangelium nach Johannes*, 13th ed. (Göttingen: Vandenhoeck & Ruprecht, 1975), 237-38.

111. Cf. George L. Carey, "The Lamb of God and Atonement Theories," *TynBul* 32 (1981): 97-122.

world.[112] As Carey contends, "In this breathtaking notion that Jesus is sinbearer of the world the evangelist announces a full-blooded concept of the atonement which is of importance to our interpretation of the cross."[113]

Turner criticizes Forestell for casting salvation by revelation and salvation by sacrificial atonement as mutually exclusive rather than embracing F.-M. Braun's view that "salvation by faith in the Word and salvation by the sacrifice of the Lamb (or by the blood) are two stages in the process of salvation."[114] Pointing to 1 John 2:2, Turner demonstrates that in Johannine thought sin broke fellowship with God and required an atoning sacrifice (ἱλασμός). In fact, Turner argues that a combination of the two views, i.e., the cross as an objective atoning event *and* as such the high point of redemptive revelation, provides a more coherent explanation of the place of the cross in John than Forestell's position does.[115]

Turner asks, "If the cross is merely a revelation of God's love, and not a sacrifice of atonement, *why is it that salvation,* for John (on Forestell's understanding), *can only be bestowed after the cross?*"[116] This author maintains, "The view Forestell opposes (namely that Jesus must effect objective redemption for sins at the cross before there can be redemption mediated by revelation and received subjectively in faith) could at least explain *why,* for John, Jesus' redemptive revelation can only become effective *after* the 'glorification.'"[117] But the sharpest question is, "[I]f the cross does not accomplish something objectively for us, *how* is it Jesus' giving of his life 'for us'; and *how* is it a revelation of *God's love for us?*"[118] Why was it Jesus' *death* that was chosen as the focal point of the revelation of God's love for humankind? Following Forestell's line of reasoning, one may well consider this mode of revelation arbitrary. Certainly it may seem capricious that God would choose as mode for his revelation a death as cruel as Jesus' if other modes of revelation would have equally served God's purpose (i.e., revealing his love).

As Turner rightly observes, Forestell, by excluding sacrificial atonement

---

112. Carey (112 and 114) notes that Schnackenburg interprets 1:29 in terms of vicarious sacrifice while Dodd, Barrett, and Brown do not (117 and 120). Cf. also the excellent treatment of 1:29 by Carson, *Gospel According to John,* 148-51.

113. Cf. Carey, 121. Cf. further Frank J. Matera, " 'On Behalf of Others,' 'Cleansing,' 'Return': Johannine Images for Jesus' Death," *Louvain Studies* 13 (1988): 161-78. Matera deals with the Fourth Gospel's use of the preposition ὑπέρ with reference to Jesus' death (164-70), the footwashing (170-72), and Jesus' exaltation and return (173-77). While Matera's discussion is helpful at many points, he concedes too much when he concludes, "The Fourth Evangelist may not explain Jesus' death as an expiatory sacrifice for sin, but he does view this death as a genuine self-sacrifice on behalf of others" (177).

114. Cf. Max Turner, 113; quoting François-Marie Braun, *Jean le théologien et son évangile dans l'église ancienne* (Paris: J. Gabalda, 1966), 172.

115. Cf. Max Turner, 115.

116. Max Turner, 115.

117. Max Turner, 116.

118. Max Turner, 116.

as a possible explanation for Jesus' death, creates an interpretational vacuum that he is unable to fill. While Forestell rightly focuses on the cross as central to Johannine soteriology, and while he correctly views the cross as a supreme revelation of God's love in the Fourth Gospel, he errs in ruling out an objective atonement accomplished by Jesus' cross-work. The Baptist's references to the "Lamb of God" and the references to Jesus' giving of his life for his sheep in the Good Shepherd discourse are best explained by viewing the cross as achieving atonement for sin. As Turner concludes, "John's . . . emphasis on the cross as salvific revelation was intended to be understood as complementary to the traditional objective explanations rather than as a denial of them."[119]

3. Conclusion

The history of the debate of the nature of Jesus' work in the Fourth Gospel has often been one of extremes and reaction.[120] While it seems inappropriate to deny that the Fourth Gospel is entirely free from the notion of salvation through sacrificial atonement, it is apparent that this aspect of Jesus' work is not focused upon as much as in other New Testament writings.[121] One should therefore be careful not to overstate one's case for the presence of atonement motifs in the Fourth Gospel.[122] Generally, John seems to assume and presuppose the notion of substitutionary sacrifice and atonement rather than elaborating upon these elements as much as the other evangelists. Especially if John knew (of) the Synoptic Gospels and wrote to supplement rather than to duplicate them, it seems reasonable to expect him to build upon their tradition rather than simply to repeat it.

The fourth evangelist appears to regard the nature of Jesus' work as unique and set apart from the activity of Jesus' followers.[123] According to the fourth evangelist, Jesus' cross-death was part of the accomplished mission of the Son

119. Max Turner, 122.

120. Cf., e.g., Morris, "Atonement in John," for an example of a reaction to Bultmann (curiously Morris does not even refer to Forestell in this article published in 1988). While Morris summarizes helpfully the Fourth Gospel's teachings on sin, judgment, and Jesus' death, he does not fully acknowledge, at least in the opinion of the present author, the distinctiveness of the Fourth Gospel's presentation of Jesus' death and its significance. Morris's essay thus has the effect of seeking to approximate John's treatment to that of the Synoptics while perhaps not fully appreciating the distinctiveness of John's perspective on the cross.

121. Cf. Grant R. Osborne, "Redactional Trajectories in the Crucifixion Narrative," *EvQ* 51 (1979): 92, who points out that John has removed the details which suggest the horror of the crucifixion: the wine mixed with myrrh, the cry of dereliction and the Elijah account, the darkness, and the taunts of the bystanders.

122. Cf. Müller, "Bedeutung des Kreuzestodes," 63.

123. Cf. Theofried Baumeister, "Der Tod Jesu und die Leidensnachfolge des Jüngers nach dem Johannesevangelium und dem ersten Johannesbrief," *Wissenschaft und Weisheit* 40 (1977): 84: "Die Einzigartigkeit Jesu in seinem Wirken und in seinem Tod ist das Thema des ganzen Evangeliums."

who was sent by the Father, as well as a station on Jesus' return to the one who had sent him.[124] It is also the Son's exaltation and the return to his pre-existent glory (cf. 12:23; 17:1, 5, 24). Finally, John's theology of the cross may be particularly designed to make as palatable as possible for his readers the notion of a crucified Messiah. Doubtless this was a serious obstacle to faith for Jesus' own contemporaries, and remained a major stumbling block for potential Jewish converts even in John's day.[125]

With regard to the work of Jesus' followers, it may be concluded that both the revelatory and redemptive aspects of Jesus' work in the Fourth Gospel are tied to the unique personal characteristics of Jesus to such an extent that the disciples can be said to participate in these only in a secondary sense. But it remains for the following chapter to develop these observations more fully.

III. THE CHARGE OF JESUS

The semantic field study conducted in the previous chapter has shown that modes of movement terminology with reference to Jesus is much more multi-faceted than that regarding the disciples. As will be further developed below, it appears that these various modes of movement in Jesus' mission are linked with certain characterizations of Jesus in the Fourth Gospel. For example, the phraseology of "sending" combines with John's representation of Jesus as "the Son" to form a portrait of Jesus as "the sent Son."

This discussion of the various modes of movement in Jesus' mission and of the resulting Christological portraits is significant for the later exploration of the mission of his followers. If the term "send," for example, is connected only to the term "Son" and not, for example, to expressions directly involving Jesus' incarnation or divinity, elements of continuity between the missions of Jesus and of the disciples should be limited to the clusters associated with the Christological portrait of the "sent Son," such as dependence and obedience, rather than being applied to the entirety of Jesus' mission.

The ensuing discussion will present the findings of the exploration of modes of movement in Jesus' mission under the following inductively developed categories. The general heading will be "Jesus the Messiah," since John's presentation of Jesus as Messiah appears to serve as his fundamental Christological purpose (cf. 20:30-31). After a general discussion of Messianic expectations in the Fourth Gospel and the designation "the Coming One," the study will attempt

---

124. On the Johannine "departure theme," cf. Nicholson, whose contribution will be discussed below.

125. See further Chapter 5 below.

to trace three interrelated but nevertheless distinct sub-portraits of Jesus, all of which combine terms denoting modes of movement in Jesus' mission with a certain characterization of Jesus:

(1) Jesus as the sent Son;
(2) Jesus as the One who comes into the world and who returns to the Father, including the descent-ascent motif; and
(3) Jesus as the eschatological shepherd-teacher.

When discussing the disciples' mission in the subsequent chapter, it will then be possible to relate corresponding elements in their mission to the framework comprising Jesus' mission presented below.

A. Modes of Movement in Jesus' Mission

The person and work of Jesus in the Fourth Gospel have already been discussed. It is now possible to deal with the various modes of movement in Jesus' mission.[126] After a brief overview of the relevant passages, the various terms denoting modes of movement will be studied with attention to the following relationships: first, terms denoting modes of movement in Jesus' mission and characterizations of Jesus; second, terms denoting modes of movement and signs and work(s) terminology; and third, terms denoting modes of movement and the purposes of Jesus' mission.[127] After this the various terms denoting modes of movement in Jesus' mission will be discussed.

A very important distinction that is not often made in the relevant literature is the one between mission terms that occur consistently throughout the Fourth Gospel and others that are used only sporadically.[128] Such a distinction may, however, help in determining more fundamental mission ter-

126. Cf. Nicholson, 51, who organizes his discussion of descent-ascent language in the Fourth Gospel under the heading "The variety of language used to describe Jesus' movement onto the stage." Nicholson's approach is similar to the one adopted in the present study. This becomes clear when he writes, "The Evangelist does not confine himself to any one word to describe this movement, nor is any one word singled out from the others as being more appropriate than them for conveying his meaning. He appears to choose a word or phrase for the task in hand with nothing more than stylistic considerations in mind" (52).

127. To the knowledge of this writer, this kind of methodical integrative study has not yet been undertaken.

128. Cf., e.g., the observation by Ernest M. Sidebottom, "The Ascent and Descent of the Son of Man in the Gospel of St. John," *ATR* 39 (1957): 122, that references to "ascent" occur very rarely in the Fourth Gospel (i.e., only in 3:13; 6:62; and 20:17). Sidebottom thinks the reason for this rarity of use lies in the Fourth Gospel's stress on the accessibility of heaven in the human person of Jesus.

minology in contrast to complementary terms. As one screens the Fourth Gospel for mission terms, one notes that there are especially three sets of mission terminology that occur throughout the Gospel: sending, coming-returning, and following, whereby the first two terms are perhaps more common than the third. One also finds occasional occurrences of the terms descending-ascending and gathering. The latter set of terms should be treated as subordinated to the terms consistently used in the Fourth Gospel in the following ways: descending-ascending under coming-returning;[129] and gathering under following.

1. Survey of Passages Featuring Terms Denoting Modes of Movement

The first references featuring a term denoting a mode of movement in Jesus' mission are already found in the prologue. There the evangelist presents Jesus as "the true light *coming into the world*," even coming "to his own." Jesus is also designated as the Logos become flesh who brought grace and truth (1:9, 11, 14, 17; cf. 3:14; 12:46). This language ("coming into the world") recurs in Jesus' testimony before Pilate (18:37).

There are also passages that simply refer to Jesus' *coming:* "I did not come from myself but the one who sent me is true. . . . I know from where I came and where I am going" (7:28; 8:14); "I came in the name of my Father" (5:43). Coming in one's own initiative is contrasted with being commissioned by someone else: "I came and have come from God; for I did not come from myself, but he sent me" (8:42). The most frequently stated purposes of Jesus' coming into the world are to save or to bring abundant life to those who believe and judgment to those who do not (cf. 3:16-17; 9:39; 10:9-10; 12:47).

The Fourth Gospel roots Jesus' coming firmly in his being *sent.* In controversy with the Jews, Jesus almost invariably claims that he was sent, to protect himself from the charge that his mission was self-appointed (note especially the formula ὁ πέμψας με πατήρ; 5:36-38; 6:38; 7:16-18, 33; 8:18, 26, 29, 42; 9:4; 12:44-45, 49). Later Jesus refers to his being sent in relation to his sending of the disciples (chap. 17; 20:21).

Specific mission terminology is clustered with certain characterizations of Jesus in the Fourth Gospel. For example, as the Son of Man, Jesus *descends and ascends* (cf. 3:13-15; 6:62; cf. 20:17). As the Bread of Life, Jesus *descends from heaven* (cf. 6:29-59). Applied to Jesus are also references to *the coming*

---

129. Cf. Forestell, 98, n. 164: "In John ἀναβαίνειν . . . is a metaphorical equivalent for πορεύεσθαι and ὑπάγειν"; Nicholson, 51: "The point . . . is that the Evangelist is not wedded to any particular word to describe the descent of Jesus. This descent can be described as 'coming down' (καταβαίνω), coming (ἔρχομαι), or 'coming out' (ἐξέρχομαι)," and 57: "As with the language of entrance, so too here, there does not appear to be any significance in the choice of one word over another." Cf. further the chart by Moule referred to below.

Prophet and the Christ (cf. 4:25; 6:14; 7:27, 31, 41-42; 11:27; 12:13, 15 [quoting Ps. 118:25-26 and Zech. 9:9]). The Farewell Discourse includes numerous references to Jesus' "*going* to the Father" (πορεύομαι, ὑπάγω).

These various strands of mission terminology should be understood in their complementary aspects as they are integrated into the Fourth Gospel. It is noteworthy that, except for "sending" (cf. 17:18; 20:21), with the possible exception of "going" (πορεύομαι; cf. 15:16), none of the terms discussed above are applied to the mission of the disciples. Clearly it is Jesus who is the towering figure in the Fourth Gospel. His mission is unrivaled.

Nevertheless, while Jesus' coming into the world, his descending and ascending, his coming as the Prophet and the Christ, and his return to the Father are all unique, the dependence theme, with its accompanying sending terminology, is prominent throughout the Gospel and forms an important bridge between the missions of Jesus and of the disciples.

2. Modes of Movement in Jesus' Mission in the Relevant Literature

Bultmann's treatment (1955) of the "Sending of the Son" and of the interrelated mission terms in the Fourth Gospel remains unsurpassed in its formidable grasp of the Greek text.[130] Bultmann categorizes the references to Jesus' coming into three modes: his "coming into the world" (3:19; 9:39; 11:27; 12:46; 16:28; 18:37); his "coming from the Father" (8:42; 13:3; 16:27-28, 30; 17:8); and his "having come" (5:43; 7:28; 8:14; 10:10; 12:47; 15:22); adding also Jesus' "coming down from heaven" (3:13; 6:33, 38, 41-42).[131] He is careful to note the relationships between the following terms: sending and coming (7:28-29; 8:42; 17:8); coming and descending (3:13; 6:33, 38, 41-42); coming and going (i.e., returning; 3:19; 8:14; 12:31; 13:1, 3; 14:12, 28; 16:5, 10, 17, 28); and descending and ascending (3:13; 6:62). He also notes the connection of these terms with "lift up" (3:14; 8:28; 12:32, 34) and "glorify" (7:39; 12:16, 23; 13:31-32; 17:1, 5, 24). The only terms denoting modes of movement in Jesus' mission that Bultmann does not connect with mission terminology in the Fourth Gospel are "gathering" and "following." Bultmann also discusses the purposes of Jesus' coming, i.e., his bearing witness (18:37) as "light" (12:46); and his giving life and salvation (3:16-17; 10:9-10).[132]

Bultmann then proceeds to relate these various modes of movement in Jesus' mission to certain characterizations of Jesus in the Fourth Gospel. He argues that the meaning of Jesus' sending is expressed in the title "Messiah" (1:41; 4:25) or "Christ." The question whether Jesus is the Christ is

---

130. Cf. Bultmann, *Theology of the New Testament*, 2:33-40.
131. Bultmann, *Theology of the New Testament*, 2:34.
132. Bultmann, *Theology of the New Testament*, 2:34-35.

entertained in the Fourth Gospel by "the Jews" in 7:26-27, 31, 41-42; 9:22; 10:24; 12:34 (cf. 1:20) and affirmed by believers in Jesus in 11:27 and 20:31 (cf. 1:49). Bultmann also refers to the important Christological titles Son of God and Son of Man.[133] What is expressed by all three phrases (Messiah, Son of God, and Son of Man), according to Bultmann, is the fact that Jesus is the eschatological salvation-bringer and that his coming is the eschatological event. First, Jesus fulfills Messianic predictions by both Moses and the prophets (1:45; 5:39, 46). He fulfills the Scriptures (4:25-26) as well as Jewish expectations of the "second redeemer" who would bestow bread from heaven as did Moses (6:31-32). Jesus' coming is "the Messiah's day" (8:56). Second, Jesus' coming is the judgment of the world (3:19; 9:39; cf. 5:24-25; cf. also 3:36; 6:47; 8:51; 11:25-26). This is the theme of entire sections of the Fourth Gospel (cf. 3:1-21, 31-36; 4:43-46; 7:15-24; 8:13-20; cf. also 6:60-71).[134]

Kuhl (1967) lists the following terms besides "sending" as relevant for mission in the Fourth Gospel: ἔρχεσθαι (cf. also ἥκω: 2:4; 4:47; 6:37; 8:42); ἐξέρχεσθαι (8:42; 13:3; 16:27, 28, 30; 17:8); ἀπέρχεσθαι (16:7); καταβαίνειν (3:13; 6:33, 38, 41, 42, 50, 51, 58); cf. also ἁγιάζειν (10:36; 17:17, 19); διδόναι (3:16, 34; 5:26; 6:37; 12:49; 13:3; 14:16); σφραγίζειν (3:33; 6:27); ἐντέλλεσθαι (14:31; 15:14, 17); and further ὑπάγειν (7:33; 8:14, 21, 22; 13:3, 33, 36; 14:4, 5, 28; 16:5, 10, 17); πορεύεσθαι (7:35; 14:2, 3, 12, 28; 16:7, 28); ἀφιέναι (16:28); ἀναβαίνειν (3:13; 6:62; 20:17); and μεταβαίνειν (13:1).[135] While this list is quite helpful, Kuhl does not provide any criteria for his choice of the above terms, nor does he consistently and consciously relate those terms to one another in the course of his study.

McPolin (1969) refers to "come (out of)," "proceed from," and "descend," noting, "These expressions of themselves denote only partial aspects of a mission for 'to come' does not necessarily imply being sent by somebody."[136] This may be so, but even if these terms constitute only a partial aspect of mission in the Fourth Gospel, they should be treated.

Miranda (1972) includes the following terms in his discussion of mission terminology in the Fourth Gospel: ἀποστέλλειν, πέμπειν, ἔρχεσθαι, καταβαίνειν, ἀναβαίνειν, φανεροῦν, φωτίζειν, φαίνειν, and διδόναι.[137] The choice of terms for revelation (φανεροῦν, φωτίζειν, φαίνειν), however, reflects Miranda's "history-of-religions" presuppositions and can hardly be justified linguistically

133. Bultmann, *Theology of the New Testament*, 2:36.

134. Bultmann, *Theology of the New Testament*, 2:37-38. Note even the division of the entire Gospel into two parts, i.e., chapters 1–12 and 13–21, the first dealing with Jesus' revelation to the world, the second with Jesus' revelation to believers.

135. Cf. Josef Kuhl, *Die Sendung Jesu und der Kirche nach dem Johannes-Evangelium,* Studia Instituti Missiologica Societatis Verbi Domini 11 (St. Augustin: Steyler, 1967), 56-57.

136. Cf. McPolin, 114.

137. Cf. Miranda, *Vater der mich gesandt hat,* 8-131.

or from the Fourth Gospel itself.[138] The term διδόναι, too, should not be considered a mission term as such but should only be considered where it is used in relation to proper mission terminology (cf., e.g., 3:16-17 where διδόναι is used in relation to ἀποστέλλειν).[139]

Arens (1976) groups together the terms ἔρχομαι, ἐξέρχομαι, ἥκω, ἀπο-στέλλω, πέμπω, and καταβαίνω.[140] He also contributes a helpful summary chart comparing the meanings of ἔρχεσθαι and ἀποστέλλω/πέμπω and a fairly detailed treatment of the term ὁ ἐρχόμενος.[141] Arens identifies two viewpoints of Jesus' mission in the Fourth Gospel: sending (prophetic) and coming (epiphanic).[142] He concludes that the ἦλθον-sayings probably reflect a Messianic consciousness.[143] Overall, his study is primarily classificatory in nature and thus provides a helpful backdrop for further investigation. The focus of Arens's treatment is on the Synoptic Gospels so that it is of only limited value for the study of Jesus' mission in the Fourth Gospel undertaken here. However, one major disagreement with Arens should be noted. He asserts that the term "sending" in the Fourth Gospel is indicative of Christ's coming from above.[144] Close scrutiny of the language of the Fourth Gospel, however, shows that it is the term "coming (into the world)," not "sending," that has this connotation.

Moule (1982) provides a list of "coming and going" terminology in the Fourth Gospel which groups together references of ἔρχομαι, ἐξέρχομαι, ἀπέρχομαι, καταβαίνω, ἀναβαίνω, ὑπάγω, πορεύομαι, ἀκολουθέω, and ἀφίημι.[145] Moule seeks to demonstrate (unconvincingly, to the mind of the present author) that all of these references relate to Jesus' incarnation, death, and resurrection rather than to Jesus' incarnation, death/resurrection, and parousia. He thus construes three categories, "coming" (from pre-existence), "going" (in death?), and "returning." The purpose of Moule's article is limited

---

138. Cf. Miranda, *Vater der mich gesandt hat*, 129: "Das ganze Leben Jesu steht nach Joh unter dem Gesichtspunkt der Offenbarung Gottes, wobei alles Interesse sich auf die Person des Offenbarers Jesu konzentriert."

139. Cf. already the comments regarding the non-inclusion or partial inclusion of certain terms in this present study in Chapter 2 above.

140. Cf. Eduardo Arens, *The ΗΛΘΟΝ-Sayings in the Synoptic Tradition: A Historico-Critical Investigation*, OBO 10 (Freiburg/Schweiz: Universitätsverlag; Göttingen: Vandenhoeck & Ruprecht, 1976), 309.

141. Cf. Arens, 288-300 and 321-22.

142. Arens, 305.

143. Arens, 324.

144. Cf. Arens, 324: "The Synoptics' weight on ἔρχεσθαι is indicative of a Christology 'from below' and its content refers to Jesus' messiahship, while the Johannine emphasis on the perf. ἐλήλυθα, ἀποστέλλειν and πέμπειν is indicative of a Christology 'from above,' which presents Jesus as the pre-existing and glorious Son of God (cf. 20, 31)."

145. Cf. C. F. D. Moule, "The Individualism of the Fourth Gospel," in *Essays in New Testament Interpretation* (Cambridge: Cambridge University Press, 1982), 105-9.

to "coming and going" terminology. His approach resembles the one by Nicholson, who pursues his analysis with greater methodological rigor.

In his 1983 study of the Johannine "descent-ascent schema,"[146] Nicholson groups the following terms under "descent language": καταβαίνω, ἔρχομαι, and ἐξέρχομαι.[147] The following terms are included under "language of departure and ascent": ἀναβαίνω, ἔρχομαι, μεταβαίνω, ὑπάγω, πορεύομαι, and ἀπέρχομαι.[148] Nicholson's organization of the various Johannine terms for coming and going, descending and descending under common headings is very helpful. Essentially, all these terms are included in this present study's category "Jesus as the Coming and Returning One." Nicholson, however, neglects a discussion of the other terms denoting movement in the Fourth Gospel, especially sending, as well as following and gathering.

Lemmer (1990) primarily studies the last part of John's Gospel, including descending and ascending, coming and going, and being sent.[149] He sees a connection especially between these terms: "the protagonist was first of all *sent* by God, the Father; then he obviously *came* (in the incarnation); and he is basically *going to return* to the Father."[150] Lemmer also investigates the implied readers of the Johannine Farewell Discourses. However, it is a weakness of his study that he does not deal with the first part of the Fourth Gospel.

Beasley-Murray (1992) contributes a very significant essay on "The Mission of the Logos-Son."[151] He notes the connection between "sending" and "Son" terminology as well as the collocation of "Son" and "works" language, arguing that "[t]his portrayal of the sending of the Son is even more unambiguously stated in those sayings wherein his 'coming' into the world is juxtaposed with his departure from the world to return to the Father," thus recognizing a second set of terms besides "the sending of the Son," i.e., Jesus' "coming into the world" and his "returning to the Father."[152] Beasley-Murray then asks, rather surprisingly, "[C]ould it be that the model of the mission of the Son in the Fourth Gospel is *the Prophet Redeemer, interpreted in the light of the Logos, the Word and Wisdom of God?*"[153] He contends that the Prologue may be seen as "an anticipatory description of the Mission of the Logos-Son to the World."[154]

Beasley-Murray's treatment is open to criticism in two respects. First,

---

146. Cf. Nicholson.

147. Cf. Nicholson, 52.

148. Cf. Nicholson, 58.

149. Cf. H. R. Lemmer, "A possible understanding by the implied reader, of the *coming-going-being sent* pronouncements, in the Johannine farewell discourses," *Neot* 25 (1992): 289-310.

150. Lemmer, 300.

151. Cf. Beasley-Murray, "The Mission of the Logos-Son," in *The Four Gospels 1992: Festschrift Frans Neirynck*, BETL C, ed. van Segbroeck et al., 3:1855-68.

152. Cf. Beasley-Murray, "The Mission of the Logos-Son," 1861-62 and 1865.

153. Cf. Beasley-Murray, "The Mission of the Logos-Son," 1866; emphasis Beasley-Murray's.

154. Cf. Beasley-Murray, "The Mission of the Logos-Son," 1867.

he neglects the passages in the Fourth Gospel that present Jesus' role in terms of the eschatological shepherd-teacher calling others to gather his eschatological harvest. Second, he unduly conflates the concepts of the Logos and of the sent Son. However, the (prologue of the) Fourth Gospel never applies "sending" language to the Logos (though the prologue uses "sending" language for the mission of John the Baptist in 1:6). Rather, "coming" terminology is used (cf. 1:9: ἐρχόμενον εἰς τὸν κόσμον; 1:11: εἰς τὰ ἴδια ἦλθεν), a fact that indicates that the concept of the Logos should be subsumed under the concept of the one who comes into the world and who returns to where he came from. Apart from the rather speculative conclusion, Beasley-Murray provides a sound study that stays close to the categories of the Fourth Gospel themselves.

The lessons learned from these contributions can be summarized as follows. While one may not follow Bultmann in all of his conclusions, he provides a very helpful treatment of the interrelations of all the terms denoting movement in Jesus' mission according to the Fourth Gospel (except for following and gathering). Also exemplary is Bultmann's effort to relate these terms denoting modes of movement in Jesus' mission to characterizations of Jesus in the Fourth Gospel. Indeed, it is the designation "Messiah" that is most important, especially in the light of 20:30-31.

Of the other authors, few seek to relate terms denoting modes of movement in Jesus' mission consistently to characterizations of Jesus or to signs and works terminology. A notable exception is Nicholson, whose treatment is however unduly limited to the Johannine descent-ascent schema, an important part of Johannine mission teaching but not the whole. The treatments of Kuhl and Miranda are both weakened by a lack of establishing criteria for selecting mission terminology. Moule's study, though limited in its scope, provides support for the present study's practice of grouping together terms of coming and going, descending and ascending. Lemmer's analysis likewise shows that in recent studies there has been an increasing sensitivity to the interrelated Johannine mission terminology, in Lemmer's case sending, coming and going, and descending and ascending. The major limitation of Lemmer's treatment is that he studies only the Farewell Discourse, thus omitting reference to Jesus' signs or Johannine sending terminology, since these occur predominantly in the first part of John's Gospel.

3. Modes of Movement and Characterizations of Jesus

The study of the Fourth Gospel, informed also by the survey of the relevant literature, yields the following insights regarding the use of terms denoting modes of movement in Jesus' mission according to John's Gospel, first in relation to characterizations of Jesus, then in relation to signs and works terminology, and finally in relation to the purpose of Jesus' mission:

**Fig. 5. Modes of Movement and Characterizations of Jesus
in the Fourth Gospel**

Mode of Movement	*Characterization of Jesus*
1. Sending[155]	the Son (of the Father) (3:16-17; 5:23, 30, 36; 10:36; 12:49; 14:24; 17:3, 18, 21, 23, 25; 20:21; cf. 7:28-29; 8:16, 18, 26, 28-29)
2. a. Coming (into the world; ἔρχομαι)/ Returning (ὑπάγω; πορεύομαι)[156]	the Logos/the Light (1:9; 3:19; 8:12; 12:46) (7:33; 8:14; chaps. 13–17)[157]
b. the Coming One	the Christ, the Prophet (4:25; 6:14; 7:27, 31, 41-42; 11:27; 12:13, 15)
3. a. Descending	the Bread of Life (6:30-59)
b. Descending and Ascending	the Son of Man (3:13; 6:62; 8:28)[158]
4. Calling to Follow	the Rabbi/Teacher (1:37-43; 8:12; 10:4, 5, 27; 12:26; 21:19-23)
5. Gathering	the Eschatological Shepherd (10:16; 11:51-52)

Arguably, any treatment of mission in the Fourth Gospel that fails to deal with all of the categories above is to that extent imbalanced and incomplete. That is especially true of studies that equate mission with sending. A one-sided emphasis on just one aspect of Jesus' mission can lead to serious distortions of the overall Johannine presentation.[159]

---

155. Note that sending and coming are linked in the following passages: 7:28 (πέμπω, ἔρχομαι), 33 (πέμπω, ὑπάγω); 8:42 (ἀποστέλλω, ἔρχομαι); 16:5 (πέμπω, ὑπάγω); and 17:8 (ἀποστέλλω, ἐξέρχομαι).

156. Note that ἔρχομαι and ὑπάγω are linked, e.g., in 8:14, 21; ἔρχομαι and πορεύομαι are connected in 16:28.

157. "Son" language is only found in conjunction with sending terminology in the Fourth Gospel. References to "the Father," however, also occur with two other terms denoting movement in the Fourth Gospel, ἐξέρχομαι (8:42; 13:3; 16:28; 17:8) and πορεύομαι (14:12, 28; 16:28; note that 16:28 combines both terms to refer to the entire cycle of Jesus' mission). In those references to Jesus' coming from and going to "the Father," the concept of "the Son" is at least implicit. Still, the fact that "Son" language is not explicitly used seems to imply that the concept of the Son itself is not in the foreground in those passages but rather Jesus' origin and destiny.

158. Cf. 1:51; 12:23, 34; but cf. 20:17, where ascending (ἀναβαίνω) is linked with "Father" terminology, perhaps because Jesus now views his crucifixion in hindsight. Note also the connection with the term "being lifted up."

159. For example, Bultmann sees the entire Fourth Gospel in the light of the gnostic Revealer, failing to balance properly the various strands of mission terminology in the Fourth Gospel.

4. Modes of Movement and Signs and Works Terminology

Regarding the collocation of terms denoting modes of movement with signs and works terminology, the following relationships can be observed:

Fig. 6. Modes of Movement and Works or Signs

Mode of Movement	Works or Signs
1. Sending	Work(s) (5:16-36; 9:3-4; 10:25-26, 32, 37-38; 15:21-24; 17:1-4)[160]
2. Coming	Signs (3:2; 7:31; cf. 9:16, 29, 33)[161]

Jesus' signs at times occasion a particular dynamic. On the one hand, people wonder whether these signs point to Jesus' divine origin or not. On the other hand, Jesus uses the interest his signs create to discuss the general nature of his "works" (cf. especially 5:16-36). The terminology of Jesus' coming is generally related to Jesus' working of signs, while the sending of the Son is related to Jesus' works.[162] It can be observed that both Jesus and the fourth evangelist move away from signs (especially their "wonder" aspect and their display of supernatural attributes) to the works of the one sent by God (cf., e.g., the progression from signs to works and sending terminology in 6:28-38).

5. Modes of Movement and the Purposes of Jesus' Mission

The purposes of Jesus' mission are linked with different terms denoting modes of movement as shown in Fig. 7.

While there is some overlap between mission terminology and the purposes linked with it (cf. especially 3:17: "For God did not *send* his Son into the world to condemn the world, but to save the world through him," and 12:47: "For I did not *come* to judge the world but to save it"; cf. also the conflation in John 6:25-59 of the sent obedient Son and the descended Bread of Life giving life), emphases on certain purposes emerge in connection with specific mission terminology.

---

160. Works terminology reflects Jesus' perspective. Jesus himself never calls his works "signs" in the Fourth Gospel. See the discussion of Jesus' works above.

161. Signs terminology reflects the human perspective on Jesus' works in the Fourth Gospel. See the discussion of Jesus' signs above.

162. This is not adequately recognized by Bittner, 105-21, in whose discussion of the σημεῖα and sending none of the passages cited (3:2; 7:31; 9:16; 10:41; 12:18) use a Johannine sending word: 3:2 and 7:31 have ἔρχομαι; 9:16 uses παρὰ θεοῦ; and 10:41 and 12:18 lack any term denoting movement, sending or otherwise.

Fig. 7. Modes of Movement and the Purposes of Jesus' Mission

Mode of Movement	*Purposes of Jesus' Mission*
1. Sending	Salvation/Judgment (3:16-17)
2. a. Coming (into the world) and Returning	Revelation of the Father (1:14, 18) Judgment (9:39); Salvation/Judgment (12:47); Abundant Life/Salvation (10:9-10) Witness to the Truth (18:37)
b. the Coming One	Fulfill Old Testament Expectations (4:25; 6:14; 7:27, 31, 41-42; 11:27; 12:13, 15)
3. a. Descending	Giving Life (6:33, 40, 44, 47, 50-58)
b. Descending and Ascending	Through Suffering to Glory (3:13; 6:62; 20:17)
4. Calling to Follow	Recreating "Israel" (chaps. 1 and 10; cf. 15) Calling People to Believe (1:37-43; 8:12; 10:4, 5, 27; 12:26; 21:19-23)
5. Gathering	Eschatological Uniting of God's People (10:16; 11:51-52)

It seems that sending terminology, usually linked with the Son (of the Father) doing his works, focuses on the way in which Jesus carries out his mission, i.e., on the quality of Jesus' relationship with his sender, namely the Father: as the obedient Son in total dependence on the Father.[163] Rarely is a purpose given in connection with sending terminology. The major exception is 3:16-17 (but there it is God's giving his unique Son; and the statement is probably by the fourth evangelist, and not from Jesus' lips, as are most other references to the sending of the Son in the Fourth Gospel).

While references to the purposes of Jesus' mission are rare in connection with sending terminology, they are more common with terms of "coming." In 1:9 it is the giving of light to every man; in 1:14, 18 it is Jesus' making known his Father and especially his Father's glory that are linked with "coming" terminology (ἔρχομαι/γίνομαι). In 9:39 judgment is the purpose given for Jesus' coming (cf. also 15:22); in 10:9-10 it is the giving of salvation and abundant life. In 12:47 the purpose of Jesus' coming is said to be salvation, not judgment;[164] in 18:37 it is Jesus' witness to the truth.

The purposes linked to other mission terminology in the Fourth Gospel

---

163. This will be important in discussing the mission of the disciples.

164. Regarding the tension between 9:39 and 12:47, note the relationship between divine sovereignty and human responsibility in John.

will be elaborated upon below so that only Jesus' practice of calling people to "follow" needs further comment here. This term involving a mode of movement[165] seems to entail two purposes: first, recreating true "Israel";[166] second, calling people to believe, with the further implications of their being trained and sent into the world to spread the word about salvation through believing in Jesus the Messiah.[167]

6. Modes of Movement in Jesus' Mission and the Fourth Evangelist

The question remains whether John held the conception of mission argued for in the present study. As one analyzes the Fourth Gospel's mission terminology and teaching, one is struck by the interrelatedness of various Johannine themes. As Meeks has well put it, "What we are up against is the self-referring quality of the whole gospel, the closed system of metaphors, which confronts the reader in a fashion somewhat like the way a Semitist once explained to me how to learn Aramaic: 'Once you know *all* the Semitic languages,' he said, 'learning any one of them is easy.' The reader cannot understand any part of the Fourth Gospel until he understands the whole."[168]

Meeks draws attention to "the stylistic structure of the whole document," elaborating, "This is the way its language, composed of an enormous variety of materials, from the standpoint of the history of traditions, has been organized, *partly by design, i.e., by the actual composition by the evangelist,* and partly by pre-redactional collocation of the different ways of talking in the life of the community."[169] These observations indicate that part of the answer to the question raised above depends on one's view of the Fourth Gospel's authorship. If one sees the Fourth Gospel written by "one large mind," be it the apostle John or an unknown fourth evangelist, a larger conception of mission would have enabled the writer or final redactor of the Fourth Gospel to unite in his Gospel the varied strands of mission terminology and teaching found in the Fourth Gospel. If one views the Fourth Gospel as a composite document of various sources, traditions, and stages of

165. Though technically, the actual movement occurs on the part of those who follow Jesus; see therefore Chapter 4 below.

166. Here the specific salvation-historical function of the disciples in the Fourth Gospel is retained. Cf. Jesus' designation of Nathanael in 1:47 (ἀληθῶς 'Ισραηλίτης); and Nathanael's confession of Jesus in 1:49 (σὺ βασιλεὺς τοῦ 'Ισραήλ) in contrast with the term οἱ 'Ιουδαῖοι in the Fourth Gospel. Cf. also the possible symbolism in "the Twelve" (οἱ δώδεκα) in 6:67, 70; and the application of the imagery of "the vine" (in the Old Testament used for Israel) to Jesus in chapter 15, with Jesus' followers as the branches of the vine.

167. Here the disciples of the Fourth Gospel are representative of believers in general. Cf. further Chapter 4 below.

168. Cf. Wayne A. Meeks, "The Man from Heaven in Johannine Sectarianism," *JBL* 91 (1972): 68.

169. Cf. Meeks, "Man from Heaven," 69.

redaction, one will explain the different mission terminologies found in the Fourth Gospel as stemming from different sources, traditions, or stages of redaction.

It is the former that is judged the more likely alternative on the basis of the present study. Even Meeks concedes, in the paragraph following the quote given above, that "the book is undoubtedly the hallmark of some one author's genius" while admitting, "Unfortunately we have no independent information about the organization of the Johannine group, and even the Johannine literature gives little description of the community."[170] Moreover, the Fourth Gospel's teaching on mission displays such a remarkable cohesiveness that it seems improbable that the Fourth Gospel represents merely a collection of disparate sources or traditions. The various modes of movement in Jesus' mission, their linkage to characterizations of Jesus as well as works and signs terminology, and the respective purposes attached to the various modes of movement are telling evidence of the fourth evangelist's deliberate attempt to display the full range of Jesus' mission in different yet complementary terms.[171]

B. The Fourth Gospel's Presentation of Jesus' Mission: Jesus the Messiah

The Fourth Gospel's purpose is explicitly stated in 20:30-31. There it is said that the evangelist selected signs to persuade his readers that the Messiah, the Son of God, is Jesus (or, that Jesus is the Messiah, the Son of God).[172] It appears that John pursues this purpose by providing three portraits of Jesus: Jesus as the Son sent from the Father, Jesus as the one coming into the world and returning to the Father (also described in terms of descent-ascent), and Jesus as the eschatological shepherd-teacher. These three portraits clarify what kind of Messiah Jesus is. The Fourth Gospel's selected signs were already discussed. The exploration of John's presentation of Jesus as Messiah may take as its proper starting point the repeated references to "the Coming One" in the Fourth Gospel.

170. Meeks, "Man from Heaven," 69.

171. The implications of these conclusions will be further discussed in the final chapter.

172. Oscar Cullmann, *The Johannine Circle* (London: SCM, 1976), 15, properly points out that 20:30-31 does not settle the issue of the Fourth Gospel's purpose conclusively. Nevertheless, the passage appears to serve as an integrative device designed to point to the fourth evangelist's overarching Christological perspective and literary strategy.

1. The Coming One: Passages Indicating
Messianic Expectations in the Fourth Gospel

Mission terminology, especially the term ἔρχομαι, is applied to Jesus a number of times in the Fourth Gospel to indicate Messianic expectations.[173] The terms "the Coming One" and "Messiah" or "Christ" are often found jointly and will therefore be treated together (cf. 4:25; 7:27, 31, 41, 42; 11:27).[174] One or both of these expressions are used in the following passages: Ἰησοῦς Χριστός in 1:17 and 17:3; Μεσσίας in 1:41 and 4:25; and Χριστός, besides in these passages, in 4:29; 7:26, 27, 31, 41, 42; 9:22; 10:24; 11:27; 12:34; and 20:31; "the Prophet who is to come into the world" in 6:14; and references to the shepherd-king, quoting the Old Testament, in 12:13 and 15. A study of these relevant passages reveals that the fourth evangelist uses the utterances of representative characters to guide his readers in their own reflection on whether Jesus is in fact the Christ or not.[175] This can be demonstrated by the following survey.

The first person in John's Gospel to refer to Jesus as the Christ is Andrew (1:41). In 4:25 it is the Samaritan woman who asks, "Could this be the Christ?" At the Feast of Tabernacles, some of the people in Jerusalem deliberate, "Have the authorities really concluded that he is the Christ?" Notably, the underlying concerns of the people uttering these statements converge: first, the Christ's origin ("When the Christ comes, no one will know where he is from"; 7:27), and second, Jesus' Messianic signs ("When the Christ comes, will he do more miraculous signs than this man?" 7:31).[176] These concerns, in turn, resemble the issues addressed in the purpose statement of 20:30-31 where the Christ is identified as "the Son of God" and where his signs are given as proof of Jesus' Messiahship. Shortly thereafter in the narrative some maintain, "He [Jesus] is the Christ." With characteristic irony, the evangelist records their concern whether the Messiah could be from Galilee (cf. also 7:52).

---

173. Cf. also Edwin D. Freed, "'Εγώ εἰμι in John 8,24 in the Light of Its Context and Jewish Messianic Belief," *JTS* 33 (1982): 163-67, who argues that the expression ἐγώ εἰμι in 8:24 reflects a Messianic claim on the part of Jesus, referring to the expectation that the Messiah would reprove sinners to PssSol. 17:25; 2 Esdr. 12:32; 13:13-38; and 4QpIsa on Isa. 11:1-5. Commenting on the possible connection between 8:18 and Isa 43:10, Freed contends, "It would be easy for John to make the transition from servant to Messiah, since for him Jesus surely fulfilled both roles. It was a foregone conclusion in all Jewish Messianic belief that the Messiah would be chosen and sent by God to be his special agent" (167).

174. Cf. also Arens, 288-300.

175. Note that the term "representative characters" does not imply a negative evaluation of the historicity of the Fourth Gospel's characters. Contra Marinus de Jonge, "Jewish Expectations about the 'Messiah' according to the Fourth Gospel," *NTS* 19 (1972/73): 246-70; Raymond F. Collins, "Representative Figures," in *These Things Have Been Written* (Grand Rapids: Wm. B. Eerdmans, 1991), 1-45.

176. On the issue of "more signs" in 7:31, cf. Bittner, 114-15.

As the narrative escalates, John notes that those acknowledging Jesus as the Christ were already destined to be put out of the synagogue (cf. 9:22).[177] The antagonism of the Jewish leadership and its obduracy are clearly revealed to the readers of the Gospel by their demand, "If you are the Christ, tell us plainly" (10:24). Throughout the Gospel up to this point, the reader has witnessed the Jewish leadership's refusal to draw the proper conclusion from the Messianic signs and words, i.e., that Jesus is the Messiah from God.[178] Their demand in 10:24 is thus immediately recognized as hypocritical. Martha, on the other hand, representing a believing confession of Jesus as Messiah, becomes a person of identification for those readers who come to the conclusion desired by the evangelist: "I believe that you are the Christ, the Son of God, who was to come into the world" (11:27). Finally, one last, and perhaps the greatest, possible objection to Jesus' Messiahship[179] is dealt with: how could the Messiah be "lifted up," i.e., crucified, when the Scriptures say he is to live forever (cf. 12:34)?[180]

All these utterances take on their full meaning in light of the purpose statement in 20:31: "But these [signs] are written that you may believe that the Christ, the Son of God, is Jesus, and that by believing you may have life in his name." This purpose statement needs to be given full weight in understanding the Fourth Gospel's structure: the record of the Messianic signs,[181] the references to Jesus' divine nature and origin,[182] and one of the major purposes of

177. Whether this is an anachronistic reference reflecting a situation in John's day toward the end of the first century or a historical reminiscence or both is disputed. Cf. Martyn, *History and Theology*, 37-62.

178. Cf. Severino Pancaro, *The Law in the Fourth Gospel: The Torah and the Gospel, Moses and Jesus, Judaism and Christianity According to John*, NovTSup XLII (Leiden: E. J. Brill, 1975), passim.

179. Jesus' origin from Galilee (cf. 7:27, 41, 52) and his signs (cf. 6:14; 7:31; 9:16) are also the subject of much discussion in John.

180. The source of this reference may be Ps 61:6-7: יֵשֵׁב עוֹלָם לִפְנֵי אֱלֹהִי. Cf. Gillian Bampfylde, "More Light on John 12, 34," *JSNT* 17 (1983): 87-89. W. C. van Unnik, "The Quotation from the Old Testament in John 12:34," *NovT* 3 (1959): 174-79 had suggested Ps. 88:37 (LXX); Brian McNeil, "The Quotation at John XII 34," *NovT* 19 (1977): 22-33, proposed Isa. 9:5 (LXX); and Bruce Chilton, "John xii 34 and the Targum Isaiah lii 13," *NovT* 22 (1980): 176-78, argued for a Targum on Isa. 52:13 as the antecedent for 12:34. However, as Bampfylde points out, only Ps. 61:6-7 contains all three elements also found in John 12:34: (1) the Christ (Ps. 61 is a Davidic psalm; reference is made not to the "seed" of the king as in Ps. 88:37 but to the king himself); (2) remains (the LXX renders יֵשֵׁב with διαμενεῖ); and (3) forever (עוֹלָם לִפְנֵי אֱלֹהִי). Cf. also Ricardo Pietrantonio, " 'El Mesías permanece para siempre' (Juan 12:12-36)," *RevistB* 47 (1985): 121-42, who refers to 1 Kgs. 2:45-46 (LXX).

181. On the Messiah and signs, cf. Bittner, 136-50. Cf. Isa. 11:2; 42:1-9; 61:1-2; and Matt. 11:2-6; Luke 7:18-23.

182. The term "Son of God" is probably added to give precision to the term "Christ." Cf. Bittner, "ὁ υἱὸς [sic] τοῦ θεοῦ als Präzisierung von ὁ χριστός," in *Jesu Zeichen*, 213-16; cf. also Brown, *Gospel According to John*, 2:1059-61. Brown notes (1060) that, "throughout the Gospel John demands not only belief that Jesus is the Messiah predicted by the prophets, but also belief that Jesus came forth from the Father as His special representative in the world (xi 42, xvi 27, 30,

his mission, i.e., the giving of life, represent the organizing principles of the Fourth Gospel. The occurrences of Χριστός in the Fourth Gospel are designed to guide the reader gradually but inevitably in his or her own decision about whether the Messiah is indeed Jesus or not (or whether Jesus is the Messiah). The signs invite such judgment. The characters featured in the Gospel themselves as well as the Gospel's readers are judged on the basis of their decision regarding the Messiahship of Jesus.[183]

But what kind of Messiah is Jesus? It appears that it is to this end that the fourth evangelist devotes his threefold presentation of Jesus' mission.

2. Jesus as the Sent Son

a. Introduction

In the study of modes of movement and characterizations of Jesus, a significant correlation of the terms "send" and "the Son" was noted. If one includes passages where "Son" terminology is implied by the use of the term "Father," both terms occur in 3:16-17; 5:23, 30, 36; 10:36; 12:49; 14:24; 17:3, 18, 21, 23, 25; and 20:21 (cf. also 7:28-29; 8:16, 18, 26, 28-29). While it is true that "Son" language is also occasionally found in conjunction with the term "come from" (ἐξέρχομαι; cf. 8:42; 13:3; 16:28; and 17:8)[184] and "return" (πορεύομαι; cf. 14:12, 28; and ἔρχομαι; cf. 17:11, 13),[185] it is certainly significant that the vast majority of instances where a term denoting movement is used with reference to Son language, it is "sending" rather than any other mission term such as "coming" or "going." Therefore "the sending of the Son" should be considered a major concept that occurs consistently throughout the Gospel.

---

xvii 8), that Jesus and the Father share a special presence to one another (xiv 11), and that Jesus bears the divine name 'I AM' (viii 24, xiii 19)," referring also to Thomas's confession of Jesus as "my Lord and my *God*" in 20:28.

183. Cf. de Jonge, "Jewish Expectations about the 'Messiah' According to the Fourth Gospel," 248, who emphasizes the literary character of the Jewish Messianic expectations referred to in the Fourth Gospel: "Representative people . . . express representative beliefs and raise representative objections." De Jonge considers the Fourth Gospel as a source for "Jewish beliefs concerning the Messiah *at the time the Fourth Gospel was written*" (247, emphasis added). However, there seems to be no good reason to doubt that the Fourth Gospel presents actual Jewish Messianic expectations prevalent at the time of Jesus' earthly ministry.

184. Note that in two of the four passages cited, "come" is used parallel to "send" (cf. 8:42 and 17:8); in 16:28, "come from the Father" is differentiated from "come into the world"; and closer scrutiny reveals that in 13:3, it is said that the Father had given all things into Jesus' (i.e., the Son's) hands but that the following phrase links "come from" with "God," not "Father."

185. Even these four passages (14:12, 28; 17:11, 13) seem different than the other occurrences of "coming" terminology in that they focus merely on Jesus' return to the Father as a Son rather than referring to Jesus' "coming into the world" from God to accomplish a particular purpose. In the latter case, Jesus may be said to have come as the Logos, as "light," or as the good shepherd, but not as the "Son."

EXCURSUS #2:
THE TWO JOHANNINE WORDS FOR SENDING

Some have maintained that in Johannine usage there are significant differences between the two Johannine verbs for sending, ἀποστέλλω and πέμπω. If this is true, the discussion of "the sending of the Son" in John should differentiate between passages where ἀποστέλλω is used and occurrences of πέμπω. If not, it will suffice to treat the Johannine sending passages without differentiating between those terms.

Is there a distinction in meaning between the two words used for "sending" in the Fourth Gospel, ἀποστέλλω and πέμπω? In a very influential *TDNT* article, Rengstorf argued for an important semantic difference in John's use of ἀπο-στέλλω and πέμπω.[186] Rengstorf's views, however, have not gone unchallenged. N. Turner has maintained that the terms constitute a "pointless variety in style," "a needless synonym," contending that "[t]here is no apparent point in these synonyms beyond the avoiding of monotony, however hard one looks for a subtle distinction."[187]

On a general linguistic level, Barr's well-known critique of the *TDNT* exposes the common fallacy of projecting one's own theology onto biblical words (a tendency from which Rengstorf may not be exempt).[188] This mindset, criticized by Barr, that frequently fails to distinguish between word meanings and concepts, and that attempts to establish a writer's theology on the basis of word studies, remains remarkably persistent to this day.[189] Indeed, as will be seen, many attempts have been made to modify Rengstorf's theses while leaving his basic approach intact.

---

186. Cf. Karl-Heinz Rengstorf, "ἀποστέλλω, et al.," *TDNT* 1:398-446.

187. Cf. Nigel Turner, *Vol. IV: Style*, in James Hope Moulton, *A Grammar of New Testament Greek* (Edinburgh: T & T Clark, 1976), 76. Some would argue that there is no such thing as a "needless synonym," since, in the words of Levinsohn, "Choice implies meaning . . . when an author has the option of expressing himself or herself in either one of two ways, the two differ in significance; there are reasons for the variations." Cf. Stephen H. Levinsohn, *Discourse Features of New Testament Greek* (Dallas, Tex.: Summer Institute of Linguistics, 1992), 8.

188. Cf. James Barr, *The Semantics of Biblical Language* (Oxford: Oxford University Press, 1961), 206-62.

189. Cf. Moisés Silva, *Biblical Words and Their Meaning: An Introduction to Lexical Semantics* (Grand Rapids: Zondervan, 1983), 18-22; cf. also Moisés Silva, *God, Language, and Scripture: Reading the Bible in the Light of General Linguistics* (Grand Rapids: Zondervan, 1990); Peter Cotterell and Max Turner, *Linguistics and Biblical Interpretation* (Downers Grove, Ill.: InterVarsity, 1989), 106-28.

1. The History of the Debate

The issue of "Johannine synonyms" in general was first addressed by Abbott (1905, 1906) at the beginning of this century.[190] Abbott maintained, "The whole of this Gospel is pervaded with distinctions of thought, represented by subtle distinctions of word or phrase-words and phrases so far alike that at first the reader may take the thought to be the same, though it is always really different."[191] This view was challenged by Tarelli (1946), who concluded that "[t]he Johannine usage . . . is dependent not upon difference of meaning, but upon difference of tense or mood, upon a preference for one verb in certain of its grammatical forms and for the other in other forms. It is probable also that this preference was not personal, but dictated by popular usage."[192] Freed (1964), in an article written half a century after Abbott's assessment, took issue with him, writing, "I fail to see these differences in most cases."[193]

In the more recent history of the debate, the spectrum of opinions has spanned the following range: the first group essentially follows Abbott in his contention that there are significant theological differences behind John's use of ἀποστέλλω and πέμπω (especially Rengstorf and many others following him); a second group, siding with Freed, fails to see any distinction at all (e.g., Turner); a third group embraces a mediating position similar to the one proposed by Tarelli, pointing to grammatical forms as explaining the different usage of the two sending words in John (e.g., Mercer); and a fourth group argues that these terms, though synonyms, play a part in John's stylistic variation in the framework of his construction of entire discourses (Louw).[194] It should be noted that the second, third, and fourth groups, while differing in their detailed explanations, concur that the two Johannine words for "sending" are synonyms.

In interaction with the major studies on the subject, the ensuing discussion will seek to explain John's varied use of ἀποστέλλω and πέμπω by answering the following questions: (1) Do the words ἀποστέλλω and πέμπω *themselves* differ in meaning? (2) If they do not, is John's use of ἀποστέλλω and πέμπω based on grammatical, stylistic, or other considerations, or a combination of these factors?

---

190. Edwin A. Abbott, *Johannine Vocabulary: A Comparison of the Words of the Fourth Gospel with Those of the Three* (London: Adam and Charles Black, 1905) and *Johannine Grammar* (London: Adam and Charles Black, 1906).

191. Cf. Abbott, *Johannine Grammar*, 645.

192. Cf. C. C. Tarelli, "Johannine Synonyms," *JTS* 47 (1946): 175.

193. Cf. Edwin D. Freed, "Variations in the Language and Thought of John," *ZNW* 55 (1964), 167. To the writers referred to here should be added those commenting on John's use of a specific pair of words such as terms for "loving," "knowing," or others. Cf., e.g., D. A. Carson, *Exegetical Fallacies* (Grand Rapids: Baker, 1984), 52-53.

194. Cf. Abbott, *Johannine Vocabulary* and *Johannine Grammar*; Freed, "Variations," 167-97; Turner, *Vol. IV: Style*, 76; Calvin Mercer, "Ἀποστέλλειν and Πέμπειν in John," *NTS* 36 (1990): 619-24; J. P. Louw, "On Johannine Style," *Neot* 20 (1986): 5-12.

2. Theological Distinctions Embedded in
Johannine Sending Terminology: Rengstorf

Rengstorf believes he has found a clear distinction in John's use of ἀποστέλλω and πέμπω. He writes,

> There is also a significant difference from πέμπειν. In the latter the point is the sending as such, i.e., the *fact* of sending, as in the transmission of an object or commission or the sending of a man. ἀποστέλλειν, however, expresses the fact that the sending takes place from a specific and unique standpoint which does not merely link the sender and recipient but also, in virtue of the situation, *unites* with the sender either the person or the object sent. To this extent it is only logical that ἀποστέλλειν should also carry with it the significance that the sending implies a commission bound up with the *person* of the one sent.[195]

Essentially, Rengstorf argues that ἀποστέλλω "is predominantly used where it is a matter of commissioning with a message or task,"[196] while πέμπω focuses on the *fact* of sending. He insists that, for ἀποστέλλω, "[T]he emphasis rests on the fact of sending in conjunction with *the one who sends*, not on the one who is sent."[197] Rengstorf finds ἀποστέλλω used equivalently to the Hebrew שׁלח, regarding which he observes, "שׁלח is less a statement concerning the mission than a statement concerning its initiator and his concern; the one who is sent is of interest only to the degree that in some measure he embodies in his existence as such the one who sends him."[198]

Simply put, Rengstorf argues that in ἀποστέλλω the emphasis is on the sender and his relationship with the one sent (i.e., unity, authority), while in πέμπω the focus is on the fact and the task of sending: "[W]e can say in general that when πέμπειν is used in the NT the emphasis is on the sending as such, whereas when ἀποστέλλειν is used it rests on the commission linked with it."[199] The use of words for "sending" in John, Rengstorf finds "[a]t first sight . . . extremely odd."[200] He concludes, "In John's Gospel ἀποστέλλειν is used by Jesus when his concern is to ground His authority in that of God as the One who is responsible for His words and works and who guarantees their right and truth. On the other hand, He uses the formula ὁ πέμψας με (πατήρ) to affirm the participation of God in His work in the *actio* of His sending."[201]

---

195. Cf. Rengstorf, "ἀποστέλλω," 1:398 (emphasis added).
196. Cf. Rengstorf, 1:400.
197. Rengstorf, 1:400 (emphasis added).
198. Rengstorf, 1:400-401.
199. Rengstorf, 1:404.
200. Rengstorf, 1:405.
201. Rengstorf, 1:405. Cf. also Josef Blank, *Krisis: Untersuchungen zur johanneischen Christologie und Eschatologie* (Freiburg im Breisgau: Lambertus, 1964), 70, n. 61, who essentially follows Rengstorf, albeit with slight modifications; Rudolf Bultmann, *Gospel of John*, 50, n. 2; and Jan Adolph

Generally, Rengstorf believes that the "sending" words were "taken out of their ordinary meaning . . . and filled with religious significance."[202] He deems his observation of a difference in meaning between ἀποστέλλω and πέμπω to be very significant not merely on a linguistic level but also theologically: "We can hardly overestimate the significance of this fact for the linguistic expression of the early Christian awareness of mission."[203] When such a distinction cannot be substantiated in the use of a given writer, such as Luke, Rengstorf concludes that Luke was insufficiently aware of such a distinction, rather than questioning the validity of his own (Rengstorf's) theory: "Lk. . . . also [like Josephus] seems to use the words as synonyms," but this is due to the fact "that neither Lk. nor Josephus has any true feeling for the special nature of ἀποστέλλειν."[204]

However, it seems precarious to charge a writer such as Luke, who displays a significant degree of literary sophistication in his writings, with linguistic incompetence in an effort to maintain the validity of one's general theory. This is all the more true since it can hardly be claimed that Luke was ignorant of the proper use of a word (ἀποστέλλω) he used twenty-six times in his writings, not counting compounds.

3. Evaluation of Rengstorf's Thesis

That the distinction in the use of ἀποστέλλω and πέμπω is at best a reflection of *John's* usage rather than pointing to a general semantic difference, is suggested by the Synoptic parallels to John 13:20. In virtually identical contexts, the Synoptic writers use ἀποστέλλω while John chooses πέμπω: compare

- Mark 9:37: καὶ ὃς ἂν ἐμὲ δέχηται, οὐκ ἐμὲ δέχεται ἀλλὰ τὸν ἀποστεί-λαντά με;
- Luke 9:48: καὶ ὃς ἂν ἐμὲ δέξηται, δέχεται τὸν ἀποστείλαντά με;
- Matthew 10:40: Ὁ δεχόμενος ὑμᾶς ἐμὲ δέχεται, καὶ ὁ ἐμὲ δεχόμενος δέχεται τὸν ἀποστείλαντά με;
- Luke 10:16: ὁ δὲ ἐμὲ ἀθετῶν ἀθετεῖ τὸν ἀποστείλαντά με; with
- John 13:20: ὁ λαμβάνων ἄν τινα πέμψω ἐμὲ λαμβάνει, ὁ δὲ ἐμὲ λαμβάνων λαμβάνει τὸν πεμψαντά με.[205]

Bühner, *Der Gesandte und sein Weg im 4. Evangelium. Die kultur- und religionsgeschichtliche Entwicklung*, WUNT 2/2 (Tübingen: J. C. B. Mohr [Paul Siebeck], 1977), 412-14; also following Rengstorf.

202. Bühner, 412-414.

203. Bühner, 399-400.

204. Bühner, 403-4. Other writers, such as Tarelli, also seem to have difficulty in subsuming Luke's use of ἀποστέλλω and πέμπω under their general theory. Tarelli, while referring to Matthew and Mark, completely ignores the references to "sending" in Luke/Acts.

205. Cf. for these Synoptic parallels to John 13:20 Eduard Schweizer, "Was meinen wir eigentlich, wenn wir sagen, 'Gott sandte seinen Sohn . . .'?" *NTS* 37 (1991): 213. Note also the further example provided by Miranda, *Vater der mich gesandt hat*, 28, who cites Rev. 22:6 where ἀποστέλλειν is used for God's sending of an angel, and Rev. 22:16, where the sender is Jesus and πέμπειν is used.

John's use of the substantival aorist participle of πέμπω in place of the Synoptists' substantival aorist participle of ἀποστέλλω suggests that the two verbs are synonymous and used interchangeably.

Even more damaging to Rengstorf's hypothesis is the frequent synonymous use of ἀποστέλλω and πέμπω in Greek writings preceding and contemporary with the New Testament.[206] This becomes important as it suggests that for Rengstorf's theory to be correct, John would have had to be exceedingly idiosyncratic. A study of Thucydides' *Historiae* (fifth century B.C.), for example, yields a number of instances where ἀποστέλλω and πέμπω are used synonymously (cf. *Hist.* 1.90, 91, 128-29; 3.4-7, 115; 4.16-17, 50, 80-81, 108; 6.93; 7.7, 19; 8.28).[207] Compare, for example,

3.4: καὶ ἀνοκωχὴν ποιησάμενοι πέμπουσιν ἐς τὰς Ἀθήνας οἱ Μυτιληναῖοι. . . . ἐν τούτῳ δὲ ἀποστέλλουσι καὶ ἐς τὴν Λακεδαίμονα πρέσβεις ("So the Mytilenaeans, having concluded an armistice, sent envoys to Athens. . . . Meanwhile they also sent envoys to Lacedaemon");

3.115: τὸν μὲν οὖν ἕνα τῶν στρατεγῶν ἀπέστειλαν Πυθόδωρον ὀλίγαις ναυσί, Σοφοκλέα δέ . . . ἐπὶ τῶν πλειόνων νεῶν ἀποπέμψειν ἔμελλον ("Accordingly they despatched one of their generals, Pythodorus, with a few ships, and were planning later on to send Sophocles . . . with the main body of the fleet"); or

7.19: μετὰ δὲ τούτους Κορίνθιοι . . . πεντακοσίους ὁπλίτας . . . ἀπέπεμψαν. ἀπέστειλαν δὲ καὶ Σικυώνιοι διακοσίους ὁπλίτας ὁμοῦ τοῖς Κορινθίοις ("the Corinthians sent out five hundred hoplites. . . . The Sicyonians also despatched at the same time as the Corinthians two hundred hoplites").

Studies of the usage of ἀποστέλλω and πέμπω in Greek literature dating from the second century B.C. to the first century A.D. yield similar conclusions. Polybius (202-120 B.C.), Diodorus Siculus (first century B.C.), and Josephus (A.D. 37-100) all use the two terms synonymously in close proximity to one another.[208] It may therefore be concluded that the data from New Testament

---

206. It should be acknowledged that, strictly speaking, *absolute synonymy* hardly ever occurs. For the present discussion, it is sufficient to argue for a substantial semantic overlap between the two Johannine words for "sending" that amounts to virtual synonymy. At any rate, these technicalities do not materially affect the argument below. On synonymy, see especially Cotterell and Turner, 159-61; Thiselton, "Semantics and New Testament Interpretation," in *New Testament Interpretation,* ed. I. Howard Marshall (Grand Rapids: Wm. B. Eerdmans, 1977), 90-93; and standard linguistic texts.

207. Cf. Tarelli, 175, who refers to Thucydides, 1.90-91. The various passages in extrabiblical Greek literature cited here and below were located by using the TLG data base of the IBYCUS system.

208. Cf. Polybius, *Historiae* 1.53, 67; 3.69, 75, 97; 4.10, 19, 22, 49, 52, 72; 5:27, 28, 35, 102, 110; 7.2-3; 8.19; 10.42; 14.1; 18.19; 20.3, 9; 21.37; 22.13-14; 25.6; 27.4; 28.15; 29.3, 24; 30.9, 19; 31.32; 32.15; 33.8; Diodorus Siculus, *Bibliotheca historica* 2.22, 26; 4.10; 11.21, 30, 92; 12.30, 41, 46-47, 60, 77; 13.1, 6-7, 9, 36; 14.8, 12, 20, 30, 35, 82, 109; 15.5, 13, 29, 45-46, 67, 73, 77, 82; 16.17-18, 27, 39, 44, 59, 65, 84; 17.12, 55, 73, 86; 18.12, 49-50; 19.61-62, 68, 71, 77, 79, 85, 97; 20.14-15, 19, 49, 79, 82; Josephus, *Antiquities* 1.255; 6.167-68, 222-23; 7.175; 8.50-51, 332-33; 9.24, 289-90; 11.317; 13.23, 45, 278; 14.126; 16.138-40; 18.112; 20.37.

and extrabiblical Greek literature invalidate Rengstorf's thesis that the Johannine words for "sending" display differences in meaning. As has been shown, ἀποστέλλω and πέμπω occur frequently in close proximity to one another with no apparent difference in meaning. These two terms should therefore be viewed as virtual synonyms,[209] despite numerous efforts to modify Rengstorf's thesis.[210]

4. The Search for Alternative Solutions

Since there appears to be no semantic difference between ἀποστέλλω and πέμπω, it is necessary to explore alternative explanations for the Johannine use of "sending" words. Can this usage be explained by a preference for those words in certain grammatical forms? Should one view the usage as serving the purpose of stylistic variation? Is John's use of ἀποστέλλω and πέμπω completely arbitrary? Or is there a combination of these or other factors at work?

a. Preference for Grammatical Forms?

That John uses πέμπω more frequently in certain grammatical forms than ἀποστέλλω and vice versa, is undeniable. Specifically, John uses ἀποστέλλω twenty-one times in the aorist indicative (75%), four times in the aorist participle (adverbial or periphrastic; 15%; three of these four occurrences are the only instances of the aorist *passive* participle for "sending" in the Fourth Gospel), and three times in the perfect indicative (10%). The term πέμπω is used by John twenty-seven times in the aorist participle (substantival; 84%), once in the aorist subjunctive (3%), once in the present indicative (3%), and three times in the future indicative (10%).[211]

---

209. Cf., e.g., Barrett, 569; Carson, *Gospel According to John,* 648, n. 1; Dodd, 254; Ferdinand Hahn, *Mission in the New Testament,* STB 47 (London: SCM, 1965), 158, n. 2; Marinus de Jonge, *Stranger from Heaven and Son of God: Jesus Christ and the Christians in Johannine Perspective,* SBL Sources for Biblical Study 11, edited and translated by John E. Steely (Missoula, Mont.: Scholars Press, 1977), 165, n. 19; Loader, 30; McPolin, 113, n. 4; Juan Miranda, *Vater der mich gesandt hat,* 28-29; Morris, *Studies in the Fourth Gospel,* 293-319; Teresa Okure, *The Johannine Approach to Mission: A Contextual Study of John 4:1-42,* WUNT 2/31 (Tübingen: J. C. B. Mohr [Paul Siebeck], 1988), 2, n. 4.

210. Among those who have attempted to modify Rengstorf's hypothesis are Jean Radermakers, "Mission et apostolat dans l'Évangile Johannique," *SE II/1,* ed. Frank L. Cross, TU 87 (Berlin: Akademie, 1964), followed by Riedl, 55; Robert Prescott-Ezickson, "The Sending Motif in the Gospel of John: Implications for Theology of Mission" (Ph.D. diss., Southern Baptist Theological Seminary, 1986), 208-11; Mercer, "Ἀποστέλλειν and Πέμπειν," 619-24; Kuhl, 54; Seynaeve, 389.

211. Note also that all four instances of πέμπω in Matthew feature the aorist participle πέμψας (Matt. 2:8; 11:2; 14:10: cf. Mark 6:27: ἀποστείλας; and 22:7). Luke exhibits greater variety in his use of πέμπω. One finds, for example, the aorist passive indicative (Luke 4:26) and participle (7:6). Interestingly, in the pericope of the parable of the wicked tenants, Mark uses ἀποστέλλω

These data cause one to ask whether or not John's preference for the two "sending" words in certain grammatical forms was predetermined by the obsolescence of certain forms at the time of writing, as Tarelli contends, or whether other reasons must be found. Going no further than the New Testament, one notes that the other New Testament writers use the alternative grammatical forms not, or virtually never, used by John, i.e., the aorist active indicative of πέμπω as well as the aorist active participle of ἀποστέλλω. John's preference for ἀποστέλλω in the aorist active indicative, while following the general preference of the Synoptic writers (but note the four uses of the aorist active indicative in Luke-Acts), is contrasted by Paul's preference for πέμπω in the same grammatical form, probably due to Paul's epistolary context and literary convention. John's preference for πέμπω in the aorist active participle actually differs from the preference of Mark and Luke-Acts.[212] Thus Tarelli's proposed rationale for John's preference of the two verbs for "sending" in certain grammatical forms, i.e., the obsolescence of the respective alternative grammatical form, must be discarded.

While John's preference for ἀποστέλλω and πέμπω in certain grammatical forms is therefore demonstrable, the question still remains *why* John preferred those forms, especially since his preference differs from that of other New Testament writers. What factor or factors should be seen as responsible for John's preference of the two verbs for "sending" in certain grammatical forms? Most likely, John's use of "sending" verbs is an instance of John's general tendency toward "stereotyping," i.e., his use of words in fixed grammatical forms due to his own personal style and for the sake of reinforcing his theological message.

Especially the substantival aorist participle ὁ πέμψας takes on an almost technical force. Convenience, consistency, clarity of expression, and other factors may have contributed to the development of Johannine sending terminology. The phenomenon of "stereotyping" is characterized well by Kraft:

> A[nother] factor contributing to communicational success and closely related to the habitual nature of our cultural activities is the fact that *what we do and say has a high level of predictability or, more technically, redundancy.* One aspect of this redundancy is the fact that we tend to deal most of the time with

five times (cf. Mark 12:1-6), while Luke uses ἀποστέλλω just once while featuring πέμπω three times (Luke 20:10-13). These observations suggest that certain grammatical forms of one particular "sending word" may generally have been used with greater frequency while there remained room for individual writers to choose either "sending" word based on their personal preference (that may have been merely an expression of an author's own preferred vocabulary, an effort to provide for stylistic variety, or have had other reasons).

212. These findings are corroborated by a representative survey of Greek literature until the first century A.D. that indicates that essentially all the grammatical forms of both verbs were still in use at the time of the writing of the Fourth Gospel. The works surveyed include the *Histories* by Thucydides, Polybius, and Diodorus Siculus, as well as Josephus's *Antiquities*.

familiar subjects and in a way that finds us frequently saying the same or similar things over and over again. The content of many conversations and a large number of books is, in fact, so highly predictable that it is often possible to get almost all of the important content in a conversation by listening no more than half the time. We can also fairly well master the content of certain books by barely skimming them. Indeed, speed reading courses are based on this fact.

Such predictability leads to the energy-saving propensity of human beings that we call *stereotyping*. Though there are many negative things to be said about stereotyping, a positive one is that stereotypes enable us to guess fairly accurately most of the time many of the things we need to know in order to interpret properly. Stereotyping at its best is merely the categorizing of people, places, times, things, and so forth in such a way that the factors held in common by the members of any given category are kept in focus and, in a communicational situation, do not need to be restated. Such predictability and the reflexive way in which we respond to it play an important part in our ability to accurately interpret communicational phenomena.[213]

Thus, for example, by repeatedly calling God "the one who sent me," and by using the term πέμπω in each case, John uses the linguistic phenomenon of "stereotyping" with considerable skill and effect in the way just described (even though the degree to which John was conscious of all these phenomena is another matter). It should be emphasized once again, however, that John's preference for ἀποστέλλω and πέμπω in certain grammatical forms does not by itself indicate that these words differ semantically.[214]

b. Stylistic Variation?

Thus far it has been argued that ἀποστέλλω and πέμπω are virtual synonyms and that John displays a preference for certain grammatical forms of the respective terms, probably owing to his tendency toward "stereotyping," i.e., the repeated use of phrases in set patterns. Nevertheless, it appears that this latter observation fails to account for John's varied use of these two "sending" words

213. Cf. Charles H. Kraft, *Communication Theory for Christian Witness*, rev. ed. (Maryknoll, N.Y.: Orbis, 1991), 104-5. Note that there is another, more narrow, use of the term "stereotype," usually bearing a negative connotation, which is touched upon by Kraft earlier in his book, i.e., with reference to the labeling of a *person* in a way which becomes a barrier to communication. The example Kraft provides is that of a student saying to him, "You don't act like a professor," thus implying that all professors are the same and act alike, plus the connotation that the way professors usually act is in accordance with their formal status and thus impersonal (19). But the way the term "stereotyping" is used in the present essay is to describe a linguistic phenomenon illustrated by the quote in the text above.

214. Note that of sixty total occurrences of ἀποστέλλω and πέμπω in John, fifty-three are in the aorist (ἀποστέλλω: twenty-five out of twenty-eight; πέμπω: twenty-eight of thirty-two instances).

in all instances. If one therefore asks the question whether John's use of stylistic variation may account for at least some of the instances of ἀποστέλλω and πέμπω in the Fourth Gospel, one faces the question of whether the use of these two words is merely arbitrary (Turner) or significant in some way (Louw).

As mentioned, Turner contends that John's use of the two "sending" words constitutes a "pointless variety in style," "a needless synonym." However, while there may not be any demonstrable semantic difference in meaning between the two verbs, it is doubtful whether John's use of ἀποστέλλω and πέμπω is always as "pointless" and "needless" as Turner suggests. As Levinsohn points out, linguistically, choice implies meaning, so that when an author has the option of expressing an idea in more than one way, the various alternatives differ in significance.[215] In other words, there are reasons for a speaker's or writer's choice of one word rather than an alternative term. Whether those reasons are semantic or linguistic is, of course, another matter.

Indeed, as Louw contends, Turner's focus on lexis and morphology causes him to neglect the larger discourse structure of the Fourth Gospel. Louw writes, "Though there seems to be no difference in lexical meaning however hard one looks for a subtle distinction [alluding to Turner], this tendency to variety in the use of similar words should rather be understood as a Johannine device to give flavor to a discussion which is syntactically very simple in structure."[216]

The element that Louw adds to the debate is that stylistic variation is not "pointless" but rather fulfills an important linguistic function, i.e., that of flavoring (Louw's term) of a discourse that otherwise would be repetitive and monotonous. In this regard Louw supplies a helpful linguistic rationale to the conviction of those who argue for stylistic variation. Louw maintains, "Perhaps the most notable [significant stylistic feature] is the tendency in the Gospel of John to employ relatively close synonyms with essentially the same meaning. . . . John seems to be very fond of varying his diction for the sake of aesthetic embellishment."[217]

Louw cites as one example the use of two different words for "to love" in 21:15-17 which, according to Louw, "seems to reflect simply a rhetorical alteration designed to avoid undue repetition."[218] He adds, "Style is not only concerned with individual words and phrases, but should also be considered in terms of a larger stretch of language such as the paragraph, and for this matter, even the total discourse . . . style involves both syntactic and semantic features, that is, the arrangement of words and of thought."[219]

---

215. Cf. Levinsohn, 8.
216. Cf. Louw, "Johannine Style," 7.
217. Louw, "Johannine Style," 6.
218. Louw, "Johannine Style," 6.
219. Louw, "Johannine Style," 10, 12.

Louw gives the following examples in John where an alteration between ἀποστέλλω and πέμπω occurs in the same discourse:

- 1:19-24: ὅτι <u>ἀπέστειλεν</u> . . . (v. 19) τοῖς <u>πέμψασιν</u> . . . (v. 22) καὶ <u>ἀπεσταλμένοι</u> (v. 24);
- 5:36-38: ὅτι ὁ πατήρ με <u>ἀπέσταλκεν</u>. καὶ ὁ <u>πέμψας</u> με πατήρ . . . (vv. 36-37) ὅτι ὃν <u>ἀπέστειλεν</u> ἐκεῖνος (v. 38); and
- 20:21: καθὼς <u>ἀπέσταλκέν</u> με ὁ πατήρ, κἀγὼ <u>πέμπω</u> ὑμᾶς.[220]

To these examples adduced by Louw the following passages may be added:

- 7:28-33: ὁ <u>πέμψας</u> με . . . (v. 28) κἀκεῖνός με <u>ἀπέστειλεν</u> (v. 29) . . . <u>ἀπέστειλαν</u> οἱ ἀρχιερεῖς (v. 32) . . . ὑπάγω πρὸς τὸν <u>πέμψαντά</u> με (v. 33); and perhaps also
- 9:4, 7: τὰ ἔργα τοῦ <u>πέμψαντός</u> με . . . <u>Ἀπεσταλμένος</u>.[221]

However, even though the use of ἀποστέλλω and πέμπω in the discourses cited by Louw can be accounted for by the Johannine practice of stylistic variation, the following cautions should be expressed regarding Louw's view. Louw has not comprehensively studied all the data in John's Gospel or even other New Testament or extrabiblical evidence. Moreover, Louw's theory tends to be monolithic, i.e., it seeks to explain *all* the instances of ἀποστέλλω and πέμπω in the Fourth Gospel on the basis of stylistic variation. Here Louw incorrectly subsumes all the other occurrences of these two terms under his general theory when only the few examples given by him may support his thesis.

5. Conclusion

It may be concluded that John's use of ἀποστέλλω and πέμπω is best explained by his preference for a word in a certain grammatical form or by stylistic variation. Of these possible reasons, the former appears to be more prominent due to John's tendency toward "stereotyping."

---

220. Louw, "Johannine Style," 10, 12. Cf. 17:18, where ἀποστέλλω is used twice in an otherwise very similar passage.
221. For other New Testament examples of the use of ἀποστέλλω and πέμπω in the same discourse, see Matt. 22:3, 4 (ἀ.), 7 (π.); Mark 5:10 (ἀ.), 12 (π.); Luke 7:3 (ἀ.), 6, 10, 19 (π.), 20 (ἀ.); 20:10 (ἀ.), 11, 12, 13 (π.), 20 (ἀ.); Acts 10:32, 33 (π.), 36 (ἀ.); 12:29 (π.), 30 (ἀ.); 15:22, 25 (π.), 27 (ἀ.); Rev. 1:1 (ἀ.), 11 (π.); 22:6 (ἀ.), 16 (π.).

b. The Contribution of John's Sending Christology to the Johannine Concept of Mission: A Survey of Theme Clusters Related to Sending in the Fourth Gospel

Having classified the Johannine usage of sending words, we resume our discussion of the Fourth Gospel's characterization of *Jesus as the Sent Son*. What is the contribution of John's sending Christology to the Johannine concept of mission? How does the Fourth Gospel's presentation of Jesus the Messiah as "the Son sent by the Father" relate to the other roles assigned to Jesus by the fourth evangelist, such as coming into the world and returning, or descending and ascending? It is apparent that John's teaching on mission unfolds in close relation to his Christology. The sending Christology of John's Gospel appears to center around the themes of obedience and dependence. Coupled with the Fourth Gospel's identification of Jesus as the "Son" of the Father (which stresses the uniqueness of Jesus, and thus the unique relationship he enjoys with "the Father"), the sending language underscores the fact that the Son, the Sent One par excellence (cf. 9:7), carried out his mission in obedience and dependence upon his sender, the Father.

John's sending terminology, with its stress on the sent one's dependence on the sender, is varied with the term "coming," at times with the added phrase "into the world," which indicates that the person's mission is undertaken with the full participation of that person's own will. Moreover, since the focus of sending terminology is on the sent one's dependent relationship with his sender, purpose statements are rarely attached to sending terminology (but cf. 3:16-17). Here the purpose statements accompanying the references to "coming" complement the Fourth Gospel's sending terminology.[222]

It will be helpful to survey briefly the relevant theme clusters related to sending in the Fourth Gospel. Sending terminology occurs frequently in the Fourth Gospel in the context of controversy (cf. 5:30, 36-38, 43; 7:16, 18, 28-30; 8:14, 16, 18, 29, 42). There is also an important link between sending and witness terminology (cf. already John the Baptist in 1:6-8; and especially 5:30-39; 8:18). The Fourth Gospel's presentation of the relationship of the Father and the Son, while certainly assuming and at times expressing their ontological unity, focuses frequently on the Father's and the Son's collaboration in the accomplishment of a mission.[223] The Father is the sender, the Son is the one sent.[224]

In the context of the larger themes of Jesus' obedience and dependence, the following emphases of sending terminology in the Fourth Gospel can be

---

222. Note, e.g., the overlap between 3:16-17 [sending] and 12:47 [coming] regarding one of the purposes of Jesus' mission, i.e., salvation rather than judgment.

223. The distinctive phrase ὁ πέμψας με πατήρ occurs in 4:34; 5:23, 24, 30, 37; 6:38, 39, 44; 7:16, 18, 28, 33; 8:16, 18, 26, 29; 9:4; 12:44, 45, 49; 14:24; 15:21; and 16:5.

224. Similarly, the Spirit's role in the Fourth Gospel is primarily presented with a view toward his contribution to the Father's and the Son's mission.

identified. Generally, the sent one is: to bring glory and honor to the sender (5:23; 7:18); to do the sender's will (4:34; 5:30, 38; 6:38-39) and works (5:36; 9:4), to speak the sender's words (3:34; 7:16; 12:49; 14:10b, 24), and to be accountable to the sender (especially chap. 17). He is to bear witness to the sender (5:36; 7:28 = 8:26), to represent the sender accurately (12:44-45; 13:20; 15:18-25), to exercise delegated authority (5:21-22, 27; 13:3; 17:2; 20:23); and finally, the sent one is to know the sender intimately (7:29; cf. 15:21; 17:8, 25), live in a close relationship with the sender (8:16, 18, 29; 16:32), and follow the sender's example (13:16).[225] These principles are laid out in the Fourth Gospel as follows.

The one sent is to bring glory and honor to the one who sent him.[226] Jesus' mission meets this requirement perfectly (cf. especially 7:18; 8:50, 54; 11:4, 40). The theme of glory in the Fourth Gospel is frequently linked with "sending" terminology (cf. 7:18; chap. 17; cf. also 5:23). In the context of controversy, Jesus repeatedly contrasts himself with those who seek their own rather than God's glory (e.g., 5:41-44; 7:18; 8:50, 54; and 12:43). Jesus claims that his sender's glory is the foremost concern of his mission (cf. 11:4, 40; 12:28, 13:31; 14:13; 17:1, 4, 5).[227]

The one sent is not to do his own will but the will of the sender, to do his works and to speak his words, and to be accountable to the sender. Again, Jesus' mission is presented by John as the epitome of these principles. For Jesus, doing the will of his Father and accomplishing his work is his very "food" (cf. 4:34). Jesus appeals to his own work for evidence that the Father has sent him (cf. 5:36). He stresses the importance of doing God's work when he says, "As long as it is day, we must do the work of him who sent me" (cf. 9:4). In the context of the "Sabbath controversy" Jesus asserts, "My Father is always at his work to this very day, and I, too, am working" (5:17). He adds, "The Son can do nothing by himself; he can do only what he sees his Father doing, because whatever the Father does the Son also does. For the Father loves the Son and shows him all he does" (5:19-20a).[228]

Not just Jesus' works but also his *words* are those of the one who sent

---

225. While many of the above statements regarding the sender-sent relationship are worded in general terms, they originally refer to Jesus' mission. Most references are found in John 1–12; all of these passages refer to Jesus. However, these references, though originally applying to Jesus, are arguably recorded with a view toward the sending of the disciples which comes in view later in the Fourth Gospel.

226. Cf. Yu Ibuki, "Die Doxa des Gesandten — Studie zur johanneischen Christologie," in *Annual of the Japanese Biblical Institute*, ed. Masao Sekine and Akira Satake, vol. 14 (Tokyo: Yamamoto Shoten, 1988), 38-81.

227. A few times the glory motif includes the disciples (cf. especially 14:13 and 15:8; cf. also 17:10, 22 and 21:19). See for this the discussion of the mission of the disciples below.

228. This paradigm is later to become the ruling pattern between Jesus and his disciples (cf. 15:5: "apart from me you can do nothing"; 15:15b: "everything that I learned from my Father I have made known to you"; cf. also 17:6-8, 22, 26).

him.[229] The Baptist already notes this: "For the one whom God has sent speaks the words of God" (3:34). Jesus himself asserts, "My teaching is not my own. It comes from him who sent me" (7:16). Recapitulating his ministry, Jesus maintains, "There is a judge for the one who rejects me and does not accept my words; that very word which I spoke will condemn him at the last day. For I did not speak of my own accord, but the Father who sent me commanded me what to say and how to say it. . . . So whatever I say is just what the Father has told me to say" (12:48-50). Later Jesus reiterates to his disciples, "These words you hear are not my own; they belong to the Father who sent me" (14:24). In the accomplishment of his entire mission, Jesus is *accountable to his sender*. Before giving his life for others on the cross, Jesus reports the fulfillment of his mission to the Father in his final prayer where he also anticipates his return to his sender.[230]

The sent one's *responsibility to represent his sender* is given clear expression in 13:20: "I tell you the truth, whoever accepts anyone I send accepts me; and whoever accepts me accepts the one who sent me." The same truth is voiced in 12:44-45: "When anyone believes in me, he does not believe in me only, but in the one who sent me. When he looks at me, he sees the one who sent me." And again, in 14:9b one reads, "Anyone who has seen me has seen the Father." An important passage referring to Jesus' representation of his sender is 5:19-23: "the Son can do nothing by himself; he can do only what he sees his Father doing, because whatever the Father does the Son also does. For the Father loves the Son and shows him all he does. . . ."

The sent one's responsibility to represent his sender is in the Fourth Gospel also referred to in terms of *bearing witness*. Jesus bore witness to the one who sent him and affirmed that he who sent him was true: "I am not here on my own, but he who sent me is true. You do not know him, but I know him because I am from him and he sent me" (7:28b-29); "He who sent me is reliable, and what I have heard from him I tell the world" (8:26). Jesus witnessed to his sender especially through his words and works (cf., e.g., 5:36). Before Pilate he summarized his mission as follows: "In fact, for this reason I was born, and for this I came into the world, to testify to the truth" (18:37).

Part of Jesus' representation of his sender is his *exercise of delegated authority*. The fact that Jesus' authority is delegated and not intrinsic to himself continues to highlight the theme of his dependence on the sender. Jesus has been given "authority over all people" to "give eternal life" to all those the Father

---

229. How closely works and words are interrelated in Jesus' ministry, can be seen in 14:10b: "The words I say to you are not just my own. Rather, it is the Father, living in me, who is doing his works."

230. As early as in 7:33 (= 16:5) and 8:21-22, Jesus had announced that his return to the Father was imminent. Most references to Jesus' return to the Father, "the one who sent" him, are found in the Farewell Discourse where "returning" terminology abounds. See further the discussion of "coming" below.

has given him (17:2; cf. also 13:3: "Jesus knew that the Father had put all things under his power"). Jesus has authority to give life: "For just as the Father raises the dead and gives them life, even so the Son gives life to whom he is pleased to give it. Moreover, the Father judges no one, but has entrusted all judgment to the Son" (5:21-22). Part of Jesus' life-giving authority is his authority to judge: "And he [the Father] has given him [the Son] authority to judge because he is the Son of Man" (5:27). This authority is displayed supremely in the raising of Lazarus (chap. 11). Jesus' authority over his own life is manifested in 10:18 when he asserts that no one takes away his life, but that he has "authority to lay it down and authority to take it up again." Jesus' authority over life is an authority delegated by the Father: "For as the Father has life in himself, so he has granted the Son to have life in himself" (5:26).

Apart from specific references to Jesus' authority in the Fourth Gospel, there are also implicit indications of Jesus' authority. One of these is Jesus' authority to forgive sins. John the Baptist introduces Jesus to some of his disciples by designating him as "the Lamb of God taking away the sin of the world" (1:29). If this expression refers to "the lamb led to the slaughter" of Isaiah 53:7 and 10, there would be a reference to the forgiveness of sins by way of a substitutionary sacrifice. If the apocalyptic warrior lamb featured in Revelation 5:6, 12; 7:17; 13:8; 17:14; 19:7, 9; 21:22-23; 22:1-3 is in view, the reference may be related to judgment and destruction rather than to atonement. Perhaps the evangelist took the Baptist's reference to the latter (the apocalyptic lamb) and interpreted it in the larger context of the former (the "lamb led to the slaughter" of Isaiah) since John draws significantly on Isaianic theology elsewhere and since the term ἀμνός is used both in Isaiah 53:7 (LXX) and in John 1:29.[231]

The corollary of Jesus' authority to forgive sins is his authority to retain them. An allusion to this authority (albeit not the actual judicial act of the retention of sins) is found in 9:41. When some Pharisees approach him after he had opened the eyes of a blind man, asking him if they were blind, too, Jesus responds: "If you were blind, you would not be guilty of sin; but now that you claim you can see, your guilt remains" (9:41; cf. also 15:21b-24). Jesus' authority to forgive or retain sins forms the basis for his commission of his disciples to do the same (cf. 20:23). Finally, Jesus, together with the Father, had the authority to give the Spirit. This is seen by his statement in 7:37-38 and confirmed by the evangelist's comment in 7:39 (cf. also 3:3, 5-8; 4:10, 13-14; and 20:22).

The Fourth Gospel indicates that *the one sent is to sustain an intimate relationship with his sender.* Jesus claimed familiar knowledge of the one who sent him: "I know him because I am from him and he sent me" (7:29).[232] The

---

231. Cf. Carson, *Gospel According to John,* 148-51.

232. Jesus refers to the "Father" more than 120 times in the Fourth Gospel. Cf. Morris, "God the Father," in *Jesus Is the Christ,* 126-44; Mlakuzhyil, 264-67.

prologue notes that Jesus "narrated" the Father on the basis of his firsthand knowledge of God: "No one has ever seen God, but God the One and Only, who is (ὁ ὤν; present participle) at the Father's side, has made him known" (1:18). For Jesus, his experience of intimate fellowship with the Father in no way ceased when "the Word became flesh." The fact that Jesus enjoyed this intimate relationship with the Father who sent him while on earth is also borne out by statements made by Jesus throughout his ministry. In 8:16 he claims, "I am not alone. I stand with the Father, who sent me." And shortly thereafter in the Gospel one reads Jesus' claim, "The one who sent me is with me; he has not left me alone" (8:29a). In the face of his disciples' desertion before his crucifixion, Jesus maintains again, "You will leave me all alone. Yet I am not alone, for my Father is with me" (16:32).

Another expression of Jesus' intimate relationship with his sender are his prayers to the Father. Besides the Final Prayer in chapter 17, prayers of Jesus are found in 11:41-42 and in 12:27-28.[233] The Fourth Gospel presents Jesus as one sent with an experiential knowledge of his sender. Jesus modeled a close, unified relationship with the Father perfectly, demonstrated by his perfect representation of the Father in word (cf. 3:34; 7:16; 12:49; 14:24) and deed (cf. 5:36; 9:4). Jesus' will was perfectly submitted to the one of "the Father who sent" him (cf. 4:34; 5:30, 38; 6:38-39). Not his own honor and glory but the honor and glory of the one who sent him were Jesus' utmost concern (cf. 5:23; 7:18).

EXCURSUS #3:
OTHER MISSION TERMINOLOGY
RELATED TO SENDING IN THE FOURTH GOSPEL

Besides the explicit references to Jesus' being sent which have been discussed above there are also other terms relevant for our study of Jesus' mission according to the Fourth Gospel. While not directly part of the semantic fields of mission identified in Chapter 2, these terms are at places used in conjunction with mission terminology. This connection warrants, even necessitates, an inclusion of such terms in the present discussion. The terms include the following: δεῖ, a term that may refer to the divine will for Jesus' mission; θέλημα, often used in conjunction with "sending" to refer to the will of the sender of Jesus,

---

233. All these prayers were answered prayers. Jesus' prayer in 11:41-42 for the Father to hear him "that they may believe that you sent me" was answered by the Father's enabling Jesus to raise Lazarus from the dead. Jesus' prayer in 12:27-28 for the Father to glorify his name (cf. also 17:1 and 5) was answered through Jesus' willing sacrifice and his own resurrection from the dead of which Lazarus's resurrection was a sign. Finally, Jesus' prayer in chapter 17 is, in some respects, still in the process of being answered by the Father.

i.e., the Father; and τελειόω, a term occasionally used in connection with Jesus' completion of the work assigned him by his sender; finally, one should note ἵνα-clauses following the terms "send" or "come" for insights regarding the specific content of Jesus' mission. Under the next heading we will discuss the use of these terms with reference to Jesus' mission according to the Fourth Gospel.

1. Δεῖ

The term δεῖ occurs ten times in the Fourth Gospel (cf. 3:7, 14, 30; 4:4, 20, 24; 9:4; 10:16; 12:34; 20:9).[234] Of these instances, the following six relate to Jesus' mission: three references are to the "lifting up" of the Son of Man (3:14; 12:34) or Jesus' resurrection (20:9); the other three passages relate to Jesus' work and mission (note the collocation of δεῖ with mission terminology in each case): in 4:4, the necessity for him to go through Samaria (with the ensuing "harvest" among the Samaritans); in 9:4, the need for Jesus to "perform the works of the one who sent" him (with the consequent opening of the eyes of a man born blind); and in 10:16, the need for the (exalted?) Jesus to "bring other sheep" into his fold as well (as has been argued, a reference to Gentile believers).

As Fascher notes, the term δεῖ refers to a necessity compelled by someone's power or will regarding a certain area of life or a task.[235] The term δεῖ may therefore be considered to function as an adumbration for the divine purpose in Jesus' mission. In this context it is significant that none of the occurrences of δεῖ relate to the aspects of Jesus' death and resurrection where the fourth evangelist stresses Jesus' own authority (e.g., in laying down his life, cf. 10:11-18). The term does not occur at all in the Farewell Discourse, a portion of the Fourth Gospel that focuses on Jesus' death as his return to the Father.

The divine will regarding Jesus is his being "lifted up" (note again the ambiguity in this term, which is used by the fourth evangelist to point to the spiritual significance of Jesus' physically being "lifted up," i.e., the honor, privilege, and exaltation bestowed by God).[236] However, even the instances of δεῖ in connection with the "lifting up" of the Son of Man (cf. 3:14; 12:34) are balanced with uses of the term ἀναβαίνειν, a word pointing rather to Jesus' own will and initiative (cf. 3:13; 6:62; cf. also 20:17).

One may contrast the Fourth Gospel's use of δεῖ to indicate the divine

---

234. Cf. Erich Fascher, "Theologische Beobachtungen zu δεῖ," in *Neutestamentliche Studien für Rudolf Bultmann*, 2d ed., ed. Walter Eltester (Berlin: Alfred Töpelmann, 1957), 228-54, and especially 242-45 and 253 on the use of δεῖ in the Fourth Gospel.

235. Cf. Fascher, 228.

236. Fascher, 244, refers to "das δεῖ ὑψωθῆναι, welches nicht zur ἐξουσία des Sohnes gehört."

will in Jesus' mission with the use of μέλλει for Judas' betrayal of Jesus (cf. 6:71; 12:4) and of ὀφείλει regarding the Jews' verdict that it would be "necessary" for Jesus to die. The sending of the Spirit is cast not in terms of divine necessity (δεῖ) but in terms of advantage (συμφέρει; cf. 16:7).[237]

2. Θέλημα

The concept inherent in the term δεῖ, i.e., that of a necessity compelled by a power or will, is closely related to the term θέλημα (cf., e.g., 4:4: δεῖ; and 4:34: θέλημα), another word that is occasionally used in conjunction with mission terminology in the Fourth Gospel.[238] One such passage is 4:34, where Jesus contends that it is his "food" to do the will of the one who sent him and to accomplish his work. This passage, and the following link with the mission of the disciples in 4:35-38, contains a remarkable concatenation of mission terminology: ποιέω, θέλημα, πέμπω, τελειόω, ἔργον (4:34); ἀποστέλλω, κοπιάω, κόπος, and εἰσέρχομαι (4:38) are all used. The pericope thus links the will of Jesus' divine sender with Jesus' obedient accomplishment of his mission ("work") which is in turn related to the disciples' "entering" into Jesus' labor and their being "sent" to "harvest" what they have not labored to produce. The will of Jesus' sender is therefore reaching into the mission of Jesus' disciples as well (cf. 20:21).

Stählin draws attention to the Son/Father metaphor used in relation to the term θέλημα in 4:34:

> Das Sohnesgleichnis, das am vollkommensten von allen menschlichen Bildern die Willensgemeinschaft zwischen Jesus und Gott veranschaulicht, hat auch darin seine Tiefe, da es die lebendige Spannung versinnbildlicht, die doch auch in der Willensgemeinschaft Jesu mit seinem Vater bestehen bleibt. Er ist Sohn, nicht der Vater, und mehr noch, er ist Mensch, für den es als eine ernsthafte Aufgabe bestehen bleibt, daß er sich diesem Willen ganz einzuordnen hat. Aber die Erfüllung dieser Aufgabe ist freilich geradezu sein Lebenselement (Joh 4, 34).[239]

Jesus' total devotion to accomplishing the will of his sender is held up as the perfect example for his disciples in their relation to their sender, Jesus (cf. 4:34; 20:21). As Stählin notes, "Es ist charakteristisch, daß gerade Johannes, der in seinem Evangelium etwas mehr von der δόξα Jesu aufleuchten läßt als die anderen Evangelisten, doch umgekehrt die Bindung Jesu an den göttlichen

---

237. Cf. Fascher, 228.
238. Cf. Gustav Stählin, "Κατὰ τὸ θέλημα τοῦ θεοῦ. Von der Dynamik der urchristlichen Mission," in *Wort und Geist: Studien zur christlichen Erkenntnis von Gott, Welt und Mensch: Festgabe für Karl Heim* (Berlin: Furche, 1934), 99-119.
239. Cf. Stählin, 103.

Willen in allem — in Lehre und Taten — am stärksten betont hat (vgl. 5, 19; 7, 16; 8, 42; 12, 49 u. ö.)."[240]

3. Ἵνα

Another construction that relates closely to the idea expressed by δεῖ or θέλημα is "send" or "come" followed by a purpose clause introduced by ἵνα. Instances of this construction are 3:17 ("God did not send his Son into the world to condemn the world but to save the world through him"); 10:10 ("I have come that they may have life, and that they may have it abundantly"); 12:47 ("I did not come to judge the world but to save it"); and 18:37 ("I came into the world to witness to the truth"). These passages are discussed under the respective modes of movement of Jesus' mission, i.e., "send" or "come."

4. Τελειόω

Finally, the term τελειόω, too, is occasionally found in conjunction with mission terminology, especially the term ἔργον (cf. 4:34; 17:4; cf. also 19:30). The Johannine usage of this word reflects the fourth evangelist's emphasis that Jesus' mission was fulfilled in his "lifting up" on the cross (cf. 19:30). This "lifting up," the fourth evangelist stresses, happened in accordance with the will of God (cf. δεῖ in 3:14; 12:34; θέλημα in 4:34). As Stählin remarks, "Die letzte Station der Mission Jesu ist sein Tod am Kreuz."[241] In the light of this present study, one may add, "Die letzte Station der Mission Jesu *als der gesandte Sohn des Vaters* ist sein Tod am Kreuz."

5. Conclusion

The study of other terms related to mission, and especially sending, terminology has further deepened the understanding of Jesus' mission and his role as the Son sent by the Father. This brief survey of sending terminology and closely related terms will help in the further investigation of the contribution of sending terminology to the Johannine mission concept which is undertaken below. The scholarly works will not be discussed in any particular order but will be used in the context of our effort to trace as accurately as possible the significance of the Johannine theme of "the sending of the Son."

---

240. Cf. Stählin, 102.
241. Cf. Stählin, 105.

c. The Fourth Gospel's Portrayal of Jesus as the "Sent Son" in Interaction with Relevant Literature

It is now possible to resume the discussion of John's sending terminology. In interaction with the insights gleaned from the relevant literature on the subject, an attempt will be made to arrive at an accurate understanding of the Fourth Gospel's portrayal of Jesus as the "sent Son." Okure gives significant attention to sending terminology. She notes that Jesus sees everything in his mission as a gift from the Father: "the 'work' and 'works' to be accomplished (5:36; 14:10; 17:4), the words he speaks (12:49; 14:11; 17:8), and even the disciples themselves (6:37; 17:6)."[242] Okure also notes that "Son" language sets Jesus apart as "the Father's sole executive agent," giving Jesus "a unique and unrivalled role in the mission." However, when Okure writes, "From the standpoint of Jesus, the phrase τοῦ πέμψαντός με [4:34], expresses both his dependence and his uniqueness in the mission," she does not adequately distinguish between sending terminology and Son language in the Fourth Gospel. The former points to Jesus' dependence, while the latter also characterizes Jesus as unique. It is exactly the conflation of the terms "send" and "Son" that is so significant in the Fourth Gospel's sending concept.

Schweizer surveys the following New Testament passages referring to God's sending of his Son: Galatians 4:4-5; Romans 8:3; John 3:16-17; and 1 John 4:9.[243] He concludes,

> Jedenfalls ist die Bezeichnung Gottes als des Jesus Sendenden früh in der Tradition verankert. Sie besagt, dass in Jesu, sekundär dann auch seiner Jünger, Reden und Wirken Gott selbst den Menschen begegnet. Sie besagt nichts darüber, ob Jesus vor seiner Sendung bei Gott gelebt hat und, wenn so, in welcher Weise. Das Wort kann so verstanden werden wie die Sendung eines Propheten, nur dass die Gleichsetzung seines Redens und Wirkens mit dem Gottes ausserordentlich stark und ohne Einschränkung betont wird.[244]

Schweizer adds, "Vorausgesetzt ist nur, dass in ihr [der Sendung des Sohnes] Gott selbst endgültig gehandelt hat. In welcher Weise die einzigartige, 'eschatologisch' abschliessende Bindung Gottes an Jesus besteht, ist nicht festgelegt. . . . Mit dem neutestamentlichen Bild des 'Sohns' wird die Einzigartigkeit des endgültigen Offenbarwerdens dieses Geheimnisses umschrieben."[245]

---

242. Cf. Okure, 143.

243. Cf. Schweizer, "Was meinen wir eigentlich, wenn wir sagen 'Gott sandte seinen Sohn . . .'?" 204-24.

244. Schweizer, 213-14.

245. Cf. Schweizer, "Was meinen wir eigentlich," 218. Schweizer sees as backgrounds for the New Testament phrase of the sending of the Son Exod. 23:20 (God's sending of his angel) as mediated by Philo's language of the sending of the Logos, the firstborn Son of God (*Agric.* 51), and Wis. 9:10, 17, where the sending of wisdom and of the Spirit are parallel (221). He writes,

In another, more recent study Schweizer confirms the finding of the present work regarding the significance of the obedience/dependence theme in John's sending terminology, observing, "The picture of Christ in the Fourth Gospel is entirely determined by the idea of obedience" (cf. 4:34; 5:19; 6:38; 8:28-29, 35; 10:17; 12:49; 15:10; cf. also 13:4-14).[246] Indeed, the climax of this obedience is Jesus' death on the cross (10:17; 13:1; 14:31).[247]

A number of authors deal with the Jewish concept of sending as a possible or probable background of the term in the Fourth Gospel. Friend, in a study of the concept of agency in Halakah and John, points to the collocation of sending and Son terminology in the Fourth Gospel: "If the agent is as the one who sent him, how much more so would the son of the household be as the father who sent him. The son as agent emphasizes both the importance of the agency and replicates in visible form the principal. Instead of the agent having merely a legal or task likeness to the sender, he additionally has an inherited likeness — a likeness of natures or being."[248] Applying these insights to the Fourth Gospel Friend observes, "The verb 'to send' is used forty-one times in the Fourth Gospel. Twenty-four of those times it is in the form of 'he who has sent him (me)' or 'the Father who has sent him (me).' Each time it is associated with Jesus as the Son or in passages in which Jesus refers to his relationship with the Father who sent him."[249] There is a oneness (cf. 10:30, 37-38; 14:10-11) and yet an obedience (cf. 3:34; 6:38; 7:16; 8:26, 29, 42; 12:49; 14:24) and dependence (cf. 5:19, 30; 13:16). Friend notes the component of filial subordination to the sending Father; "but the subordination of the one sent is not one of a servant, rather it is one of a loving son" (cf. 8:35; 15:15).[250] Finally, Friend notes that John's sending terminology is also linked with works terminology: "Jesus

---

"Eine Weisheits- oder Logos-Christologie bildet also die sprachliche Matrix für die neutestamentliche Aussage von der Sendung des 'Sohns' " (221). We cannot pursue this matter here; it must remain doubtful, however, whether Schweizer has proven his case.

246. Cf. Eduard Schweizer, "Jesus as the One Obedient in Suffering and Therefore Exalted to the Father," in *Lordship and Discipleship*, SBT 28 (Naperville, Ill.: Alec R. Allenson, 1960), 68.

247. Schweizer, "Jesus as the One Obedient," 69. Note also that Jesus' obedience is connected with his exaltation and glorification.

248. Helen S. Friend, "Like Father, Like Son: A Discussion of the Concept of the Agency in Halakah and John," *Ashland Theological Journal* 21 (1990): 21.

249. Friend, 21. Also Peder Borgen, "God's Agent in the Fourth Gospel," in *Logos Was the True Light and Other Essays on the Gospel of John* (Trondheim: Tapir, 1983), refers to Théo Preiss, *Life in Christ*, SBT 13 (London: SCM, 1954), 9-31, who discusses the idea of the Son as commissioned by the Father within the wider framework of the juridical aspects of Johannine thought. Cf. also Nils Alstrup Dahl, "The Johannine Church and History," in *Current Issues in New Testament Interpretation: Essays in Honor of Otto A. Piper,* ed. William Klassen and Graydon F. Snyder (New York: Harper & Brothers, 1962), 130-36.

250. Cf. Friend, 22. Cf. also Borgen, "God's Agent in the Fourth Gospel," 124, who maintains that obedience is intrinsic to the Jewish concept of sending. Borgen also observes that thoughts of unity and identity between agent and sender are modified by an emphasis on the superiority of the sender (cf. especially 13:16).

being the agent of the Father — sent by God — points to both his relationship of Son to the Father and to his mission or works. . . . In turn, both the mission and works bear witness to him as the agent of the Father."[251] Friend adds yet another aspect of Jesus' agency according to the Fourth Gospel that will be important in the treatment of the mission of his followers: the fact that one of the components of the Son's agency is the *extending of his agency.*[252]

Borgen, too, draws attention to the same principle, referring to 13:16, 20; 17:16 [sic], 21; and 20:21.[253] At the conclusion of his study, Borgen comments, "Thus there are striking similarities between the halakhic principles of agency and ideas in the Fourth Gospel, as (a) the unity between the agent and his sender — (b) although the agent is subordinate, (c) the obedience of the agent to the will of the sender, (d) the task of the agent in the lawsuit, (e) his return and reporting back to the sender, and (f) his appointing of other agents as an extension of his own mission in time and space."[254]

Ibuki contributes an important study on the glory of the sent one in the Fourth Gospel.[255] He maintains that the δόξα of Jesus is displayed through Jesus' unique relationship as the "Son" with the Father and is linked with sending terminology by way of the obedience/dependence theme.[256] As does Friend, Ibuki sees a combination between sending and Son terminology in the Fourth Gospel.[257] More specifically, Ibuki views sending as a function of the Fourth Gospel's conception of δόξα: the Son does not seek his own glory; he is *sent.*[258] Ibuki also surveys the theme clusters associated with sending, i.e., words/speak (3:34; 5:24; 7:16; 8:26-27; 12:49; 14:24; 17:8; cf. 5:38; 8:26); works/do (4:34; 5:36; 8:29; 9:4; 10:36-37); will (4:34; 5:30; 6:38-39; cf. 8:29); doxa (7:18); and witness (5:37). He notes the formula "not by myself" regarding Jesus' works in 5:19, 30; and regarding his words in 7:16-17; 12:49; 14:10. Ibuki observes that being sent is more than just the accomplishment of individual commissioned

---

251. Cf. Friend, 23.

252. Cf. Friend, 24-25.

253. Cf. Borgen, "God's Agent in the Fourth Gospel," 127-28.

254. Borgen, "God's Agent in the Fourth Gospel," 128-32, speculates that Merkabah mysticism may have influenced the writer of the Fourth Gospel, especially the combination of sending language (halakah) and concepts as the Logos or the Son of Man (the heavenly world). Borgen finds a similar combination in Philo. Yet the parallels Borgen adduces are strenuous indeed. For example, the Fourth Gospel never says that the Logos was *sent.* See further the discussion of coming and going (descent-ascent) below, and the critique of Beasley-Murray, "Mission of the Logos-Son," 1855-68, above.

255. Ibuki, "Doxa des Gesandten," 38-81.

256. Ibuki, "Doxa des Gesandten," 56. Cf. the study by Thüsing, especially 41-296, which studies the Fourth Gospel's references to δόξα or δοξάζω regarding their relationship to ὑψόω, focusing on what Ibuki calls the "glory" aspect of these references. Ibuki, on the other hand, also includes the "honor" aspect of this terminology and links both aspects to Johannine sending terminology.

257. Ibuki, "Doxa des Gesandten," 59.

258. Ibuki, "Doxa des Gesandten," 59.

works — rather, the latter serve to reveal Jesus' *person*, including his unique relationship with the Father.[259]

Bühner provides a helpful discussion of the sending concept and Johannine Christology.[260] In a section on the agent's commission and authority, Bühner contends that the Johannine sent one is a Son in terms of his participation in the possessions of the Father.[261] The author also argues that the transformation of the σημεῖα tradition into the ἔργα of the sent one serves the crystallization of the juridical principle of legitimization, thus distancing the works of Jesus from "wonders."[262] Bühner finds the following aspects of the principle of legitimization relevant for Johannine Christology: the Son's participation in cosmological events, i.e., creation and judgment; the Son's pre-existence as prerequisite for his sharing in his Father's possessions; the issue of the sent one's authority in relation to his legitimacy; the figure of the בן בית ("son of the house") which Bühner sees as providing the background for 3:35 and 13:3; and terms denoting transfer of property used in the Fourth Gospel such as διδόναι, ἑλκύειν, and perhaps ὑψοῦν.

Bühner maintains that it is Jesus' obedience that proves his legitimacy as one commissioned by God (cf. the collocation between sending and θέλημα: 4:34; 5:30; cf. 6:38, 40; between sending and ἐντολή: 10:18; 12:49; and the frequently recurring phrase καθώς . . . οὕτως or equivalents: 5:30; 8:28; 12:50; 14:23; 20:21).[263] Bühner then deals with the sent one as a representative of his sender. As Friend and Borgen above, Bühner notes that the Father-Son language in the Fourth Gospel is closely related to the sending theme. The sent one is not only a representative of the sender but he is Son of the Father. Thus their relationship transcends mere representation. It is a relationship unique to Father and Son (cf. especially 5:22-23). The Son's being "in" the Father also refers to the obedience of the one sent (i.e., staying within the mandate of the sender; cf. 10:38; 14:10, 20; 17:21-23; cf. also 10:30).[264] Bühner concludes that the Fourth Gospel links the sending concept with the apocalyptic-prophetic theme of the revelation of seen glory and with the Son of Man tradition (the Son of

259. Cf. Ibuki, "Doxa des Gesandten," 67.

260. Cf. Bühner, 191-267, who deals with the agent's commission and his delegated authority (191-207), the obedience of the sent one (207-9), the sent one as representative of his sender (209-35), and other principles of sending (235-67).

261. Bühner, 198.

262. Cf. Bühner, 202. While one may disagree with Bühner regarding his tradition-critical views (note the discussion of signs and works above), this author provides further corroboration that in the Fourth Gospel sending and works terminology are interrelated.

263. If Bühner (208) is correct, the phrasing used in 20:21 (i.e., sending terminology in combination with καθώς . . . κἀγώ) would be an allusion to the obedience of the Son to the Father in commissioning his disciples, an important insight which will be taken up in Chapter 4.

264. Cf. Bühner, 208: "Das Ineinander-Sein wird 14,10 also aus dem Sachverhalt des Botengehorsams als Bleiben im Bereich der Rechtsgültigkeit des Mandats und des Auftrags als autoritativem Beteiligtsein des Sendenden am Handeln des Gesandten hergeleitet."

Man commissioned by God as a gatherer of the flock of the righteous).[265] But it is far from established whether Jewish apocalyptic influenced the Fourth Gospel's mission concept or whether John's teaching drew primarily and more directly on Old Testament antecedents themselves. And it is doubtful whether it can be demonstrated from the Fourth Gospel that Son of Man terminology is linked with a commission to gather the flock of the righteous. It seems more appropriate to link the latter aspect to following terminology and to see it as part of the Fourth Gospel's presentation of the Messiah as the eschatological shepherd-teacher calling his followers to help him gather his Messianic harvest.

Meeks and Michel study the concept of agent in the ancient world with reference to the Johannine descending and ascending sent one.[266] Meeks compares the Fourth Gospel and Philo and finds "remarkable differences in their use of similar motifs."[267] He contends that Moses traditions are used in the Fourth Gospel in the context of sectarian controversy.[268] According to Meeks, the Farewell Discourses present the disciples as a group to whom the Messenger has delivered the name of God and his Word, "in the context of the mission of the Johannine Christians within a Jewish community."[269] But the data allow for different reconstructions: why should it be "Johannine Christians" who advance these claims and not the fourth evangelist? Why would this have taken place "within" a Jewish community rather than having been directed *to* Jews?

Michel explores the Fourth Gospel's descent-ascent pattern in terms of "myth."[270] He follows Burney in postulating an Aramaic original of the Fourth Gospel and finds in the Fourth Gospel a targumic development of the Jewish apocalyptic descent-ascent motif (cf. especially *1 Enoch* 14; *Jub.* 1:1-4).[271] The Fourth Gospel's "sending" terminology, according to Michel, should be understood within this Jewish apocalyptic framework.[272] However, Michel does not demonstrate the probability that the Fourth Gospel's descent-ascent motif has Jewish apocalyptic roots rather than being derived directly from the Old Testament.[273]

265. Bühner, 233. See the discussion below.
266. Cf. Wayne A. Meeks, "The Divine Agent in the Fourth Gospel," in *Aspects of Religious Propoganda in Judaism and Early Christianity*, ed. Elisabeth Schüssler-Fiorenza (Notre Dame: University of Notre Dame Press, 1976), 43-67; Otto Michel, "Der aufsteigende und herabsteigende Gesandte," in *The New Testament Age: Essays in Honor of Bo Reicke*, vol. 2, ed. W. C. Weinrich (Mercer: Macon, 1984), 335-61.
267. Meeks, "Divine Agent," 46.
268. Meeks, "Divine Agent," 54.
269. Meeks, "Divine Agent," 58-59.
270. Cf. Michel, "Aufsteigende und herabsteigende Gesante," 335-61. Cf. also Michel's survey, "Die Botenlehre des vierten Evangeliums," *TBei* 7 (1976): 56-60.
271. Cf. Michel, "Aufsteigende und herabsteigende Gesandte," especially 352, n. 32.
272. Michel, "Aufsteigende und herabsteigende Gesandte," 353: "Die himmlische Welt, die den Aufsteigenden aufnimmt, ist die Voraussetzung des Botenrechtes, das der Absteigende nun zur *Legitimierung* aufweisen kann."
273. Cf. especially the discussion of Burkett below.

An excellent contribution to the study of the Fourth Gospel's sending terminology is made by A. E. Harvey.[274] In using the term "agent," Harvey insists on making a distinction between communicating one's intentions through another person (a messenger) and having one's interests promoted by an agent.[275] Harvey summarizes, "the secular concept of 'messenger,' which influenced the concept of prophecy, underwent further development in post-biblical Judaism and became juridically defined in terms of Representation."[276] The author translates ἀπόστολος in 13:16 as "agent" but notes that Jesus is never called "agent" in the Fourth Gospel.

Harvey's work builds on, and yet transcends, the work by Bühner. While Bühner discusses sending in general, Harvey focuses on the sending *of the Son* (cf. Mark 12:6). Harvey contends that only the son, and especially an only son, beloved by his father, could be fully trusted to promote the father's interests.[277] Indeed, the title for the Sent One in the Fourth Gospel is the "Son," not "agent."[278] Harvey thinks the reason for this is that a use of the agency model would imply that God is absent.[279] Jesus' signs in the Fourth Gospel are to be interpreted as signs of authority enabling the audience to assess the genuineness of Jesus' agency from God. Once this genuineness is established, Jesus the sent one becomes like his sender and is to be obeyed (cf. also 2 Cor. 5:19; Col. 1:19-20). God's sending of his Son also carries salvation-historical connotations: the Son is the ultimate messenger (cf. also Mark 12:6). He is doing God's work, speaking God's word, as did the obedient prophet of old.

The implications of Harvey's work are very significant: first, one should understand the Fourth Gospel's sending theme in the (Jewish) context of someone's sending his (only, beloved) son (not just any messenger or agent); second, a study of "sending" in the Fourth Gospel is by itself inadequate — the proper subject of study ought to be the sending of the *Son*.[280] Harvey's insights also put in perspective the above mentioned studies by Ibuki and Thüsing. Ibuki's study had focused more on the sending of the son who could be trusted to

274. Cf. Anthony E. Harvey, "Christ as Agent," in *The Glory of Christ in the New Testament: Studies in Christology in Memory of George Bradford Caird,* ed. L. D. Hurst and N. T. Wright (Oxford: Clarendon, 1987), 239-50.

275. Harvey, "Christ as Agent," 240.

276. Harvey, "Christ as Agent," 240.

277. Cf. already the statement by Friend, 21, quoted above. Cf. also Betz, 412: "Dabei wird deutlich, daß Jesus mehr ist als der Bote, den ein σημεῖον legitimiert. Er ist der Sohn, der im Reden und Handeln und mit der Hingabe des Lebens das Werk des Vaters tut."

278. Cf. Betz, 243.

279. Cf. Betz, 243-44.

280. Cf. in this context also Rudolf Schnackenburg, " 'Der Vater, der mich gesandt hat'. Zur johanneischen Christologie," in *Anfänge der Christologie: Festschrift für Ferdinand Hahn zum 65. Geburtstag,* ed. Cilliers Breytenbach and Henning Paulsen (Göttingen: Vandenhoeck & Ruprecht, 1991), 275-91, who investigates the relationship between the Fourth Gospel's sending Christology and its "Son" Christology, concluding that the latter represents a "Neugestaltung und Veränderung" of the former.

represent his father's interests (δόξα as "honor"); Thüsing developed the son's "being lifted up" and the "glorification of the son" (δόξα as "glory").[281]

Within the framework of Johannine teaching on mission, the sending of the Son seems to represent the element focusing on the "human" side of Jesus' mission, i.e., the aspects of obedience and dependence of the sent one on his sender. The terminology of coming-going and descending-ascending appears to be employed in order to balance the sending terminology by putting it in the context of one who was heaven-sent and who even in his earthly days shone forth his divine glory.

After this assessment of the contribution of "the sending of the Son" to Johannine teaching on mission, the second aspect of the Fourth Gospel's presentation of Jesus the Messiah will now be considered, i.e., "Jesus as the one coming into the world and returning to the Father" (at times also described in terms of descent and ascent). It is argued that while these two aspects of the Fourth Gospel's presentation of Jesus as Messiah are related, they are nevertheless distinct. Only when one understands the complementary nature and the interplay between the portraits of Jesus as the sent Son and Jesus as the Coming and Going one (as well as Jesus as the eschatological shepherd-teacher) will one arrive at a balanced account of the Fourth Gospel's presentation of Jesus and his mission.

3. Jesus as the One Who Comes into the World and Returns to the Father (Descent-Ascent)

The terminology of coming and going is used consistently throughout the Gospel. Occasionally, descent-ascent language is interspersed. The latter terminology should therefore be viewed as supplementary to the broader conceptuality of coming and returning.[282] While sending terminology focuses more on the human side of Jesus' mission, coming and going terminology appears to emphasize Jesus' divine provenance and destination. The references to Jesus' coming (into the world) and his return to the Father will now be discussed, followed by a treatment of the Fourth Gospel's descent-ascent terminology.

a. Coming (into the World) and Returning to the Father

The first reference to Jesus' *coming into the world* is found in the prologue: "the true light . . . was coming into the world" (1:9). The statement is reiterated in 3:19: "Light has come into the world." In both cases, the Evangelist links this assertion with the fact that the light was not received but rejected (cf. 1:5, 9, 11; 3:19). This theme of rejection, with resulting judgment, is also expressed in 9:39

---

281. Cf. Ibuki, "Doxa des Gesandten"; and Thüsing.

282. For this reason Nicholson's terminology — i.e., "descent-ascent schema," which for Nicholson comprises all of the references to Jesus' coming and going as well as descent-ascent language in the Fourth Gospel — appears to be inadequate.

where Jesus indicts those who, due to spiritual pride, fail to receive him: "For judgment I have come into this world, so that the blind will see and those who see will become blind." Jesus' healing of a blind man thus becomes an acted parable of salvation as well as of judgment. Again, 12:46-47, in the concluding section of the "Book of Signs," links Jesus' coming into the world with the concept of light: "I have come into the world as a light, so that no one who believes in me should stay in darkness. . . . For I did not come to judge the world, but to save it." Other references to Jesus' "coming into the world" are found in 16:28, where Jesus summarizes his mission as follows: "I came from the Father into the world; now I am leaving the world and am returning to the Father"; and in 18:37, where Jesus asserts before Pilate: "In fact, for this reason I was born, and for this I came into the world, to testify to the truth."[283]

Apart from these occurrences of "coming into the world" terminology, there are also numerous references to Jesus' *coming and going*. In his introduction to the Farewell Discourse the evangelist writes, "Jesus knew that the time had come for him to leave this world and go to the Father. . . . Jesus knew that the Father had put all things under his power, and that he had come from God and was returning to God" (13:1, 3). The remainder of the Discourse includes a number of references to Jesus' return ("going") to the Father (cf. 14:4, 5, 12, 28; 16:5, 7, 10, 17, 28; 17:11, 13; cf. already 7:35-36; 8:14, 20-21).[284] There are also references to a brief temporary return of Jesus (his resurrection appearances; cf. 14:18, 28; and John 20–21), and to Jesus' "coming again" (14:3; 21:22) after ascending to the Father (cf. 20:17).[285]

The different kinds of references to Jesus' coming and going in John's Gospel may be grouped thematically as follows.[286] First, there are references to

---

283. This passage (18:37) would certainly not fail to provide great reassurance to Jesus' followers at the time the Fourth Gospel was written and began to circulate in their own struggle to testify to the truth in a world just as hostile to them as it was to Jesus (cf. also 15:18-27).

284. Cf. Ulrich Müller's thesis that 7:31-35 and 8:21-24 represent an "Entrückungstheologie" which draws on Old Testament Enoch (cf. Gen. 5:24) as a precedent of one who was pleasing to God and who was therefore taken up to be with God. But there are many obvious differences between Enoch and the Fourth Gospel's presentation of Jesus. Cf. also Roland Mörchen, " 'Weggehen': Beobachtungen zu Joh 12, 36b," *BZ* 28 (1984): 240-42, who argues that ἀπέρχομαι in 12:36b, besides referring to Jesus' literal leaving, also carries connotations of the completion of Jesus' public ministry so that "12, 36b [dürfte] auf zwei verschiedenen Bedeutungsebenen anzusiedeln sein" (241).

285. Contra Moule, "Individualism," 171-90.

286. Cf. for a classification of Jesus' ἦλθον-sayings in John see Arens, 303-7, who notes that there are twelve ἦλθον-sayings in John, six in the aorist (8:14; 9:39; 10:10b; 12:27, 47; 15:22) and six in the perfect (5:43; 7:28; 8:42; 12:46; 16:28; 18:37). The purposes of Jesus' coming are addressed (with ἵνα) in the aorist in 9:39; 10:10b; 12:47 (salvation/judgment); in the perfect in 12:46 (cf. 1:9; 3:19; 8:12; light); and 18:37 (witness to truth). Of these purpose sayings, 9:39; 12:46; and 18:37 include "into the world." The following sayings relate to the origin of Jesus: 5:43; 7:26b-29; 8:14b; 16:27b-28a. References to Jesus' coming which are not in the first person singular include 1:9, 11; 3:2, 19; 7:27, 31, 41, 42. Note also the chart (Arens, 321-22) comparing the meaning of ἔρχεσθαι and ἀποστέλλω/πέμπω.

Jesus' "coming into the world" (1:9; 3:19; 9:39; 12:46; 16:28; and 18:37). Second, sometimes the term "come" occurs absolutely (10:10; 12:47; 15:22). In both kinds of uses one finds occasionally an attached purpose statement (cf. 9:39; 10:10; 12:46, 47; 18:37). The fact that instances of both phrases at times carry a purpose statement as well as the use of "coming into the world" in 12:46 and "come" in 12:47 in parallel fashion suggest that these two groups are equivalent. The emphasis seems to lie in Jesus' coming from another sphere (i.e., heaven; cf., e.g., 3:31) into the world to accomplish a purpose. Third, there are instances where "come" is used parallel to sending (cf. 5:43; 7:28). In those cases, the context indicates that the contrast is between one's coming in one's own authority or on one's own initiative and one's having been sent. Thus these instances of "come" do not allude to an other-worldly provenance as such. Fourth, there are references where coming and going occur together or one term is used while implying the other (cf. 7:35; 8:14, 21-22; 13:33; 14:2, 3, 12, 28; 16:7, 28; 17:11, 13). The emphasis of this kind of usage appears to be on the cyclical dimension of Jesus' mission, i.e., his return to where he came from. What this category has in common with the first two is a reference to Jesus' otherworldly provenance.

Generally, studies of the Fourth Gospel's portrayal of Jesus' coming and going or his descent and ascent frequently appear to suffer from one or more of the following deficiencies. First, some treatments are reductionistic, i.e., they take the Fourth Gospel's portrait of Jesus in terms of coming and going or descent and ascent as a reflection of John's entire teaching on mission when, as is contended in the present study, it is actually only a part. Second, there is insufficient integration between the various elements within this aspect of the Fourth Gospel's teaching on mission. The Logos hymn, the Farewell Discourse(s), the figure of the Son of Man and its descent and ascent, the Bread of Life discourse, or other references to Jesus' coming (into the world) and his return to the Father are studied in isolation from one another rather than with a view toward their relationship with one another in the Fourth Gospel's teaching on mission. Third, sometimes the opposite flaw can be detected: an inappropriate blending or lack of discrimination of elements in the Fourth Gospel's teaching on mission that should be kept distinct (albeit interrelated). Finally, fourth, the putative historical background of a given concept may inappropriately supersede biblical-theological considerations within John's Gospel.

The first deficiency, reductionism, may be found in Bultmann's famous essay "Die Bedeutung der neuerschlossenen mandäischen und manichäischen Quellen für das Verständnis des Johannesevangeliums." After enumerating as many as twenty-eight supposed parallels between the language and theology of the Fourth Gospel and Mandean and Manichean writings, Bultmann concludes, "Die Hauptabsicht der vorausgehenden Ausführungen ist erreicht, wenn deutlich geworden ist, daß das Joh.-Ev. den skizzierten Erlösungsmythos voraus-

setzt *und nur auf seinem Hintergrund verständlich ist.*"287 An undue generalization is also found in Bultmann's description of the Fourth Gospel's portrait of
Jesus: "In all that he is, says, and does, he is not to be understood as a figure of
this world, but his appearing in the world is to be conceived as an embassage
from without, an arrival from elsewhere."288 But as has been shown, the concept
of the sending of the Son is a thoroughly this-worldly motif applied to Jesus.

The second shortcoming, i.e., insufficient integration, is common especially in Christological treatments where a list of Christological titles or designations is provided and each is discussed in turn without an effort to relate the
various elements of the Fourth Gospel's Christology and teaching on mission
to one another.289

The third, opposite imbalance, i.e., the improper blending of distinct
elements, can be seen in Schnackenburg's summary statements of Jesus' mission
according to the Fourth Gospel. Schnackenburg identifies the following pattern:
"der Abstieg und Aufstieg des 'Menschensohnes,' das Kommen des göttlichen
Gesandten in die Welt, die 'Reise' des Sohnes Gottes aus der Welt zum Vater
und seine Verherrlichung beim Vater."290 He also refers to "die 'mythologische'
Vorstellung vom himmlischen Gesandten, der auf die Erde kommt und uns die
'himmlischen' Dinge offenbart."291 However, close scrutiny of the Fourth
Gospel reveals that Schnackenburg's statement regarding the "himmlischen
Gesandten" is not a phrase used by the evangelist. One rather finds one cluster
of references to the Son sent by the Father and another strand of motifs referring
to Jesus' coming into the world and returning to the Father which is also
described metaphorically in terms of descent and ascent.

Finally, the fourth flaw, that of improper weight given to historical background matters, can be illustrated by a perusal of Talbert's work on "Descending-Ascending Redeemer Figures" and its application to the Fourth
Gospel's presentation of Jesus' mission.292 Talbert writes,

> A number of lines of evidence points to the roots of the Fourth Gospel's
> Christology in the Hellenistic Jewish *katabasis-anabasis* mythology. . . .

---

287. Cf. Rudolf Bultmann, "Verständnis des Johannesevangeliums," *ZNW* 24 (1925): 100-
146; the citation is from a reprint of this article in *Johannes und sein Evangelium*, ed. Karl Heinrich
Rengstorf (Darmstadt: Wissenschaftliche Buchgesellschaft, 1973), 455 (emphasis added). Cf. also
the studies of Kuhl and Miranda on the sending motif in John and Nicholson's treatment of the
Johannine descent-ascent schema.

288. Cf. Bultmann, *Theology of New Testament*, 2:33.

289. Cf., e.g., David L. Mealand, "The Christology of the Fourth Gospel," *SJT* 31 (1978):
449-67; or James Parker, "The Incarnational Christology of John," *CrisTR* 3 (1988): 31-48.

290. Cf. Schnackenburg, "Gedanke des Sühnetodes Jesu," 220.

291. Cf. Schnackenburg, "Gedanke des Sühnetodes Jesu," 224.

292. Cf. most recently Charles H. Talbert, "Appendix: Descending-Ascending Redeemer
Figures in Mediterranean Antiquity," in *Reading John: A Literary and Theological Commentary on
the Fourth Gospel and the Johannine Epistles* (New York: Crossroad, 1992), 265-84.

(a) The background for the logos/word in 1:1-18 is almost certainly the Wisdom myth assimilated with logos thought such as one finds in Hellenistic Judaism. (b) The clue to the Son of God language in the Gospel seems to be two formulae . . . which have their background in Wisdom-Logos speculation. (c) The background for the Johannine Son of Man sayings . . . may very well be that the apocalyptic tradition has been assimilated to the "Man" of Hellenistic Judaism.[293]

Talbert appears to believe that, by identifying a possible or probable historical background for an element of Johannine Christology, he has also explained it. However, the task still remains to explore the connections between different aspects of John's presentation of Jesus to one another.

The present study seeks to avoid these kinds of shortcomings by making an effort to appreciate the complexity of the Fourth Gospel's presentation of Jesus and his mission. It will be necessary to show the interrelationships between various components of the Fourth Gospel's teaching on mission without improperly blending elements that the Fourth Gospel distinguishes, and to combine matters of historical background with biblical-theological considerations. Reference has already been made to the study by Nicholson, who demonstrates the integrative nature of the Fourth Gospel's "descent-ascent schema."[294] As one traces the occurrences of mission terminology denoting coming and going (metaphorically expressed in terms of descent-ascent), one finds a string of references that pervades the entire Gospel. The Gospel opens with a reference to the Logos-become-flesh who came from the Father (1:14). After some precursors of descent-ascent language (cf. 1:32-33, 51), this terminology is first applied to Jesus in 3:13. References to Jesus' ascent are also found in 6:62 and 20:17 (cf. also the connected "lifted up sayings": besides 3:13 and 8:28 also 12:32-34). The descent of the Bread of Life is the subject of an extended discourse in chapter 6. Intermittently one finds statements regarding Jesus' coming into the world; relatively early in the narrative there are also scattered references to Jesus' going back to from where he came. These references abound in the Farewell Discourse.

It seems best to understand the varied terminology as composing one conglomerate picture of a coming and returning, descending and ascending Messiah whose purpose on earth is the accomplishment of a task. While the emphasis of John's sending terminology appears to be on Jesus' relationship with his sender as well as on the fulfillment of Old Testament expectations,[295] "coming and going" language may be viewed as accentuating Jesus' heavenly

---

293. Cf. Talbert, "Appendix: Descending-Ascending," 283.

294. One may still differ with Nicholson regarding the relative weight of this motif within Johannine mission teaching as a whole.

295. The exception to this is the technical term "the Coming One." Fulfillment of Old Testament prophecy is in view with the third role of Jesus the Messiah discussed below.

origin. The divine purpose embodied in Jesus' coming, Jesus' accomplishment of his divine mission, and his return to heavenly glory with the Father are primarily in view.

b. Descent and Ascent

Jesus' coming and going as well as his descent and ascent may be viewed as part of an overarching "journey theme" in the Fourth Gospel.[296] After three trips "up" to Jerusalem, Jesus' fourth trip to Jerusalem is presented by the fourth evangelist as indeed a journey back to the Father via the cross.[297] The cross is thus in the Fourth Gospel viewed as part of a journey, a "way" (cf. 14:6).[298] This way, first traveled by Jesus, is also to be followed by his disciples (cf. 12:26). According to John, the cross is a station along the way to Jesus' return to the Father's glory rather than a place of shame and humiliation. By presenting the cross as a station along the way to the Father's glory and as the culmination of the Son's obedience to the Father, John maintains a thoroughly theocentric focus. Not man's need is the ultimate reference point of Jesus' mission, but rather the Father's will.

Besides "coming and going" terminology, the Fourth Gospel also uses the word pair "descend" and "ascend" to characterize Jesus' mission.[299] However, unlike "coming and going," the terms "descend" and "ascend" are used infrequently in John's Gospel and should therefore be seen as subordinate to the Fourth Gospel's portrait of Jesus the Messiah as coming into the world and returning to the Father. The use of descent-ascent language clusters around two characterizations of Jesus: the Son of Man (3:13; 6:62; cf. 20:17?); and the Bread of Life (6:33, 38, 41, 42, 50, 51, 58).[300]

---

296. Nicholson.

297. Cf. Nicholson, 145.

298. Cf. also the discussion of the contributions by Pamment and Rissi below.

299. These terms are also used for the Spirit in 1:33 and 34, and for angels in 1:51. On descent-ascent, cf. Willem Grossouw, "La glorification du Christ dans le quatrième évangile," in L'Évangile de Jean, études et problèmes, ed. Marie-Émile Boismard et al., RBib III (Bruges: Desclée de Brouwer, 1958), 131-45; Martin McNamara, "The Ascension and Exaltation of Christ in the Fourth Gospel," Scripture 19 (1967): 65-73; Nicholson; Sidebottom, "The Ascent and Descent of the Son of Man," 115-22; Charles H. Talbert, "The Myth of a Descending-Ascending Redeemer in Mediterranean Antiquity," NTS 22 (1976): 418-40; and "Appendix: Descending-Ascending," 265-84; Thüsing.

300. In the light of this very limited use of descent/ascent terminology and the distinct Jewish flavor of both contexts in which this terminology is used, the suggestion that Gnostic conceptualities constitute the background for this terminology appears rather improbable. Rudolf Schnackenburg, "Das Brot des Lebens," in Das Johannesevangelium, vol. 4, Ergänzende Auslegungen und Exkurse, HTKNT (Freiburg im Breisgau: Herder, 1984), 119-31, in the search for a possible background of the term "Bread of Life" investigates Jewish mysticism, Qumran-Essenism, Pharisaic rabbinism, and Jewish diaspora Hellenism. Noting that there appears no instance of the term "Bread of Life" in rabbinic writings, Schnackenburg finds the sole parallel

The term "Son of Man," with its intriguing conflation of the concepts of humanity and divinity, including its possible Danielic apocalyptic overtones, holds in tension the divine and human aspects in Jesus' person and mission. It is not necessary to agree with Bultmann and Talbert, who point to the gnostic descending-ascending revealer myth as the background for the Johannine descent-ascent motif. The Son of Man in the Fourth Gospel fulfills the following roles: he is the gate of heaven of Jacob's vision (1:51), he alone descended and ascended (3:13; cf. 6:62), he is to be lifted up and glorified (3:14; 8:28; 12:34), he is judge (5:27), and he provides the Bread of Life, i.e., his flesh (6:27, 53).[301] This considerable range in the Fourth Gospel's description of the Son of Man appears too broad to be easily accommodated by the kind of generalization postulated by Bultmann and Talbert.

Writers disagree in their general assessment of the emphasis in the Fourth Gospel's "Son of Man" concept. Moloney finds the humanity of Jesus accentuated: "The Johannine Son of Man is the human Jesus, the incarnate Logos, he has come to reveal God with a unique and ultimate authority and in the acceptance or refusal of this revelation the world judges itself."[302] Mlakuzhyil regards the Johannine "Son of Man" as fulfilling a bridge function between the titles "Messiah" and "Son (of God)": "[B]ecause 'the Son of Man' has a mysterious heavenly origin (3, 13; 6, 62), this Christological title may be considered a theological bridge between the Messianic title 'the Christ' and the divine title 'the Son' (of God)."[303] Most helpful for the purposes of the present work is the discussion by Burkett, since this writer provides a separate treatment for those passages in John's Gospel where "Son of Man" terminology is linked with descent-ascent language. According to Burkett, there is not just one single source for the idea of the descending and ascending Son of Man in the Fourth Gospel but rather three different Old Testament passages: for 1:51, Genesis 28:12; for 3:13, Proverbs 30:4; and for 6:26-65, Numbers 11:9 and Isaiah 55:10-11.[304] Burkett also notes that part of the Old Testament passages underlying 3:13 and 6:26-65 are associations with the word of יהוה and with God himself.[305] If Burkett is correct, at least in principle, one should avoid the tendency of forcing the various Johannine references to a descending and ascending Son of Man

---

in terminology in the Jewish-Hellenistic work *Joseph and Aseneth*. He conjectures that the writer of this work and John may both have drawn on the Jewish concept that the manna gives a part in the heavenly life and that it promises the life to come (cf. 3:16, 36; 5:24, 26; 6:63, 68; 8:12; 10:10; 11:25; 14:6; cf. also *2 Bar.* 29:8). Cf. also Peder Borgen, *Bread from Heaven: An Exegetical Study of the Concept of Manna in the Gospel of John and the Writings of Philo*, NovTSup 10 (Leiden: E. J. Brill, 1965), who sets forth the thesis that the passage represents a midrash on Ps. 78:24 as quoted in 6:31.

301. Cf. Sidebottom, "Ascent and Descent."
302. Cf. Moloney, *Johannine Son of Man*, 220.
303. Cf. Mlakuzhyil, 270-71.
304. Cf. Burkett, 38; but cf. the review by Douglas R. A. Hare in *JBL* 112 (1993): 158-60.
305. Burkett, 48.

into one explanatory grid. In fact, it may be best to treat these instances separately from designations of Jesus as "Son" or "Son of God."

As Meeks observes, the *pattern* of descent and ascent is already introduced in the Fourth Gospel in 1:51, albeit of angels, as is the term Son of Man. Both of these concepts recur in 3:13 with reference to Jesus.[306] The Son of Man who descends (ὁ καταβάς) is in turn presupposed in chapter 6.[307] It appears therefore that the fourth evangelist wants the readers of his Gospel to understand the pericope regarding the descending Bread of Life in the context of the descending and ascending Son of Man. Indeed, the purposes of both figures are identical: the giving of life (cf., e.g., 3:15; 6:33). Notably, the Bread of Life pericope is framed by references to the Son of Man in 6:27 and 62. These two passages, 3:13 and 6:30-59, also develop the concept of the Son of Man's "exaltation": he will be "lifted up" (3:13), giving his "flesh" "for the life of the world" (6:51; cf. 6:52-58). In 6:53, reference is even made to "the flesh of *the Son of Man*" and to "his blood." In connection with the recurrence of the term "lifted up" (ὑψοῦν) in 8:28 and 12:32, 34 (in both contexts also with "Son of Man" language), one is further able to trace the fourth evangelist's gradual development of the theme of the Son of Man being lifted up for the purpose of giving life.[308] The "lifting up" of the Son of Man on the cross combines two elements of Jesus' mission. As Lindars observes, John "adopts an unusual word for 'lifted up,' which normally refers to exaltation in an honorific sense, and thereby contrives to combine the two notions of crucifixion and exaltation in a single ambiguous word."[309] Thus the "lifting up" of Jesus is not to be understood merely in terms of Jesus' exaltation but

306. Cf. Meeks, "Man from Heaven," 51; cf. Meeks's treatment of John 3:13 (52-57).

307. Cf. Meeks, 57.

308. Cf. especially Thüsing, 3-40, who sees Jesus' mission in the Fourth Gospel proceed along two stages: his being "lifted up" and his being "glorified" (cf. especially 311-15). For a generally very competent treatment of the Johannine "lifted up sayings," cf. Nicholson, 75-144, and especially the summary on 141-44, who argues, "since all allusions to the crucifixion contained in the LUS [i.e., "lifted up sayings"] are embedded in sections which deal with the return of Jesus to the Father, they emphasize that the crucifixion of Jesus is to be understood in terms of exaltation/ascent/return. . . . Thus, what might appear to have been an ignominious death, was in reality a return to glory" (142 and 144). Nicholson's final point is doubtless true; however, regarding his contention that the crucifixion of Jesus is to be understood in terms of exaltation, one may ask if John in fact drains Jesus' death *completely* of notions of atonement and suffering. The exaltation of the Son of Man in the Fourth Gospel is also discussed by Antoine Vergote, "L'exaltation du Christ en croix selon le quatrième évangile," *ETL* 28 (1952): 5-23. He concludes, "[L]a croix constitue l'apogée de toute l'activité du Christ telle que la dépeint le IVe évangile" (22). According to Vergote, Jesus' crucifixion and resurrection are merged in the Fourth Gospel, "absorbé dans la théologie de l'exaltation" (23). Cf. also Burkett, 120-28; Bampfylde, 87-89; George R. Beasley-Murray, "John 12, 31-34: The Eschatological Significance of the Lifting Up of the Son of Man," in *Studien zum Text und zur Ethik des Neuen Testaments: Festschrift zum 80. Geburtstag von Heinrich Greeven,* ed. Wolfgang Schrage (Berlin/New York: de Gruyter, 1986), 70-81.

309. Cf. Barnabas Lindars, *Jesus Son of Man,* 146.

also as the completion of the obedient, dependent mission of the Son sent by the Father.[310]

Meeks finds in the descent-ascent pattern a "cipher for Jesus' unique self-knowledge as well as for his foreignness to the men of this world" (cf. 3:8; 7:23-29, 37-52; 8:14; 9:29; 19:9).[311] He states categorically, "in every instance the motif points to contrast, foreignness, division, judgment," maintaining, "The descent and ascent of the Son of Man thus becomes not only the key to his identity and identification, but the primary content of his esoteric knowledge which *distinguishes* him from the men who belong to 'this world.'"[312] Indeed, "[i]n this manner the descent, as a 'coming into the world,' is clearly identified as the judgment of the world (9:39, but adumbrated already in 3:14-21)."[313] As Ruckstuhl contends, however, chapters 3 and 6 should be viewed in the light of assurances in the Fourth Gospel that everyone can come to Jesus and is welcome (cf. 3:16; 6:37; 12:32; et al.).[314]

Since sending terminology is a feature pervading the entire Fourth Gospel while the theme of the descent of the Bread of Life is only found in chapter 6, one should seek to understand the descent motif in the larger context of the Fourth Gospel's sending terminology. The Son of Man's descent and ascent as well as the Bread of Life's descent are to be seen in the context of the obedient, dependent Sent One who came into the world for the purposes outlined above. Yet the opposite is true as well. As Meeks observes, "Ch. 17 as a whole is only intelligible within the descent/ascent framework, for it is the summary 'de-briefing' of the messenger who . . . has accomplished his work in the lower regions and is returning."[315] The descent-ascent motif should therefore be allowed to make its own contribution to the Fourth Gospel's teaching on mission and not be totally subsumed under sending terminology.

Finally, the question arises whether the crucifixion and resurrection are

---

310. This is insufficiently recognized by some who talk about "lifting up" in John exclusively in terms of exaltation. Cf., e.g., Nicholson. Forestell, 81, whose general thesis has been critiqued already, is balanced here: "The cross is . . . the way by which Jesus returns to the Father. . . . On the cross Jesus fulfils the mission for which he was sent into the world. . . ." It should also be noted that the Bread of Life discourse is precipitated in the Fourth Gospel by people's failure to understand the sign Jesus had done in feeding the multitude. Indeed, the "food that endures to eternal life, which the Son of Man will give you" (6:27), is the Bread of Life (cf. 6:35, 48), i.e., Jesus, who is also the Son of Man. One also notes the interweaving of sending terminology with references to the Bread of Life's descent (cf. 6:29, 38-39, 57).

311. Forestell, 60. In general, Meeks's analysis of the Johannine descent-ascent pattern provides many helpful insights ("Man from Heaven," 46-66). But when Meeks launches into his own sociological application of the Fourth Gospel's textual data, his treatment becomes increasingly speculative (67-72).

312. Meeks, 67 and 60-61.

313. Meeks, 61.

314. Cf. Ruckstuhl, "Abstieg und Erhöhung des johanneischen Menschensohnes," 339, in response to Meeks.

315. Cf. Meeks, "Man from Heaven," 66.

linked in the Fourth Gospel with sending language or with coming and going/descending and ascending terminology. While these events may be included in the "work" of the obedient Sent One (cf. 4:34; 17:4), it appears that the connections of the crucifixion and resurrection with descent-ascent language by way of ὑψοῦν are more pronounced. In light of these observations, it is possible to conclude that the perhaps most central feature of the Johannine mission concept, i.e., the sending of the Son, is put into perspective by other mission terminology such as "coming into the world" or descent/ascent language.[316] Moreover, it is apparent that these terms emphasize the eschatological character of Jesus' coming. The fourth evangelist blends sending language with "coming and going" terminology, also developing the latter metaphorically by way of descent and ascent language. Only a treatment that considers both sets of terminologies is an adequate treatment of the Fourth Gospel's teaching on mission.

4. Jesus the Eschatological Shepherd-Teacher Calling Followers to Gather "Fruit"

One may at first sight conclude that one of the ways in which Jesus is presented in the Fourth Gospel is that of a Jewish rabbi who gathers around himself a group of followers.[317] It seems, however, that John has interwoven this aspect of Jesus' mission with the role of the Messianic shepherd. This is clearest in chapter 10, where "following" and "gathering" terminologies intersect (cf. 10:4, 5, 27; and 10:16; cf. also 11:51-52). A very important connection between following and shepherding (which in turn is linked with gathering; cf. 10:16) is also found in 21:15-19 where Jesus calls one of his *followers* to be a *shepherd*.[318] Integrated into the strand of passages which deal with Jesus' calling of others to follow him are also references to these followers' "bearing fruit," i.e., participating in the Messianic "harvest" (cf. especially 4:34-38; cf. also chap. 15). Thus the emphasis is laid not so much on Jesus' teaching as such, but on his launching of the reaping of the eschatological Messianic harvest.

---

316. On the relationship between coming and returning terminology and descent-ascent language, cf. Meeks, "Man from Heaven," 63: "the identity of Jesus . . . in . . . the ascent/descent motif . . . is bound up with the pattern of his coming from heaven and going back there."

317. On Jesus as a rabbi in the Fourth Gospel, see my forthcoming article with this title in *BBR* 8 (1998).

318. These crucial kinds of connections are frequently missed by those who focus exclusively on the Fourth Gospel's sending or coming references. These interpreters' failure to account for the presence of 1:37-43 or especially chapter 21 becomes a major liability of the explanatory power and extent of their studies. Many works only account for chapters 2 through 20 (or chapters 2 to 12 with the addition of 20:30-31) or for 1:1-18 and the Farewell Discourse (13–17) respectively. What is needed, however, is not a treatment of just *one* aspect of Jesus' mission in the Fourth Gospel as if it were what the Fourth Gospel has to say about Jesus' mission in its *entirety* but investigation of Jesus' entire mission according to John.

Many of these passages involve the disciples very prominently. For this reason it seems reasonable to delay dealing with them in detail until Chapter 4. The primary concern in the present context, i.e., the mission of Jesus, is to show with reasonable plausibility that the role of the eschatological shepherd-teacher is indeed a distinct way in which the fourth evangelist shows what kind of Messiah Jesus is. First a brief survey of the two terms denoting movement that are relevant for the portrait of Jesus as the eschatological shepherd-teacher will be given: "following" and "gathering."[319] An effort will then be made to show in greater detail how the fourth evangelist weaves references including these terms denoting movement into a coherent picture of Jesus as the eschatological shepherd-teacher who calls his followers to participate in bringing in the eschatological Messianic harvest.

a. Following

The accomplishment of Jesus' mission involves his calling of others to follow him (cf. 1:37-43; 8:12; 10:4, 5, 27; 12:26; 21:19-23).[320] This "following" terminology is never applied to Jesus (i.e., Jesus is never said to "follow" anyone, including the Father), just as the "descending and ascending" terminology, as well as "coming into the world" terminology are never applied to the disciples. Jesus begins his public ministry by calling others to follow him (1:37-43). The fourth evangelist's record of Jesus' first "sign" concludes with the statement that Jesus "thus revealed his glory, and his disciples put their faith in him" (2:11). By implication, the disciples also are to follow Jesus in his evangelistic mission (cf. especially John 3 and 4, but also chapters 6, 9, and 11). In 8:12, Jesus promises that anyone who follows him will not "walk in darkness," but have "the light of life." In the Good Shepherd Discourse, Jesus repeatedly refers to "his sheep" who know his voice and follow him (10:4, 5, 27). Jesus' public ministry ends with his call to a radical commitment on the part of his followers that does not even hold one's own life dearer than loyalty to Jesus (12:26). Finally, Jesus' disciples are to follow him until his return (cf. 21:22).

---

319. It should be noted that in the case of "following," Jesus is the one who calls *others* to follow and not the one who himself follows others. Therefore the term "following" will primarily be discussed when dealing with the disciples in Chapter 4. However, the fact that it is in the Fourth Gospel without exception *Jesus* who calls disciples to follow him seems to warrant the inclusion of "following" under the present heading, especially since the term occurs in the Fourth Gospel in conjunction with Jesus' gathering activity (a term denoting a mode of movement), as will be seen below. Moreover, it would be difficult to separate Jesus' gathering from his calling others to follow him, since those whom Jesus calls to follow will be the very ones through whom the exalted Jesus will bring in his eschatological Messianic harvest.

320. Cf. Anselm Schulz, *Nachfolgen und Nachahmen: Studien über das Verhältnis der neutestamentlichen Jüngerschaft zur urchristlichen Vorbildethik*, SANT VI (München: Kösel, 1962), 172-75.

It has been argued that there is a broader conceptuality in the Fourth Gospel involving movement or direction which includes but transcends the term "follow" alone. This has most recently been set forth by Pamment, who explores "path and residence metaphors" in the Fourth Gospel.[321] Focusing on Jesus' statement, "I am the way" (14:6), she notes, "the way can be completed in the same manner as a task is accomplished."[322] She relates the Fourth Gospel's way metaphor to following terminology in the Fourth Gospel (cf. especially John 10) and observes that statements such as 8:42 or 13:1, 3 are indicative of a pattern "which integrates the path metaphor into those of mission and descent-ascent."[323] Pamment also seeks to relate the Fourth Gospel's residence and path metaphors to one another. She finds that "following and dwelling are mutually exclusive activities."[324] Pamment's exploration of two metaphors in the Fourth Gospel, though suggestive, appears not fully successful in showing from the Fourth Gospel that a "path metaphor" is deliberately and consistently sustained by the fourth evangelist.[325] Nevertheless, Pamment illumines the fact that Jesus' statement in 14:6 should be integrated into the references to following in the Fourth Gospel since "movement after Jesus" is in view in both terminologies.

Also worthy of note is Rissi's contention that the travels of Jesus in the Fourth Gospel are designed according to a certain plan and that this plan determines the structure of the entire Gospel.[326] Rissi argues that the Fourth Gospel presents four trips of Jesus that all lead him to the same place, i.e., Judea and Jerusalem. While a number of details in Rissi's analysis appear contrived in order to accommodate his overall thesis, Rissi does provide a helpful discussion of the place of geographical movement in the Fourth Gospel's design. It is indeed instructive to observe the relationship between geographical movement in John and possible "theological" uses of movement terminology. For example, one may ask whether there is significance in the fact that the term ἀναβαίνειν is used for Jesus' first three journeys to Jerusalem (cf. 2:13; 5:1; and 7:14) but not for his final journey, which the fourth evangelist considers to be Jesus' return to the Father (but cf. 20:17).[327]

---

321. Cf. Margaret Pamment, "Path and Residence Metaphors in the Fourth Gospel," *Theology* 88 (1985): 118-24.

322. Pamment, "Path and Residence Metaphors," 119.

323. Pamment, "Path and Residence Metaphors," 120.

324. Pamment, "Path and Residence Metaphors," 123. This observation provides support for the decision of the present author not to include μένειν in the purview of this study.

325. Thus one wonders whether 1:23, for example, where John the Baptist is said to "prepare *the way*" of the Lord should be subsumed under a "path motif" in John.

326. Mathias Rissi, "Der Aufbau des vierten Evangeliums," *NTS* 29 (1983): 48. Cf. also Nicholson, 48-51.

327. Cf. Nicholson's distinction between geographical and nongeographical occurrences of descent and ascent terminology in the Fourth Gospel (52 and 58).

b. Gathering

Terms of "bringing" and "gathering" reveal a further aspect of Jesus' mission. In 10:16, Jesus says, "I have other sheep [Gentiles?] that are not of this sheep pen [Judaism?]. I must *bring* them also. They too will listen to my voice, and there shall be one flock and one shepherd."[328] Later in his Gospel, the fourth evangelist expands a comment by the Jewish high priest in the following way: "He did not say this on his own, but as high priest that year he prophesied that Jesus would die for the Jewish nation, and not only for that nation but also for the scattered children of God to *bring them together and make them one*" (11:51-52). Yet a little later, the coming of some Greeks (Hellenistic Jews or Gentile Greeks?) signals to Jesus that "the hour has come for the Son of Man to be glorified" (12:23).[329] Using metaphorical language, Jesus speaks of the fact that he will "bear much fruit" through his death (12:24: πολὺν καρπὸν φέρει). This statement may be regarded as a reference to the inclusion of diaspora Jews and Gentile proselytes into the orbit of God's salvation and community. It is also noteworthy that the same terminology of bearing much fruit is later used for the disciples' future mission (cf. 15:5: φέρει καρπὸν πολύν; 15:8: καρπὸν πολὺν φέρητε; 15:16: καρπὸν φέρητε; cf. also 4:36: ὁ θερίζων μισθὸν λαμβάνει καὶ συνάγει καρπὸν εἰς ζωὴν αἰώνιον). The implication that can be drawn from these kinds of passages (cf. also the "greater works" of 14:12) is that Jesus' followers will have a part in Jesus' fruitful "gathering" activity, especially after his life-giving death. Finally, the reference to the "scattering" of Jesus' disciples in 16:32 also implies the imagery of a flock tended by a shepherd.

Further development of these arguments has to await Chapter 4. In the remainder of this chapter some of the connections in the Fourth Gospel will be drawn out that combine to present Jesus' mission in terms of the eschatological Messianic shepherd-teacher calling his followers to participate in gathering the Messianic harvest.

c. Calling Followers to Gather (Fruit)

It is argued that the two roles of Jesus already discussed, i.e., Jesus as the sent Son, and Jesus as the one who comes into the world and returns to the Father, are complemented in the Fourth Gospel by a third description of Jesus the Messiah: the eschatological shepherd-teacher.[330] The relevant passages range from 1:37-43

---

328. Cf. Otto Hofius, "Die Sammlung der Heiden zur Herde Israels (Joh 10,16; 11,51f.)," *ZNW* 58 (1967): 289-91.

329. Cf. Ulrich Busse, "Die 'Hellenen' Joh 12, 20ff. und der sogenannte 'Anhang' Joh 21," in *The Four Gospels 1992: Festschrift Frans Neirynck*, BETL C, ed. van Segbroeck et al., 3:2083-2100.

330. Jesus is addressed as "teacher" (ῥαββί; in 20:16, ῥαββουνί; translated as διδάσκαλε in 1:38 and 20:16) in 1:38, 49; 3:2 (διδάσκαλος); 4:31; 6:25; [8:4: διδάσκαλε;] 9:2; 11:8, 28 (διδάσκαλος); 13:13, 14 (διδάσκαλος) and 20:16. Jesus is presented as the good shepherd in chapter 10,

over 4:34-38, chapter 10, 12:26, chapter 15, and 21:15-23, to name but a few of the most important ones. It seems hard to include these passages in the Fourth Gospel's presentation of the first two roles of Jesus. References to "sending" or "coming" are conspicuously absent from these passages (except for "coming" in 10:10; note also the references to "sending" framing 4:34-38).[331] Thus without the third dimension added by Jesus' role as the Messianic shepherd-teacher a discussion and understanding of the Fourth Gospel's presentation of Jesus' mission remains incomplete. It is therefore noteworthy that few studies of Jesus' mission in the Fourth Gospel have given significant attention to this third role assigned to Jesus by the fourth evangelist. However, it is this very role that enshrines important references to Jesus' giving of his life for others (cf. especially 1:29, 36; 10:11, 15, 17; 12:24; 15:13).[332] It may therefore be no coincidence that those who neglect a discussion of this third role of Jesus often appear to neglect the Fourth Gospel's teaching on the redemptive aspect of Jesus' death.[333]

Jesus' role as a shepherd is most clearly developed in the Fourth Gospel in chapter 10. This passage blends motifs found primarily in Ezekiel, Zechariah, and Isaiah.[334] It should be noted that chapter 10 is intricately linked with the preceding chapter (cf. 10:19-21). There Jesus' healing of the blind man had led to the man's excommunication from the local synagogue.[335] This act by the Jewish religious leaders, in turn, had provoked Jesus' response. He saw in their excommunication of this formerly blind man an arrogant assertion of usurped authority. This he used as an occasion for recalling God's promise of judgment on the irresponsible religious leaders of Israel (9:39-41; cf. Ezek. 34). While "the

---

where "following" terminology is prominently used (cf. also 16:32). The fact that both Jesus' activity as a teacher and his (metaphoric) description as a shepherd are linked closely with "following" terminology supports the claim that Jesus' role can be described as that of shepherd-teacher in the Fourth Gospel.

331. The argument is *not* that there is no relationship between Jesus' roles as sent Son, as one coming into the world and returning to the Father, and as eschatological shepherd-teacher. On the contrary, these roles complement each other in that *together* they show what kind of Messiah Jesus is. It is argued, however, that three distinct roles of Jesus the Messiah are presented in the Fourth Gospel and that these roles should be distinguished rather than blended together indiscriminately.

332. Cf. similarly the juxtaposition of 20:20 (Jesus' showing his wounds and his side to his followers) with 20:21-23 (Jesus' commissioning of his followers, including their pronouncement of forgiveness of sins in Jesus).

333. See the discussion of the nature of Jesus' work above.

334. Cf. France, 103-10, 148-50, 208-9, following Lamarche.

335. There is no reason why excommunication from the local synagogue might not have been practiced as early as during the later stages of Jesus' ministry as a local, isolated phenomenon, foreshadowing what was to come (cf. John 16:2). There is therefore no need to follow Martyn and others who see John 9 as a later projection on the part of the "Johannine community" onto the time of the historical Jesus (cf. Martyn, *History and Theology*, 2d ed., 24-62). Cf. especially the treatment of Martyn's hypotheses in Carson, *Gospel According to John*, 35-38, 360-61, and especially 369-72. Cf. also D. A. Carson, "Historical Tradition in the Fourth Gospel: After Dodd, What?" in *Gospel Perspectives: Studies of History and Tradition in the Four Gospels*, Volume II, ed. R. T. France and David Wenham (Sheffield: JSOT, 1981), 98-99.

Jews" were trying to guard their religious system, i.e., the temple which was soon to be destroyed (cf. 2:19-22), the Law of Moses (cf. 1:17; 5:16; 7:19; 9:28-29), and their national autonomy (cf. 11:49-50; 19:15), their day of reckoning was near. Jesus' sharp polemic calls "Israel's shepherds" to account for their failure to follow the Davidic/prophetic tradition: "All who came before me are thieves and robbers, but the sheep did not hear them" (10:8). This prophetic word of judgment is firmly placed within John's "eschatology of decision." It is decision time for Israel's religious leaders (cf. also Mark 12:1-12 in allusion to Isa. 5).

Yet while the earlier part of chapter 10 is polemically directed against the Pharisees who are questioning Jesus (cf. 9:41-42), Jesus' teaching is not limited to the conflict at hand. In 10:16, he transcends the immediate context of the blind man's healing and the Pharisees' opposition, when he talks of "other sheep that are not of this fold" (i.e., Judaism; cf. 10:1) which he must bring also, "and there will be one flock, one shepherd."[336] The passage is similar, though not identical in import, to 11:52, where the evangelist points out that Jesus' death would not only benefit the nation of Israel but also occur "in order to gather into one the scattered children of God." While John's comment in 11:52 betrays hindsight, referring to a universal gathering of the scattered children of God in general (but cf. John 12:32), Jesus' statement in 10:16 appears to be historically fixed in a context where the exalted Lord would in the near future unite two kinds of "sheep" into one "flock." Thus 10:16 is an instance in the Fourth Gospel where reference is made to the future mission of the exalted Lord through his disciples (cf. 4:34-38; 14:12; 17:20; 20:21-23; 21:15-19).[337]

As France argues, the four figures from Zechariah 9–14 (further developing Ezek 34) were merged into one coherent picture of the coming Messiah in Old Testament tradition: the king riding on a donkey (Zech. 9:9; cf. John 12:15); the good shepherd (Zech. 11:4-14; cf. John 10); the martyr ("the one whom they have pierced" of Zech. 12:10; cf. 19:37; cf. also Rev. 1:7); and the smitten

---

336. For a listing of alternative views concerning the identity of the "other sheep," however unlikely, cf. Carson, *Gospel According to John*, 390. Cf. also Kuhl, 226-29; and Odo Kiefer, *Die Hirtenrede: Analyse und Deutung von Johannes 10, 1-18* (Stuttgart: Katholisches Bibelwerk, 1967), 72, n. 113 for the broad scholarly consensus that John 10:16 refers to the Gentile mission. For dissenting views, cf. John Painter, "Tradition, History and Interpretation in John 10," in *The Shepherd Discourse of John 10 and Its Context*, SNTSMS 67, ed. Johannes Beutler and Robert T. Fortna (Cambridge: Cambridge University Press, 1991), 65-66, who sees the "Johannine community" as the sheepfold and the "other sheep" as prospective converts to the "Johannine community"; Severino Pancaro, "The Relationship of the Church to Israel in the Gospel of St. John," *NTS* 21 (1975): 396-405; and Raymond E. Brown, "'Other Sheep Not of This Fold': The Johannine Perspective on Christian Diversity in the Late First Century," *JBL* 97 (1978): 5-22.

337. Concerning the mission of Jesus' disciples, especially to the Gentiles, cf. Hofius, "Sammlung der Heiden," 289-91; Hahn, *Mission in the New Testament;* Joachim Jeremias, *Jesus' Promise to the Nations,* SBT 24, trans. S. H. Hooke (London: SCM, 1958); McPolin, 113-22; Kuhl, 141-49; and Max Meinertz, "Zum Ursprung der Heidenmission," *Bib* 40 (1959): 762-77. See further Chapter 4 below.

shepherd (Zech. 13:7; cf. also John 10).[338] France makes reference to Lamarche, who argues that these four passages should be viewed as four aspects of a single Messianic conception, "the Shepherd-King," presenting successive phases of the Messiah's coming and the reaction of the people. Lamarche further sees a relationship between Zechariah 9–14 and the Servant Songs in Isaiah.[339]

Attention may also be drawn to another Isaianic passage, 56:8, that expresses the expectation of an eschatological ingathering of people beyond the boundaries of Israel: "The Lord God, who gathers the dispersed of Israel, declares, 'Yet others I will gather to them, to those already gathered.' "[340] Thus there is the notion of "others" besides the "dispersed of Israel" that God pledges to gather as well. It is crucial to read verse 8 in the context of verses 3-7, which emphatically affirm the inclusion of "foreigners" in God's covenant:

> Let not the foreigner who has joined himself to the Lord say, "The Lord will surely separate me from his people". . . . I will give them an everlasting name which will not be cut off. Also the foreigners who join themselves to the Lord, to minister to him, and to love the name of the Lord, to be his servants, every one who keeps from profaning the sabbath, and holds fast my covenant, even those I will bring to my holy mountain, and make them joyful in my house of prayer. Their burnt offerings and their sacrifices will be acceptable on my altar; for my house will be called a house of prayer *for all the peoples*.[341]

It is those previously excluded from God's covenant with Israel that God will gather. The basis for being joined to the Lord will not be ethnic heritage but loving service to God and holding fast to his covenant. This passage, then, links the "divine shepherd motif" with the inclusion of non-Jews ("foreigners")

---

338. Cf. France, 103-10; cf. also Leonhard Goppelt, *Typos: The Typological Interpretation of the Old Testament in the New* (Grand Rapids: Wm. B. Eerdmans, 1982 [1939]), 88-89; Douglas J. Moo, *The Old Testament in the Gospel Passion Narratives* (Sheffield: Almond, 1983), 174-78.

339. Cf. France, 109-10, citing Lamarche, 138-39. France also refers to the important article by F. F. Bruce, "The Book of Zechariah and the Passion Narrative," *BJRL* 43 (1960/61): 336-53, especially 342-49, where Bruce traces the figure of Zech. 9–14 in Jesus' thought during the closing phases of his ministry. Cf. also the helpful summary statement by Hassell Bullock, *An Introduction to the Old Testament Prophetic Books* (Chicago: Moody, 1986), 322: "The image of the shepherd-king had already been set forth by Ezekiel (34:23-31; 37:24), and Zechariah mixes the hues of that imagery with those of the Suffering Servant to paint the portrait of the Messiah on his apocalyptic canvass. The gospel writers knew those precious phrases from Zechariah, and in them they heard the traumatic events of the passion of Christ expressed." Cf. also F. F. Bruce, *The New Testament Development of Old Testament Themes* (Grand Rapids: Wm. B. Eerdmans, 1968), 100-14. Along different lines, André Feuillet, "Deux références évangeliques cachées au Serviteur martyrisé (Is 52,13–53,12). Quelques aspects importants du mystère rédempteur," *NRT* 106 (1984): 549-65, sees Isaianic language reflected in Jesus' expression "give my life for," found four times in 10:11-18 (cf. especially 556-61).

340. Cf. Hofius, "Sammlung der Heiden," 289-91. Note also Isa. 46:6 (cf. Jesus of himself in John 8:12, to his disciples in Matt. 5:14).

341. Cf. also the quote of Isa. 56:7 in the Synoptics at the occasion of Jesus' cleansing of the temple (Mark 11:17 = Matt. 21:13 = Luke 19:46).

into the orbit of God's covenant. As Jeremias points out, the universal expansion of the shepherd motif belongs to the conception of the eschatological pilgrimage of the nations to God's mountain.[342] Within the framework of Johannine "inaugurated eschatology," Jesus indicates that in his coming the hour of the eschatological ingathering of God's flock has indeed dawned.

While the Pharisees who held to particularistic views were closed to the notion of a united "flock" under Jesus including Jews and Gentiles alike, such a prospect, far from being absent from Old Testament teaching, is positively predicted in passages such as Isaiah 56:3-8. Their conscious rejection of God's revelation renders the Jewish religious leaders therefore morally culpable. Indeed, the evangelist explicitly links the Jews' response to Jesus' ministry with Isaiah's own experience (cf. the quote of Isa. 53:1 in John 12:38): "He has blinded their eyes, and he hardened their heart, lest they see with their eyes, and perceive with their heart, and be converted, and I heal them."[343] In contrast to the Jewish religious leaders, Jesus is found to represent the universal perspective that has already found expression in Isaiah 56:3-8.[344]

France's main concern is with Jesus' own Messianic consciousness in relation to motifs found in the Old Testament. The concern of this present monograph lies in the Fourth Gospel's portrait of one of the roles of Jesus, i.e., that of the eschatological shepherd-teacher. Of course, if the Fourth Gospel should be found to be an accurate reflection of Jesus' mission, one would expect to find a certain convergence between Jesus' own Messianic consciousness and the Fourth Gospel's portrait of Jesus' mission. It appears that the fourth evangelist integrates the notion of Jesus as the Messianic shepherd-king into his passion and pre-passion narratives (cf. especially the quotes of Zech. 9:9 and 12:10 in John 12:15 and 19:37), which are in turn incorporated into the larger framework of the Gospel narrative. This larger framework spans from the references to Jesus' calling of others to follow him at the beginning of John's Gospel (cf. 1:37-43; note that Jesus had previously been identified as the "Lamb of God" in 1:29 and 36) to Jesus' calling of his followers to follow him until his return, a passage that is found at the end of the Gospel (cf. 21:19, 20, 22). Moreover, as already mentioned, at the conclusion of the Fourth Gospel Jesus calls one of his *followers* to be a *shepherd* (cf. 21:15-19).[345] Thus the notion of the shepherd-*king*, though surfacing during the passion narrative, seems to

---

342. Cf. Jeremias, 64-65; cf. also Hofius, "Sammlung der Heiden," 289, 291.

343. Cf. especially Craig A. Evans, "Obduracy and the Lord's Servant: Some Observations on the Use of the Old Testament in the Fourth Gospel," in *Early Jewish and Christian Exegesis: Studies in Memory of William Hugh Brownlee,* ed. Craig A. Evans and William F. Stinespring (Atlanta: Scholars, 1987), 221-36.

344. This great "paradigm shift" from particularism to universalism is realized at Pentecost (Acts 2) and confirmed at the Jerusalem council (Acts 15). As the Fourth Gospel indicates, the historical Jesus clearly anticipated these developments.

345. Note also the parallel references to the kinds of death Jesus and Peter would die in 12:33 and 21:19. See Chapter 4 below.

retreat into the background over against the shepherd-*teacher* (cf. especially chap. 10 with 13:1-17).[346]

Finally, in light of the fact that the present work subsumes this third role of Jesus under the overall purpose of the Fourth Gospel of presenting Jesus as the Messiah by way of selected signs, the question arises whether the term σημεῖον is related in any way to the figure of the eschatological shepherd-teacher in the Fourth Gospel. A connection between Jesus as teacher and the doing of signs is explicitly drawn in 3:2, where Jesus is called "a teacher (διδάσκαλος) come from God" who is performing "signs."[347] In 6:25, 9:2, and 11:8, Jesus is called "teacher" in the context of pericopae that narrate his performance of signs. Thus, it seems that the working of signs is part of Jesus' role as the eschatological shepherd-teacher in John.

IV. CONCLUSION

It has been suggested that the evangelist's overall purpose is to demonstrate that Jesus is the Messiah, "the Coming One" (cf. 20:30-31). Through his distinctive use of modes of movement terminology, John carries out his general purpose by presenting Jesus in the following roles: "Jesus as the Sent Son," "Jesus as the Coming and Returning One," and "Jesus as the Eschatological Shepherd-Teacher." This overall presentation of Jesus' mission in the Fourth Gospel can be diagrammed as follows:

Fig. 8. The Mission of Jesus according to the Fourth Gospel

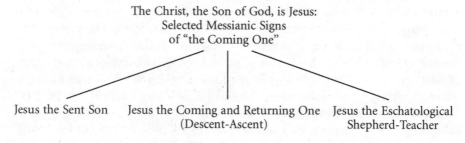

The Christ, the Son of God, is Jesus:
Selected Messianic Signs
of "the Coming One"

Jesus the Sent Son   Jesus the Coming and Returning One   Jesus the Eschatological
                       (Descent-Ascent)   Shepherd-Teacher

---

346. As Riesner, following Hengel, demonstrates, early Judaism also expected from the coming Messiah a teaching activity (cf. 2 Sam. 23:1-2; Isa. 11:1-5). Cf. Rainer Riesner, *Jesus als Lehrer: Eine Untersuchung zum Ursprung der Evangelien-Überlieferung*, WUNT 2/7, 3d ed. (Tübingen: J. C. B. Mohr [Paul Siebeck], 1988), 304-30; cf. also Martin Hengel, "Jesus als messianischer Lehrer der Weisheit und die Anfänge der Christologie," in *Sagesse et Religion*, Colloque de Strasbourg, Octobre 1976 (Paris, 1979), 148-88; and Bittner, 108. Riesner refers especially to Jesus' call for people to come to him and drink in John 7:37-39 as evidence, noting that water was a common image both for wisdom and teaching, especially teaching of the Torah. Cf. Riesner, 343-44.

347. Cf. Bittner, 112, who notes the connection but adds, "ohne dass erkennbar wird, was damit genau gemeint ist."

The three portraits of Jesus outlined above serve the purpose of the fourth evangelist to present Jesus as the Messiah by clarifying *what kind of* Messiah Jesus is. He is not just a human figure but heaven-sent (coming-returning, descending-ascending). Yet he is not just a healer or wonder-worker. His Messianic signs are rather works wrought as the obedient, dependent Son sent by the Father (sending). Jesus is also the eschatological shepherd-teacher who calls followers to bring in his Messianic "harvest." The function of the mission theme in the Fourth Gospel with reference to Jesus thus appears to be that of providing a multifaceted comprehensive portrayal of the person and mission of the Messiah for the purpose of leading others to believe.

In this final section, it may be appropriate to entertain the question of how the death of Jesus (which was discussed when dealing with the nature of Jesus' work above) relates to the various terms denoting modes of movement in Jesus' mission. The following correspondences can be seen. Regarding the Fourth Gospel's depiction of Jesus as the Son sent by the Father, the death of Jesus is the culmination of Jesus' life of obedient submission to the will of his sender (cf. 4:34; 17:4; 19:30). Regarding the presentation of Jesus as the coming and returning one, the death of Jesus is simply his departure and return (cf., e.g., 14:12c). Finally, regarding the portrait of Jesus as the eschatological shepherd-teacher, the death of Jesus is an act of self-giving love of the Master for his disciples and of the "shepherd" for his "sheep" (cf. 10:11, 15-18; 16:33; 17:12), making possible the eschatological harvest (cf. especially 12:20-32; cf. also 4:38; 14:12; 15:16). The "lifting up" of the Son of Man probably should be put in the third category (cf. 12:20-32).[348]

Attention may also be drawn to 13:1-3, a passage that sets the stage for the second part of the Gospel. There Jesus is presented as the one who came from God and who would return to God. His work is portrayed as the revelation of the full extent of his love for "his own."[349] This kind of love, in turn, Jesus' disciples are to imitate (cf. 13:12-15, 34-35). While 3:16 speaks of God's love *for the world*, 13:1-3 focuses on Jesus' love *for his own*. Indeed, in 17:6-19 it is his own for whom Jesus prays. It is only said of *God* in the Fourth Gospel that he loves the world. The missions of Jesus and of the disciples are to be directed primarily toward their respective senders in order to do *their* will and to please and love *them*. Yet these loving, obedient relationships are presented in the Fourth Gospel not as an end in themselves but as a means to draw from the world those who would believe in Jesus the Messiah and be incorporated into the Messianic community (cf. 13:34-35; 17:21, 23).

It has become apparent that the Fourth Gospel's teaching on mission

---

348. If this were accurate, Nicholson would stand corrected in subsuming the "lifting up" sayings under the Johannine descent-ascent scheme.

349. Cf. Peter G. Ahr, " 'He Loved Them to Completion': The Theology of John 13–14," in *Standing before God: Studies on Prayer in Scriptures and in Tradition with Essays in Honor of John M. Oesterreicher,* ed. Asker Finkel and Lawrence Frizzell (New York: Ktav, 1981), 73-89.

focuses on the mission of Jesus. One may view the two parts of the Gospel as each highlighting one aspect of Jesus' mission: chapters 1–12 present the mission of the earthly Jesus; chapters 13–21 portray the mission of the exalted Jesus. Notably, his cross-death, which is developed in the first part in terms of the "lifting up" of the Son of Man (cf. 3:13; 8:28; and 12:32), as well as the passion narrative (albeit largely emptied of the aspects of humiliation and shame) and the resurrection appearances are all presented from the viewpoint of Jesus' exaltation.

The mission of the earthly Jesus in the first part of the Gospel has as its major antagonists "the Jews." In this aspect of Jesus' mission, the disciples have no part. Indeed, as will be discussed below, the sole references to their mission in the first part of the Gospel are proleptic (cf. 4:38; and, perhaps by implication, 10:16; 11:51-52; and 12:20-32). The governing conflict in the second part of the Gospel is between Jesus and his followers and "the world." One notes the universal aspect of the mission of the exalted Jesus through his disciples given expression by the substitution of "the world" for "the Jews," an element that is present in the first part of the Gospel only in the form of veiled references.

Correspondingly, the Fourth Gospel's portrayal of Jesus in chapters 1–12 focuses on Jesus the Messiah as the Son sent by the Father, with a stress on the "horizontal" dimension of Jesus' mission, while chapters 13–21 view Jesus primarily as the one who came into the world and who returns to the Father, with an emphasis on the "vertical" dimension of the mission of Jesus. Notably, however, 20:30-31 subsumes both 1–12 and 13–20 under the Fourth Gospel's purpose for writing. The presentation of Jesus as the eschatological shepherd-teacher spans chapters 1–21 and thus provides a unifying element within the framework of the Gospel narrative, encompassing the gathering of Jesus' disciples as well as the disciples' gathering of fruit for Jesus.

With these comments the investigation of Jesus' mission according to the Fourth Gospel comes to a close. The present study has found a rich variety in the fourth evangelist's teaching on mission, with the various mission terms cohering and mutually complementing each other. A study of "sending" terminology alone would not have revealed these interdependences. It took a more comprehensive view of the conceptual world of the Fourth Gospel to grasp its complex theological structure regarding mission. The study of mission in the Fourth Gospel, however, is not yet complete. Since the fourth evangelist links Jesus' mission repeatedly to that of his disciples, it is this latter mission that needs to be considered next.

CHAPTER 4

The Mission of the Disciples according to the Fourth Gospel

As the previous chapter has shown, it is Jesus' mission, not the disciples', that is the central mission presented in the Fourth Gospel. Every other mission is derivative of his: the Baptizer's, the Spirit's, and the disciples'.

Nevertheless, John makes clear that Jesus' mission, while pre-eminent, was not to stand alone; it was to be continued in the mission of his followers. In the present chapter, the subject of investigation will be the disciples' mission in relation to that of Jesus.

That the mission of Jesus is cast in the Fourth Gospel as fundamental and more comprehensive than the mission of the disciples, is partly evidenced by the more multifaceted usage of mission vocabulary in reference to Jesus. Certain terminology is reserved for the mission of Jesus: "descend" (καταβαίνω) and "ascend" (ἀναβαίνω), "come into the world" (ἔρχομαι εἰς τὸν κόσμον) and "return" (πορεύομαι). Other terminology is exclusively used for the disciples and occurs throughout the Fourth Gospel: "follow" (ἀκολουθέω). Yet other terminology is shared: "to be sent" (ἀποστέλλω, πέμπω) or "to be sent into the world" (ἀποστέλλω εἰς τὸν κόσμον). Further evidence for the primacy of the mission of Jesus in the Fourth Gospel is provided by the semantic clustering of mission terminology in the Fourth Gospel. Almost all of the instances of mission terminology in chapters 1–12, and a majority of the references in the rest of the Fourth Gospel, refer to Jesus' mission. The mission of the disciples is virtually never mentioned other than with reference to the mission of Jesus.

The Fourth Gospel describes the mission of the disciples in terms of "harvesting" (θερίζω; 4:38), "fruitbearing" (καρπὸν φέρω; 15:8, 16), and "witnessing" (μαρτυρέω; 15:27). All of these terms place the disciples in the humble position of extending the mission of Jesus. The disciples are to "harvest the crop" they did not work for (cf. 4:38). They are to "bear fruit" they did not produce (cf. 15:8, 16). They are to do "greater works" than Jesus in dependence on the exalted Lord who answers their prayers (cf. 14:12-13). They are to extend the forgiveness (or retention) of sins made possible by their Lord who presented his pierced hands and side as living proof of the completion of his own mission (cf. 20:19-23).

It remains to develop these observations in greater detail. The definition formulated in Chapter 2 will function, as in the discussion of Jesus' mission, as a heuristic guide. In analogy to the study of the mission of Jesus according to the Fourth Gospel, the investigation of the disciples' mission will begin with the Fourth Gospel's portrait of the disciples as a group. Then the task of the disciples will be treated, followed by a discussion of the modes of movement associated with the disciples' mission.

I. THE GROUP OF THE DISCIPLES

There is a significant number of studies on the Johannine characterization of the disciples.[1] The difficult hermeneutical issue of the relationship between the

---

1. From the growing body of literature on the church and the disciples of the Fourth Gospel, see especially Rudolf Schnackenburg, "The Disciples, the Community and the Church in the Gospel of John," in *The Gospel According to St. John*, vol. 3, HTKNT (New York: Crossroad, 1990 [1975]), 203-17; and the more recent treatment by R. Alan Culpepper, *The Anatomy of the Fourth Gospel: A Study in Literary Design* (Philadelphia: Fortress, 1983), 99-148, especially 115-23 and 132-44. Cf. also Jean-Louis d'Aragon, "Le caractère distinctif de l'église johannique," in *L'Église dans la Bible, Communications présentées à la XVIIe réunion annuelle de l'Acébac* (Montréal: Desclée de Brouwer, 1962), 53-66; Günther Baumbach, "Gemeinde und Welt im Johannesevangelium," *Kairos* 14 (1972): 121-36; Henri van den Bussche, "Die Kirche im vierten Evangelium," in *Vom Christus zur Kirche: Charisma und Amt im Urchristentum*, ed. Jean Giblet (Wien: Herder, 1966), 79-107; Alf Corell, *Consummatum Est: Eschatology and Church in the Gospel of St. John* (London: SPCK, 1958); Nils Alstrup Dahl, "The Johannine Church and History," in *Current Issues in New Testament Interpretation: Essays in Honor of Otto A. Piper*, ed. William Klassen and Graydon F. Snyder (New York: Harper & Brothers, 1962), 124-42 and 284-88; Doris Faulhaber, *Das Johannes-Evangelium und die Kirche* (Ph.D. diss., Heidelberg, 1935); Ernst Gaugler, "Die Bedeutung der Kirche in den johanneischen Schriften," *IKZ* 14 (1924): 97-117; *IKZ* 14 (1924): 181-219; and *IKZ* 15 (1925): 27-42; Herbert Giesbrecht, "The Evangelist John's Conception of the Church as delineated in his Gospel," *EvQ* 58 (1986): 101-19; Heinrich Greeven, "Die missionierende Gemeinde nach den apostolischen Briefen," in *Sammlung und Sendung. Vom Auftrag der Kirche in der Welt: Eine Festgabe für Heinrich Rendtorff*, ed. Joachim Heubach and Heinrich Hermann Ulrich (Berlin: Christlicher Zeitschriftenverlag, 1958), 59-71; Klaus Haacker, "Jesus und die Kirche nach Johannes," *TZ* 29 (1973): 179-201; Ramón Moreno, "El discípulo de Jesucristo, según el evangelio de S. Juan," *EstBib* 30 (1971): 269-311; Severino Pancaro, "'People of God' in St John's Gospel?" *NTS* 16 (1970): 114-29; and "The Relationship of the Church to Israel in the Gospel of St. John," *NTS* 21 (1975): 396-405; John W. Pryor, "Covenant and Community in John's Gospel," *RTR* 47 (1988): 44-51; and, *John: Evangelist of the Covenant People: The Narrative and Themes of the Fourth Gospel* (Downers Grove, Ill.: InterVarsity, 1992), 157-80; Rudolf Schnackenburg, "Is there a Johannine Ecclesiology?" in *A Companion to John: Readings in Johannine Theology*, ed. Michael J. Taylor (New York: Alba, 1977), 247-56; Udo Schnelle, "Johanneische Ekklesiologie," *NTS* 37 (1991): 37-50; Eduard Schweizer, "Der Kirchenbegriff im Evangelium und den Briefen des Johannes," in *SE I*, TU 73, ed. Kurt

Fourth Gospel's disciples and later generations of believers, however, is rarely discussed and will therefore need to be treated in greater detail. The present investigation begins with a survey of the instances in the Fourth Gospel where the term μαθητής is used to designate the followers of the historical Jesus (i.e., "the twelve" as well as a broader, less clearly defined circle of followers). Next addressed is the Fourth Gospel's widening of the term to include later believers (i.e., post-resurrection disciples), followed by a discussion of the disciples as figures of identification for John's readers. The section concludes with a treatment of Johannine corporate metaphors.

A. Introduction

It is frequently observed that the term ἐκκλησία is not used in the Fourth Gospel.[2] It should be noted, however, that the expression is likewise absent from Mark and Luke while occurring only twice in Matthew (cf. 16:19; 18:18). Moreover, it appears that the absence of ἐκκλησία from the Fourth Gospel can be explained by the fact that the Gospel purports to set forth primarily the life and passion of Jesus rather than dealing directly with issues in the later church. The Fourth Gospel contains a number of corporate metaphors for Jesus' Messianic community such as "the flock" (chap. 10) or "the vine" (chap. 15). These metaphors transfer descriptions of Old Testament Israel to the group of Jesus' followers, thus marking an important salvation-historical development. Attention will also be given to the Johannine characterization of the disciples as a group and of individual disciples such as Peter or the Beloved Disciple.

Recent scholarship has increasingly viewed the Fourth Gospel's disciples as figures representing the "Johannine school,"[3] "circle,"[4] or "community."[5] Within such a framework, the Fourth Gospel's disciples become vehicles of the history of the "Johannine community."[6] In these treatments, the focus tends to

---

Aland et al. (Berlin: Akademie, 1959), 363-81; Jeffrey S. Siker-Gieseler, "Disciples and Discipleship in the Fourth Gospel: A Canonical Approach," *SBT* 10 (1980): 199-227; Adela Yarbro-Collins, "Crisis and Community in John's Gospel," *CurTM* 7 (1980): 196-204.

2. For general treatments of Johannine ecclesiology, cf. d'Aragon; van den Bussche; Gaugler; Haacker, "Jesus und die Kirche nach Johannes."

3. Cf. R. Alan Culpepper.

4. Cf. Oscar Cullmann, *The Johannine Circle* (London: SCM, 1976).

5. This term seems to have carried the day in recent discussion. It is used almost universally. Cf. Raymond E. Brown, *The Community of the Beloved Disciple* (New York: Paulist, 1979).

6. Cf. J. Louis Martyn, *History and Theology in the Fourth Gospel*, 2d ed. (Nashville: Abingdon, 1979); and "Glimpses into the History of the Johannine Community," in *L'Évangile de Jean: Sources, Rédaction, Théologie*, BETL 44, ed. Marinus de Jonge (Leuven: University Press, 1977), 149-75; David Rensberger, *Overcoming the World: Politics and Community in the Gospel of John* (London: SPCK, 1989); and *Johannine Faith and Liberating Community* (Philadelphia: Westminster, 1988); Takashi Onuki, *Gemeinde und Welt im Johannesevangelium: Ein Beitrag zur Frage nach der*

shift from the historical level in the life of Jesus to the time of writing.[7] John's representation of the disciples is consequently viewed as an expression of the "Johannine community's" self-understanding in the light of its faith in Jesus.[8] This "Johannine community," it is maintained, should be understood as a "sect" defining itself in contrast to the surrounding world, a mindset that some scholars trace to a possible dependence on gnostic thought.[9] While often very insightful, these studies, however, appear to make too little of the care taken by the fourth evangelist to preserve the distinction between the understanding of the disciples during the time *before* and *after* Jesus' resurrection. Also, many of these studies focus on the fourth evangelist's literary art to the extent that historical matters are neglected.[10] However, the possibility that the fourth evangelist retains historical points of reference while engaging in more sophisticated literary strategies of characterization should at the very least not be ruled out a priori.

In light of these preliminary observations, it is now possible to consider the Fourth Gospel's characterization of Jesus' followers.

B. The Fourth Gospel's Characterization of Jesus' Followers

The Fourth Gospel's disciples, like the disciples in the other Gospels, are part of a story line that is inextricably linked with the events surrounding Jesus' earthly ministry.[11] Nevertheless, as will be seen, especially as the Gospel progresses, there is an increasing widening of the designation "disciples" that transcends the followers of the historical Jesus. There are also instances where a historical disciple or the disciples of the Fourth Gospel as a group, besides

---

theologischen und pragmatischen Funktion des johanneischen "Dualismus," WMANT 56 (Neukirchen-Vluyn: Neukirchener, 1984); Brown, *Community of the Beloved Disciple;* and " 'Other Sheep Not of This Fold': The Johannine Perspective on Christian Diversity in the Late First Century," *JBL* 97 (1978): 5-22.

7. This is the sense in which the term "history" is used by Martyn in *History and Theology in the Fourth Gospel,* who advocates a reading of the Fourth Gospel on two levels, i.e., the purported life-setting in Jesus' day and the setting contemporary to the writing of the Gospel.

8. Thus Baumbach, 128, for example, sees the figure of the Beloved Disciple in the Fourth Gospel as an expression of the Johannine community's self-understanding.

9. In addition to the works of Martyn, Meeks, Brown, Onuki, and Rensberger that have already been discussed, cf. also the essays by Baumbach and Andreas Lindemann, "Gemeinde und Welt im Johannesevangelium," in *Kirche: Festschrift für Günther Bornkamm zum 75. Geburtstag,* ed. Dieter Lührmann and Georg Strecker (Tübingen: J. C. B. Mohr [Paul Siebeck], 1980), 133-61.

10. Cf. Raymond F. Collins, "Representative Figures," *These Things Have Been Written — Studies on the Fourth Gospel* (Louvain: Peeters; Grand Rapids: Wm. B. Eerdmans, 1990); de Jonge, "Messianic Expectations"; Baumbach, 128.

11. Cf. Karl-Heinz Rengstorf, "μανθάνω, et al.," TDNT 4:390-461; Michael J. Wilkins, *The Concept of Disciple in Matthew's Gospel as Reflected in the Use of the Term Μαθητής,* NovTSup 59 (Leiden: E. J. Brill, 1988).

constituting historical disciples of the earthly Jesus, function as representative figures and figures of identification for the Fourth Gospel's readers.

1. The Term Μαθητής *Designating the Historical Followers of Jesus in the Fourth Gospel*

The term μαθητής occurs seventy-eight times in the Fourth Gospel.[12] Most of these references are to the followers of Jesus, usually with the pronoun αὐτοῦ.[13] As do the other Gospels, the Fourth Gospel features the disciples as significant characters. After their call (cf. 1:37-43), they accompany Jesus (cf. 2:2, 11, 17). They begin to participate in his work (cf. 4:2, 8, 27, 31, 33, 38) and gradually step into the foreground (cf. 6:3, 8, 12, 16, 22, 24, 60-71). Contrasted with the unbelief of Jesus' own brothers is the loyalty of Jesus' inner circle (cf. 7:2-5), and discipleship is the subject of various discourses (cf. 8:12, 31; 9:27-29; and chap. 10). The disciples play an important role on the way to Jerusalem (cf. 9:2; 11:7-16, 54; 12:16, 21-22) and during their time of preparation and instruction in Jesus' farewell discourse (chaps. 13–17). Judas, one of Jesus' disciples, betrays him (cf. 6:70-71; 12:4-8; 13:21-30; 17:12). Finally, the risen Jesus appears to his disciples and commissions them (chaps. 20–21; especially 20:19-23).

The way the fourth evangelist distinguishes between Jesus' close followers and those who follow him from a distance can be illumined by his use of the term ὄχλος. One writer identifies the following characteristics of this term in John, all of which entail a somewhat distant relationship to Jesus: (1) the crowd follows Jesus only externally (6:2, 5, 22, 24); (2) it is only impressed by Jesus' miracles (cf. 7:31; 12:9, 12, 17-18); (3) otherwise its opinion is divided (7:12, 40-43); (4) the crowd is without understanding (cf. 11:42; 12:29, 43).[14] The predominant characteristic of the crowds in the Fourth Gospel is unbelief, which is all the more striking since they witness a number of Messianic signs performed by Jesus. Crowds are at hand when Jesus heals a man on the Sabbath

---

12. The term μαθηταί (pl.) is applied to followers of Jesus in the following passages: 2:2, 11, 17, 22; 3:22; 4:1, 2, 8, 27, 31, 33; 6:3, 8, 12, 16, 22 [twice], 24, 60, 61, 66; 7:3; 8:31; 9:2, 27, 28; 11:7, 8, 12, 54; 12:4, 16; 13:5, 22, 23, 35; 15:8; 16:17, 29; 18:1 [twice], 2, 17, 19, 25; 20:8, 10, 18, 19, 20, 25, 26, 30; 21:1, 2, 4, 8, 12, 14. The term μαθητής (sg.) occurs in 18:15 [twice], 16; 19:26, 27 [twice], 38; 20:2, 3, 4, 8; 21:7, 20, 23, 24. All the references in the sg. refer to the "disciple whom Jesus loved" who is simply called "another disciple" when appearing with Peter.

13. Cf. the designation of Jesus as teacher (ῥαββί, διδάσκαλος) and Lord (κύριος) in the Fourth Gospel. Jesus is called ῥαββί by Andrew, Nicodemus, the disciples, and Mary Magdalene (cf. 1:38, 49; 3:2; 4:31; 6:25; 9:2; 11:8; and 20:16). In Matt. only Judas calls Jesus ῥαββί (cf. 26:25, 49), in Mark also Peter (cf. 9:5; 11:21). Luke never uses ῥαββί; he always employs the Greek equivalent διδάσκαλος, a term also used by John in 1:38; 3:2, 10; 8:4; 11:28; 13:13, 14; 20:16. Cf. now also Andreas J. Köstenberger, "Jesus as Rabbi in the Fourth Gospel," *BBR* 8 (1998): forthcoming.

14. Cf. Schnackenburg, *Gospel According to St. John*, 3:208, n. 5. The μαθηταί of 6:60-61, 66 are probably those that had identified themselves more closely with Jesus. The same kinds of people are probably also referred to in 7:3.

(5:13). Multitudes are fed by Jesus (6:2, 5, 22, 24, 26). Crowds are also present at various feasts in Jerusalem (7:12, 20, 31, 32, 40, 43, 49; 12:12, 17, 18, 29, 34) and at the raising of Lazarus (11:42; 12:9). While Jesus wanted people to believe (cf. 7:31; 11:42), the fourth evangelist notes that, despite Jesus' many signs, the crowds would still not place their faith in him (cf. 12:36b-41). At times the crowds in the Fourth Gospel express Messianic expectations. They wonder whether the Messiah will perform more signs than Jesus (cf. 7:31) and marvel at Jesus' statement that the Son of Man must be "lifted up" (cf. 12:34-35).[15] In those instances, the crowds' reluctance to believe becomes prominent. Generally, the crowds seem to function in Johannine characterization as an example of "following Jesus" that falls short of actual discipleship, or, as in the case of 8:31, of discipleship that proves spurious.

Generally, the Fourth Gospel's characterization of the disciples appears to be consistent with the way these figures are cast in the Synoptics. As Anselm Schulz comments,

> The use of the term μαθητής in the Fourth Gospel provides an impressive corroboration of this document's historical and theological accuracy. To begin with, the expression designates in John in the vast majority of cases the disciple of Rabbi Jesus, in agreement with the Synoptic tradition (cf. 2:2, 11, 12, 17, 22; 3:22; 4:2, 8, 27, 31, 33; 6:3, 8, 16; etc.). The disciple's most salient characteristic is captured by the term ἀκολουθεῖν, i.e., the close relationship with his Messianic teacher. . . . The disciples live together with their teacher (cf. 2:2, 11; 6:3, 60, 66; 11:7, 54; 13:1; 18:2). They accompany him on his travels (cf. 2:12; 3:22; 11:7; 12:16; 18:1). They carry out various services for their teacher (cf. 4:8, 27, 31, 33; 6:10, 12). Finally, they witness his teachings and address their questions to him (cf. 6:60; 9:2).[16]

The disciples also share in their teacher's sufferings (cf. 13:16; 15:20).

The extent of the group referred to by the term μαθητής in the Fourth Gospel is fairly ambiguous. The designation "disciples" may be taken to refer in John, as in Luke, to Jesus' inner circle, i.e., the twelve (cf. 6:22, 24; 9:2; 11:7, 8, 12, 54; 12:4, 16; 13:5, 22, 23; 16:17, 29; 18:1, 2; 20:18, 19; 20:25, 26), or it may extend to a larger group of Jesus' followers (cf. 4:1; 6:60, 61, 66; 7:3; 9:27, 28;

---

15. Other terms referring to (otherwise unidentified) characters in the Fourth Gospel include πολλοί (15 times; 8 times with πιστεύω: 2:23; 4:39; 7:31; 8:30; 10:42; 11:45; 12:11, 42); τινες (used absolutely 6 times; often describing elements hostile to Jesus: 6:64; 7:25, 44; 9:16; 11:37, 46); ἄλλοι (12 times: 4:38; 7:12, 41; 9:9 [2], 16; 10:21; 12:29; 18:34; 20:25; 21:28); and οὗτοι (4 times: 6:5; 12:21; 17:25; 18:21). All of these terms refer to persons with varying degrees of interest in or hostility toward Jesus while falling short of being actual μαθηταί.

16. Cf. Anselm Schulz, *Nachfolgen und Nachahmen: Studien über das Verhältnis der neutestamentlichen Jüngerschaft zur urchristlichen Vorbildethik*, SANT VI (München: Kösel, 1962), 137 and 143. Cf. also Hans-Dieter Betz, *Nachfolge und Nachahmung Jesu Christi im Neuen Testament*, BHT 37 (Tübingen: J. C. B. Mohr [Paul Siebeck], 1967), especially 36-40.

18:17, 19, 25; 19:38). At times it is difficult to know which exact group is referred to (cf. 18:15, 17, 25; 19:26; 20:2, 3, 4, 30).[17] While the lines between a narrow and a broader circle of Jesus' followers are often fluid, the distinction that is more significant for the purposes of this present study is that between the Fourth Gospel's disciples, wide or narrow, and later believers. In this regard, the question arises as to whether or not what is predicated about the Fourth Gospel's disciples necessarily extends to post-resurrection disciples. This issue therefore will be addressed immediately after the discussion of the references to "the twelve" in the Fourth Gospel below.

2. "The Twelve" in the Fourth Gospel

There are only two pericopae in the entire Gospel where reference to "the twelve" is made. The first, 6:67-71, is set in a context where many of Jesus' disciples desert him due to his "hard teachings" (cf. 6:60). Peter, on the other hand, speaking for "the twelve," pledges loyalty to Jesus, acknowledging him as "the holy one of God" (6:69). The designation "the twelve" may be used at this point in the narrative to point to the symbolism inherent in the number twelve, relating the twelve tribes of Old Testament Israel to "the twelve" as the representatives of Jesus' new Messianic community. In the second occurrence of the term, Thomas is almost incidentally identified as "one of the twelve" (20:24), similar to Judas in 6:71.

That the expression "the twelve" is used in only one significant pericope in the entire Gospel, apart from the incidental reference in 20:24, suggests that the twelve are not viewed by John as the only ones who are sent or participate in Jesus' mission. The Fourth Gospel does, however, emphasize that, at a critical juncture, the twelve followed Jesus while disciples with inadequate faith fell away (cf. similarly, Matt. 16:13-16; Mark 8:27-30; Luke 9:18-20). This becomes especially significant in light of the references to discipleship in the following chapters, where many of "the Jews" fail to arrive at full faith in Jesus (cf. 8:31-59; 9:1-41; 10:1-39; and 12:39-50).

The inclusion of these passages in the Fourth Gospel indicates that the fourth evangelist recognized the historical configuration of twelve disciples who were especially chosen by Jesus (cf. 6:70). Nevertheless, in light of the scarcity of the expression in John's Gospel, care should be taken not to place an undue emphasis on the Johannine characterization of the twelve. Rather, it appears that John's Gospel, being a Gospel, assumes this important part of tradition and refers to it incidentally without pursuing any elaborate literary strategies of characterization.

---

17. Cf. A. Schulz, 137-38; Schnackenburg, *Gospel According to St. John*, 3:207-8; Kevin Quast, *Peter and the Beloved Disciple: Figures for a Community in Crisis*, JSNTSup 32 (Sheffield: JSOT, 1989), 23.

But this has not prevented some scholars from trying. Bauder, for instance, finds a theological distinction between "the disciples" and "the twelve" in the Fourth Gospel. He contends, "*[H]oi mathetai* are not simply the equivalent of *hoi dōdeka*, the Twelve. . . . The circle of the Twelve was both a symbolic representation of the twelve tribes of Israel, and thus of the whole people of God, and also a section of the larger circle of disciples which Jesus summoned to discipleship from a still wider group of adherents. . . . The disciples would have been a circle of immediate followers who were commissioned to particular service."[18]

Collins holds that the twelve of the Fourth Gospel actually "represent a group among Jewish Christians."[19] He interprets the fourth evangelist's portrayal of "the twelve" as negative, especially in comparison with the Synoptics: "Simon Peter's confession does not earn the response of Jesus' self-revelation. Rather Jesus responds by speaking about his betrayal. The response indicates that the faith of those for whom Peter serves as spokesperson is not all that it ought to be. From the standpoint of the Fourth Gospel, the corporate faith of the twelve is somehow inadequate."[20] However, as has already been pointed out, the twelve do pledge allegiance to Jesus at a critical juncture in the Johannine narrative (cf. 6:69).[21]

It may be concluded that the fourth evangelist portrays the twelve rather positively. John appears to view them as the core group of Jesus' Messianic community, an entity that is also discussed in terms of the corporate metaphors of a "flock" or a "vine" later in the Gospel.[22] Indeed, the group of the twelve extends beyond the historical followers of Jesus, fulfilling an important representative function in the Fourth Gospel. In this, John does not differ significantly from the other Gospels. Instead of reflecting sophisticated literary strategies on the part of the fourth evangelist, the references to the twelve in John's Gospel should probably be viewed as hints to the tradition common to all four Gospels which John assumes and which at times surfaces almost incidentally.

The issue to be discussed next is the characteristic widening of the term μαθητής in the Fourth Gospel. As will be seen, this "widening" functions as a bridge between the followers of the historical Jesus and later disciples.

18. Cf. Wolfgang Bauder, "Disciple," *NIDNTT* 1:489.
19. Cf. Bauder, 81.
20. Cf. Collins, 83.
21. Note also that one may infer from the Synoptics that it was the twelve who were the primary audience of the farewell discourses (cf. Mark 14:17). Although this is not explicitly mentioned in the Fourth Gospel, it may be suggested by the parallel between the sayings "I know the ones I have chosen," plus a reference to Judas the betrayer (cf. 13:18) and "Did I not choose you, the twelve, and yet one of you is a devil?" (6:70). However, even if this is so, the twelve would still function as representatives of later followers of Jesus so that the teachings of the discourse would extend to subsequent generations of believers as well.
22. See the discussion of corporate metaphors in the Fourth Gospel below.

3. The Widening of the Term Μαθητής in the Fourth Gospel

A characteristic and very significant feature of John's portrayal of Jesus' followers is his widening of the term μαθητής during the course of his Gospel. This movement from the concept of a mere physical following of Jesus to an adherence to Jesus with a more explicitly spiritual connotation facilitates the transition from the disciples of the historical Jesus to later believers. Thus one can discern a development in John's Gospel from a physical remaining with Jesus (cf. 1:37-43) to a spiritual remaining in Jesus' word (cf. 8:31) and a remaining "in Jesus" beyond the time of his earthly ministry (cf. 15:4-7). Gradually, the designation "disciple" is released from a following of the historical Jesus to a spiritual "following" that is not constrained by boundaries of time and space (cf., e.g., 8:31; 13:35; 15:8; chap. 17).[23]

Indeed, the activity of the disciples will transcend that of Jesus' earthly ministry, since it is no longer limited to the spatial-temporal form of the incarnate Word but is transformed into the work of the exalted Lord through his disciples and thus lifted out of its historical boundaries (cf. 14:12b).[24] According to the fourth evangelist, the believing response of the first disciples to Jesus functions as a model for the discipleship of later generations of believers. In the case of subsequent followers of Jesus, their lives of discipleship are no longer rooted in personal eyewitness experience or a call of Jesus. In fact, the faith of such believers is not based on any direct personal experience of Jesus but on the obedient reception of another's testimony to Jesus.[25] "Following Jesus," no longer limited to people who leave their profession for the sake of attaching themselves to their Lord, becomes in Johannine theology the spiritual exodus from a world alienated from God that is motivated by faith in the one sent from God who bequeathes on his followers the salvific blessings of eternal life.[26]

This widening of the Fourth Gospel's concept of discipleship, however, does not entail a complete obliteration of the function and figures of Jesus' first disciples. As Schnackenburg maintains, "Disciples are initially the close followers of Jesus, subsequently also his committed adherents, finally all of those who believe in him. This 'widening' is grounded in theological reflection and deliberate formulation. . . . While the fourth evangelist is certainly aware of the historical followers of Jesus, later believers are incorporated into discipleship. This is a development of ecclesial significance."[27]

Inherent in the gradual widening of John's concept of discipleship is a certain degree of ambiguity. If the exact delineation of the group of Jesus'

---

23. Cf. Schulz, 139; Moreno, 276-83.
24. Cf. Schulz, 141.
25. Schulz, 142.
26. Schulz, 175.
27. Cf. Schnackenburg, *Gospel According to St. John* 3:208-9; the translation is the present author's from the German original (*Johannesevangelium*, 3:237).

μαθηταί occasionally appears unclear and imprecise, the reason is probably that the concept of "disciple" is already opened up, widened, and prepared for a new point of reference.[28] This becomes apparent in passages where discipleship is spoken of in a way that does not limit it to Jesus' historical audience, as is the case, for example, in 8:31. Originally and in context, the statement is addressed to Jews who turned out to be spurious believers. Since the statement is phrased in general terms, however, it is relevant for every potential follower of Jesus (cf. also 8:12, 51). Thus the concept of discipleship is transferred to any person who would believe.

It may be asked whether the general Johannine practice of widening the term μαθητής *necessarily* extends to post-resurrection disciples.[29] In 15:26-27, the disciples' witnessing activity in conjunction with the Spirit is predicated on their having been with Jesus "from the beginning," a possible allusion to the twelve. In the context of the Fourth Gospel, this points to those disciples who had been called by Jesus at the beginning of his public ministry (cf. 1:37-43) and had persevered in following him (cf. 6:60-71). But does that mean that the Fourth Gospel presents the task of witnessing as limited to the twelve or to those who followed Jesus during his earthly ministry? At first glance, this seems to be the case, since witnessing is in the Fourth Gospel usually related to the historical Jesus (cf. 1:7, 8, 15, 32, 34; 3:11, 26, 28, 32; 15:26-27; 19:35; 21:24) and since the term "witness" (μαρτυρέω) is frequently in the Johannine writings tied to "seeing" (cf. 3:11, 32; 19:35; 1 John 1:1-3; 4:14).

However, as has been argued, the twelve, as well as the μαθηταί of John's Gospel in general, besides retaining their historical point of reference, also function as representatives of Jesus' Messianic community. Thus the responsibility of witnessing, while given primarily to Jesus' first disciples, derivatively also extends to later generations of believers.[30] Still, it is only on the basis of the word of the first disciples that later believers are able to bear witness (cf. 17:20). This line between first and later generations of believers drawn in John's Gospel also serves the function of authorizing the witness of the first disciples, including that of the fourth evangelist.

---

28. Schnackenburg, 3:207.

29. Cf. Siker-Gieseler, who contends that the Fourth Gospel's *disciples* are largely negative models while persons embodying *discipleship,* such as the Samaritan woman or the man born blind, are positive reflections of what it will mean to follow Jesus after his departure. However, this distinction can hardly be sustained. Certainly the concept of *discipleship* in the Fourth Gospel is also related to the Fourth Gospel's *disciples.* After all, only the characters designated "disciples" are traced in the Fourth Gospel from their "coming" to Jesus over their "following" Jesus to their being "sent" by Jesus. It would be better to distinguish between pre- and post-glorification disciples. Cf. also Moreno.

30. Cf. D. A. Carson, *The Gospel According to John* (Grand Rapids: Wm. B. Eerdmans, 1991), 529; Matthew Vellanickal, "Evangelization in the Johannine Writings," in *Good News and Witness,* ed. Lucien Legrand, J. Pathrapankal, and Matthew Vellanickal (Bangalore: Theological Publications in India, 1973), 142-46.

Stott keeps those dimensions in proper balance when he distinguishes between the "primary witness" of the apostles and the "secondary" and "subordinate" witness of later believers:

> We have no liberty to preach Jesus Christ according to our own fantasy, or even according to our own experience. Our personal witness does indeed corroborate the witness of the biblical authors, especially that of the apostles. *But theirs is the primary witness,* for they were "with Jesus" and knew him, and they have borne witness to what they heard with their ears and saw with their eyes. Our witness is always secondary and subordinate to theirs.[31]

Indeed, the original disciples are to witness to what they have heard and seen. Yet, as may be inferred from 20:29, faith in Jesus after his ascension will be based on hearing the apostolic message regarding Jesus rather than seeing Jesus. And such hearing, too, must result in witnessing to what one has heard.[32] In characteristic Johannine dual reference, the healed blind man's statement, "Once I was blind, but now I see" (9:25), too, has overtones of spiritual "seeing" (cf. 9:39-41). Thus physical seeing by those who have been with Jesus from the beginning is not a necessary prerequisite for witnessing.

Similarly, Jesus' statement to his disciples that the coming παράκλητος would teach them all things and bring to their remembrance all that Jesus had told them (cf. 14:26; cf. also 16:12-15), while originally referring to the first disciples, probably also extends derivatively to later believers. These later believers will, through the instrumentality of the original disciples, be taught all things and be "reminded" of all Jesus had said.[33]

Do the privileges and responsibilities conferred upon the first followers of Jesus therefore extend also to post-resurrection disciples? On the one hand, the Fourth Gospel preserves the original disciples' historical function as witnesses to the historical Jesus. The notion is retained that they alone followed Jesus during his earthly ministry, including his crucifixion and resurrection (cf. 18:19; 19:35; 20:30). This historic specificity also extends to the references in the Farewell Discourse regarding "the little while" during which Jesus would be absent and "the little while" for which he would be reunited with his disciples (cf. 7:33; 12:35; 13:33; 14:19; 16:16-19) or even to the fourth evangelist himself (cf. 21:24). Thus the general references in the Fourth Gospel to believers should not be taken to imply that all boundary lines between the first and later disciples

---

31. Cf. John R. W. Stott, *Christian Mission in the Modern World* (London: Church Pastoral Aid Society, 1975), 48.

32. The importance of trusting in Jesus' *word* is already related to "the Twelve" (cf. 6:68). It is again noted in 17:20, where the original disciples have become the bearers of Jesus' word to others.

33. Carson, *Gospel According to John,* 505, may draw the line a bit too sharply when he writes, "[T]he promise of v. 26 has in view the Spirit's role to the first generation of disciples, not to all subsequent Christians."

are removed. On the other hand, the original disciples, while primary, also function in John's Gospel as representatives and models for later generations of believers. Thus what is *primarily* true for Jesus' original followers, extends *derivatively* also to later believers.

These observations have important implications for the study of the Fourth Gospel's teaching on mission. For example, the major "sending" passages in the Fourth Gospel (cf. 4:38, 17:18, and 20:21), while originally referring to the first followers of Jesus, extend, due to this group's representative function, also to later believers. Indeed, all those who believe in Jesus will form the newly created Messianic community. The eleven are merely its first historic representatives. Therefore all believers, too, are sent into the world to bear witness to Jesus (cf. 17:18, 20). Moreover, all believers are to pattern their relationship with Jesus, *their* sender, after Jesus' relationship with *his* sender, the Father (cf. 20:21).

The reference to the "greater works" also pertains to every believer regardless of his or her position before or after Jesus' cross and resurrection (cf. 14:12).[34] Moreover, numerous benefits are extended indiscriminately to every believer. For example, every believer has the privilege of becoming a child of God (cf. 1:12) and of receiving the gift of eternal life (cf. 3:16; 20:31). Likewise, many responsibilities are given to every believer alike. Thus all of Jesus' disciples share the duty of serving one another (cf. 13:14-17), of loving one another (cf. 13:35), of obeying Jesus' commandments (cf. 15:14), and of living with one another in unity (cf. 17:20-25).

In the original historical setting, the important question arose of what it meant to "follow" Jesus after his physical departure. The answer was that following Jesus would be possible by the Spirit whom Jesus would send. This Spirit would continue many of the same functions Jesus had fulfilled while physically with his disciples (cf. 14:16-17). The Johannine widening of the term "disciple" to include later believers together with Jesus' original followers is an important device used by the fourth evangelist in order to facilitate the transition from the followers of Jesus during his earthly ministry to those disciples who would depend on the witness of the original disciples. The relationship of later disciples to their glorified Lord, already anticipated in 14:12 and chapter 15, is thus shown to be mediated by the first disciples. Both original and later disciples, in turn, are united in their believing, dependent relationship with their glorified Lord by the Spirit.

The fourth evangelist also asserts the primacy of Jesus' first followers by exercising his own witnessing role while at the same time pointing out the important connection between original and later disciples. Perhaps the insistence in 1:37-43 that even the original disciples came to believe in Jesus through the witness of another can be seen in this context. The word of the risen Lord himself in 20:29, "Blessed are those who have not seen and yet

---

34. See the discussion of 14:12 below.

believe," functions as a further indication that having been a follower of the historical Jesus does not guarantee faith in him. Jesus elevates "believing" over mere "seeing," rebuking Thomas's unbelief. The superiority of believing over mere seeing was doubtless of great importance for the first and subsequent readers of the Gospel.

Moreover, there seems to be a progression in the characterization of the disciples from the first to the second part of the Gospel. While the disciples are in chapters 1–12 set in relation to the earthly Jesus, chapters 13–21 find them as participants with the Father, the exalted Jesus, and the Spirit in their mission. Their love for one another as well as their being sent into the world are shown to be grounded in the Father-Son relationship between Jesus and his sender (cf. 13:35; 17:18; 20:21). This transformation of followers and disciples of the earthly Jesus into representatives of the exalted Jesus (cf. 13:16, 20; 15:20) is made possible by Jesus' "glorification" and follows Jesus' return to the Father.

The second part of the Fourth Gospel also shows a change from a teacher-disciple relationship between Jesus and his followers to a more intimate relationship, as is indicated by the more endearing terms used by Jesus for his followers (ἴδιοι in 13:1; τεκνία in 13:33; φίλοι in 15:15; τοῖς ἀνθρώποις οὓς ἔδωκάς μοι in 17:6 and τὰ ἐμά in 17:10; ἀδελφοί in 20:17; and παιδία in 21:4-5).[35] However, even at the end of the Gospel Jesus' disciples are still called to "follow" Jesus (cf. 21:19, 22).

Two more aspects of Johannine characterization remain to be discussed, i.e., the characterization of individual disciples in the Fourth Gospel and corporate metaphors. A study of the Johannine characterization of individual disciples, especially that of Peter and of the Beloved Disciple, is important since such an investigation will help clarify whether passages regarding the mission of individual disciples in John's Gospel should be restricted to these individuals or whether these disciples should be regarded as having a representative function for later believers as well.

4. Johannine Characterization of Individual Disciples

a. Introduction

Johannine characterization, i.e., the fourth evangelist's literary development of characters featured in the Fourth Gospel, is a subject that has attracted considerable attention in recent years. Collins seeks to show that the Fourth Gospel

---

35. Regarding ἴδιοι, cf. 1:11, where reference is made to Jesus' "own" who "did not receive him." As Pryor, *John: Evangelist*, 55, contends, the probable reference to Israel in 1:11 may be set in antithesis to 13:1, where ἴδιοι refers to Jesus' disciples. Moreover, Jesus' use of ἴδιοι for his own disciples in the second part of the Gospel is already foreshadowed by the reference to Jesus' "own sheep" (τὰ ἴδια or τὰ ἴδια πρόβατα; cf. 10:3, 4, 12) in contrast to "the Jews" who do not belong to Jesus' "sheep" (οὐκ ἐστὲ ἐκ τῶν προβάτων τῶν ἐμῶν).

was originally a series of homilies highlighting the faith response of certain individuals, with the goal of strenghtening the faith of the "Johannine community."[36] He contends that each original homily selected a particular individual as a type of faith or lack of faith in Jesus. However, of the fifteen figures Collins identifies, not all appear to fit this pattern.[37] Does only Philip represent "the disciple who misunderstands" in the Fourth Gospel?[38] Is it accurate to consider Mary as the one who "symbolizes the one who faithfully awaits the messianic times"?[39] On a larger scale, Collins's work appears to be aimed at shifting the emphasis from the Fourth Gospel's Christology to reader-response patterns.

Nevertheless, there appear to be a number of characters in the Fourth Gospel who, besides representing historical persons, are used by the fourth evangelist to show the issues involved in a person's becoming a disciple of Jesus or growing into such discipleship. One writer names the Samaritan woman (from questioning Jesus to leading others to Jesus), the Capernaum official (the issue of giving priority to faith in Jesus as a person over "signs"), the man born blind (progressive understanding and faith), and Martha (right confession but not necessarily an adequate grasp of who Jesus is) as figures fulfilling this function.[40] Thus persons other than Jesus' disciples (μαθηταί) may be used by the fourth evangelist to teach about "discipleship."

b. Peter and the Beloved Disciple

For the purposes of the present study, the most important aspect of Johannine characterization is the fourth evangelist's development of the characters of Peter and the Beloved Disciple.[41] This development is sustained throughout the

36. Cf. Collins, 1-45 and 56-78.

37. The figures Collins identifies are: John the Baptist, Nathanael, Mary (the mother of Jesus), Nicodemus, the Samaritan woman, the royal official, the lame man, Philip, the man born blind, Lazarus, Judas, Mary Magdalene, Thomas, Peter, and the Beloved Disciple. Each of the homilies, according to Collins, highlight one core characteristic in these persons' faith. Thus John the Baptist is a type of the witness to Jesus; Nathanael is the true, Scripture-literate Israelite (in contrast to "the Jews"); Nicodemus is a type of the (Jewish) unbeliever (cf. also Collins's separate article, "Jesus' Conversation with Nicodemus"); the Samaritan woman is a type of the Christian messenger who brings others to faith in Jesus; etc.

38. Collins, 25.

39. Collins, 32-33.

40. Cf. Siker-Gieseler, 215-20. To Siker-Gieseler's list other figures such as Nicodemus or disciples like Thomas may be added. On Nicodemus, cf. Jouette M. Bassler, "Mixed Signals: Nicodemus in the Fourth Gospel," *JBL* 108 (1989): 635-46.

41. Cf. also the interesting suggestion by J. S. Billings, "Judas Iscariot in the Fourth Gospel," *ExpTim* 51 (1939-40): 156-57, who argues that the Fourth Gospel's characterization of Judas as ὁ υἱὸς τῆς ἀπωλείας indicates that the fourth evangelist saw the antichrist (referred to by the same term in 2 Thess. 2:3) as already incarnate in Judas in the light of the Fourth Gospel's realized eschatology (cf. also 6:70, where Judas is called διάβολος; 12:4, where he is called a robber; and 13:11, where he is called "unclean"). Another possible representative type of characterization is the

Gospel, culminating in the concluding pericope (21:15-23).[42] This consistent characterization of Peter in relation to the Beloved Disciple appears to point to the Gospel's coherent perspective, which would have remained incomplete had the final chapter not been included.[43] The major interest of the present monograph is whether the characterization of these two figures involves their function as representative characters for the readers of John's Gospel. If this were in fact the case, it would be highly relevant for the Fourth Gospel's teaching on mission, since Peter and the Beloved Disciple would be invested with a message transcending their historical significance.

Generally, it appears that that the fourth evangelist probably wanted to convey a particular understanding of the relationship between Peter and the Beloved Disciple, since the Beloved Disciple is in all but one occurrence closely identified with Peter (cf. 1:37-42; 6:68-70; 13:6-10, 23-25, 36-38; 18:15-18, 25-27; 19:26-27, 35; 20:2-10; 21:7-24).[44] The question remains, however, what kind of relationship the Fourth Gospel ascribes to Peter and the Beloved Disciple. This relationship has been variably described as one of rivalry, as that of assuming the same basic function in their respective communities, as that of differentiated roles, or as essentially unrelated.

One of the proponents of the view that Peter and the Beloved Disciple are cast in terms of rivalry speaks of the strong "anti-Petrinism" of the Fourth Gospel. This writer argues that "the figure of the Beloved Disciple, as one more authoritative than the other disciples, especially those later designated as apostles, is an

---

emphasis on one disciple's leading another person to Jesus in chapter 1 (cf. Culpepper, 115-16). It is especially Andrew who is cast as leading others to Jesus: his own brother (cf. 1:41); a boy (cf. 6:8); and the "Greeks" (cf. 12:22). On Andrew in the Fourth Gospel, cf. Peter M. Peterson, *Andrew, Brother of Simon Peter: His History and His Legends,* NovTSup 1 (Leiden: E. J. Brill, 1963), 4-5. Other figures include Nathanael, the "true Israelite" (cf. Paul Trudinger, "An Israelite in whom there is no Guile: An Interpretative Note on John 1, 45-51," *EvQ* 54 [1982]: 117-20) and Thomas, a disciple who demands tangible evidence for believing (cf. Culpepper, 123-24).

42. Quast. Cf. also the helpful study by Thorwald Lorenzen, *Der Lieblingsjünger im Johannesevangelium: Eine redaktionsgeschichtliche Studie,* SBS 55 (Stuttgart: Katholisches Bibelwerk, 1971); and Collins, 46-55. A recent study on the characterization of the Beloved Disciple in the Fourth Gospel is William S. Kurz, "The Beloved Disciple and Implied Readers: A Socio-Narratological Approach," *BTB* 19 (1989): 100-107.

43. Cf. Culpepper, 96; Paul S. Minear, "The Original Functions of John 21," *JBL* 102 (1983): 85-98; Willem S. Vorster, "The Growth and Making of John 21," in *The Four Gospels 1992: Festschrift Frans Neirynck,* BETL C, ed. F. van Segbroeck, C. M. Tuckett, G. van Belle, and J. Verheyden, vol. 3 (Leuven: University Press, 1992), 2207-21. Minear argues that only John 21 provides a sense of closure regarding the relationship between Peter and the Beloved Disciple (91-93); and that chapter 21 clarifies the relationship between the fourth evangelist and the Beloved Disciple (95). Cf. also Gabriel M. Napole, "Pedro y el discípulo amado en Juan 21,1-25," *RevistB* 52, NS 39 (1990): 153-77, who points to the *inclusio* between 21:1 and 14 and the chiasm between 20:30-31 and 21:24-25.

44. The references to "another disciple" in 18:15-16 and 20:2-8 should probably be taken as referring to the Beloved Disciple, since 20:2 combines both expressions (τὸν ἄλλον μαθητὴν ὃν ἐφίλει ὁ Ἰησοῦς). Moreover, Peter and the Beloved Disciple/other disciple are consistently featured jointly in the Fourth Gospel, as the present discussion shows.

absolute necessity to the structure of the Gospel of John."[45] Moreton maintains that "the figure of the beloved disciple in the Fourth Gospel is basically a device, intended to correct a growing reverence for Peter."[46] Agourides, too, contends "that its [the Fourth Gospel's] author or editors were trying to combat the prestige and authority of Peter among the readers to whom the Gospel was addressed, on the basis of the superior position of this 'beloved disciple' of Jesus."[47] According to Agourides, "one of the aims of the Evangelist was to correct certain false impressions in the Church concerning the position of Peter, interpretations based perhaps on texts of the synoptic tradition such as Matt. 16, 18."[48] Brown suggests that the Beloved Disciple's portrayal in the Fourth Gospel seeks to counteract the dominance of "the Twelve" in the developing church.[49]

Many see Peter and the Beloved Disciple as assuming the same basic function in their respective communities. Bultmann interprets the Beloved Disciple as an ideal figure representative of Gentile Christianity and Peter of Jewish Christianity, an interpretation that is integral to his basic understanding of the Gospel.[50] Watty views the portrayal of the anonymous Beloved Disciple as the "response to a pastoral situation which seems to have necessitated a corrective to a developing Petrine tradition."[51] Similarly, a group of interpreters believes "the [Johannine] community secured its own position by placing the Beloved Disciple alongside Simon Peter. . . . Chapter 21 is not an attack on the pastoral authority of Peter; it is a demand for the recognition of another type of discipleship, just as authentic as that of the original apostles."[52] Gunther understands the superiority of the Beloved Disciple in the Johannine tradition in terms of spiritual insight, perception, and interpretation of the events of the life of Jesus.[53] Quast, taking his cue from 1 John 2:19, hypothesizes that the schism of Johannine community led to its absorption either into the apostolic churches or gnosticism. The death of the Beloved Disciple, according to Quast,

---

45. Cf. Graydon F. Snyder, "John 13.16 and the Anti-Petrinism of the Johannine Tradition," *BibRes* 16 (1971): 14.

46. Cf. M. B. Moreton, "The Beloved Disciple Again," in *Studia Biblica 1978. II. Papers on the Gospels,* JSNTSup 2, ed. E. A. Livingstone (Sheffield: JSOT, 1980), 218.

47. Cf. Savas Agourides, "Peter and John in the Fourth Gospel," in *SE IV,* ed. Frank L. Cross (Berlin: Akademie, 1968), 3.

48. Agourides, 3.

49. Brown is, of course, supposing that the Beloved Disciple was not a member of "the Twelve." Cf. Brown, *Community of the Beloved Disciple,* 191.

50. Cf. Rudolf Bultmann, *The Gospel of John* (Oxford: Basil Blackwell, 1971), 483-85; followed by Margaret Pamment, "The Fourth Gospel's Beloved Disciple," *ExpTim* 94 (1983): 363-67.

51. Cf. William W. Watty, "The Significance of Anonymity in the Fourth Gospel," *ExpTim* 90 (1979): 209-12.

52. Cf. Raymond E. Brown, Karl P. Donfried, and John Reumann, eds., *Peter in the New Testament* (Minneapolis, Minn.: Augsburg, 1973), 147.

53. Cf. John J. Gunther, "The Relation of the Beloved Disciple to the Twelve," *TZ* 37 (1981): 135.

led the final editors, representatives of the Johannine Community, to look at Peter as a potential figure for identification.[54] Thus, according to Quast, the Fourth Gospel "confronts an exclusivist attitude within the Johannine community" and constitutes an effort to bring apostolic and Johannine Christians together (cf. especially John 21).[55]

Others see the relationship between Peter and the Beloved Disciple in the Fourth Gospel as one of differentiated roles. As Hartin notes, the relationship is not one "of rivalry, nor of opposition," but rather "each has a distinctive function to perform."[56] Kragerud sees the Beloved Disciple as the representative of a pneumatic circle *(Geist)* while Peter functions as the holder of an ecclesiastical office *(Amt)*.[57] Lindars distinguishes between the "prophetic ministry" of the Beloved Disciple and the local "pastoral ministry" of Peter.[58] Thus the "rivalry" is not in terms of competition but in terms of differentiation of functions. Peter's ecclesiastical authority contrasts with the Beloved Disciple's didactic authority.

Yet others do not detect any rivalry at all between Peter and the Beloved Disciple in the Fourth Gospel. These scholars argue that the Beloved Disciple may be symbolically significant while not being in direct relationship with Peter.[59] Culpepper views the Beloved Disciple as "the ideal disciple, the paradigm of discipleship."[60] F.-M. Braun maintains that the Beloved Disciple is not a rival to Peter, but the image of the believer in his love, faith, and attachment to Jesus.[61] Peter serves as a subordinate spokesman, representing the twelve in the common tradition. Cullmann asserts that the Fourth Gospel "nowhere attempts to deny directly the special role of Peter within the group of disciples. It only has the tendency to lessen this role, in so far as it seeks to show that beside the unique position of Peter there is the somewhat different special role of the 'Beloved Disciple.' "[62]

---

54. Cf. Quast, 165-70.

55. Cf. Quast, 170. However, Quast appears to move too easily from the rhetoric of the text to a supposed situation in the life of the community.

56. Cf. P. J. Hartin, "The Role of Peter in the Fourth Gospel," *Neot* 24 (1990): 58.

57. Alv Kragerud, *Der Lieblingsjünger im Johannesevangelium: Ein exegetischer Versuch* (Hamburg: Grosshaus Wegner, 1959), 65-67.

58. Cf. Barnabas Lindars, *The Gospel of John*, NCBC (Grand Rapids: Wm. B. Eerdmans, 1981 [1972]), 602.

59. Cf. Schnackenburg who sees a relationship of coordination and mutual recognition between the Beloved Disciple and Peter. The association of the anonymous Beloved Disciple with Peter would increase the former's prestige. Cf. "Der Jünger, den Jesus liebte," in EKKNT.V, vol. 2 (Zürich: Neukirchener, 1970), 105-7.

60. Cf. Culpepper, 121. He observes, "He [the Beloved Disciple] has no misunderstandings." The Beloved Disciple could, however, be viewed as included in the misunderstandings of the Fourth Gospel's disciples (cf. 2:22; 4:33; 11:12; 12:16; 16:17-18; 20:9; cf. also 13:22).

61. Cf. François-Marie Braun, *Jean le théologien et son évangile dans l'Église Ancienne* (Paris: J. Gabalda, 1959), 302-3, 327.

62. Cf. Oscar Cullmann, *Peter: Disciple, Apostle, Martyr* (London: SCM, 1976), 27.

Indeed, a discussion of the relationship between Peter and the Beloved Disciple merely in terms of "rivalry" or "contrast" may be too simplistic. On the one hand, it appears likely that the fourth evangelist conceived of the Beloved Disciple, like Peter, as a historical figure. This can be seen, for example, in the passion narrative, where both figures function side by side. It is difficult to imagine a procedure that would have inserted the Beloved Disciple as an ideal figure alongside Peter, a historical figure. At the same time, the fourth evangelist appears to invest these two figures also with representative roles.[63]

This can be seen especially in those passages where explicit parallels or analogies are established between Jesus on the one hand and Peter or the Beloved Disciple on the other. Regarding the Beloved Disciple, the major analogy is that of his closeness to Jesus (cf. 13:23: ἐν τῷ κόλπῳ τοῦ ᾽Ιησοῦ), similar to Jesus' closeness to the Father (cf. 1:18: ὁ ὢν εἰς τὸν κόλπον τοῦ πατρός). This analogy, an unmistakable allusion, is accentuated by the fact that both of these references occur at the respective openings of the two parts of the Gospel and by the fact that the Beloved Disciple is only introduced by that designation in the second part of the Gospel.

Jesus' closeness to the Father is presented in 1:18 as providing the perfect qualification and legitimization for Jesus to "narrate" (ἐξηγήσατο) the Father. The Beloved Disciple is, on the surface level of the narrative, simply physically closer to Jesus and thus in a position to pass on another's inquiry to his Master. But in light of Johannine multilayered language, it is hard to escape the notion that 13:23, in allusion to 1:18, also presents the Beloved Disciple, who is later identified as the Fourth Gospel's author (cf. 21:24), as in a position of proximity to Jesus that enables him to provide a close-up account of the life and mission of the Messiah.[64]

The major analogy between Jesus and Peter concerns the kinds of deaths Jesus and Peter were to die. The fourth evangelist's comment on Jesus' death is worded thus: τοῦτο δὲ ἔλεγεν σημαίνων ποίῳ θανάτῳ ἤμελλεν ἀποθνῄσκειν

---

63. Cf. Brown, *Community of the Beloved Disciple*, 83: "The Beloved Disciple was no less a real human being than was Simon Peter, but the Fourth Gospel uses each of them in a paradigmatic capacity."

64. Cf. Schnackenburg's comment, quoted in Lorenzen, 100, n. 11: "Er [the Beloved Disciple] galt ihnen als zuverlässiger Traditionsträger, mehr noch als der geisterleuchtete Künder und Deuter der Botschaft Jesu." Note, however, that the term used for Jesus is "narrate" (cf. 1:18) while the expression used for the Beloved Disciple is "witness" (cf. 19:35; 21:24-25). But in 18:37 it is also said of Jesus that he came to "witness to the truth." There may also be a relationship between the roles of "John" (i.e., the Baptist) and of the Beloved Disciple, both of whose functions it is to witness to Jesus. John 1–12 may be considered as presenting Jesus as witnessed to by John (the Baptist), while John 13–21 may be seen as portraying Jesus as witnessed to by the Beloved Disciple. Note also that both John and the Beloved Disciple were aided in this witnessing role by the Spirit (cf. 1:32-33; 15:26-27). John's role was "to baptize with water" with the purpose "that he [Jesus] might be revealed to Israel." Perhaps this is still the (primary) purpose of the Beloved Disciple in his writing of the Gospel.

(12:33). Peter's death is spoken of in almost identical terms: τοῦτο δὲ εἶπεν σημαίνων ποίῳ θανάτῳ δοξάσει τὸν θεόν (21:19). In the context of 21:15-23, this kind of death is seen within the scope of yet another analogy between Jesus and Peter, i.e., their role as "shepherds." Jesus is presented as the "good shepherd" in chapter 10, while Peter is commissioned by Jesus in 21:15-17 to "tend" Jesus' "sheep" (Ποίμαινε τὰ πρόβατά μου; 21:16). Thus the disciple's calling extends to dying the same kind of death Jesus died — though in Peter's case without any atoning significance[65] — as well as to "shepherding" Jesus' "flock." In one sense, Peter's salvation-historical role as the one first commissioned by Jesus and the one leading the early church is distinct. Yet he also functions as a representative for subsequent believers, whom Jesus likewise calls to "shepherd" his people.

Another passage where the Beloved Disciple and Peter are featured together in the Fourth Gospel is 21:15-23. Whichever source- or redaction-critical explanations for the inclusion of this section in the final text of the Fourth Gospel may be given, it still remains to account for the theological reason why the final redactor included this pericope. At the culmination of the Fourth Gospel's consistent characterization of Peter and the Beloved Disciple in relation to one another, this passage characterizes the roles of Peter and of the Beloved Disciple with the accompanying exhortation that each disciple should fulfill the role assigned him by his Lord while not questioning the role of the other.

As a part of his overall presentation of mission, the fourth evangelist here shows that the two disciples, and the callings they represent, have different, complementary roles within the Messianic community's mission. The Beloved Disciple's role is that of bearing faithful witness to Jesus, a role the Beloved Disciple discharged, among other things, by writing the Fourth Gospel. Peter's ministry, too, has as a component the faithful bearing of witness to Jesus. His role is one of loving, faithful "shepherding" of Jesus' "flock"[66] and of bold, courageous witness ending in a violent, Christ-like (though not atoning), God-glorifying death.[67] Peter's role as a shepherd should probably not be seen as

65. On the issue of whether Peter's death was "for the community" or not, cf. Baumeister, 96, n. 50.

66. The emphasis is not on Peter's representative rule but on his obligation to love and care for Jesus' "flock." Cf. the Johannine characterization of Jesus as the shepherd who gives his life for his sheep (cf. 10:11, 15-18), who protects his own (cf. 10:28-29; cf. also 17:12), and who cares for those entrusted to him even beyond his physical presence with them (cf., e.g., Jesus' provision of care for his own mother; of the Spirit for the disciples; of salvation for the world; and of Peter for his "flock"). Cf. also the emphasis in 1 Pet. 5:2-3 on shepherding not by lording over the "flock" but by example; and the charge in Acts 20:28 for the elders to "watch over" their "flock" (i.e., provide spiritual protection; both passages share with John 21:15-17 the use of ποιμαίνω or variants). Cf. George Beasley-Murray, *John*, WBC 36 (Waco, Tex.: Word, 1987), 406-7.

67. Cf. Lindars, 637, who observes, "Peter's death is to reproduce the act by which Jesus most fully revealed God's glory . . . it reflects the meaning of Jesus' death, on the principle that true discipleship continues Jesus' mission (17.10)." As Carson, *Gospel According to John*, 678-79,

merely pastoral in the sense of nurturing believers only. Rather, as in the case of Jesus, the role of a shepherd also entails his bringing to the flock yet other dispersed sheep (cf. 10:16). Thus 21:15-23 transcends mere nurture of believers to include outreach to unbelievers.[68]

In light of the above observations it may be concluded that both Peter and the Beloved Disciple, in addition to having their historical and specific identities, also appear to fulfill a representative role in the Fourth Gospel. Thus their respective roles serve likewise as models for subsequent believers. As one surveys the Fourth Gospel, it appears that some duties are shown to pertain to every disciple of Jesus, such as the duty to obey Jesus and to love one's fellow-disciples, while other callings are specific to the individual disciple, such as certain kinds of witness, be it by pastoring or other forms of representing Jesus. This becomes apparent in the fourth evangelist's characterization of individual disciples, especially Peter and the Beloved Disciple.[69]

In both cases, the Fourth Gospel is careful to highlight both an analogous element between Jesus and the Beloved Disciple or Peter and yet to include hints regarding the limitations of this analogy.[70] Jesus, who is described in the Fourth Gospel as the unique Son, shares with the Beloved Disciple a proximity to the person they "narrate" or bear witness to. However, only Jesus is witnessed *to*. Jesus, the eschatological shepherd-teacher, and Peter both fulfill a shepherding role and die violent deaths. Yet only Jesus' death is of atoning significance.[71]

---

contends, Peter is given neither founding preeminence nor comparative authority. His is a rein-statement to service, not an elevation to primacy. The three pledges of loyalty to Jesus correspond to the three denials (cf. C. K. Barrett, *The Gospel according to St. John*, 2d ed. [Philadelphia: Westminster, 1978], 553). Cf. also Beasley-Murray, 405, who refers to the fact that Peter's "re-establishment [was] commensurable with the seriousness of the defection." Bultmann, *Gospel of John*, 714, notes that 21:19 echoes 13:36.

68. Cf. Beasley-Murray, 405, who refers to Jesus' preparation of Peter "for responsible leadership among the people of the Kingdom and for the mission to Israel and the nations," and who, commenting on 21:15-23, draws attention to "the aspect of the Shepherd's calling to seek the lost sheep and gather them into the flock, hence the aspect of *mission* (cf. 407, emphasis Beasley-Murray's)" Beasley-Murray concedes, however, that this is not the primary emphasis of John 21:15-17. Cf. also Barrett, 583, who contends: "The interest here lies not in the mission of the church (as in 20.21) but in leadership and pastoral care within it (Bultmann)." Cf. also Luke 21:32 and Peter's activities narrated in Acts 3 and 4.

69. It is more difficult to know *why* the fourth evangelist characterizes Peter and the Beloved Disciple the way he does, and *why* he seeks to impart the lessons described here. Did the fourth evangelist seek to correct an undue regard for Peter among his readers? It is true that this was part of the Corinthian problem (cf. the reference to a "Cephas party" in 1 Cor. 1:12). Certainty regarding this is elusive. But the lessons transcend any one historical setting, so that it may be best to emphasize the timeless lessons over a speculative *Sitz im Leben*.

70. Another analogy drawn between Jesus and the disciples, i.e., that of the way in which they are "sent" (cf. 17:18 and 20:21), is likewise not without its boundaries, as will be discussed below.

71. Perhaps the term "glorify," too, is deliberately used to focus on the revelatory rather than the atoning function of Peter's death. On this, cf. Baumeister, 97, n. 55.

Fig. 9. The Roles of the Beloved Disciple and Peter in Relation to Jesus

	Characterization of Jesus	*Analogous element*	*Limitation*
Jesus and the BD	the unique Son	a proximity to the person they narrate or bear witness to	only Jesus is witnessed *to*
Jesus and Peter	the eschatological shepherd-teacher	a shepherding role a violent death	only Jesus' death has atoning value

Before treating the disciples' task and the modes of movement in the disciples' mission according to the Fourth Gospel, one last aspect of the Fourth Gospel's treatment of the group of Jesus' followers remains, viz. its use of corporate metaphors.

C. Corporate Metaphors in the Fourth Gospel

The corporate metaphors used in the Fourth Gospel to describe the disciples include that of the "flock" and the "branches." The imagery of the flock pervades chapter 10, where Jesus is referred to as "the good shepherd" (ὁ ποιμὴν ὁ καλός), with his followers as "sheep" (τὰ πρόβατα). The metaphor of a "flock" (ποίμνη) in 10:16 occurs in the context of Jesus' desire of uniting his present "sheep" with yet other "sheep" in "one flock" under "one shepherd." References to the imminent "scattering" of Jesus' disciples (cf. 16:32: σκορπισθῆτε) and to Jesus' protection of his own (cf. 17:12: ἐτήρουν, ἐφύλαξα) also may imply the imagery of a flock. Finally, Jesus gives Peter charge over his "flock," appointing him as an undershepherd (21:15: βόσκε τὰ ἀρνία μου; 21:16: ποίμαινε τὰ πρόβατά μου; 21:17: βόσκε τὰ πρόβατά μου).[72]

At the outset, John's use of corporate metaphors appears to function as a device to balance the Fourth Gospel's emphasis on the individual with the communal dimension of a believer's life.[73] As is suggested in a recent study on the Fourth Gospel's Old Testament background, however, the Fourth Gospel's corporate metaphors may be part of a larger framework which casts the Fourth Gospel's disciples as God's new covenant people. This can be illustrated by the following examples:

---

72. For Old Testament references to Israel as God's "flock," cf., e.g., Ps. 23; Jer. 23:1; Ezek. 34:11; and Isa. 40:11.

73. Cf. Schnackenburg, *Gospel According to John*, 3:209; Dan O. Via, "Darkness, Christ and Church in the Fourth Gospel," *SJT* 14 (1961): 172-93. Contra C. F. D. Moule, "The Individualism of the Fourth Gospel," in *Essays in New Testament Interpretation* (Cambridge: Cambridge University Press, 1982), 91-109; and Schweizer, 371, who both view the Johannine corporate metaphors in the light of the Fourth Gospel's emphasis on the individual.

(1) the use of ἴδιοι in 1:11 with reference to Israel and in 13:1 with regard to Jesus' followers;[74]

(2) the insistence of 15:1 that Jesus is the "true" vine embodying the true Israel;[75]

(3) the "creation" of the new Messianic community by breathing on it the Spirit (cf. 20:22);[76]

(4) the Fourth Gospel's portrayal of Jesus as the Mosaic Prophet[77] (even though Jesus exceeds both Moses and Abraham categories in the Fourth Gospel: cf. 1:17; 8:58; chaps. 13–17 patterned after the book of Deuteronomy);[78]

(5) the implication of 1:51 that Jesus replaces Israel as the locus of the revelation of God's glory;[79]

(6) the use of "shepherd" and "flock" imagery for the relationship between Jesus and a community that transcends Jewish ethnic lines;[80]

(7) the claim that Jesus' glory "dwelt among us" (i.e., the Messianic community), in allusion to God's dwelling among his (old) covenant people, Israel (cf. 1:14);[81]

(8) the insistence that Jesus' sonship is unique (cf. the term μονογενής in 1:14, 18; 3:16, 18);[82] and

(9) the Fourth Gospel's adaptation of the covenantal terminology and patterns found in the primary texts of Judaism, i.e., Exodus and Deuteronomy.[83]

As this writer suggests, "For John, physical Israel is not the people of God (see on 11:48-52), nor did it ever properly have that status. . . . Israel was not in any sense God's own possession but simply that nation through whom the revelation and salvation of God would come (4:22). The true Israel . . . was yet

---

74. Pryor, *John: Evangelist*, 55.

75. Pryor, *John: Evangelist*, 64.

76. Pryor, *John: Evangelist*, 89.

77. Pryor, *John: Evangelist*, 119.

78. Pryor, *John: Evangelist*, 119-20. Cf. also Aelred Lacomara, "Deuteronomy and the Farewell Discourse (Jn 13:31–16:33)," *CBQ* 36 (1974): 65-84. But cf. Carson, *Gospel According to John*, 480, who notes that, unlike Moses, Jesus fully expected to return shortly so that the title "farewell discourse" only partially captures the occasion in John 14–16. Thus there is a point where the analogy between Jesus' and Moses' "farewell discourses" breaks down.

79. Pryor, *John: Evangelist*, 126.

80. Pryor, *John: Evangelist*, 158.

81. Pryor, *John: Evangelist*, 158.

82. Pryor, *John: Evangelist*, 130-31.

83. Pryor, *John: Evangelist*, 160 and 166. Pryor notes, for example, that the five major verb themes of 14:15-24 (to love, obey, live, know, and see) have their basis in the covenant theology of Exod. 33–34 and Deuteronomy (216, n. 8). Cf. also Edward Malatesta, *Interiority and Covenant: A Study of εἶναι ἐν and μένειν ἐν in the First Letter of Saint John*, AnBib 69 (Rome: Biblical Institute Press, 1978), 42-77.

to come in the person of Jesus. The people of God who gather in him . . . have no racially unifying factor. They are both Jew and Gentile and have only one thing in common, faith in Jesus Christ (1:12)." The Fourth Gospel's disciples appear thus to be conceived by the fourth evangelist as God's new covenant people.[84]

In light of this general framework, the Fourth Gospel's corporate metaphors can now be examined in greater detail. As mentioned, the imagery of the flock is most prominent in chapter 10. There the fourth evangelist casts Jesus as the fulfillment of the Messianic promise, i.e., as the Messianic shepherd in contrast to the faithless leaders of the Jewish people (cf. Ezek. 34:23-24; Zech. 13:7-9).[85] Remarkably, the impact of the Messianic shepherd transcends the boundaries of ethnic Israel, even to the extent that ethnic Jews can be said not to be of Jesus' sheep (10:26; cf. 8:31-59). This opens a new horizon of prophecy. The fulfillment is not only explication, but also transposition of the original promise.[86] In continuity with, even in escalation of, the Old Testament theme of the faithlessness of Israel's leaders, "the Jews" fail to believe in Jesus. Those who do believe, on the other hand, know themselves to be a new community, belonging to the Messianic eschatological shepherd. These believers, while still being Jews, no longer define themselves by their ethnic background but rather simply by their faith in Jesus. This perspective opens up the possibility of membership in the Messianic community to a universal and diverse group of people, a fact that would be further accentuated if the "other sheep" in 10:16 were to be interpreted as Gentiles.[87]

---

84. In this, the fourth evangelist does not differ substantially from the other evangelists. Cf., e.g., the conclusion by Gerhard Maier, "The Church in the Gospel of Matthew: Hermeneutical Analysis of the Current Debate," in *Biblical Interpretation and the Church: Text and Context,* ed. D. A. Carson (Exeter: Paternoster, 1984), 60: "When we speak about the 'church in Matthew's Gospel' we do not mean a church which is fundamentally different from the 'church in John's Gospel' and so on. Rather it has become clear that Jesus established 'the church' very much in the sense of the New Testament covenant community and with common characteristics in its various local manifestations."

85. Cf. Schnackenburg, *Gospel According to St. John,* 3:210. Contra Günter Reim, *Studien zum alttestamentlichen Hintergrund des Johannesevangeliums,* SNTSMS 22 (Cambridge: Cambridge University Press, 1974), 183-86. Cf. also Birger Gerhardsson, *The Good Samaritan — The Good Shepherd?* ConNT 16 (Lund: Gleerup, 1958), 1-31, who contends that John 10:1-16 is a Messianic midrash on Ezek. 34; and the bibliographical references given in the discussion of Jesus as the eschatological shepherd-teacher in Chapter 3.

86. Cf. Schnackenburg, *Gospel According to St. John,* 3:211.

87. Cf. Schnackenburg, "Johannine Ecclesiology," 251. The reference to "other sheep" in 10:16 refers back to 10:1-5, where Jesus speaks of "sheep" following him out of the "sheep pen" of Judaism. Thus, as Carson, *Gospel According to John,* 390, contends, the category presupposed by "other sheep" is Gentiles. Contra Robinson, *Twelve New Testament Studies,* SBT 34 (London: SCM, 1962), 114-15. J. Louis Martyn's thesis that the "other sheep" are Christians in other Christian communities who have been scattered by the persecution of the 80s appears needlessly anachronistic (*The Gospel of John in Christian History: Essays for Interpreters* (New York: Paulist, 1978), 115-21). Brown, "Other Sheep," 5-22, developing Martyn's thesis further, claims to be able to "read

In terms of individual discipleship as well as in terms of belonging to the corporate Messianic community, the criteria for membership in the new Messianic community have been extended beyond ethnic boundaries to assume universal dimensions. Indeed, one may view the entire Gospel as a presentation of the movement from old definitions of discipleship and belonging to the people of God to a new understanding of such categories. Judaism is viewed as a system that has been transcended by the appearance of the Messiah, which left Judaism an empty shell and exposed its futile adherence to customs now obsolete as well as its clinging to power that would soon be gone. Even the figures Judaism claimed as its own founding fathers, Abraham and Moses, Jesus denied to them by claiming that these characters pointed toward himself and were preparatory for him.[88]

The metaphor of the "vine" (ἄμπελος) and the "branches" (τὰ κλήματα) pervades chapter 15.[89] The barely concealed reference to Israel (cf. Isa. 5:1-7; 27:2-6; Jer. 2:21; Ezek. 15; 19:10-14; Hos. 10:1; Ps. 80:9-16) casts Jesus as the true vine, i.e., the representative of Israel, and his disciples as the branches, i.e., participants in Jesus, the "new" Israel.[90] The Father is the "vinedresser" as well as the one to whose glory the disciples are to "bear fruit." The metaphor of the vine illustrates even more vividly than that of the shepherd and his flock the unity between Jesus and his disciples.[91] The fourth evangelist emphasizes that

off" six different groups from the Fourth Gospel: the synagogue of "the Jews"; crypto-Christians; Jewish Christians; Christians of apostolic churches; Johannine Christians; and secessionist Johannine Christians. He identifies the "other sheep" of 10:16 with Christians of apostolic churches with which the Johannine Christians hoped to be reconciled and ecclesiastically united. However, this hypothesis, too, appears unduly speculative.

88. Thus Klaus Haacker, *Die Stiftung des Heils: Untersuchungen zur Struktur der johanneischen Theologie* (Stuttgart: Calwer, 1972), properly draws attention to the "founder motif" in the Fourth Gospel. It seems unwarranted, however, to characterize Jesus and Moses exclusively in those terms. The Fourth Gospel presents Jesus not just as the antitype of the Moses typology but also as the true heir of Abraham and the replacement of many Jewish institutions and festivals. On Moses and exodus typology in the Fourth Gospel, cf. also Jacob J. Enz, "The Book of Exodus as a Literary Type for the Gospel of John," *JBL* 76 (1957): 208-15, T. Francis Glasson, *Moses in the Fourth Gospel*, SBT 40 (London: SCM, 1963); Marinus de Jonge, "Jesus as Prophet and King in the Fourth Gospel," *ETL* 49 (1973): 160-77; Wayne A. Meeks, *The Prophet-King: Moses Traditions and the Johannine Christology*, NovTSup 14 (Leiden: E. J. Brill, 1967); Rudolf Schnackenburg, "Die Erwartung des 'Propheten' nach dem Neuen Testament und den Qumran-Texten," in *SE I*, TU 73, ed. Frank L. Cross (Berlin: Akademie, 1959), 622-39; Robert H. Smith, "Exodus Typology in the Fourth Gospel," *JBL* 81 (1962): 329-42.

89. Cf. Corell, 26-29.

90. Cf. Pryor, "Covenant and Community," 49; contra Rainer Borig, *Der wahre Weinstock. Untersuchungen zu Jo 15,1-10*, SANT 16 (München: Kösel, 1967). Pryor's view that 15:1-17 sees "the JohCom . . . in Israel categories" is doubtful; it seems more likely that the community of believers in general is in view. Cf. now also Pryor's book *John: Evangelist of the Covenant People* in which the author develops his insights in greater detail; and the summary and interaction with Pryor above.

91. Some have seen this passage as the Johannine equivalent to the Pauline "body of Christ" metaphor in the way it expresses the organic unity between Christ and his disciples (cf. Schweizer,

Jesus is not merely the person in whom the faith of his followers is rooted but that he should also be the continuing source of nurture and strength in the life of individual believers and of the community.[92]

Thus both the "flock" and the "vine" metaphors accentuate elements of unity between Jesus and his followers. One may also detect another common element between these metaphors. In both of these allegories, one finds a reference to Jesus' giving of his life for others (cf. 10:11, 15, 17, 18; 15:13). These passages thus appear to underscore the significance of Jesus' death for the community's birth and subsequent life.[93] Moreover, both metaphors are significant for John's teaching on mission. The shepherd motif of chapter 10 is applied to Peter in 21:15-17, while the vine metaphor of chapter 15 is linked with references to the disciples' "going" and bearing of fruit (cf. 15:8, 16). These two connections indicate that the circle begun with Jesus' death is not closed until his redeemed community goes and accomplishes its mission.

The expression "his own" (οἱ ἴδιοι), while not metaphoric, should also be included in the present discussion, since it frequently occurs in close connection with the Fourth Gospel's corporate metaphors. For example, the expression is found in relation to the shepherd motif in 10:3 (cf. also 10:12, 14; cf. further 17:6, 10). The phrase also stands programmatically at the beginning of both the first and the second parts of the Gospel (cf. 1:11; 13:1).[94] The expression accentuates both the close relationship between Jesus and his covenant community and the disciples' distinctness from the world (cf. 17:6a; see also 15:18-25). Thus Jesus' "own," i.e., both original disciples and later believers, are to define their identity in relation to the Father and Jesus on the one hand and in relation to the world on the other (cf. 14:16-17). The Father and Jesus are to be the disciples' constant source of strength and sustenance (cf. 15:5; 17:16), while the world is alien territory, hostile to Jesus and his followers. Nevertheless, the disciples, like Jesus, are sent into the world (cf. 3:16; 17:18). As one writer notes, "The disciples were commissioned as a group to continue the mission

---

368-70; Haacker, "Jesus und die Kirche," 183). However, in contrast to Paul who develops the body metaphor primarily in terms of the relationship of the various members to one another (but cf., e.g., Eph. 5:21-33 where besides this metaphor a second one, that of the body's relationship to the "head," i.e., Jesus Christ, is used; cf. Edmund P. Clowney, "Interpreting the Biblical Models of the Church: A Hermeneutical Deepening of Ecclesiology," in *Biblical Interpretation and the Church,* ed. D. A. Carson [Exeter: Paternoster, 1984], 81), John focuses on the necessary connection of each individual to Jesus. Nevertheless, there are similarities between the Pauline metaphor and Johannine imagery. Both presuppose that the historical Jesus has become the exalted, glorified Christ, who will continue and extend his work through his disciples.

92. Cf. Schnackenburg, *Gospel According to St. John,* 3:212. Cf. also Pryor, "Covenant and Community," 49-50, who notes the term μένειν in chapter 15 and other texts in the Fourth Gospel. Following Malatesta, *Interiority and Covenant,* he argues that this term (as well as εἶναι ἐν) suggests the presence of new covenant theology in John. Cf. also Pryor, *John: Evangelist,* 63-65.

93. Cf. Corell, 25-26.

94. Cf. Haacker, "Jesus und die Kirche," 137; Pryor, "Covenant and Community," 48; Pryor, *John: Evangelist,* 55.

task. They could not achieve this end as individuals. The whole emphasis on unity in John 17 shows how indispensable a corporate community is for the continuation of the mission of Jesus."[95]

Another expression with ecclesiological significance is "children of God" (τέκνα θεοῦ; cf. 1:12; 11:52; cf. also τεχνία in 13:33).[96] While traditionally applied to Israel (cf. Deut. 14:1; Hos. 2:1), this term was in New Testament times disputed between the church and Israel (cf. Rom. 9:4, 8; Gal. 3:26–4:7). The Fourth Gospel presents this controversy most extensively in chapter 8, where "the Jews" who claim to be children of God are called by Jesus children of the devil.[97] By implication, the locus of identity for the true children of God shifts from historical Israel to Jesus, the Son of God.[98] The concept of being "children of God" is discussed in the Fourth Gospel in terms of spiritual generation in relation to physical procreation (cf. 1:13; 3:3, 5-6).

It may be concluded that the significance of the Johannine corporate metaphors for the Fourth Gospel's teaching on mission lies primarily in the fact that the conventional referents of these metaphors are replaced with new referents. The corporate metaphors of John's Gospel therefore replace Old Testament Israel with believers in Jesus (regardless of their ethnic, racial, or gender identity) as new referents.[99] By establishing one sole criterion for belonging to what is described by various corporate metaphors, viz. believing in Jesus the Messiah, and by pointing to the world as the destination where both Jesus and the disciples are sent (cf. 3:16; 17:18; 20:21), the fourth evangelist reveals the universal scope of Jesus' mission and work, yet without sacrificing its historical particularity.

The message for Jews and proselytes reading the Fourth Gospel is clear. A reversal has taken place that requires a rethinking of categories. The issue is no longer one of others joining *Jews* in *their* special and privileged position with God, but one of *Jews* being invited to join the universal Messianic community that had been inaugurated by the mission of the Messiah, the Son of God, viz. *Jesus*. "The Jews," i.e., the Jewish nation represented by the religious and political leadership, had rejected the Messiah, but God had raised him from the dead. The effects of Jesus' death extend to the world, *through the disciples,* who are sent into the world to do greater works than even Jesus did during his earthly

---

95. Cf. Donald Guthrie, *New Testament Theology* (Downers Grove, Ill.: InterVarsity, 1981), 724.

96. Cf. Haacker, "Jesus und die Kirche," 181-82.

97. Haacker, "Jesus und die Kirche," 182.

98. Son of God typology may be brought into play in the Fourth Gospel. If so, perhaps the term should be seen not as an appeal to the Hellenistic world but as an appeal to Jews. Very possibly there is a deliberate double reference on the part of the fourth evangelist who would have been well aware of the expression son of God in the Hellenistic world but who also would have been familiar with Son of God typology (cf. John 10 and 15).

99. Cf. also the Johannine characterization of "the world" and of "the Jews."

ministry, in the power of his Spirit. The eschatological time of harvest has dawned — and the readers of the Fourth Gospel, too, should believe that the Messiah, the Son of God, is Jesus (cf. 20:30-31).

D. Concluding Reflections

The Fourth Gospel's characterization of the disciples, of "the twelve," and of Peter and the Beloved Disciple, as well as the Fourth Gospel's corporate imagery have been discussed. Before the disciples' task and the modes of movement in their mission are considered, we may provide a brief summary of the findings up to this point.

The fourth evangelist appears to show a concern with both the disciples' historical role and their representative function for later believers. As the Gospel progresses, one notes a widening of the Fourth Gospel's characterization of Jesus' followers. Regarding John's characterization of individual disciples, it appears that the figure of the Beloved Disciple is intended, among other things, to serve as a figure of identification for the reader. The Beloved Disciple is also often set in relation to Peter, a fact that may be seen in part as as reflecting the actual relationship between these figures during Jesus' earthly ministry.

John is a master of double meanings, of symbolism and irony. Moreover, the Fourth Gospel is *interpreted* history, i.e., a spiritual reflection and interpretation of Jesus' life and mission. One should therefore expect to find the disciples cast in a way that exposes their relevance not just in the set context of Jesus' life but also for the Gospel's readership. This is accomplished without leveling the distinctions between the original followers of Jesus and later believers. The occasional, at times almost incidental references to "the twelve" in the Fourth Gospel are evidence of the fourth evangelist's awareness of this group of Jesus' close original followers. Nevertheless, the fourth evangelist also addresses his reader's concern regarding their own relationship to these original followers.

As argued, John meets this need in the following ways. On the one hand, he assigns the primary responsibility of witnessing to those who have been with Jesus from the beginning (cf. 15:27; cf. also 1 John 1:1-4). He also places his whole account squarely in its historical context (cf. the references to the "little while"). On the other hand, John develops the concept of following Jesus and of remaining with and "in" him so that it transcends an experience of the historical Jesus. To be sure, that experience of the historical Jesus is mediated through the apostolic witness (cf. also 1:14), but the condition of faith in Jesus the Messiah does not hinge on having seen him in the flesh (cf. 20:29), nor do the works of the believer depend on this (cf. 14:12). In the era of the Spirit, the exalted Christ, risen, glorified, and ascended, is no longer subject to physical limitations.

Moreover, since the Fourth Gospel presents the giving of the Spirit as still future even for the original disciples of Jesus (cf. 7:37-39; chaps. 14–16; and probably also 20:22, though this is disputed), both original followers and later believers share in common the Spirit's ministry to them and through them. And while the Spirit's guidance of the disciples into all truth and his conviction of the world of its sin by the disciples are doubtless originally attributed to the original followers of Jesus, there seems to be no reason to limit the reference to them, especially in the light of the fourth evangelist's widening of the concept of discipleship in the course of his Gospel. This is also true in the case of the disciples' being sent, as well as for other aspects of their mission. The original followers are the ones who were commissioned by the historical Jesus (cf. 20:21), but those who come to believe through them enter into that commission (cf. especially 17:20; 20:29). There are also several hints of the Gentile mission (cf. 10:16; 11:51-52; 12:20-21).

Nevertheless, the Fourth Gospel is not an idealized, ahistorical account where symbolism and allegory replace historical reference. This is perhaps supremely illustrated in the final pericope of the Gospel, 21:15-23, featuring Peter and the Beloved Disciple. This account fulfills the necessity of reporting Peter's reinstatement to service after his denial of Jesus (cf. 13:36-38; 18:15-27). The important lesson taught through Peter in the Fourth Gospel is that "following" Jesus (cf. 13:36-37) is only possible *after* the cross, thus pointing to the unique and essential role of Jesus' cross-death. Eventually Peter's following of Jesus will extend even to sharing with Jesus his manner of death (cf. 12:33; 21:19). The fourth evangelist preempts, however, the notion that faithful following of Jesus *necessarily* involves martyrdom. Hence his "representative rebuke" of Peter (cf. 21:20-23). The emphasis that there are different ways of following Jesus would be perennially relevant.

Perhaps the most significant conclusion that can be drawn from the study of the fourth evangelist's characterization of the disciples is that of the priority of salvation history over literary strategy. It has been suggested that the fourth evangelist conceived of the disciples as the representatives of the Messianic community in relation to Old Testament Israel. The correspondences are many: the Fourth Gospel's corporate metaphors, the respective endings of chapters 6 and 12, and numerous others.[100] Thus the Fourth Gospel's characterization of Jesus' disciples turns out to be very similar to his portrayal of Jesus. In both cases, the fourth evangelist places these figures in a matrix of fulfillment language and replacement terminology. Jesus is God's dwelling with his own (1:14), the fulfillment of the Old Testament temple (cf. 2:19), the antitype of the serpent in the wilderness (cf. 3:14-15) and of the heavenly manna (6:29-59). The Messianic community called out by Jesus, likewise, is cast by the fourth evangelist in terms of fulfillment of Old Testament metaphors for God's people. Yet there

---

100. Cf. also the possible connection between the Fourth Gospel's disciples and the Old Testament prophets in 4:38 which will be discussed below.

is one important distinction: according to the fourth evangelist, it is *Jesus,* not the Messianic community, who replaces Old Testament Israel (cf. 15:1).[101] In the Fourth Gospel's inaugurated eschatology, the harvesting has already begun in Jesus and continues in his Messianic community (cf. 4:38). Through his community, the Messiah will bear fruit (cf. chap. 15; cf. also 12:24-26). Finally, discipleship is at least potentially extended beyond the confines of Israel to include anyone who believes in Jesus, regardless of that person's race, ethnic origin, or gender. Samaritans, Jews, and Greeks, women and men alike are to be disciples of the Messiah.

II. THE TASK OF THE DISCIPLES

Jesus' task is referred to in the Fourth Gospel in terms of "works" (ἔργον/ἔργα) or "signs" (σημεῖον/σημεῖα). The range for describing the task of the disciples is much more limited. The disciples do not perform any "signs" in the Fourth Gospel. There is no mention of their "work" (in the sg.; but cf. 6:29). Even reference to the disciples' "works" is limited to one, albeit very significant, passage (14:12). There are, however, passages in the Fourth Gospel that characterize the disciples' task: Jesus' followers are sent to harvest (4:38), they are appointed to go and bear fruit (15:16), they must testify (15:27), and they are to forgive others their sins (20:23).[102] In analogy with the treatment of Jesus' mission, and consistent with the working definition of mission used here, the various aspects of the disciples' task according to the Fourth Gospel will now be considered. This will be followed by a discussion of the various modes of movement in the disciples' mission, especially "being sent" (4:38; 17:18; 20:21), "going" (15:16), and "following" (chap. 10; 12:26; 21:15-23).

A. No "Signs" by the Disciples

What is the significance of the fact that the Fourth Gospel restricts the working of "signs" to Jesus? It is hardly possible to improve upon Schnackenburg's comments:

101. Thus the fourth evangelist's theology regarding the relationship of Israel and the Messianic community turns out to be compatible with Paul's development of this issue in Rom 9–11 (cf. also Gal 6:16).

102. Cf. also Vellanickal, "Evangelization in the Johannine writings," 121-68, who divides "the Johannine vocabulary of evangelization" into three categories: (1) process: δίδωμι, λαλέω, λέγω, μαρτυρέω, κράζω, ἀπαγγέλλω, διδάσκω, ἀναγγέλλω; (2) object: ἀγγελία, ἀλήθεια, λόγος, ῥῆμα, μαρτυρία; (3) recipient: λαμβάνω, ἀκούω, ὁράω. He does, however, not provide any criteria for selecting these particular terms.

Thus the later heralds of the faith can only recount, attest and recall the revelation given by Jesus in "signs" (and words), which becomes thereby "present" in their own day. It is presupposed implicitly that he who once wrought these "signs" on earth has in the meantime been glorified, that he still lives and still effects the salvation of believers. But his revelation, as a historical and eschatological event, is closed, and it only remains to explain it further, disclose its riches and explicitate its full truth.[103]

The fact that no "signs" are performed by the disciples in John's Gospel constitutes a crucial element of dissimilarity between the task of Jesus and that of his followers. As argued in the previous chapter, the fourth evangelist appears to conceive of "signs" as confined to the historical point in time prior to Jesus' glorification. The "signs," a unique part of Jesus' ministry, point beyond themselves to Jesus and his sender (the signs' revelatory function). By healing a lame man, by opening a blind man's eyes, and by raising a dead man to life, Jesus moves to increasingly greater demonstrations (cf. 5:20), not so much of his power (cf. the Synoptic Gospels), but of his role as the authentic representative of his divine sender (cf. 11:42).[104]

Jesus' working of "signs" is also significantly linked in the Fourth Gospel to expectations related to his Messianic identity (the signs' Christological function; cf. 7:31; 20:30-31). This may be one reason why the fourth evangelist is careful never to apply the working of "signs" to Jesus' disciples: he takes pains not to rival Jesus' role as the God-sent Messiah. The Fourth Gospel thus reserves the accomplishment of "signs" for Jesus the Messiah. A more humble task is reserved for others, i.e., that of witnessing to Jesus.[105] While the term "signs"

---

103. Cf. Schnackenburg, Gospel According to St. John, 1:524.

104. The function of this progressive dynamic in the Fourth Gospel seems to be at least partly one of theodicy. As the closing of the "Book of Signs" indicates, the author viewed Jesus' ever more demonstrative signs in the context of the obduracy motif and in the service of vindicating God's sovereignty and justice (cf. 12:37-41). Cf. Craig A. Evans, "Obduracy and the Lord's Servant: Some Observations on the Use of the Old Testament in the Fourth Gospel," in Early Jewish and Christian Exegesis: Studies in Memory of William Hugh Brownlee, ed. Craig A. Evans and William F. Stinespring, 221-36 (Atlanta: Scholars, 1987), 221-36; D. A. Carson, Divine Sovereignty and Human Responsibility: Biblical Perspectives in Tension (Atlanta: John Knox, 1981).

105. John the Baptist (cf. 1:7, 8, 15, 32, 34; 3:26; 5:33), the Spirit (cf. 15:26), and the disciples (cf. 15:27; cf. also 19:35 and 21:24) alike are said in the Fourth Gospel to "witness" to Jesus, as are the Father (cf. 8:18), the Scriptures (cf. 5:39), and Jesus' own works (cf. 5:36 and 10:25). On the witness motif in the Fourth Gospel, cf. Johannes Beutler, Martyria: Traditionsgeschichtliche Untersuchungen zum Zeugnisthema bei Johannes, FTS 10 (Frankfurt am Main: Josef Knecht, 1972); J. Daryl Charles, "'Will the Court Please Call in the Prime Witness?' John 1:29-34 and the 'Witness'-Motif," TrinJ 10 NS (1989): 71-83; Martin Hengel, "Maria Magdalena und die Frauen als Zeugen," in Abraham unser Vater: Juden und Christen im Gespräch über die Bibel: Festschrift für Otto Michel zum 60. Geburtstag, ed. Otto Betz, Martin Hengel, and Peter Schmidt (Leiden: E. J. Brill, 1963), 243-56; Ignace de la Potterie, "La notion de témoignage chez Saint Jean," in Sacra Pagina II (Paris: J. Gabalda, 1959), 193-208; Albert Vanhoye, "Témoignage et vie en Dieu selon le IV Évangile," Chr 16 (1951): 155-71.

is never related to the disciples and even the term "work" is not used for them, there is a reference to the disciples' "greater works" in 14:12.

B. The "Greater Works" of the Believer (14:12)

From the patristic period onward, the "greater works" have been interpreted as the missionary successes of the disciples. The Fathers as well as medieval commentators understood the "greater works" as referring to the miracles performed by the apostles accompanying their missionary activities.[106] Later the idea of the extension of faith and salvation gained greater prominence. Augustine and Aquinas saw a reference to justification and sanctification in these "works."

In recent years, the passage's eschatological dimension has been increasingly recognized. Contextually, the reference to Jesus' "going to the Father" (a rather oblique way of referring to Jesus' cross and resurrection) at the end of the verse connotes an eschatological dimension.[107] Moreover, in light of the similar wording in 5:20 (μείζονα τούτων), one probably should interpret 14:12 against the backdrop of this earlier passage.[108] There, in "the parable of the apprenticed son," the disciple is said, as in 14:12, to perform the works of his master. In the latter instance, the disciples' performance of "greater works" may be taken to refer to the gap Jesus' followers would fill between his ascension and return. Thus the work of Jesus, which was only foreshadowed in his "signs," would continue to be carried out through the disciples. This interpretation would put the entirety of the earthly Jesus' work in perspective, considering it in a sense as foundational for the later, "greater" works.

Another relevant passage where a similar wording occurs is 1:50. There the fourth evangelist narrates Jesus' prophesy to Nathanael that he would see "greater things than these" (μείζω τούτων). Reference is thus made to eschatological events relating to the Son of Man. The concept found in 1:51 and 14:12 may further be illumined by comparison with Matthew 11:11, where Jesus compares the ministry of John the Baptist with the role of the "least in the kingdom of heaven," concluding that the relative impact of the latter exceeds by far the role of the former.[109] Analogously, the reference to the "greater works" of the believer should probably likewise be taken in its eschatological frame of reference, i.e., as pointing to a new era based on Jesus' completed life work (cf. 17:4).

---

106. Bultmann, 610: "Most exegetes [refer to] missionary successes and miracles."

107. Cf. Godfrey C. Nicholson, *Death as Departure. The Johannine Descent-Ascent Schema,* SBLDS 63 (Chico, Calif.: Scholars Press, 1983), and the discussion in Chapter 3.

108. Cf. Christian Dietzfelbinger, "Die größeren Werke (Joh 14.12f.)," *NTS* 35 (1989): 28; Lindars, 475.

109. Cf. F. F. Bruce, *The Hard Sayings of Jesus* (Downers Grove, Ill.: InterVarsity, 1983), 112-14, who comments on Matt. 11:11 and its parallel in Luke 7:28, drawing the implication that the disciples were privileged to participate in Jesus' "new age of salvation" (cf. also Luke 10:23-24).

Finally, the "forerunner motif" which pervades the Fourth Gospel may find its climax here: John was the forerunner of Jesus, while Jesus in turn will be followed by the Spirit and the disciples.[110] Indeed, the ministries of Jesus and of the disciples are set in relation to one another elsewhere in the Gospel. Thus it is said that servant and master alike must serve humbly (cf. 13:16; 15:13) and that both will be persecuted (15:20). On the basis of these observations, it may be concluded that the comparative "greater" in 14:12 relates the works of Jesus and those of believers to each other with respect to an eschatological framework, i.e., different phases in God's economy of salvation in which Jesus and his followers are operative.

The disciples' "greater works" are therefore not simply *more* works, nor are they merely *more spectacular* or *more supernatural* works or "miracles."[111] Neither is the primary reference to raw numbers of converts made or to the larger geographical dimension of the disciples' mission.[112] As Brown points out, the emphasis is less on the marvelous character of the "greater works" and more on their eschatological dimension.[113] Bultmann agrees, calling the "greater works" an eschatological event not limited to a historical point in time and linking them to the Spirit's work described in 15:26-27 and 16:7-11.[114] Schnackenburg, too, cautions against an external orientation that interprets the "greater works" primarily in terms of external expansion or numerical successes.[115]

It follows from the above observations that the disciples' "greater works" are constrained by salvation-historical realities. This is seen by Barrett, who maintains, "The death and exaltation of Jesus are the condition of the church's mission," adding, "Thus the 'greater works' are directly dependent upon the 'going' of Jesus, since before the consummation of the work of Jesus in his ascent to the Father all that he did was necessarily incomplete. The work of the disciples on the other hand lies after the moment of fulfilment. . . . Their works are

---

110. Cf. Gary M. Burge, *The Anointed Community: The Holy Spirit in the Johannine Tradition* (Grand Rapids: Wm. B. Eerdmans, 1987), 23-25.

111. At any rate, the function of the Fourth Gospel's "signs" is to point to Jesus as the Messiah and life-giver; and not all "signs" are "miracles." For example, the temple cleansing is a Johannine "sign" but not a "miracle" (cf. the discussion in Chapter 3 above). Cf. Adolf Schlatter, *Der Evangelist Johannes: Wie er spricht, denkt und glaubt*, 2d ed. (Stuttgart: Calwer, 1948), 295. Beasley-Murray, 254, identifies the works in 14:12a with Jesus' "signs." But the word is ἔργα, not σημεῖα. Surely the "signs" are included; but ἔργα is a broader term that views Jesus' activities in a less differentiated fashion (cf. Chapter 3 above). Unfortunately, Beasley-Murray's assumption regarding the works of 14:12a being Jesus' "signs" unduly influences his conclusion that the "greater works" are "the conveying to people of the spiritual realities of which the works of Jesus are 'signs' " (254).

112. Cf. Carson, *Gospel According to John*, 495-96; Bultmann, 610; Beasley-Murray, 254. Contra Lindars, 475, who calls the "greater works" "more extensive."

113. Cf. Raymond E. Brown, *The Gospel According to John*, 2 vols. (New York: Doubleday, 1966, 1970), 2:633.

114. Cf. Bultmann, 610.

115. Cf. Schnackenburg, *Gospel According to St. John*, 3:72.

greater not because they themselves are greater but because Jesus' work is now complete."[116] Schnackenburg concurs, noting that it is only *after* Jesus' glorification that the full fruit can be harvested (cf. 12:24, 31-32; 17:2).[117]

Significantly, the reference in 14:12 elevates the future works of the disciples in one sense above Jesus' "signs" presented in chapters 1–12. It also reveals Jesus' perspective of his own work in relation to that of the disciples to be accomplished after the accomplishment of his earthly mission. Jesus' death and resurrection are thus set in the context of not just *salvation* but *mission*. On the one hand, Jesus' work is unique and foundational, since Jesus alone is the sower of the eschatological harvest (cf. 4:34-38) as well as the grain of wheat that falls into the ground and dies (12:24). Yet, in eschatological perspective, it is only the age of the Spirit that will see the disciples help gather the eschatological harvest and thus perform "greater works" even than Jesus.[118]

Beasley-Murray sets the "greater works" in proper perspective:

> The contrast accordingly is not between Jesus and his disciples in their respective ministries, but between Jesus with his disciples in the limited circumstances of his earthly ministry and the risen Christ with his disciples in the post-Easter situation. Then the limitations of the Incarnation will no longer apply, redemption will have been won for the world, the kingdom of God opened for humanity, and the disciples equipped for a ministry in power to the nations.[119]

He adds, "It is this setting that is presupposed in the striking words of 14:12-14: the disciples go forth to their mission and seek the Lord's aid therein, and in response to their prayers *he* will do through them 'greater things' than in the days of his flesh, 'that the Father may be glorified in the Son' — in the powerful mission that *he* continues!"[120]

In this context, reference should also be made to the role of the Spirit. John's acknowledgment of the disciples' misunderstandings *before* the giving of the Spirit points to the *Spirit* as the source of the disciples' subsequent understanding and ability. The emphasis appears to be on the Spirit's continuation of the revelation and work of Jesus after his exaltation. This work of the Spirit keeps Jesus the Messiah from being just a past chapter of history that fades forever from living memory. The Spirit's mission includes the roles of teaching

116. Cf. Barrett, 460.

117. Cf. Schnackenburg, *Gospel According to St. John*, 3:72.

118. Dietzfelbinger, 38, interprets 14:12 as reflecting the perspective of the Johannine community on the limitations of the pre-Easter period, ruling out the possibility that 14:12 may represent an authentic logion of Jesus. However, the criterion of dissimilarity suggests the implausibility of the attribution of such a statement to Jesus by the post-Easter community. Thus the authenticity of the substance of 14:12 should be affirmed.

119. Beasley-Murray, 255.

120. Beasley-Murray, 380.

the disciples and of reminding Jesus' followers of all that Jesus had taught them (14:26). The Spirit would also bear witness to Jesus (15:26), convicting the world, through the disciples, regarding its sin of unbelief in Jesus, its lack of righteousness, and its judgment (16:8-11).[121] Finally, the Spirit would guide the disciples into all truth and declare to them the things to come (16:13), thus glorifying Jesus by taking what is Jesus' and declaring it to the disciples (16:14). Therefore the primary function of the Spirit is that of ensuring the continuity of Jesus' work in his disciples. Moreover, the Spirit would also legitimize Jesus' followers as representatives of the Messiah.[122]

The fourth evangelist's decision to give equal space to chapters 1–12 and 13–21 may be explained by his desire to show that the signs of the historical Jesus are continued in the "greater works" of the exalted Jesus, and that Jesus' suffering of persecution is continued in the persecution suffered by his followers. Indeed, the disciples' identification with Jesus in their sending suggests a close connection between the tasks carried out by Jesus and by his disciples. Moreover, the statement in 20:30-31 places chapters 13–20 in the context of chapters 1–12. Thus chapters 13–20, too, are seeking to show that Jesus is the Messiah, adding to the "signs" of the earthly Jesus the "greater works" of the exalted Jesus accomplished through his followers. Thus the fourth evangelist closes the gap between A.D. 30 and 90 by interpreting the work of the Christian community as the continued work of the exalted Messiah. Still, he begins by presenting the Messianic signs of Jesus: people cannot start believing in the exalted Christ who is operative in the contemporary community until they have come to believe in the Son sent from the Father, the heaven-sent, "signs"-working, Coming and Returning One, the Descending and Ascending One, the "lifted up" Son of Man.[123]

---

121. Cf. D. A. Carson, "The Function of the Paraclete in John 16:7-11," *JBL* 98 (1979): 547-66.

122. Contra Dietzfelbinger, 44-45, who distinguishes between the old Jesus tradition and the new revelations by the Spirit in the community, postulating that the Fourth Gospel may have been written in opposition to a group or groups referring back to the traditions authorized by the circle of "the Twelve." This, however, appears to be at odds with the Fourth Gospel's insistence that it is the Spirit's task *both* to remind the disciples of Jesus' words *and* to guide them into all truth. The fourth evangelist, rather than setting an old "Jesus tradition" against new revelation by the Spirit, appears to accentuate the deep underlying continuity between the words of Jesus and the teaching of the Spirit. This, of course, is not to deny that according to the Fourth Gospel the exalted Jesus is said to be present and at work in and through the believing community and its mission.

123. In this context one should also note that the often-applied charge that the Fourth Gospel is "anti-Semitic" can be countered at least in part by the observation that the term "the Jews" is totally absent from the entire Farewell Discourse (13–17; the only reference in 13:33 is no real exception). Thus the contrast between Jesus and "the Jews" in 1–12 is replaced in 13–17 by the contrast between "the world" and the Spirit/the disciples. In the new era of the Spirit, the era of the disciples' "greater works," the fourth evangelist contends that there will only be two kinds of people, believers in the Messiah and unbelievers. Thus the references to "the Jews" in 1–12 primarily have a salvation-historical thrust.

The "greater works" of 14:12 thus refer to the activities of believers, still future from the vantage point of the historical Jesus, that will be based on Jesus' completed redemptive work (cf. 14:12c). Seen in eschatological perspective, these works will be "greater" than those of Jesus because they will take place in a different, more advanced phase of God's economy of salvation. In a very real sense, these "greater works" will be works *of the exalted Christ* through believers.[124] Importantly, the fourth evangelist draws an inseparable distinction between the foundation laid by Jesus (cf. 12:24; 15:13; 19:30) and the work done by his disciples. Jesus' followers reap what they have not sown (cf. 4:31-38). They can do so only because Jesus is going to the Father from where he, in answer to prayer, will supply all that is needed for his disciples' mission to be accomplished (cf. 14:13).

C. Other References to the Disciples' Task

Remarkably little is said about the purpose or content of the disciples' mission. More information about the disciples' task can be gained from passages in the Fourth Gospel that include together with a term denoting a mode of movement a reference to a specific activity to be carried out by the disciples. These passages, 4:36-38; 15:16, 27; and 20:21-23, will all be treated in detail under "The Charge of the Disciples" below. A brief summary of the various tasks to which they refer will therefore suffice here.

Both 4:36-38 and 15:8, 16 use agricultural metaphors to describe the disciples' task. In 4:36-38, Jesus tells his disciples that they have entered into the labor of others and envisions sending them to "harvest" (4:38).[125] In a similar metaphor, Jesus speaks in 15:8, 16 of the disciples' "bearing of fruit." The point of similarity, apart from terminology (4:36: συνάγει καρπόν; 15:8, 16: καρπὸν [πολὺν] φέρητε), is that in both 4:36-38 and 15:8, 16 the disciples are not credited with producing anything: they are harvesting for what they did not labor, and they are bearing fruit only by remaining in Jesus (cf. 15:5: φέρει καρπὸν πολύν).[126]

Another task assigned to the disciples is that of bearing witness to Jesus. The disciples' future witnessing activity is cast within the purview of the Spirit's

---

124. If the later reference to the disciples' being appointed to "go and bear fruit" further specifies the general designation "greater works" in 14:12, the latter passage would be even more tightly linked to the mission theme in the Fourth Gospel.

125. Regarding the identity of the "others" in 4:38, see the discussion under "sending" below.

126. The only other pericope besides 4:36-38 and chapter 15 where the term καρπός is used is 12:24 (πολὺν καρπὸν φέρει). There, in yet another agricultural metaphor, it is the death of Jesus, "the grain of wheat falling into the ground and dying," that produces much fruit. One may therefore conclude that it is Jesus' sacrifice that is the fundamental work. The disciples' mission involves the harvesting of the fruit resulting from it. Cf. further the interpretation of 4:38 below.

witnessing role in 15:26-27.[127] This reference to the disciples', and the Spirit's, witness is placed in the context of the world's hatred of Jesus and of his representatives and of the persecution that can be expected. The disciples' witnessing activity is also set in relation to the Spirit's activity of convicting the world of its unbelief in Jesus (cf. 16:8-11). Moreover, by witnessing to Jesus, the disciples enter into one of the major purposes of Jesus' mission, the giving of life. This is apparent in 20:30-31 where the writing of the Gospel is said to have as its purpose that people would believe and "have life."

Finally, the disciples' task includes, in addition to their participation in the eschatological harvest by bearing fruit and their witness to Jesus together with the Spirit, the commission to forgive others their sins in Jesus' name (cf. 20:23). Like the other passages briefly surveyed here, this aspect of the disciples' mission will be considered more fully below.

III. THE CHARGE OF THE DISCIPLES

There are two modes of movement in the disciples' mission according to the Fourth Gospel: "following" and "being sent." The term "coming" to Jesus will also be briefly discussed, since it frequently in the Fourth Gospel refers to potential followers of Jesus. "Coming" is used both literally and figuratively (cf., e.g., 1:39, 46, 47; 6:35, 37). The passages developing the "following" conceptuality include 1:37-43; 8:12; chapter 10; 12:24-26; 13:36-38; and 21:15-23. The references to the disciples' "being sent" are 4:38; 17:18; and 20:21. To these should probably also be added 15:16, though the term used there is "going" (ὑπάγητε), since it is linked with the term "appoint," which denotes a commission. First the instances of "coming" to Jesus will briefly be dealt with. Since the term "follow" is logically prior to the term "being sent,"[128] "follow" will be discussed before the "sending" references.

A. Coming (to Jesus)

"Coming" to Jesus may in the Fourth Gospel be the beginning of "following" Jesus, as is the case in 1:39, 46, 47 or presumably in 4:40. This "coming" to Jesus may simply amount to an inquisitive visit (cf. 3:2; 7:50) or a crowding to see Jesus in action (cf. 3:26; 4:30; 6:5). Even so, an attitude of expectation when

127. Terms that relate to the witnessing theme in the Fourth Gospel are μαρτυρία (1:7, 19; 3:32, 33; 5:31, 32, 34, 36; 8:13, 14, 17; 21:24); and μαρτυρέω (1:7, 15, 32, 34; 2:24; 3:26, 28, 32; 4:39, 44; 5:31, 32, 33, 36, 37, 39; 7:7; 8:13, 14, 18; 10:25; 12:17; 13:21; 15:26, 27; 18:23, 37; 21:24); cf. also the terms ἐξηγέομαι (1:18); ἀναγγέλλω (4:25; 5:15; 16:13, 14, 15); and ἀπαγγέλλω (16:25).

128. This is reflected in the use of "follow" as early as 1:37-43 in the Fourth Gospel while the primary references to "being sent" are not found until 17:18 and 20:21.

coming to see Jesus may lead to placing one's faith in him (cf., e.g., 10:41). Increasingly, the term "come" to Jesus is associated with other terms that lend the whole expression in context a spiritual flavor (as, e.g., in 5:40 for "come to me and have life"; cf. also 6:35, 37, 44, 45, 65; 7:37). It is noteworthy that all the references to "coming" to Jesus occur in chapters 1–12. The only partial exception is 14:6, which refers to people's coming to the Father through Jesus.

The Fourth Gospel's use of "coming" (to Jesus) is thus an example of the evangelist's choice of simple terms (in the present case, terms denoting modes of movement) while investing these expressions with figurative meanings and spiritual overtones. Thus "coming" to Jesus can end up being used almost synonymously with "believing" in Jesus (cf., e.g., 6:35: "He who comes to me will never go hungry, and he who believes in me will never be thirsty"). One also notes a development during the course of the Gospel from more literal (1:39–6:5) to more figurative meanings (5:40–7:37). The Gospel thus knows of a very early stage of a potential follower's response to Jesus, a "coming" to Jesus that may or may not lead to "believing" in him. Believing, in turn, may lead to a person's "following" of Jesus. Conversely, following may lead to believing.

B. Following

The disciples are to follow Jesus (references range from 1:37-43 until 21:19-21) and to believe in him (cf. 2:11; 6:67-68; 14:1, 11).[129] However, the disciples' failure to understand is repeatedly emphasized by the fourth evangelist.[130] Moreover, the Fourth Gospel makes it clear that not all disciples *kept* following Jesus (cf., e.g., 6:60-71 or 8:31-33). Before his passion, Jesus predicts that even his close disciples will be scattered and that all will leave him (cf. 16:32). Only later, through the "reminding" ministry of the Spirit (cf. 14:26), will Jesus' disciples remember what Jesus had said and understand the significance of Jesus' words (cf. 2:22; 12:16). Thus, according to the Fourth Gospel, faithful following of Jesus is only possible *after* the cross and Jesus' glorification. In order to gain a comprehensive understanding of what it means to follow Jesus according to the Fourth Gospel, the various references to the disciples' following will be

129. Cf. Schulz, 172-75. The Fourth Gospel does not dichotomize between "discipleship" on the one hand and "evangelism" or "missions" on the other. Those who follow Jesus closely are at the end commissioned to be sent into the world. Thus while a disciple's being sent out is preceded by a time of following Jesus ("discipleship"), a person's "discipleship" *includes* and *entails* that person's ("evangelistic") mission to the world.

130. Cf. especially D. A. Carson, "Understanding Misunderstandings in the Fourth Gospel," *TynBul* 33 (1982): 59-89. The disciples' remembering is possible through the "reminding" ministry of the Spirit (cf. 14:26). The theme of the disciples' misunderstanding further accentuates the difference between them and Jesus. It points to Jesus' work as fundamental and highlights the disciples' need for dependence on the Spirit for insight and understanding of Jesus' works and words.

traced, with special emphasis on the major point made by the fourth evangelist in each case.

A study of the occurrences of "follow" in the Fourth Gospel yields the following insights. First, there is a movement from literal to figurative following in the Fourth Gospel (cf. 1:37, 40, 43 and 8:12; cf. also 13:13-38).[131] In the opening call narrative (1:35-51), the emphasis is still on a literal following, though the stage is already set for overtones of figurative following later in the Gospel. In 8:12, reference is made to the fact that the one who follows Jesus will not "walk in darkness" but have "the light of life" (i.e., salvation; cf. 10:9-10). The literal meaning of "follow" and the figurative meaning with attached spiritual overtones are used side by side in 13:36-38 (see below).

Second, there is a widening from the "following" of Jesus' original disciples (cf. 1:37-43) to the "following" of every believer (cf. 8:12; chap. 10). Not only is there a movement from literal to figurative following from 1:37-43 to 8:12, there is also a widening of the term from Jesus' historical disciples to the following of every believer. This can also be seen in chapter 10, where Jesus elaborates on the kind of trust relationship characterizing his relationship with believers in him individually, and corporately between him and his "flock."

This wider concept of "discipleship" is also found in 12:26. There the point is made that following Jesus involves "death" to one's self-interest (cf. also 21:15-23). This "death" is not linked, as in Jesus' case, with the "bearing of much fruit," thus preserving an important distinction between Jesus' and the believer's "deaths."[132] Jesus' challenge, "If anyone would like to serve me, let him follow me," is linked with a promise, "and where I am, there my servant will be as well." In life and death, in humiliation and glory, Jesus' disciple is to be with his Master (cf. 14:3; 17:24).[133]

It should be pointed out that the context of 12:24-26 is one of (Gentile)

---

131. Cf. Oscar Cullmann, "Der johanneische Gebrauch doppeldeutiger Ausdrücke als Schlüssel zum Verständnis des 4. Evangeliums," *TZ* 4 (1948): 367, where Cullmann notes this movement from 1:37-38 to 1:40, 44 and within 13:36-38. Similarly, Earl Richard, "Expressions of Double Meaning and their Function in the Gospel of John," *NTS* 31 (1985): 100.

132. Cf. F. F. Bruce, *The Gospel of John* (Grand Rapids: Wm. B. Eerdmans, 1983), 265, who comments that Jesus' followers "must be prepared to renounce present interests for the sake of a future inheritance." Cf. also Carson, *Gospel According to John*, 438, who adduces 1 Pet. 2:21-25 as a parallel to 12:24-26 in that passage's movement from the unique and redemptive sacrifice of Christ to its exemplary significance for Jesus' followers. Note also the similar wordings of 12:25 (φιλῶν, ψυχήν) and 15:13 (φίλων, ψυχήν) and the movement from Jesus' giving his life to the implications for his followers in both passages (cf. 12:26 and 15:16).

133. Cf. Barrett, 424; Schlatter, 268. Note the emphatic position of ἐμοί in both parts of the phrase in 12:26: ἐὰν ἐμοί τις διακονῇ, ἐμοὶ ἀκολουθείτω. See also the partial Synoptic parallels to 12:25-26, i.e., Mark 8:34-35 par.; 10:43-45; Matt. 10:39 = Luke 17:33; Matt. 16:25; Luke 9:24; 14:26; 22:26-27. Unique to John are the phrases "in this world" and "unto eternal life" in 12:25. The term "serve" is also found in Mark 10:43-45, the term "follow" especially in Matt. 16:24 = Mark 8:34. Cf. Lindars, 429; C. H. Dodd, *Historical Tradition in the Fourth Gospel* (Cambridge: Cambridge University Press, 1963), 338-43.

mission (cf. 12:20-21; cf. already 10:16; 11:49-52).[134] Notably, the "Greeks" first approach the disciples. Indeed, it is the disciples who will mediate access to Jesus — but not now. First comes the "hour" of Jesus' glorification (cf. 12:23).[135] The passage is followed by Jesus' reference to his being "lifted up" and his subsequent drawing of "all men" to himself (cf. 12:32-33).[136] Doubtless this is at least part of what is in view in the reference to the "much fruit" that Jesus' death will bear (cf. 12:24).[137] Thus 12:32 can be taken as an indirect answer to the Greeks' request in 12:21.[138] Paradoxically, it is through his *exaltation* that Jesus will become accessible to the "Greeks." Read in connection with 14:12 and 15:16, it may be concluded that the "following" of 12:26 includes the disciples' participation in Jesus' drawing of "all men" to himself after Jesus has been "lifted up."[139]

Following Jesus involves following him in his death, i.e., *after* Jesus' glorification. This involves a lifestyle of self-sacrifice, albeit not of atoning value, and service (cf. 13:1-15; 15:13). This way of life Jesus himself has modeled: he is "the way" (cf. 14:6). Following Jesus, in turn, is part of a disciple's individual prerequisite for mission. As can be seen in the Fourth Gospel, the disciples who keep following Jesus are sent by him into the world (cf. 17:18; 20:21). They thus have the honor of entering into their Master's labor of bringing in the eschatological harvest (cf. 4:38).

134. Cf. especially Johannes Beutler, "Greeks Come to See Jesus (John 12, 20f)," *Bib* 71 (1990): 333-47, who argues that "[t]he wording of the approach of the Greeks to Jesus echoes in an astonishing way Isa 52,15 LXX": "those to whom the news had not yet been announced about him will see, and those who have not yet heard will understand" — i.e., the Gentiles (ἔθνη πολλά; 342). Cf. also Ulrich Busse, "Die 'Hellenen' Joh 12, 20ff. und der sogenannte 'Anhang' Joh 21," in *The Four Gospels 1992: Festschrift Frans Neirynck*, BETL C, ed. F. van Segbroeck, C. M. Tuckett, G. van Belle, and J. Verheyden, vol. 3 (Leuven: University Press, 1992), 2083-2100. As Bultmann, 423, notes, the "Greeks" of 12:20 are probably proselytes. Bultmann also draws attention to the connection between 12:19 and 20. Finally, Brown, *Gospel According to John*, 1:472, notes the parallel wording to 12:24 ("bear much fruit") in Dan. 4:12 (both Theodotion: ὁ καρπὸς αὐτοῦ πολύς and LXX) to describe the great tree of Nebuchadnezzar (cf. also the probable allusion to this verse in Mark 4:32). He contends that in all three passages, Dan. 4:12, Mark 4:32, and John 12:24, the coming of the Gentiles to God is in view. This possible connection between John 12:24 and Dan. 4:9 [sic] had already been noted by Schlatter, 268. Note also the similar wording in Matt. 13:23: καρποφορεῖ.

135. Cf. Bultmann, 423.

136. See also the culminating reference to the persistent Jewish unbelief despite Jesus' working of Messianic signs in 12:37-50. Cf. further Schnackenburg, *Gospel According to St. John*, 2:383, who interprets the "fruit" of 12:24 as the fruit of mission: "Jesus' death is necessary to bring rich missionary fruit," referring also to 12:32; and Lindars, 429: "The context into which John has inserted the parable implies that he is thinking of the Gentile mission."

137. There remains, however, an important difference between Jesus' calling of others to follow and the disciples' calling of others to follow. While Jesus during his earthly ministry called others to follow him, the disciples are to call others to follow, not themselves, but *Jesus*. The disciples, together with those they call, are still to follow Jesus.

138. Cf. Bultmann, 423.

139. Cf. also 10:16 where the disciples' participation in Jesus' future mission to the "other sheep" may be implied. Cf. further Baumeister, 95, who notes that the "following" spoken of in 12:24-26 does not presuppose the fellowship of a disciple with the historical Jesus.

Finally, in another lesson on "following," the fourth evangelist uses Peter to illustrate the impossibility of an adequate following of Jesus before Jesus' glorification (cf. 13:36-38). Moreover, as already mentioned, the final pericope featuring Peter and the Beloved Disciple indicates that there are different ways of following the crucified and risen Messiah, and that following Jesus does not *necessarily* entail *physical* death (though it entails "death" to self, cf. 12:26).[140]

In conclusion, it may be noted that both 1:19–6:71 (ranging from John the Baptist's "referral" of some of his disciples to Jesus to the abandonment of Jesus by many of his disciples except for the twelve) and 7:1–12:50 (a section extending from the antagonism of Jesus' own brothers to the Jews' final rejection of Jesus), focus on the relative "failure" of Jesus' earthly mission, except for the twelve. In a sense, the first part of the Gospel may be seen as a narration of 1:11: "He came to that which was his own, but his own did not receive him."[141] On the other hand, chapters 13–21 show the success of the mission of the exalted Jesus through his Messianic community represented by "the Twelve."

One final mode of movement in the disciples' mission remains to be considered: "being sent."

C. Being Sent

While the references to the disciples' being sent are rare in comparison to the host of references to Jesus' being sent from the Father, the fact that both 17:18 and 20:21 link the disciples' being sent with Jesus' being sent places "sending" at the center of mission terminology applied to the disciples in the Fourth Gospel. The link between Jesus' and the disciples' "works" in 14:12 has already been discussed. Just as that reference observes a distinction between the time before and the time after Jesus' glorification and return to the Father, so the "sending" references of 4:38, 17:18 and 20:21 presuppose Jesus' completed work (cf. 17:4), i.e., his crucifixion, resurrection, and ascension (cf. 20:17, 19-20).

1. Entering into Jesus' Labor: Sent to Harvest (4:38)

Before studying 17:18 and 20:21, we will consider the only other reference to the "sending" of the disciples, 4:38.[142] The passage is part of a pericope narrating Jesus' Samaritan mission (cf. 4:1-42). For Jesus, to go through Samaria was God's will

---

140. On the references in 12:24-26 to the "losing" or "keeping" of one's life, cf. Gerhard Dautzenberg, *Sein Leben bewahren: ΨΥΧΗ in den Herrenworten der Evangelien*, SANT 14 (München: Kösel, 1966).

141. Cf. also 4:44: "a prophet has no honor in his own country"; Matt. 13:57; Luke 4:24. On 1:11 and οἱ ἴδιοι as a reference to "the Jews" with overtones or echoes of "the world," cf. John W. Pryor, "Jesus and Israel in the Fourth Gospel — John 1:11," *NovT* 32 (1990): 201-18.

142. We will also briefly treat 15:16. The rationale for this will be given below.

(cf. δεῖ in 4:4). In a book as given to multiple levels of meaning as the Fourth Gospel, one may detect an *inclusio* between the reference to Jesus' being tired (cf. 4:6: κεκοπιακώς) and the references to the labor of others into which the disciples are to enter (cf. 4:38: κεκοπιάκατε, κεκοπιάκασιν, κόπον).[143]

Another possible *inclusio* may be found in the reference to the sender of Jesus in 4:34 (τοῦ πέμψαντός με) and the statement made by Jesus regarding his sending of his disciples in 4:38 (ἐγὼ ἀπέστειλα ὑμᾶς). The Fourth Gospel's portrait of Jesus as the sent Son has already been discussed in the previous chapter. The theme of the obedient, dependent sent Son is more fully developed in 5:19-27 (cf. especially 5:36; cf. also 6:38; 8:29; 9:3-4; 10:25, 32, 37-38; 14:10; 17:4). In the present context the reference is to the Father's sending of his Son *to harvest*.[144] Already there is an indication that the Son envisions his sending of the disciples to enter his harvest (cf. 4:38). This reference is anticipatory of 20:21 where Jesus, who has been consistently portrayed in the Fourth Gospel as the one sent, becomes the sender of his disciples (cf. also 17:18).

The verb tenses in 4:38 have led many to believe that the verse does not reflect the time of the historical Jesus but rather a later perspective at the time of writing the Fourth Gospel (cf. especially ἀπέστειλα; cf. also εἰσεληλύθατε).[145] However, the perfect forms of κοπιάω should probably be considered to have stative force ("you are not in a state of laboring"; "others are in a state of laboring") while the aorists may be viewed from a global aspect and not necessarily as referring to past *time* ("I send you"; "you enter").[146] Besides allowing for the possibility that the saying may reflect the perspective of the

143. This is the only pericope in the Fourth Gospel where the κοπιάω word group is found. Cf. Lindars, 197, who considers κοπιάω in 4:38 to be a possible allusion to Josh. 24:13 (LXX), where the same term is used. This suggestion was already made by Bultmann, 199, n. 1.

144. Note the progression from "will" (θέλημα) and "work" (ἔργον) in 4:34 to "harvest" (θερισμός) in 4:35. From 4:35 on, the term "harvest" (noun as well as verb) dominates (six occurrences in 4:35-38: twice in v. 35, twice in v. 36, once in v. 37, and once in v. 38). In 4:36, a distinction is introduced between "sowers" and "harvesters." After the last use of "harvest" in v. 38, there are three occurrences of "labor" (noun as well as verb). The term "labor" may well encompass both "sowing" and "reaping" and refer to the whole harvesting process.

145. Cf., e.g., Teresa Okure, *The Johannine Approach to Mission: A Contextual Study of John 4:1-42*, WUNT 2/31 (Tübingen: J. C. B. Mohr [Paul Siebeck], 1988), 158-59, who argues, on the basis of the verb tenses found in 4:38, for viewing "all of v 38 as clearly reflecting the post-Easter standpoint from which the Gospel is written." Other commentators holding this view include Schnackenburg, who believes that Jesus projects himself into the future, or Cullmann, who holds that the statement is a post-resurrection utterance made in the light of the early church's Samaritan mission. For a helpful discussion and critique of these views, see Beasley-Murray, 64.

146. Thus categories such as the ones used by Schnackenburg (who refers to the aorist in ἀπέστειλα as reflecting "prophetic prevision" and who sees the perfect as "looking back") are unnecessary. For a thorough treatment of verbal aspect theory, an alternative to conventional time-based verbal theories, cf. especially Stanley E. Porter, *Verbal Aspect in the Greek of the New Testament, with Reference to Tense and Mood* (New York: Peter Lang, 1989), 233. Cf. also the future-referring aorists in 13:31, 32 (ἐδοξάσθη); 15:6 (ἐβλήθη, ἐξηράνθη), 8 (ἐδοξάσθη) and 17:14 (ἐμίσησεν).

historical Jesus, this understanding also has implications for one's interpretation of the "others" in 4:38.

The ἄλλοι of 4:38 have been variously identified as the Old Testament prophets (perhaps culminating in the ministry of John the Baptist),[147] John the Baptist and his disciples,[148] John the Baptist and Jesus,[149] Jesus and the Father,[150] or Jesus alone.[151] Some of those who take the view that 4:38 reflects a later perspective have identified the "others" with the Hellenists of Acts 6 (cf. also 8:14-17).[152]

In light of the comments on the verb forms represented in 4:38, it seems needlessly anachronistic to view the present passage as referring to the Hellenists of Acts 6. It is also not likely that the activities of Jesus and the Father are grouped together under the term "laboring,"[153] since the Fourth Gospel usually presents the Father as working in and through Jesus rather than working alongside him.[154] Indeed, Jesus is the obedient sent Son whose "food" it is to accomplish the work given him by his sender, the Father. The notion of Jesus' colaboring with the Father seems foreign to the thought of 4:34.[155]

---

147. Cf. Lindars, 197, who refers to Luke 10:23-24 as a supposed parallel; Bruce, *Gospel of John*, 115; Carson, *Gospel According to John*, 231, apparently following Bruce, who argues that the "others" of 4:38 are "a long succession of prophets and righteous leaders who led up to the ministry of Jesus. . . . John is the last in the succession of prophets and of others who sowed the seed but did not live long enough to participate in the harvest."

148. Cf. John A. T. Robinson, "The 'Others' of John 4.38," *SE I*, TU 73, ed. Frank L. Cross (Berlin: Akademie, 1959), 510-15.

149. Cf. Brown, *Gospel According to John*, 184; Beasley-Murray, 64, who adds to John the Baptist and Jesus also "others who spread their message, such as the woman at Sychar."

150. Cf. Wilhelm Thüsing, *Die Erhöhung und Verherrlichung Jesu im Johannesevangelium*, NTAbh 21, 1/2 (Münster: W. Aschendorff, 1979), 54-55; Okure, 145-64.

151. This seems to be the conclusion by Barrett, 243: "ἄλλοι represents Jesus (perhaps together with the Baptist, or the Old Testament writers, though again there is nothing to suggest this)." Cf. also Schnackenburg, *Gospel According to St. John*, 1:453: "If this point is missed [i.e., that the aorist ἀπέστειλα in 4:38 is future-referring], and the text explained as the conferring of a mission at the present juncture, one has to fall back, like the Fathers and many later exegetes, on the untenable explanation that the 'others' who laboured before the disciples are the prophets, John the Baptist and eventually Jesus. But the inclusion of the prophets and John the Baptist is very far from mind [sic] of the evangelist. Jesus alone accomplishes the eschatological work of salvation. . . ." However, Schnackenburg then proceeds to argue in favor of Cullmann's conclusion that the reference is to the conditions of the early church's Samaritan mission, an inference unnecessary in the light of the text itself.

152. Cf. Oscar Cullmann, "Samaria and the Origins of the Christian Mission," in *The Early Church*, ed. A. J. B. Higgins (London: SCM, 1956), 185-92.

153. However, cf. 5:17, where ἐργάζομαι is used. Cf. Schnackenburg, *Gospel According to St. John*, 1:453; Bultmann, 199.

154. Cf. Bultmann, 199: "These ἄλλοι surely cannot refer to the Father and Jesus, since the Father's work is neither antecedent nor complementary to Jesus' work; rather the Father works through him." Bultmann cites as example for this also 5:17.

155. These factors invalidate the interpretation by Okure, 162-63, who fails to consider the objections just stated.

Once the interpretations of the ἄλλοι of 4:38 as referring to the Hellenists of Acts 6 or to Jesus and the Father have been eliminated, one is left with a spectrum of views that place a varying degree of emphasis on the respective predecessors of Jesus. The contention that ἄλλοι should be taken as referring to Jesus alone correctly perceives that Jesus is the focus of the whole section (4:34-38). The view is, however, rendered rather improbable by the fact that a self-reference in the third person plural ("others") is unparalleled in the Fourth Gospel.[156] Moreover, as will be further argued below, the objections advanced by some that would exclude the Old Testament prophets from the purview of the ἄλλοι in 4:38 are not insurmountable, especially in the light of the massive fulfillment structures in the Fourth Gospel.[157]

Among the remaining interpretive options, the view that the "others" of 4:38 are John the Baptist and Jesus receives support by the joint mention of John's and Jesus' ministries in 4:1-3 (cf. also 3:22-24). However, one need not limit the scope of Jesus' predecessors to the Baptist. The discussion of the reference to the disciples' "greater works" in 14:12 has already indicated that the fourth evangelist perceives the work of Jesus and of the disciples along a salvation-historical grid where advances are made within an eschatological framework. It has been argued that the fourth evangelist essentially shares the perspective reflected in Matthew 11:12-13, where John the Baptist is portrayed as the last in a long succession of Old Testament prophets and where Jesus is presented as the one of whom "all the prophets and the law prophesied until John" (Matt. 11:13; cf. also Luke 16:16). Likewise, the ἄλλοι of John 4:38 are best taken as Jesus and his predecessors, i.e., the Old Testament prophets up until John the Baptist.

It is helpful to see the passage in its context in chapter 4. Jesus had "labored," during the absence of his disciples, by seeking to persuade a Samaritan woman of his Messiahship. The woman had left to summon the people in her village. In the interim, the disciples had returned with the food Jesus had sent them to buy. At the end of Jesus' instruction of his disciples in 4:34-38, the Samaritans are on the horizon (cf. 4:39-41).[158] Many would believe in Jesus as "the Savior of the world" (cf. 4:42). This course of events illustrates, according to Jesus, two important principles of mission, first, that with Jesus' coming the eschatological harvest had dawned and was already here (cf. 4:35-36; contrary

---

156. In 3:11 and 9:4, passages containing possible self-references by Jesus, it is the first, not the third, person plural that is used ("we").

157. Cf. Brown, *Gospel According to John*, 1:183, who notes that an interpretation of the "others" of 4:38 with reference to the Old Testament prophets is weakened by the fact that the Samaritans accepted only the Pentateuch; and Bultmann, 199, n. 2: "There can be no question here of any reference to the prophets of the OT; a correlation of Jesus and the prophets would be quite contrary to the Johannine view."

158. Cf. Beasley-Murray, 63, who even speculates that Jesus' statement that the fields are "white for harvest" is matched by the white clothes of the approaching Samaritans!

to the fact that, by ordinary reckoning, four months would have remained until harvest time)[159] and, second, that in this harvest there would be a collaboration between "sowers" and "reapers" (though a distinction between these roles remains, as the saying quoted in 4:37 illustrates). In this context, Jesus acknowledges that his own eschatological "reaping" occurs in fulfillment of the contributions made by his predecessors (cf. 4:36). In a further development of this principle, Jesus then envisions his sending of his disciples who in turn would enter into the labor of their predecessors (cf. 4:38).

The "fruit" of mission is probably indicated through the phrase συνάγει καρπὸν εἰς ζωὴν αἰώνιον, where the "crop" seems to represent converts, with the Samaritans in immediate view.[160] However, as 17:18 and 20:21 indicate, Jesus' sending of his disciples to harvest had to await Jesus' glorification. The present passage is consistent with the message of 14:12 that it is ultimately the exalted Jesus who will continue his mission through the disciples. There a comparison is made between the works of the earthly Jesus and those of the exalted Jesus through his followers. Analogously, it is indicated in 4:38 that the disciples merely "enter" into the harvest of their predecessors so that the conclusion seems warranted that Jesus remains the eschatological harvester who brings in his harvest through his commissioned disciples.

The relationship of 4:38 to other mission passages in the Fourth Gospel can thus be summarized as follows: "Jesus' view [reflected in 4:38] already takes in the coming time of fruitfulness, in which he, as the exalted Lord, draws all men to him (12:32), does still greater works through his disciples (cf. 14:12) and gathers the one flock of believers (cf. 10:16; 17:21)."[161] Indeed, it may be argued that what in 4:38 is referred to as being "sent to harvest" is in 15:16 termed "going to bear fruit" (cf. also 14:12). Before turning to 17:18 and 20:21, the other two references to the disciples' "being sent," we may therefore briefly consider 15:16.

2. Commissioned to Go and Bear Fruit (15:16)

Even though the term "send" is not directly used in 15:16, there are two reasons why it seems appropriate to subsume the present passage under the references to the disciples' being sent in the Fourth Gospel. First, the words "send" and "go" are at times used in a parallel fashion in the Fourth Gospel (cf. especially

159. It seems best to take the phrase "Do you not say?" (οὐχ ὑμεῖς λέγετε) in 4:35 as indicating "by ordinary reckoning" rather than reflecting a common proverb in Jesus' day. Contrast with this the reference to "the saying" (ὁ λόγος) in v. 37. Cf. Carson, *Gospel According to John,* 229-30. On the "inaugurated eschatology" of 4:35-36, cf. Beasley-Murray, 63.

160. Cf. Barrett, 242. Cf. also Schlatter, 132, who argues that καρπός in John does not mean fruit but harvest (cf. Rev. 22:2).

161. Cf. Schnackenburg, *Gospel According to St. John,* 1:452. Cf. also Beasley-Murray, who groups 4:38, 12:24-26, and 14:12 all under "mission."

4:38: ἀπέστειλα, εἰσεληλύθατε). Second, the word "appoint" (ἔθηκα) almost certainly has connotations of a commission,[162] especially since it is linked with the term ὑπάγειν.[163]

As one writer comments, "the fruit primarily in this verse is the fruit that emerges from mission, from specific ministry to which the disciples have been sent. The fruit, in short, is new converts."[164] Noting the reference to "fruit that remains" in the latter part of the verse, this writer contends "that these closing allusions to the vine imagery ensure that, however comprehensive the nature of the fruit that Christians bear, the focus on evangelism and mission is truly central."[165]

It seems therefore safe to conclude that 15:16 sustains close ties with 14:12 and that the passage relates primarily to the notion of the disciples' mission, specifically the making of converts, even though the term "sending" is not used in 15:16. While there is a string of passages throughout the earlier parts of the Gospel that treat elements of the disciples' mission (i.e., 4:38; 12:24-26; 14:12; and 15:7-8, 16), it is not until 17:18 and especially 20:21 that the disciples' mission is fully focused upon. The task of the disciples had been set in connection with Jesus' task in 4:36-38 ("harvesting"; there also including the task of Jesus' predecessors) and 14:12 ("greater works"). The concept of "fruitbearing," too, was applied both to Jesus (cf. 12:24) and to the disciples (cf. 15:8, 16). But it is not until 17:18 and 20:21 that the disciples' sending is comprehensively related to the sending of Jesus.

---

162. Cf. the use of the same word in 15:13 where it refers to Jesus' setting aside of his life for others. The term is used in terms of a commission of the setting apart of a person for a task in Num. 8:10 (Levites); Num. 27:18 (Joshua by Moses); Acts 13:47 (quoting Isa. 49:6; the "Servant of the Lord" to be a light and salvation for the nations); 20:28 (Ephesian elders); 1 Cor. 12:18 (members of the body), 28 (apostles, prophets, teachers); 1 Tim. 1:12 (Paul); 2 Tim. 1:11 (Paul).

163. Cf. Barrett, 478: "ὑπάγητε refers to the mission of the apostles to the world." Barrett also relates the wordings of 15:16 (ὁ καρπὸς ὑμῶν μένῃ) and 4:36 (συνάγει καρπὸν εἰς ζωὴν αἰώνιον). Cf. also Lindars, 492: "Here go . . . is meant literally, to go on mission"; and Brown, *Gospel According to John*, 2:683: "Both the notions of going and of bearing fruit have connotations of a mission to others. The use of the Greek verb 'to appoint' in OT passages for commission and ordination lends another hint of mission to this verse." Contra Bultmann, 545, n. 2, who denies that ὑπάγητε is the disciples' going on a mission; he conjectures that the phrase may simply be a Semitic pleonasm. Similarly Schnackenburg, *Gospel According to St. John*, 3:111-13, who considers the phrase "go and bear fruit" to function analogously to ὕπαγε φώνησον in 4:16 or ὕπαγε νίψαι in 9:7, i.e., as a Semiticizing imperative which gives greater weight to the following imperative. But it must be noted that in neither of these supposed parallels is there a coordinating conjunction between the two linked verbs as there is in 15:16 (ἵνα ὑμεῖς ὑπάγητε καὶ καρπὸν φέρητε). Schnackenburg concludes, "The terminology in this verse hardly entitles us to tie the bearing of fruit down to missionary activity" (112). According to this interpreter, the emphasis is on the fruitfulness of the Christian life, especially brotherly love (cf. 15:13).

164. Cf. Carson, *Gospel According to John*, 523. Cf. also Beasley-Murray, 275: "the employment of ἔθηκα and ὑπάγητε suggests that the sending of the disciples on mission is to the fore here (so Westcott, 2:207; Bernard, 2:489; Lagrange, 408; Barrett, 478, etc.)."

165. Carson, *Gospel According to John*, 523. Cf. also Brown, *Gospel According to John*, 2:684.

3. Sent (into the World) as Jesus Was Sent (into the World) (17:18; 20:21)

The two major "sending" passages of 17:18 and 20:21 link the way in which the disciples are sent with the way Jesus is sent. The adverb "just as" (καθώς), which occurs in both passages is found in the Fourth Gospel also in 1:23; 3:14; 5:23, 30; 6:31, 57, 58; 7:38; 8:28; 10:15; 12:14, 50; 13:15, 33, 34; 14:27, 31; 15:4, 9, 10, 12; 17:2, 11, 14, 16, 21, 22, 23; and 19:40. The relationships drawn in the Fourth Gospel by way of καθώς between Jesus and the disciples, besides sending in 17:18 and 20:21, include those of life (6:57), knowledge (10:14-15), love (15:9; 17:23), and unity (17:22).

The meaning of καθώς may be paraphrased as "in like manner," or "in the same way as," as is illustrated by the following examples: "Just as Moses lifted up the snake in the desert, so the Son of Man must be lifted up" (3:14); "I have set you an example that you should do as I have done for you" (13:15); "as I have loved you, so you must love one another" (13:34). Care should be taken not to push the relationship established by καθώς between two words, concepts, or statements too far. For example, when Jesus says in 17:16 that "they are not of the world, even as I am not of it," it would be inappropriate to argue that Jesus ruled out any distinction whatsoever between the exact way in which he could be said not to be "of the world" and the way in which the same thing could be said about his disciples. One should not require perfect correspondence in every detail between these relationships but only seek to grasp the perceived commonality between them.

The criterion for interpreting the meaning of καθώς involves therefore the question of what, from the perspective of the speaker or writer, is the perceived commonality between the two clauses related by καθώς. In 15:9, it is the kind of love Jesus showed the disciples. In 17:18, it is the way Jesus sent his disciples: he set them apart (cf. for his own setting apart, 10:36); he imparted to them the Spirit (cf. for Jesus' impartation with the Spirit, 1:34-36; 3:34); and he sent them out. In 20:21, the point seems to be that the same kinds of parameters guiding the sender-sent relationship between the Father and Jesus now also are to govern the relationship between Jesus and his disciples.[166]

While the wording of 17:18 and 20:21 is almost identical, and while 20:21 doubtless builds on 17:18, a closer scrutiny of the exact wordings and the respective contexts reveals that the respective passages nevertheless contain distinctive emphases. The major difference is that the former passage (17:18) includes the further qualifier "into the world," while the latter (20:21) simply links the sendings of Jesus and the disciples in general terms.

---

166. Cf. Bultmann, 382, n. 2, who argues that καθώς has both a comparing and at the same time a causal or explanatory sense, pointing also to 13:15, 34; 15:9-10, 12; 17:11, 21.

a. Sent into the World as Jesus Was Sent into the World (17:18)

It appears that 17:18 speaks to the process of sending, i.e., being set apart from the world and then sent back into the world (ἁγιάζω occurs three times in 17:16-19; cf. 10:36), while 20:21 focuses on the sender/sent relationships between the Father and Jesus on the one hand and between Jesus and his disciples on the other. The disciples must first be purified and set apart from the world (ἁγιάζω; cf. also καθαρός in 13:8-14; 15:3) before they can be sent (back) *into* the world (cf. also 6:60-71).[167] The frequency of ἀποστέλλω (seven times in John 17) indicates that John 17 is the focal point for the "sending" theme in the Fourth Gospel. Retrospectively, Jesus has accomplished his mission (cf. 17:4). Prospectively, the disciples' mission is about to begin.

According to 17:18 the disciples are sent by Jesus "into the world." The term κόσμος occurs frequently in the Farewell Discourse (cf. especially 15:18-27). Chapter 17 alone contains eleven out of the thirty-six occurrences found in the entire Gospel. The world is consistently characterized as a dark place that is alienated from God but nevertheless remains an object of his love (cf. 3:16). The Fourth Gospel portrays "the world" as in bondage to sin (cf. 8:23-24, 34-47; 9:39-41; 15:22; 16:8-11); under judgment (cf. 3:18) and God's wrath (cf. 3:36); "blind" (cf. 9:39-41) and unregenerated (cf. 3:3, 5); undiscerning regarding the true worship of God (cf. 4:24); and as hating Jesus, his followers, and the truth (cf. 1:10-11; 15:18-25; and 16:8-11).[168] While the Fourth Gospel emphasizes

---

167. As Brown, *Gospel According to John*, 2:762, points out, the consecration in truth mentioned in 17:17-18 is more than simply a purification from sin (cf. 15:3); it also involves a consecration *to* a mission (cf. Exod. 28:41). Cf. also Beasley-Murray, 300, who contends that consecration in the truth involves a spiritual separation from the world as well as growing conformity to the revelation of God in Christ and in dedication to his service. Finally, Lindars, 528-29, emphasizes that the consecration of Jesus and of the disciples is not the same. Only Jesus was consecrated to the task of sacrificing his life on behalf of others (ὑπέρ; cf. 10:11, 15-18; 11:51-52; 15:13; 17:19); Jesus' sacrifice will be the disciples' "constant inspiration to maintain their separation from the world and their devotion to their mission."

168. For an inventory of the occurrences of κόσμος in the Fourth Gospel, cf. Ned H. Cassem, "A Grammatical and Contextual Inventory of the Use of κόσμος in the Johannine Cosmic Theology," *NTS* 19 (1972/73): 81-91. However, Cassem's analysis, while claiming to be a simple "inventory," contains a number of questionable interpretive conclusions. Most importantly, Cassem fails to distinguish between a term's intrinsic meaning (its sense) and the role played by a passage's context. For example, he classes 3:16-17 as an instance of the Fourth Gospel's positive characterization of the world. At the surface, such a categorization appears plausible since 3:16-17 speaks of God's love for the world. However, closer scrutiny reveals that the fact that the world is the object of God's love should in no way be taken to imply that the world is viewed positively by the fourth evangelist in that passage. As a matter of fact, God's sending of his Son on a saving mission involving a violent cross-death rather presupposes the world's sinfulness and need for redemption. Cassem's failure to discern between the sense of the term κόσμος in 3:16-17 and other words in the passage's context causes him to misidentify the term's connotation in that passage. The same can be said of Cassem's classification of the references to Jesus' being "the light of the world." Cassem classes these references, too, as positive. Yet the fact that the world needs light presupposes

the need for believers to love one another and to be unified, these qualities are presented not as ends in themselves but as prerequisites for the church's mission in and to the world. The "destination" of the church's mission is not primarily defined in geographical but in spiritual terms.

The most important implication from the wording in 17:18 for the mission of the disciples is drawn by Carson, who writes, "Use of the phrase *into the world* for the mission of the disciples shows that there is no *necessary* overtone of incarnation or of invasion from another world. Only the broader descriptions of the coming of the Son 'into the world' betray the ontological gap that forever distances the origins of Jesus' mission from the origins of the disciples' mission."[169] As this writer points out, seekers reading the Gospel are introduced to mutually exclusive circles that demand a choice: "the circle of the world, in all its rebellion and lostness, and the circle of the disciples of Jesus, in all the privilege of their relationship to the living, self-disclosing, mission-ordaining, sanctifying God."[170]

Barrett addresses the issue whether 17:18 refers just to the original disciples or whether, as Käsemann asserts, the verse applies to *all* disciples and therefore presupposes the priesthood of all believers. According to Barrett, 17:20, with its reference to later believers, makes it doubtful whether John has in mind more than the original witnesses.[171] However, Brown is surely right when he contends, commenting on 15:16, that the original disciples "are being given a mission that all Christians must fulfill."[172] Similarly, Lindars asserts, commenting on 20:21, "The commission is of the disciples in the name of the whole Church for its mission to the world. . . . The disciples, and the whole Church following them, carry on the mission of Christ, which he received from the Father."[173] This is also the view held by Bultmann, who argues that 20:21, like chapters 13–16, rather than referring to a special apostolic mandate, features

---

that, by itself, it is dark! Again, Cassem has failed to distinguish properly between the sense of the word itself and that of other terms in the context. These kinds of shortcomings largely invalidate this author's conclusion that the fourth evangelist views κόσμος more favorably in chapters 1–12 and more negatively in chapters 13–21 (89) and that the Fourth Gospel's characterization of "the world" reflects a certain "ambivalence" (85). In light of the above critique, it seems rather warranted to find a unified Johannine perspective on "the world" pervading the entire Gospel, as indicated in the brief summary just presented. Cf. also Brown, *Gospel According to John*, 1:508-10.

169. Cf. Carson, *Gospel According to John*, 566. On the "incarnational model" for mission, cf. already Chapter 1 and again Chapter 5 below.

170. Carson, *Gospel According to John*, 567.

171. Cf. Barrett, 510-11.

172. Cf. Brown, *Gospel According to John*, 2:684. Cf. also Brown, *Gospel According to John*, 2:1034: "The characteristically Johannine outlook does not demote the Twelve, but rather turns these chosen disciples into representatives of all the Christians who would believe in Jesus on their word. And so, sometimes it is very difficult to know when John is speaking of the disciples in their historical role as the intimate companions of Jesus and when he is speaking of them in their symbolic role."

173. Cf. Lindars, 611.

the μαθηταί as representatives of the believing community.[174] This does not mean that the Fourth Gospel fails to distinguish between the missions of Jesus and of the disciples, and between the original and later disciples. It does mean, however, that 17:18 applies also to later believers, albeit derivatively.

Before discussing 20:21, it will be helpful to deal briefly with two foundational aspects of the disciples' mission that are highlighted in the Farewell Discourse and especially chapter 17, mutual love and unity.

b. Foundations for the Disciples' Mission: Love and Unity

As with the disciples' being sent (cf. 17:18; 20:21), the Fourth Gospel establishes connections with Jesus' relationship with the Father regarding love (cf. 13:34; 15:12) and unity (17:11, 22-23; in all these instances, καθώς is used). It seems closest to the Fourth Gospel's theological message to view the disciples' mutual love and unity as important foundations for their mission. As Popkes points out, the term καθώς establishes a correlation containing elements of participation and of analogy or correspondence.[175] The disciples are brought by Jesus into the unity and love of the Father-Son relationship. Moreover, the disciples are also brought into Jesus' relationship with the Father as a sent one. This spiritual participation places the entire mission of the disciples in the orbit of the love and unity between Father and Son. The disciples' love for one another and their unity with one another will be the foundation for their re-presentation of Jesus to the world (cf. 13:35; 17:21, 23).

Yet, importantly, love and unity are not in and of themselves the mission as if the revelation of the nature of God were merely an existential component of the believing community. The disciples are rather sent into the world with a message to proclaim (cf. 17:20) and commissioned to extend forgiveness (20:23). While love and unity are to be the foundation, they must be accompanied by an actual "going" (cf. 15:16) in order for fruit to be borne. Indeed, there are "works" to be done (cf. 14:12). Also, the disciples must "witness" in conjunction with the Spirit (cf. 15:26-27).

While one may therefore agree with Popkes that love and unity are an important element in the disciples' mission, disagreement must be registered with his contention that for John the disciples' internal relationships are more important than their external relationships.[176] The disciples' internal relationships are rather presented as foundational for their potential impact on the world and for the possible fruit resulting from their proclamation of the message about the Messiah. Thus Popkes is not completely correct when he contends,

---

174. Cf. Bultmann, 693.

175. Cf. Wiard Popkes, "Zum Verständnis der Mission bei Johannes," *Zeitschrift für Mission* 4 (1978): 66.

176. Cf. Popkes, 66.

"Das johannäische Missionsverständnis kann man mit dem Stichwort 'Mission durch Attraktion' verstehen."[177]

It is true that love and unity may and should have an initial appeal for those in the world. Yet, as the fourth evangelist himself demonstrates by his example of writing the Gospel (cf. 20:30-31), this "corporate witness" must be complemented by the verbal proclamation and exposition of the significance of Jesus' death and resurrection. Perhaps John indeed incorporates the Old Testament "centripetal" concept of mission resulting in the nations' flocking to Zion. But surely John transcends this concept and develops it further in terms of the *sending* of the Messianic community to re-present Jesus the Messiah to the world by *going* and "bearing fruit." Popkes' one-sided focus on the community's love and unity and his total neglect of the Fourth Gospel's sending passages cannot be justified and leads to a very serious distortion of the Fourth Gospel's presentation of the disciples' mission.

In this context it must be maintained that the Fourth Gospel's teaching on predestination does not preclude Jesus' sending of his disciples into the world. The disciples' separation from the world is a spiritual separation from the world that is necessary for their effectiveness in the world, not an expression of a negative attitude toward the world or evidence for a lack of concern for the world. Thus the fourth evangelist does not advocate indifference toward the world or even the believing community's withdrawal or seclusion from the world, even though the term "love" is not applied to the disciples with reference to the world.

The proper objects of the disciples' love are neither self (cf. 12:25-26) nor the world but only Jesus and fellow believers. Moreover, the disciples were first loved by Jesus (cf. 13:1-3). It is his love for them which is to be the ground and model for their love for one another (cf. 13:34-35). This love, in turn, together with their unity, will be the foundation for their own mission to the world. However, as already mentioned, as in the case of Jesus (cf. 3:16), their love is to be followed by works (14:12), going (15:16), witnessing (15:27), and the proclamation of a message (17:20; 20:23).

c. Sent as Jesus Was Sent (20:21)

While 17:18 sets the disciples' mission in the context of their being sent into the "world," 20:21, while building on this reference, focuses more on Jesus' investing of the disciples with authority and legitimation.[178] This more general

---

177. Cf. Popkes, 67.

178. Cf. Schnackenburg, *Gospel According to St. John*, 3:324, who argues that while 17:18 has overtones of the disciples' being sent into a world alienated from God, 20:21 is concerned for the passing on of the *Vollmacht* and *Auftrag Jesu*. According to Schnackenburg, the disciples are to represent Jesus in the world and to continue his work of salvation. While the former is doubtless true, the latter notion must be rejected, since Jesus' work of salvation is everywhere in the Fourth Gospel presented as completed (cf., e.g., 17:4; 19:30).

reference to "sending" ties the disciples' mission in with earlier statements regarding Jesus' being sent as well as with comments regarding the nature of the sender/sent relationship. When dealing with Jesus' mission, four basic characteristics of the sent one were identified: (1) bringing glory and honor to the sender; (2) doing the sender's will, working his works, and speaking his words; (3) witnessing to the sender and representing him accurately; and (4) knowing the sender intimately, living in close relationship with the sender, and following his example. All these aspects of what one sent is required to be and do, are applicable to the disciples as they are sent by Jesus.

Brown's careful exposition of the force of καθώς in 20:21 deserves to be quoted in full:

> The special Johannine contribution to the theology of this mission is that the Father's sending of the Son serves both as the model [the comparative aspect of καθώς] and the ground [the explanatory aspect of καθώς] for the Son's sending of the disciples. Their mission is to continue the Son's mission; and this requires that the Son must be present to them during this mission, just as the Father had to be present to the Son during his mission.[179]

The implications of Brown's observation may be summarized as follows: the disciples are not just to *represent* Jesus (thus the Jewish sending concept is transcended), they are to *re-present* him, i.e., Jesus will be present in and through them in his Spirit as they fulfill their mission in the world. This fact is underscored by the "in" language used frequently in the Farewell Discourse with reference to the disciples and the stress on the disciples' need for dependence and obedience to Jesus, their sender.[180]

Of great importance is the fact that 20:21 (cf. also 20:24-31) identifies *Jesus* as the sender of the disciples. Ahr, referring also to 13:16 and 20, notes this "shift in the theology of sending": "he [Jesus] now becomes, like the Father, the sender."[181] Therefore the disciples are to bring glory and honor to *Jesus* (as well as to the Father; cf. 15:8, 16). They are to do *Jesus'* will, perform *Jesus'* works, and speak *Jesus'* words. The disciples are to witness to *Jesus* and to

179. Cf. Brown, *Gospel According to John*, 2:1036. Brown refers to 12:45; 13:20; and 20:22. For the Father's presence with Jesus, cf. especially 1:18; for the Spirit's presence with Jesus, cf. 1:32-33; 3:34. Cf. also Vellanickal, 150, who reproduces the entire (!) quote verbatim without crediting Brown.

180. Regarding Brown's use of language the following caution may be registered. As already asserted, a distinction should be made between the terms "sending" and "mission." While Jesus' *sending* can be seen as the model and ground for the disciples' mission in his dependent, obedient relationship to his sender (even as Son to Father), Jesus' *mission* (and especially the incarnation, i.e., his "coming into the world") is never in the Fourth Gospel presented as the model for the mission of the disciples or believers in general.

181. Cf. Peter G. Ahr, " 'He Loved Them to Completion': The Theology of John 13–14," in *Standing Before God: Studies on Prayer in Scriptures and in Tradition with Essays in Honor of John M. Oesterreicher*, ed. Asker Finkel and Lawrence Frizzell (New York: Ktav, 1981), 80.

represent *him* accurately. And they are to know *Jesus* intimately, live in close relationship with *him,* and follow *his* example. In a word, *their* relationship to *their* sender, Jesus, is to reflect *Jesus'* relationship with *his* sender, the Father.[182]

Beasley-Murray notes two important ramifications of 20:21. First, the Son's mission does not end with his being "lifted up." While the form of fulfillment is to be changed, the mission will nevertheless continue and be effective. Thus the disciples are commissioned to carry on Christ's work, not to begin a new one. Second, the giving of the Spirit is linked with the disciples' mission (cf. 20:22; cf. already 15:26-27; 16:8-11), so that 20:23 should be interpreted in the light of 20:21-22. As Beasley-Murray points out, the Spirit provides a crucial element of continuity between the ministry of Jesus in the flesh and the work of the exalted Jesus through his disciples: "The risen Lord, in associating his disciples with his continuing mission in the world, bestows the Spirit, through whom his own ministry in the flesh was carried out in the power of God."[183] Bruce concurs: "The Son's mission in the world is entrusted to them, since he is returning to the Father, but as the Son had received the Spirit . . . for the discharge of his own mission (John 1:32-34; 3:34), so they now receive the Spirit for the discharge of theirs."[184]

Doubtless the sending of the Spirit is presented by the fourth evangelist as the key element in the disciples' mission.[185] The sending of the Spirit is one of the major subjects of the Farewell Discourse. Reference is made to the Spirit in the immediate context of 14:12 and 20:21. The disciples' consecration in the truth, i.e., God's word, should also be seen in the context of the Spirit, who is repeatedly in the Fourth Gospel called "the Spirit of truth" (cf. 14:17; 15:26; 16:13). Nevertheless, the sending of the Spirit occurs with reference to the missions of Christ and of the disciples. As Vellanickal observes, "It is worth noting that in Jn the work of the Spirit is entirely subordinated to the work of Christ and strictly related to the disciples' life of faith in Christ."[186]

---

182. Regarding the disciples' obligation to follow their sender's example in the Fourth Gospel, cf. Schulz, 298-301. This theme is only prominent in 13:1-15 in terms of service and in 13:34 and 15:12-13 in terms of love (cf. 1 John 3:16).

183. Cf. Beasley-Murray, 380. Regarding the interpretation of 20:22, cf. Carson, *Gospel According to John,* 649-55.

184. Cf. Bruce, *Gospel of John,* 391.

185. Cf. Hahn, "Sendung des Geistes — Sendung der Jünger," in *Universales Christentum angesichts einer pluralen Welt,* Beitrage zur Religionstheologie 1, ed. Andreas Bsteh (Mödling bei Wien: St. Gabriel, 1976), 87-106; Jean Giblet, "Les promesses de l'Esprit et la mission des apôtres dans les Évangiles," *Irénikon* 30 (1957): 20-43. Cf. also the recent structural-critical study by Mark Stibbe, " 'Return to Sender': A Structuralist Approach to John's Gospel," *Biblical Interpretation* 1 (1993): 189-206. Stibbe concludes that the missions of Jesus and of the disciples can be mapped out structurally in parallel fashion except for the Spirit's role in the disciples' mission. While this observation is interesting, Stibbe makes too little of the Fourth Gospel's references to the Spirit's role in the mission of Jesus (cf., e.g., 1:32-33; 3:34).

186. Cf. Vellanickal, 136. Thus the procedure followed in this present study, i.e., to study the missions of Jesus and of the disciples with secondary reference to the sending of the Spirit where it relates to these missions, seems justified.

At the occasion of his commissioning of the disciples, Jesus gave them the authority to forgive or retain sins (cf. 20:23).[187] Only Jesus is "the Lamb of God that takes away the sins of the world" (1:29). Nevertheless, the disciples have the privilege of extending the forgiveness made possible by Jesus' sacrificial death to others.[188] While some focus in their discussion of this mandate on forgiveness within the (Johannine) community,[189] the disciples' forgiveness or retention of sins should probably be seen in the context of people's reception or rejection of Jesus as the Christ, i.e., in the context of belief or unbelief in Jesus.[190] This seems to be consistent with the event immediately preceding the mandate, i.e., the disciples' imminent reception of the Spirit (cf. 20:22) whose mission to the world was described in 16:8-11 as convicting the world of its unbelief in Jesus.[191] It also seems to cohere with the fact that Jesus' mission is consistently in the Fourth Gospel presented in terms of bringing salvation or judgment (cf. 3:17; 9:39; 12:31).[192]

Finally, Beasley-Murray counters the view of Seidensticker that that passage does not refer to a comprehensive sending of the disciples by Jesus but only reflects a pastoral concern of the Johannine community.[193] Seidensticker argues that Jesus' commission to his disciples to forgive sins limits the sending

187. Cf. the instances of the terms ἁμαρτία (1:29, 36; 8:21, 24, 34, 46; 9:34, 41; 15:22, 24; 16:8, 9; 19:11; 20:23); ἁμαρτάνω (5:14; [8:11]; 9:2, 3); ἁμαρτολός (9:16, 24, 25, 31); ἀναμάρτητος (8:7). Cf. also the terms potentially implying sin or the need for forgiveness, σῴζω (3:17; 5:34; 10:9; 11:12; 12:27, 47); ἀπόλλυμι (3:16; 6:39; 10:10, 28; 11:50; 12:25; 17:12; 18:9); and ἀπώλεια (17:12). Note also 1:5, 11; 2:24-25; 3:19-21; and the Jews' persecution and crucifixion of Jesus throughout.

188. For a discussion of whether this commission is entrusted to the disciples *qua* apostles or *qua* believers, cf. F. W. Beare, "The Risen Jesus Bestows the Spirit: A Study of John 20:19-23," *CJT* 4 (1958): 99.

189. Cf. Barry F. Sullivan, "Ego Te Absolvo: The Forgiveness of Sins in the Context of the Pneumatic Community" (Th.M. thesis, Grand Rapids Theological Seminary, 1988).

190. Cf. Carson, *Gospel According to John*, 655; Bruce, *Gospel of John*, 392: "whereas the Matthaean contexts [16:19 and 18:18] point to an interpretation in terms of church discipline, the present context is related to the disciples' mission in the world." Contra Brown, *Gospel According to John*, 2:1044 who argues that 20:23 should be understood not from a purely missionary situation but in the light of an established ecclesiastical community so that the forgiveness referred to in 20:23 applies to the time of admission to the community and afterwards in the life of the community. Also contra Beasley-Murray, 384; and Schlatter, 360, who adduces 1 John 5:16 as a supposed instance where 20:23 is applied in the Johannine community. Cf. further Lindars, who cites the view of John N. Sanders, *A Commentary on the Gospel According to St. John* (London: Adam & Charles Black, 1968), 434, that 20:23 refers to the church's mission preaching and proceeds to argue, without substantiation, that reference is *also* made to the preaching within the life of the church.

191. Cf. Brown, *Gospel According to John*, 2:1035, who argues that 20:22 is a later addition by the evangelist for the purpose of modifying 20:21 by widening the horizon of the original appearance scene to include not only "the Twelve" but those whom they represent. However, this view is without substantiation from the text and is completely unnecessary.

192. Cf. Beasley-Murray, 383.

193. Cf. Beasley-Murray, 380; Philip Seidensticker, *Die Auferstehung Jesu in der Botschaft der Evangelisten*, SBS 26 (Stuttgart: Katholisches Bibelwerk, 1968), 122-44.

of 20:21. However, as Beasley-Murray shows, Seidensticker fails to consider 20:22, a passage which, in connection with 15:26-27 and 16:8-11, should be understood in the context of the disciples' comprehensive mission *to the world,* not just as operative within the confines of a believing community. Moreover, Seidensticker does not give adequate weight to 17:18 which speaks of the disciples as being sent *into the world,* a passage that 20:21 surely builds upon and develops. Also, Jesus' own mission is presented in the Fourth Gospel as a mission with ramifications for *the world* (cf. 1:29; 3:16; 12:31-32).

4. General Observations on the Sending Theme and the Missions of Jesus and of the Disciples

The sending theme thus provides a major bridge between the missions of Jesus and of the disciples. It is the matrix of themes connected with the sending theme in the Fourth Gospel, especially the sent Son's obedient, dependent relationship with his sender, the Father, that provides the proper informing context for the sending of the disciples.[194] This is emphasized by Barrett, who writes,

> It follows further that as Jesus in his ministry was entirely dependent upon and obedient to God the Father, who sealed and sanctified him (4.34; 5.19; 10.37; 17.4, and other passages: 6.27; 10.36), and acted in the power of the Spirit who rested upon him (1.32), so the church is the apostolic church, commissioned by Christ, only in virtue of the fact that Jesus sanctified it (17.19) and breathed the Spirit into it (v. 22), and only so far as it maintains an attitude of perfect obedience to Jesus (it is here, of course, that the parallelism between the relation of Jesus to the Father and the relation of the church to Jesus breaks down).[195]

The matrix of sending references applied to the mission of Jesus has already been studied. Through the explicit connection established by 20:21, one may extend these characteristics to the mission of the disciples.

Like Jesus, the disciples are to bring glory to the sender (humility), do the sender's will (obedience; cf. 4:3; 5:30, 38), make the sender known, witness to, and represent the sender accurately (cf. 12:44, 45; 13:20), know him intimately (cf. 15:15; 17:7, 8, 25), and follow his example (cf. 13:12-17). At the heart of 20:21 is the message that, while formerly the Father had been the sender and Jesus the one sent, now *Jesus* is the sender (κἀγώ, πέμπω) and the disciples the sent ones. From now on and in the future, the disciples are to relate to Jesus the way Jesus, while on earth, related to the Father. They are chosen, set apart,

---

194. Cf. Carson, *Gospel According to John,* 648. However, since there is no mention of the incarnation in connection with the disciples' mission, any parallel from it must remain entirely derivative.

195. Cf. Barrett, 569.

and sent into the world by Jesus (cf. 17:18). They are to be totally dependent on him, as evidenced by their prayer to Jesus and in Jesus' name (cf. 14:13-14; 15:7-8, 16). They are to live in obedience to Jesus and his word (cf. 14:21, 23-24; 15:14, 20; 17:6; cf. 14:31). And they are to relate to one another in humble service, love, and unity (cf. 13:12-17, 34-35; 15:9-10, 12-13, 17; 17:11, 21-23, 26).

As Jesus was completely devoted to do the will of the one who sent him (cf., e.g., 4:34), the disciples, too, are to subordinate themselves in the accomplishment of their mission to the will of their sender, i.e., Jesus. Jesus' call of people to follow him constitutes their decisive encounter with the will of God.[196] From this call onward, the personal life of the messenger is determined exclusively by his charge. The disciple is to be completely subordinated to the will of his Lord until death.[197] However, while thus the disciples are to continue Jesus' mission, this is presented in the Fourth Gospel in such a way that the uniqueness and once-for-all nature of Jesus' work is preserved.[198]

Jesus, a unique person, shared his intimate knowledge of *his* sender with his disciples, with whom he would in turn initiate a sending relationship. This intimate relationship is not acquired at once, nor is it forever won, once achieved. Rather, it needs to be carefully maintained. Jesus desires no less of his sent ones. He wants them to represent him accurately (cf. 12:44-45; 13:20; cf. also 20:21). Jesus is presented in the Fourth Gospel as the Sent One par excellence (cf. 9:7) whose relationship with his sender forms the model for the relationship Jesus himself, once turned sender, desires to have with those he is to send (cf. 20:21: "As the Father sent me, so send I you"). Therefore the thoughtful reader — and disciple — is expected to view Jesus throughout the Fourth Gospel as worth imitating in his dependent relationship with his sender.

The fact that Jesus shows to his disciples his pierced hands and his side (cf. 20:19), as well as his commission to forgive or retain sins, ties the disciples' mission to Jesus' death (cf. chaps. 18–20; cf. also 17:4 and 19:30). Jesus' mission is unique, irreplaceable, and fundamental for the church's mission. His sacrifice makes the disciples' mission possible. As the passion narrative is careful to maintain, this sacrifice was accomplished in fulfillment of Scripture, in accordance with God's will, and with the full and active cooperation of Jesus himself. Jesus' crucifixion and resurrection form an integral part of the disciples' mission. Jesus is the center of their mission as well as their message regarding Jesus' Messiahship.

The commissioning is the climax of the relationship the resurrected yet departing Jesus sustains with his disciples (cf. 1:18; 14:10-11; 15:15; chap. 17).

---

196. Cf. Gustav Wilhelm Stählin, "Κατὰ τὸ θέλημα τοῦ θεοῦ: Von der Dynamik der urchristlichen Mission," in *Wort und Geist: Studien zur christlichen Erkenntnis von Gott, Welt und Mensch: Festgabe für Karl Heim,* ed. Adolf Köberle and Otto Schmitz (Berlin: Furche, 1934), 107.

197. Cf. Stählin, 108.

198. Stählin, 105.

Jesus has revealed the Father fully to them (cf. 15:15; 17:6-8). Now he can send them as the Father sent him, since they fully know Jesus as the one who was sent from the Father (cf. 17:6-8; cf. also 14:6-14). And this is the goal of their mission: that through them others may come to know Jesus (cf. 17:20; 20:29; cf. also 20:30-31). This full revelation of the Father is climaxed in Jesus' death for them (cf. 3:16) which, among other things, reveals God's love for a sinful world. Now the disciples are to be "the continuing locus of 3:16: 'God so loved the world that he sent. . . .'"[199] Jesus is both the *perfect* revelation and the *ultimate* sacrifice — the disciples are to witness to Jesus' person and work through their words, works, and lives (cf. 14:12; 15:26-27; 16:8-11; 17:18).

While the disciples share in the likeness of Jesus' sending from the Father — with no direct implications as to Jesus' divine nature and thus his unique revelatory or redemptive work — and thus in the manner of his sending, they share only mediately in the purpose of Jesus' mission by being his instruments of further extending it. Jesus' mission itself is never rescinded or abandoned in the Fourth Gospel. Jesus is still, through the Spirit and his disciples, carrying out his mission, though now from heaven.[200] The disciples do not replace Jesus — his ministry continues and is effective in their ministry (14:12-14). Jesus is still the "Sent One" par excellence (cf. 9:7). It is still Jesus, the exalted, glorified crucified, risen, and coming one, who forgives and who gives salvation and eternal life. The disciples have simply entered into his mission (cf. 4:38), a mission that Jesus has never abandoned.

The Spirit and the disciples will represent Jesus (cf. the sending theme), but they will not replace him. The Spirit represents Jesus in that he will remind the disciples of what Jesus said (cf. 14:26). Like Jesus, he will teach them and lead them into all truth (cf. 8:31; 17:17). He also will convict the world of its unbelief in Jesus (cf. 16:8-11), again a function that Jesus had already fulfilled throughout his earthly ministry, and especially in his death on the cross (cf. 12:31). Again, Jesus is "the good shepherd." Yet his commissioning of Peter to "tend his lambs" does not imply that Jesus abandons his role as the Shepherd (cf. 10:16). He simply confers this task to Peter as his representative.

As noted, the mission theme in the Fourth Gospel comprises components of "sending," as well as other terminologies, such as "descending" and "ascending," "coming" or "coming into the world," and "returning." It is vital to distinguish among these various components and to relate them accurately to one another in order to arrive at a proper understanding of the relationship between the missions of Jesus and of the disciples. Perhaps one can compare and contrast the relationship between the missions and sendings of Jesus and of the disciples this way: while the ways in which they are sent contain elements of analogy, their missions are still distinct. If the missions of Jesus and of the disciples were

---

199. Cf. Carson, *Gospel According to John,* 567.
200. Cf. Thüsing.

identical, the disciples could replace Jesus. But since important distinctions remain, the disciples merely enter into Jesus' mission (cf. 4:38).

The identities of Jesus and of the disciples are different — thus they have different parts in God's mission. Importantly, Jesus is identified with God the Father in a way in the Fourth Gospel that the disciples are not. However, the disciples are to be identified with Jesus in the way they are sent (cf. 17:18; 20:21), and, by way of instrumentality, also in the purpose of his sending (cf., e.g., 20:31 and Jesus' giving of life elsewhere in the Fourth Gospel). They are to extend Jesus' mission as they are equipped, led, and taught by the Spirit. By virtue of Jesus' unique personhood, his mission continues through the disciples, having modelled, as part of his own mission, the role of a sent one for them while on earth so that they might have his example and follow it.

IV. CONCLUSION

How does the disciples' mission relate to the mission of Jesus? One should be careful not to force these missions into a general scheme that fits both. Neither should one expect to find a total correspondence between the various elements of the missions of Jesus and of the disciples. Nevertheless, the following patterns illustrate the respective missions and their relationship.

Fig. 10. The Mission of Jesus and the Mission of the Disciples

Jesus' Mission

coming (into the world) and returning (descent-ascent) (signs)	The Son sent (into the world) by the Father (works)	The shepherd-teacher calling followers to gather harvest	

The Disciples' Mission

	sent (into the world) by Jesus (greater works)	following Jesus	coming to Jesus (and believing)

Jesus' descent-ascent (his coming into the world and returning, the logos becoming flesh) as well as his Messianic signs are unparalleled in the disciples' mission. They are simply to come to Jesus and to believe. Jesus' role as the shepherd-teacher who calls followers to gather his eschatological harvest corresponds to the disciples' following Jesus. The Son's being sent into the world by the Father to do his (i.e., the Father's) works is paralleled by the disciples' being sent into the world by Jesus to do "greater works" in dependence on Jesus. This latter correspondence, of course, is explicitly noted in the Fourth Gospel in 17:18 and 20:21.

The disciples' participation in Jesus' mission is almost exclusively discussed in the second part of the Gospel (except for the proleptic reference in 4:38 and the possible implications drawn from 12:20-32). The disciples' participation in the mission of the earthly Jesus in chapters 1–12 is limited to the ordinary tasks of disciples, such as the buying of food (cf. 4:8) or helping Jesus to distribute food and gathering leftovers (cf. 6:5-13). By contrast, the disciples' participation in the exalted Jesus' mission according to chapters 13–21 is much more significant than the accomplishment of these ordinary tasks. The disciples will do even "greater works" than their Master did during his earthly mission (cf. 14:12).

The disciples' following of Jesus and their gathering of fruit, already referred to in the first half of the Gospel, are set on a higher, more advanced plane in the second part (cf. 13:36-38 and 21:15-23 for following; 15:5, 8, 16 for bearing fruit). Part two of the Fourth Gospel thus can be said to show not just the exaltation of Jesus but *the implications* of Jesus' exaltation for the mission of his followers and thus the *significance* of Jesus' work not just for believers' salvation but for their mission as well, both individually (cf. especially Peter and the Beloved Disciple) and corporately. Finally, for John there is no separate class of "missionaries": *all* believers are sent.

With these general observations regarding the mission of the disciples and its relationship to the mission of Jesus according to the Fourth Gospel the study of the disciples' mission according to the Fourth Gospel may be concluded. It remains for the final chapter to explore some of the implications of the present study. Specifically, the implications for the purpose of the Fourth Gospel and for the mission of the contemporary church will be considered.

CHAPTER 5

Conclusions and Implications from the Study of Mission in the Fourth Gospel

The study of the missions of Jesus and of the disciples in the Fourth Gospel has been completed. This final chapter, after briefly revisiting definitional matters, will address the implications from the present study for the Fourth Gospel's purpose and for the mission of the contemporary church.

I. THE DEFINITION OF MISSION REVISITED

The working definition of mission reads as follows: "Mission is the specific task or purpose which a person or group seeks to accomplish, involving various modes of movement, be it sending or being sent, coming and going, descending and ascending, gathering by calling others to follow, or following." The study of mission in the Fourth Gospel in Chapters 3 and 4 then proceeded along the following lines: the *person* of Jesus or the *group* of the disciples, their respective *tasks,* and the *various modes of movement* involved. These terms proved to function as an appropriate framework for the study of the Fourth Gospel's presentation of the missions of Jesus and of the disciples.

Jesus' mission is presented in a way that promotes the Fourth Gospel's readers' faith in Jesus as Messiah. The Fourth Gospel portrays Jesus' mission according to three major emphases, each involving a certain *mode of movement*: Jesus as the Son *sent* from the Father, Jesus as the one who *came* into the world and *returned* to the Father, and Jesus as the eschatological shepherd-teacher who called others to *follow* him in order to help *gather* the eschatological harvest.

The major modes of movement in the disciples' mission according to the Fourth Gospel were determined to be *following* Jesus and *being sent* by Jesus. In a comparison of the mission of Jesus with that of the disciples, the following relationships emerge. The disciples' *being sent* involves components of all three

199

aspects of Jesus' Messianic mission: an obligation to reflect Jesus in his obedient, dependent relationship to his sender (cf. "Jesus the sent Son"; cf. 20:21), a sharing in Jesus' otherworldly orientation (cf. "Jesus who came into the world and returned"; cf. 17:18), and a call to help gather the Messianic eschatological harvest (cf. "Jesus the eschatological shepherd-teacher"; cf. 4:38).

The working definition in Chapter 2 thus proved to be generally valid in the study of the missions of Jesus and of the disciples in Chapters 3 and 4 and can therefore be adopted permanently.

II. IMPLICATIONS FOR THE PURPOSE
OF THE FOURTH GOSPEL

Should the Fourth Gospel's mission emphasis be understood within the framework of a missionary purpose or should it be seen as part of a document whose intent it is to strengthen the faith and mission of an already believing community? It is now possible to explore some of the implications from the study of the Fourth Gospel's teaching on mission for an identification of the Fourth Gospel's purpose. It will be useful to trace briefly the alternative views held regarding the Fourth Gospel's purpose, giving special attention to the way each view corresponds with a certain assessment of mission in John.

Essentially, the proposed solutions fall into two categories: (1) the Fourth Gospel as "Missionsschrift," i.e., as designed to lead its recipients to faith, whatever group the author(s) may have had in mind; (2) the Fourth Gospel as a "Gemeindeschrift," i.e., as written to strengthen the — already existing — faith of a community of believers.[1] Under the second view, one may distinguish further between writers who believe that John or an unknown "fourth evangelist" wrote the Fourth Gospel to strengthen the faith of his recipients and those who view the document's setting in light of the "Johannine community hypothesis."[2] Although there are various versions of the hypothesis, it seems

1. It must be noted that these two terms, "Missionsschrift" and "Gemeindeschrift," are not always defined the same way by different scholars. It seems best to understand the former term as referring to the Fourth Gospel's supposed intention to lead unbelievers to faith in Jesus the Messiah and the latter expression as speaking of the Fourth Gospel's purported design to deepen the faith of its postulated believing recipients. But especially the latter term has sometimes been taken to imply also that the Fourth Gospel is the *product* of a believing community, a view that is even held by van Unnik, a pronounced proponent of the "Missionsschrift" hypothesis. It appears that there has been a considerable amount of terminological confusion that has hindered clarity of discourse among proponents of different views. A proper definition of terms is therefore imperative.

2. Note, however, that there are many variations of the "Johannine community hypothesis" so that it is highly advisable to speak of different schools of thought in this regard, such as the "Martyn/Brown school" (referring to the work of J. Louis Martyn and Raymond E. Brown) or others. For convenience's sake, when general reference to the "Johannine community hypothesis" is made in the discussion below, the hypothesis championed by Martyn and Brown is the one in

best to group the adherents of this Johannine community hypothesis together under one separate heading, "The Fourth Gospel as a Sectarian Document," and to deal with differences in detail there.

A. Missionary (Missionsschrift)

The view that the Fourth Gospel is designed for a missionary purpose received pronounced expression earlier this century by Bornhäuser (who held that the Fourth Gospel was designed as a "Missionsschrift" for Israel),[3] Oehler (who argued that the Fourth Gospel was written as a "Missionsschrift" for the Hellenistic world of John's day),[4] and Oepke (who saw the Fourth Gospel as addressed to a wide array of recipients, even within the church).[5] Later Oehler published three small volumes in which he sought to highlight the missionary nature of the Fourth Gospel, arguing that John is telling the story of the savior of the world.[6] Bowman, at least partially followed by Freed as well as Meeks, expressed his view that the Fourth Gospel may have been largely composed with the Samaritan mission in mind.[7]

Bornhäuser's thesis was given a new lease on life almost thirty years later by van Unnik and Robinson. Van Unnik, in an article that remains very influential even today, argued that the Fourth Gospel was written to missionize visitors to a Jewish-Hellenistic synagogue in the diaspora, including both Jews and

---

mind (for a description, see below). However, as will become evident, there are many variations to their version of the "Johannine community hypothesis" so that it is precarious to streamline all of its proponents into one school of thought.

3. Karl Bornhäuser, *Das Johannesevangelium: Eine Missionsschrift für Israel*, BFCT 2/15 (Gütersloh: Bertelsmann, 1928).

4. Wilhelm Oehler, *Das Johannesevangelium, eine Missionsschrift für die Welt, der Gemeinde ausgelegt* (Gütersloh: Bertelsmann, 1936); Wilhelm Oehler, *Zum Missionscharakter des Johannesevangeliums* (Gütersloh: Bertelsmann, 1941).

5. Albrecht Oepke, "Das missionarische Christuszeugnis des Johannesevangeliums," *EMZ* 2 (1941), 4-26.

6. Wilhelm Oehler, *Das Johannesevangelium, eine Missionsschrift für die Welt*, 3 vols. (Württemberg: Buchhandlung der Evangelischen Missionsschule Unterweissach, 1957). Oehler points especially to the nature of the prologue and epilogue, the references to "the Jews" in the Fourth Gospel, the book's eschatology, and the message to the "Johannine community" in the Farewell Discourse.

7. John Bowman, "The Fourth Gospel and the Samaritans," *BJRL* 40 (1958): 298-308. Cf. also Edwin D. Freed, "Samaritan Influence in the Gospel of John," *CBQ* 30 (1968): 580-87; and "Did John Write His Gospel Partly to Win Samaritan Converts?" *NovT* 12 (1970): 241-56; and Wayne A. Meeks, *The Prophet-King: Moses Traditions and the Johannine Christology*, NovTSup 14 (Leiden: E. J. Brill, 1967): 313-19; and "'Am I a Jew?' Johannine Christianity and Judaism," in *Christianity, Judaism, and Other Greco-Roman Cults*, ed. Jacob Neusner (Leiden: E. J. Brill, 1975), 163-86, especially 178. Cf. also Teresa Okure, *Johannine Approach to Mission: A Contextual Study of John 4:1-42*, WUNT 2/31 (Tübingen: J. C. B. Mohr [Paul Siebeck], 1988) 11, who further lists the contributions by Cullmann, Brown, and Olsson.

proselytes.[8] Thus he pioneered the idea that the missionary life-setting for the Fourth Gospel was the controversy of the "Johannine community" with the synagogue. Robinson developed Bornhäuser's views in a different direction than van Unnik. He maintained that the Fourth Gospel is a "Missionsschrift" composed by the apostle John in Ephesus and addressed to diaspora Jews after Palestinian Judaism had rejected Jesus as Israel's Messiah.[9] The Fourth Gospel's message, according to Robinson, is therefore that true Judaism finds its fulfillment in faith in Jesus as Israel's Messiah and king, and that the promise of Israel's gathering was fulfilled through the death of Jesus. Robinson sees the distinction made in the Fourth Gospel not as between Jews and Gentiles but as between Palestinian and diaspora Jews.[10] Finally, C. H. Dodd believes the Fourth Gospel was addressed to a wide, non-Christian readership of the Hellenistic world of the day.[11]

B. Edificatory (Gemeindeschrift)

Schnackenburg, in discussion with van Unnik and Robinson, rejects the views of both. He maintains that the Christological presentation of the Fourth Gospel as well as the self-revelation of the Johannine Jesus can only be understood by believers. Thus the Fourth Gospel is not a "Missionsschrift" but a "Gemeindeschrift" written to deepen the faith of believers.[12] Conzelmann agrees: "Dem johanneischen Kirchengedanken entspricht nicht der Gedanke der Mission, sondern das 'Zeugnis,' die Stärkung des Glaubens."[13] Schneider states categorically, "Das vierte Evangelium hat verhältnismäßig wenige Texte, die auf die Mission bezogen sind. Es ist keine 'Missionsschrift.'"[14] Bowker contributes a rather speculative thesis which has been adopted by some very influential Jo-

8. W. C. van Unnik, "The Purpose of St. John's Gospel," in *SE I*, TU 73, ed. Kurt Aland et al. (Berlin: Akademie, 1959), 382-411. Van Unnik interprets 20:30 as well as 10:16 and 11:52 in the light of his thesis. He also draws attention to the titles Μεσσίας and Χριστός found in the Fourth Gospel and argues that these would have been most meaningful for Jews and proselytes.

9. John A. T. Robinson, "The Destination and Purpose of St John's Gospel," *NTS* 6 (1959-60): 117-31.

10. Correspondingly, he interprets 10:16 and 11:52, as well as 7:35 and 12:20ff., as references to diaspora Jews.

11. C. H. Dodd, *The Interpretation of the Fourth Gospel* (Cambridge: Cambridge University Press, 1953), 9. Cf. also the works by Oehler and Oepke cited above.

12. Rudolf Schnackenburg, "Die Messiasfrage im Johannesevangelium," in *Neutestamentliche Aufsätze: Festschrift für Josef Schmid,* ed. J. Blinzler, O. Kuss and F. Mußner (Regensburg: Friedrich Pustet, 1963), 240-64.

13. Cf. Hans Conzelmann, *Grundriß der Theologie des Neuen Testaments* (München: Chr. Kaiser, 1967), 362.

14. Cf. Gerhard Schneider, "Der Missionsauftrag Jesu in der Darstellung der Evangelien," in *Mission im Neuen Testament,* ed. Karl Kertelge, QD 93 (Freiburg im Breisgau/Basel/Wien: Herder, 1982), 90.

hannine scholars, including R. E. Brown and J. L. Martyn. He postulates that the Fourth Gospel was not designed to missionize Jews but that it constitutes a reflection of Jewish Christians about their relationship to Judaism.[15] Finally, Wind manages to argue that the Fourth Gospel was written to *both* believers and unbelievers alike![16]

Some scholars maintain that, while the Fourth Gospel is a "Gemeindeschrift," it nevertheless reflects a strong "Missionsgedanke," i.e., a very positive attitude toward mission, albeit not a direct missionary intent.[17] Okure recognizes a "missionary thrust" in the Fourth Gospel without being prepared to accept the Fourth Gospel as an evangelistic document.[18] She seeks a solution in redefining one's definition of mission from "outreach to unbelievers" to "continuing to believe in Jesus." Another mediating position is represented by the source critics Wilkens, Fortna, and Nicol, who hold that the Fourth Gospel's σημεῖα-source was essentially a missionary document, designed to win Hellenists (Wilkens), Jews (Nicol), or both Jews and Gentiles (Fortna), but that the Fourth Gospel in its final form was intended to serve the needs of the "Johannine community."[19]

C. Sectarian

Others have argued that the Fourth Gospel is essentially a sectarian document. Most of these writers follow J. L. Martyn's view that the Fourth Gospel, as a "two-level drama," reflects not so much the history of the historical Jesus but that of the "Johannine community."[20] According to Martyn, the "Johannine

15. J. W. Bowker, "The Origin and Purpose of St John's Gospel," *NTS* 11 (1964/65): 398-408.

16. A. Wind, "Destination and Purpose of the Gospel of John," *NovT* 14 (1972): 26-69. Cf. also the discussion of Wind's work by Okure, 16.

17. Cf., e.g., Miguel Rodriguez Ruiz, *Der Missionsgedanke des Johannesevangeliums: Ein Beitrag zur johanneischen Soteriologie und Ekklesiologie*, FB 55 (Würzburg: Echter, 1986), his mentor Schnackenburg, and Rensberger. See also the survey of Rensberger below.

18. Cf. Okure, 16.

19. Cf. Wilhelm Wilkens, *Zeichen und Werke. Ein Beitrag zur Theologie des 4. Evangeliums in Erzählungs- und Redestoff*, ATANT 55 (Zürich: Zwingli, 1969); Robert T. Fortna, *The Gospel of Signs: A Reconstruction of the Narrative Source Underlying the Fourth Gospel* (Cambridge: Cambridge University Press, 1970); and Willem Nicol, *The Semeia in the Fourth Gospel: Tradition and Redaction*, NovTSup 32 (Leiden: E. J. Brill, 1972).

20. This is the sense in which "history" is used in J. Louis Martyn's landmark work *History and Theology in the Fourth Gospel* (New York: Harper & Row, 1968; rev. ed. Nashville: Abingdon, 1979). Cf. also J. Louis Martyn, "Glimpses into the History of the Johannine Community," in *L'Évangile de Jean: Sources, Rédaction, Théologie*, BETL 44, ed. Marinus de Jonge (Leuven: University Press, 1977), 149-75. Martyn has been followed by Raymond E. Brown, whose work on this subject includes *The Community of the Beloved Disciple* (New York: Paulist, 1979) and " 'Other Sheep Not of This Fold: The Johannine Perspective on Christian Diversity in the Late First Century," *JBL* 97 (1978): 5-22. Cf. also Oscar Cullmann, *The Johannine Circle* (London: SCM, 1976).

204 THE MISSIONS OF JESUS AND THE DISCIPLES

community" consisted of believers who were expelled from the Jewish synagogue in the process of a traumatic conflict.[21] Along these lines, Rensberger maintains, "Johannine Christianity bears many of the marks of a sect [which Rensberger defines as "a minority counterculture consciously opposed to much of the status quo in its environment"], of a movement that finds light and truth within its own community and falsehood and darkness outside."[22] Besides Martyn's work, the most influential contribution has doubtless been that of Meeks, who views "[o]ne of the primary functions of the book . . . to provide a reinforcement for the community's social identity."[23]

Commentators who see the Fourth Gospel as a reflection of the "Johannine community's" sectarian consciousness find differing degrees of mission-mindedness in the Fourth Gospel. Some writers detect very little material on mission. They believe that the Fourth Gospel focuses primarily on love and unity within the "Johannine community."[24] K. G. Kuhn writes, "Johannesevangelium und -briefe zeigen uns eine Gemeinde, die im Grunde gar nicht missionarisch denkt. Diese Gemeinde weiß sich streng geschieden von der Welt, ausgegrenzt aus ihr im Gegensatz zu ihr stehend . . . darum gibt es hier auch keine eigentliche Mission im Sinn des werbenden Gewinnens neuer Gläubiger."[25]

Others, like Onuki, see the entire Fourth Gospel as a the "Johannine community's" reflection on Johannine tradition in terms of its characteristic dualism and symbolism. Onuki conjectures that this reflection serves to facilitate the reintegration of the community into its situation, with its dialectic of proclamation and unbelief, salvation and judgment.[26] For example, the Farewell Discourse in 13:31–14:31 functions, according to Onuki, as a device to distance the community from the situation of its proclamation to the Jewish community,

21. Cf. Kenneth L. Caroll, "The Fourth Gospel and the Exclusion of Christians from the Synagogues," *BJRL* 40 (1957/58): 19-32.

22. Cf. David Rensberger, *Overcoming the World: Politics and Community in the Gospel of John* (London: SPCK, 1988), 135. Rensberger's definition of a sect is found on page 136. For his development of his views on the mission concept in the Fourth Gospel, see especially Chapter 7, "Sect, World, and Mission: Johannine Christianity Today," 135-54.

23. Cf. Wayne A. Meeks, "The Man from Heaven in Johannine Sectarianism," *JBL* 91 (1972): 69, following Martyn. Meeks is in turn followed, among others, by Marinus de Jonge, "Jewish Expectations about the 'Messiah' according to the Fourth Gospel," *NTS* 19 (1973): 264-65.

24. Cf. especially Meeks, "Man from Heaven." But see the strong refutation of the view that the Fourth Gospel is a sectarian document by Rudolf Schnackenburg, "Der Missionsgedanke des Johannesevangeliums im heutigen Horizont," in *Das Johannesevangelium*, vol. 4, *Ergänzende Auslegungen und Exkurse*, HTKNT (Freiburg im Breisgau: Herder, 1984), 58-72.

25. Cf. Karl Gustav Kuhn, "Das Problem der Mission in der Urchristenheit," *EMZ* 11 (1954): 167-68. Quoted in Werner Bieder, *Gottes Sendung und der missionarische Auftrag der Kirche nach Matthäus, Lukas, Paulus, und Johannes*, ThStud 82 (Zürich: EVZ, 1965): 41.

26. Cf. Takashi Onuki, *Gemeinde und Welt im Johannesevangelium: Ein Beitrag zur Frage nach der theologischen und pragmatischen Funktion des johanneischen "Dualismus,"* WMANT 56 (Neukirchen-Vluyn: Neukirchener, 1984). Cf. also David Rensberger, Review of *Gemeinde und Welt im Johannesevangelium* by Takashi Onuki, *JBL* 105 (1986): 728-31.

leading it to reflect on the meaning of its largely negative experience. In essence, John enables the community to reflect theologically on the rejection of its message and so to return to its proclamation in the world. Onuki may best be represented as advocating a mediating position among those who view the Fourth Gospel as a sectarian document. While the Fourth Gospel is not a missionary tractate as such, it is not a sectarian tractate either. The community is not closed to the world surrounding it. Recovering from its trauma, it prepares to reach out to its neighbors once again.

Rensberger, too, taking his cue from Onuki, sees the function of the Fourth Gospel in the life of the "Johannine community" as a *katharsis* leading to a renewed focus on the community's mission. While conceding that "[t]he image of the Johannine community as an introversionist sect would not seem to encourage the idea of a Johannine mission," Rensberger argues, "Johannine Christianity is not a pure example of introversionism."[27] He concludes,

> Thus the community's mission is, like that of Jesus, to "take away the sin of the world," to draw people from darkness into light (1:29; 12:46). Like Jesus, the community is sent into the world with the revelation of God, and like him, it meets with rejection. The function of the Fourth Gospel, then, is to enable the community to step back from its situation of rejection, reflect upon it in the light of the fate of Jesus, and to be *sent out again with its faith renewed.* The fourth evangelist's dualism thus works not only to distance the community from the world but also to affirm both the community's identity and the possibility of conversion and salvation for people in the world.[28]

Finally, it has been speculated that it was the "Johannine community's" missionary failure that "led the community to turn in upon itself in an attitude of antagonism towards the world and the synagogue."[29]

Generally, proponents of the "Johannine community hypothesis" tend to gravitate toward one of three major options in their efforts to explain the "mission" material in the Fourth Gospel.[30] First, this community may have

---

27. Rensberger, *Overcoming the World,* 140.
28. Rensberger, *Overcoming the World,* 144.
29. Nicol, 143, approvingly quoted by Okure, 15; cf. also her own comments, 232.
30. See fig. 11. Cf. also Okure, 28-34. Those who consider the "Johannine community" to be mission-minded include, according to Okure, Bornhäuser, Oehler, Robinson, Freed, Wind, Dodd, and Cullmann, as well as Anton Fridrichsen, "La pensée missionnaire dans le Quatrième Évangile," in *Arbeiten und Mitteilungen aus dem neutestamentlichen Seminar zu Uppsala* VI, ed. Anton Fridrichsen (Uppsala, 1935), 39-45. In a second group (those holding that the Fourth Gospel is a "Gemeindeschrift" with a "Missionsgedanken") Okure includes Schnackenburg, Kümmel, and Meeks. She then treats Brown, *Community of the Beloved Disciple,* who holds to a series of redactions of the Fourth Gospel. Both Brown and J. Louis Martyn believe that the "Johannine community" may have been mission-minded earlier in its history but that in its later history — which is reflected in the final version of the Fourth Gospel — the community was a closed sectarian group struggling to recover from the trauma of its expulsion from the Jewish synagogue (cf. Okure, 33).

pursued a direct evangelistic purpose by addressing the Fourth Gospel to a Jewish synagogue with which the "Johannine community" was in conflict (*View #1* in fig. 11 below).[31] Second, the Fourth Gospel may have been written by a group within the community that sought to stir up their fellow group members to greater faith and missionary zeal.[32] Thus, while the Fourth Gospel's intent was not primarily evangelistic, according to those holding this second view, there is nevertheless a strong "Missionsgedanke" which reveals a dynamic within the "Johannine community," i.e., its inner discussion and struggle concerning its relationship to the surrounding world (*View #2*). Third, the Fourth Gospel was written *by* the community and *for* the community, but mission is insignificant or absent from the book (*View #3*).[33] These three views can be diagrammed as follows:[34]

Fig. 11. The "Johannine Community Hypothesis": Three Views of the Fourth Gospel's Purpose

	View #1	*View #2*	*View #3*
Purpose of the FG:	Missionary document	Gemeindeschrift with "Missionsgedanke"	Sectarian document
Author of the FG:	Johannine community (mission-minded as a whole community)	Johannine community (mission-minded group)	Johannine community (sectarian)
Recipients of FG:	a Jewish synagogue	Johannine community (the rest needing new zeal in their mission)	Johannine community (sect)

D. Implications from the Present Study

One's view of the Fourth Gospel's purpose has important implications for one's understanding of the function of the mission theme in John. If the purpose of John is missionary, the mission theme may be seen as primarily related to Jesus

31. Cf. already the view of van Unnik discussed above.

32. This is the view of Okure. See the discussion below.

33. Cf. the works by W. A. Meeks and K. G. Kuhn referred to above.

34. To these options should be added the view held by some on source- and redaction-critical grounds that the community's mission-mindedness was limited to the earlier stage of its history while its traumatic expulsion from the synagogue caused it to turn its focus inward. Cf. the works of Raymond E. Brown and J. Louis Martyn listed above.

and his followers, whom the recipients of the Fourth Gospel are invited to join. In the case of an edificatory purpose, the Johannine emphasis on mission may reinforce the mission practice of the community to whom the Gospel is addressed. Finally, if the nature of the Fourth Gospel is sectarian, the work may be written by a mission-minded community to its Jewish parent synagogue, it may be directed from a mission-minded segment within the community to the rest of the group, or one may view the mission theme as only a marginal part of a sectarian document.

The traditional view of the Fourth Gospel, while by no means without its contemporary supporters, has become a minority position. As observed, recent years have witnessed a gradual recasting of the Fourth Gospel.[35] No longer does the majority of scholars view the Gospel as the eyewitness account of the apostle John, a Gospel that focuses on Jesus and that seeks to lead its readers to believe in him.[36] Instead, the Fourth Gospel is now widely regarded as the product of a "Johannine community" engaged in polemic with its parent synagogue, the result of numerous stages of revision.[37] Moreover, in recent Johannine scholarship the question of the Fourth Gospel's historical purpose has been replaced by relatively ahistorical concerns.[38]

The present study of the Fourth Gospel's teaching on mission indicated that the mission of Jesus, not the mission of Jesus' followers, is the focal point of John's mission presentation. At the same time, it was found that John's interest was not merely to set forth a self-contained Christological portrait. The fourth evangelist rather links the missions of Jesus and of his disciples, casting the latter mission in relation to the former and characterizing Jesus' mission in a way that is relevant for the mission of his followers.[39] Which of the above views of the Fourth Gospel's purpose best accommodates these findings?

It seems important here to strike a proper balance between an assessment that accentuates unilaterally either mission. While the Fourth Gospel is a *Gospel*, it was written with the interest of the believing community at the end of the first century in mind. The question remains, was the motivation behind the final Gospel missionary, edificatory, or sectarian? Of course, this question cannot be fully dealt with here. It is merely possible to draw some implications from the study of one significant theme, i.e., that of mission. One may begin to formulate a tentative answer by pointing to the significant amount of material on mission in John. This phenomenon appears to render a radical sectarian view, one that denies any missionary interest on the part of the community, rather implausible.

---

35. Cf. Chapter 4.

36. Cf. the relevant sections in Chapter 4 above.

37. But cf. now Martin Hengel, *Die johanneische Frage*, WUNT 67 (Tübingen: J. C. B. Mohr [Paul Siebeck], 1993).

38. Cf. D. A. Carson, "The Purpose of the Fourth Gospel: Jn 20:31 Reconsidered," *JBL* 106 (1987): 639.

39. Cf. Chapters 3 and 4 above.

This, of course, has been recognized by many proponents of the "Johannine community hypothesis." Efforts have therefore been made to accommodate the Fourth Gospel's mission material *within* an overall sectarian framework. Several stages of redaction have been postulated, with accompanying scenarios that would explain the mission material generated at the respective levels of redaction. In the light of the pervasiveness and coherence of the Fourth Gospel's teaching on mission discovered in the present study, however, it appears doubtful whether these efforts have been successful. At the very least, John's presentation of mission suggests that the final redactor did not espouse a radical sectarian outlook but rather advocated a mission to the world (cf. 17:18; cf. also 3:16).

The final author's definition of the community over against "the Jews" (chapters 1–12) and "the world" (chapters 13–21) probably should not be understood primarily in sociological terms but along salvation-historical lines. This is suggested, for example, by the evangelist's insistence at the end of the first part of his Gospel that the Jewish rejection of the signs-working Messiah fulfilled Isaianic prophecy. Likewise, the Fourth Gospel's corporate metaphors are built upon Old Testament metaphors for God's people Israel, thus pointing to a salvation-historical link between the old and the new Messianic community. While these considerations do not by themselves exclude the possibility of a sectarian interpretation along the lines of a "Johannine community hypothesis," they do shift the focus significantly away from intracommunity matters to larger salvation-historical dimensions.

The findings of the present study appear therefore to lend support to Pryor's thesis that John was the "evangelist for the covenant people." When there are some strong separating lines drawn in the Gospel, this may point primarily to a concern to delineate as clearly as possible who is, and is not, part of the new Messianic community. This concern could have been shared by a final redactor within or without a "Johannine community." The important thing appears to be that the evangelist's teaching on mission, besides being configured along salvation-historical lines, embraces at the same time a realistic attitude toward "the Jews" during the earthly Jesus' mission and "the world" at the time of the mission of the later community, *and* an interest in a mission to the world.

It seems therefore doubtful that the Fourth Gospel is rooted in a sectarian mindset. The strong salvation-historical consciousness evidenced in the final Gospel rather suggests a broader background for John's Gospel. The author's horizon appears to have been the world, not merely his community. Moreover, whether John's critical attitude toward "the Jews" or "the world" is rooted in the traumatic experience of expulsion from a non-Messianic Jewish synagogue toward the end of the first century A.D., or whether John seeks to draw those lines for other reasons, should not be considered an established fact, since the data do allow for other legitimate conclusions. There is something to be said for the view that such a drawing of lines would be an important prerequisite even for missionizing diaspora Jews and proselytes, since only a clear demonstration of the differences between Judaism and the new Messianic community would necessitate the choice of the latter over the former. Thus a missionary purpose of the Fourth Gospel does appear to be allowed for in the light of the present study of John's mission teaching.

It should be pointed out once again in this context that the emphasis on the community on the part of many proponents of the "Johannine community hypothesis" does not seem to be supported by the Fourth Gospel's teaching on mission, which is centered around the mission of Jesus. While the disciples, according to the fourth evangelist, are to be involved in a mission to the world, John casts this mission as merely the continuation, albeit in escalated form (cf. 14:12), of Jesus' mission (cf. 17:18; 20:21). While it is true that the Fourth Gospel devotes much space to Jesus' instructions to the community (cf. 13–16), the fact remains that chapters 1–12 set forth the signs of the historical Jesus, while 18–19 present Jesus' passion, albeit with the evangelist's own emphases.

In light of this redressed balance suggested by the findings of the present study, both a missionary and an edificatory purpose are quite possible. It is unclear whether the data surfaced in this monograph allow for a decision for one over the other. Is the fourth evangelist himself pursuing a missionary purpose by writing his Gospel? This, of course, is even held by some proponents of the "Johannine community hypothesis," even though these writers hold that the Fourth Gospel's recipients are merely the members of the community's parent synagogue, not, for example, Jews and proselytes in the diaspora at large.

The decisive factor is usually seen in John's inclusion of the Farewell Discourse, a feature that by itself is often taken as conclusive evidence against a missionary purpose of the Fourth Gospel. However, it may be argued that the issues discussed in the Farewell Discourse would be of some interest for prospective Jewish converts, especially since the section seems to be patterned after the Deuteronomic farewell discourses. Jesus' intimacy with his new Messianic community could thus be seen as being in sharp contrast with his rejection of non-Messianic Jews. This presentation, coupled with convincing evidence, on Jewish terms, that the Messiah, the Son of God, is in fact *Jesus*, could be expected to lead some Jews to reconsider their position, with the possible result of embracing faith in Jesus and of joining the new Messianic community. Thus the inclusion of the Farewell Discourse in the Fourth Gospel does not appear to be as insurmountable an obstacle to a missionary purpose of John as is often contended.

Thus the question remains whether the Fourth Gospel was written for a missionary or an edificatory purpose. While some look to the purpose statement in 20:30-31 for a solution, it appears that this passage by itself is not able to supply conclusive evidence.[40] The matter must be settled on other grounds.[41] For example, one may argue that the sustained emphasis on a personal decision for Jesus can best be accommodated by a missionary purpose. On the other hand, it may be held that the recipient community could be strengthened in its mission by a clarified understanding of Jesus and his mission. The first part of the Gospel, however, does not just read like a clarification but rather like an effort to lead people to first-time faith by way of literary techniques such as representative questions regarding Jesus' Messiahship or the escalating presentation of selected signs of Jesus. Perhaps, then, it is a missionary purpose that best accommodates the findings of the present study, but certainty remains elusive.

III. IMPLICATIONS FOR THE MISSION OF THE CONTEMPORARY CHURCH

The Fourth Gospel's contribution to a clarification of the contemporary church's mission can now be explored. This final section will include a discussion of implication from the present study as well as critiques of current missiological paradigms.

A. Implications from the Present Study

The comprehensive implication for the mission of the contemporary church from the present study is its need to see itself more consciously in relation to the mission of Jesus. The fourth evangelist conceived of the mission of the Christian community as ultimately the mission of *the exalted Jesus* carried out through his followers. As is apparent also in Paul's teaching of the headship of Christ over his church, Jesus has not relinquished the ultimate control and direction of the mission of the church (cf. also Matt 28:18-20). Rather than operating on the basis of marketing surveys or mere human strategizing, the contemporary church therefore needs to subordinate itself consciously to the salvation-historical purposes Jesus seeks to pursue in our day.

  Another implication for the church's mission from the Fourth Gospel is the contemporary church's need to acknowledge anew the sovereignty of God

---

40. Cf. Gordon D. Fee, "On the Text and Meaning of John 20.30-31," in *The Four Gospels 1992. Festschrift Frans Neirynck,* BETL C, ed. F. van Segbroeck, C. M. Tuckett, G. van Belle, and J. Verheyden, vol. 3 (Leuven: University Press, 1992), 2193-2205, who argues from the present subjunctive πιστεύητε in 20:31 for an edificatory purpose. The evidence, however, is not as conclusive as Fee suggests (cf., e.g., 11:42 πιστεύσωσιν with 17:21 πιστεύῃ in virtually identical contexts).

41. Cf. Cullmann, *Johannine Circle,* 15.

in its mission. The fourth evangelist's affirmation that the rejection of Jesus by his own people, including his crucifixion, occurred according to God's predestinatory counsel, should give the church new strength, especially in parts of the world where it is currently suffering. The assurance permeating the Fourth Gospel that God draws people to himself and that he "gives" people to Jesus, too, should encourage the church in her resolve to proclaim the gospel. Moreover, as the church carries out its mission, it can be assured that all of the resources needed for its outreach will be provided for (cf. 14:13; 15:7, 16b).

The fourth evangelist's teaching on mission calls the church to greater humility in the conception of its task. The church does not operate alongside, or even as a replacement for, Jesus. It rather remains a church under orders. Its main role is the extension of forgiveness in Jesus' name to repentant sinners (cf. 20:23) and the proclamation of the gospel message (cf. 17:20). This proclamation should be given credibility by the relationships of the church's members. A humble servant spirit (cf. 13:1-15), mutual love (cf. 13:35; 15:13), and unity (cf. 17:21, 23, 25) need to be pursued if the church's mission is to be successful.

The mission of God in this world cannot be thwarted. Even sinful human resistance to God's salvific plans is incorporated into God's inscrutable predestinatory counsel. Thus even the world's rejection of the church and its mission should not cause the church to reject the world. On the contrary, Jesus' followers must bear witness to Jesus (cf. 15:18-27). Like Jesus, they are sent into the world (cf. 17:18). The church's mission, however, is to be based on a spiritually separated life, one that is based on God's word (cf. 17:17). John's Gospel provides a timely reminder that the church must preach Jesus as the *only* way to the Father (cf. 14:6) regardless of the popularity of this message in its modern context. While dialogue and contextualization are important, accommodation and compromise should be avoided.

Another lesson that emerges from a study of the Fourth Gospel's mission theology is that the church's mission is not to be carried out as an individualistic enterprise. The mission should rather be supported by the corporate life of the community as believers reflect God's love and unity (cf. 13:34-35; 15:12; 17:11, 20-26). Where direct proclamation of the word may fail to persuade, the more indirect, corroborative approach of providing an example of loving, unified relationships may succeed, or both aspects jointly may be effective. Moreover, the Christian community is to follow its calling to represent Christ actively in the world. A merely passive reflection of Christ in the community's life falls short of the church's mandate (cf. 15:16; 17:18; 20:21).

The study of the Fourth Gospel's presentation of Jesus' mission showed that the fourth evangelist conceived of Jesus as thoroughly unique. Jesus, a unique person combining within himself attributes of divinity as well as humanity, was called to carry out a unique mission, culminating in his "exaltation" and "glorification" and his founding of the new Messianic community. The implications for an age where pluralism makes rapid gains are profound.[42] It seems difficult to see how anyone who takes his or her cue from the biblical material, in the present case John's Gospel, can dispute that the New Testament writers viewed Jesus as unique in his personhood and redemptive work (cf., e.g., 1:14, 18; 3:16; 14:6).

For the fourth evangelist, God's work for humanity is centered in Christ's cross-work (cf. 3:13-17; 4:34; 6:51-58; 8:28; 10:11, 15, 17-18; 12:32; 17:4; 19:30) and in his revelation of God in word and work (cf. 1:14, 18; cf. also Jesus' "signs" and "I am-sayings"). The paradigm for the church's mission is to be the sender-sent relationship sustained between God the Father and Jesus during the latter's earthly ministry (cf. 20:21). The church's obedient response needs to mirror Jesus' in his total dependence upon God. At the same time, the church's mission appears to be perceived by the fourth evangelist more humbly than in terms of Christ's incarnation, since the Fourth Gospel retains the uniqueness of the Word's becoming flesh and of Christ's salvific work (cf. 1:14, 18; 3:16, 18). This issue, however, needs to be treated more fully below due to its importance for contemporary missiological discussion.

B. Critique of the "Incarnational Model"

The "incarnational model" considers Jesus' incarnation as the model for the church's mission. The "representational" model, on the other hand, contends

---

42. The rapidly growing literature includes Carl Braaten, *No Other Gospel: Christianity Among the World's Religions* (Minneapolis: Fortress, 1991); Frederic B. Burnham, ed., *Postmodern Theology: Christian Faith in a Pluralistic World* (San Francisco: Harper, 1989); Nigel M. de S. Cameron, ed., *Universalism and the Doctrine of Hell* (Grand Rapids: Baker, 1992); D. A. Carson, *The Gagging of God: Christianity Confronts Pluralism* (Grand Rapids: Zondervan, 1996); Andrew D. Clarke and Bruce W. Winter, eds., *One God, One Lord: Christianity in a World of Religious Pluralism,* 2d ed. (Grand Rapids: Baker, 1993); William V. Crockett and James G. Sigountos, eds., *Through No Fault of Their Own? The Fate of Those Who Have Never Heard* (Grand Rapids: Baker, 1991); Jacques Dupuis, *Jesus Christ at the Encounter of World Religions,* trans. Robert R. Barr (Maryknoll, N.Y.: Orbis, 1989); Chester Gillis, *Pluralism: A New Paradigm for Theology* (Louvain: Peeters; Grand Rapids: Wm. B. Eerdmans, 1993); John H. Hick, *The Myth of God Incarnate* (London: SCM, 1977); and *God Has Many Names* (Philadelphia: Westminster, 1982); and "The Non-Absoluteness of Christianity," in *The Myth of Christian Uniqueness,* ed. John H. Hick and Paul F. Knitter (Maryknoll, N.Y.: Orbis, 1987), 16-36; Paul F. Knitter, *No Other Name? A Critical Survey of Christian Attitudes Toward the World Religions* (Maryknoll, N.Y.: Orbis, 1985); Stephen Neill, *Christian Faith and Other Faiths* (London: Oxford University Press, 1961); Harold A. Netland, *Dissonant Voices: Religious Pluralism and the Question of Truth* (Grand Rapids: Wm. B. Eerdmans, 1991); Clark Pinnock, *A Wideness in God's Mercy* (Grand Rapids: Zondervan, 1992); and "The Finality of Jesus Christ in a World of Religions," in *Christian Faith and Practice in the Modern World,* ed. Mark A. Noll and David F. Wells (Grand Rapids: Wm. B. Eerdmans, 1988), 152-68; Gregory D. Pritchard, ed., *Hermeneutics, Religious Pluralism, and Truth* (Winston-Salem, N.C.: Wake Forest University, 1989); John Sanders, *No Other Name: An Investigation into the Destiny of the Unevangelized* (Grand Rapids: Wm. B. Eerdmans, 1992).

that the fourth evangelist presents Jesus' incarnation as unique, viewing the relationship between Jesus and his followers merely in terms of representation. In the light of the findings of the present study, which of these models reflects John's teaching on mission most accurately?

The following quote illustrates the incarnational approach:

> For Jn, evangelization is *the process of an ever-renewed incarnation of the Word*, of which Christ was the perfect expression, in a given nation, in a particular place and time, through the sharing of Christian experience. This is effected in dialogue with other religious experiences of the Word present in the world from the beginning. Hence evangelization in Jn presupposes dialogue with other cultural and religious traditions.[43]

However, it is very difficult to find precise definitions of the "incarnational model" in the relevant literature. Perhaps due to this lack of terminological clarity, evaluations of the "incarnational model" differ. At the core of this approach seems to be the advocacy of "an identification that transcends the superficial material culture and behavior roles and focuses on the underlying attitudes that should characterize missionaries as servants."[44] Also, reference is frequently made to passages such as Philippians 2:5-11 or 1 Corinthians 9:19-22.

Stott, doubtless one of the most pronounced advocates of this approach, contrasts "two extreme views," "the older or traditional view" that equates mission and evangelism with a concentration on verbal proclamation, and the position that identifies the church's mission as the establishment of *shalom*, i.e., social harmony.[45] Seeking to mediate between these two "extreme" positions, Stott argues that Jesus is the model of the church's mission. Using John 20:21 as his paradigm passage, he maintains,

> The crucial form in which the Great Commission has been handed down to us (though it is the most neglected because it is the most costly) is the Johannine. . . . In both these sentences [17:18 and 20:21] Jesus did more than draw a vague parallel between his mission and ours. Deliberately and precisely

43. Cf. Matthew Vellanickal, "Evangelization in the Johannine Writings," in *Good News and Witness*, ed. Lucien Legrand, J. Pathrapankal and Matthew Vellanickal (Bangalore: Theological Publications in India, 1973), 168.

44. Cf. Kenneth McElhanon, "Don't Give Up on the Incarnational Model," *EMQ* 27 (1991): 391. Cf. also Harriet Hill, "Incarnational Ministry: A Critical Examination," *EMQ* 26 (1990): 196-201.

45. Cf. John R. W. Stott, *Christian Mission in the Modern World* (London: Church Pastoral Aid Society, 1975), 15-17; see also John R. W. Stott, *The Contemporary Christian: Applying God's Word to Today's World* (Downers Grove, Ill.: InterVarsity, 1992), especially 264-65, 341-43, and 357-74, where Stott reiterates and further develops his arguments. Cf. further Jose M. Abreü, "La misión cristiana en el pensamiento juanino," in *Hacia una teología de la evangelización*, ed. Orlando E. Costas (Buenos Aires: Editorial La Aurora, 1973), 55-66, who focuses on the incarnation and continued presence of Jesus in the church's mission through the Holy Spirit.

he made his mission the *model* of ours, saying "*As* the Father sent me, *so* I send you." Therefore our understanding of the church's mission must be deduced from our understanding of the Son's. Why and how did the Father send the Son?[46]

Stott qualifies his remarks as follows: "Of course the major purpose of the Son's coming into the world was unique. Perhaps it is partly for this reason that Christians have been hesitant to think of their mission as in any sense comparable to his. For the Father sent the Son to be the Saviour of the world, and to that end to atone for our sins and to bring us eternal life. . . . We cannot copy him in these things. We are not saviours."[47] What the church is to imitate, acccording to Stott, is the principle of incarnation, i.e., that Christ came and was sent into the world. He "made his mission the *model* of ours, saying 'As the Father sent me, *so* I send you,'" but since Christ is unique in providing redemption, the church's model should be found in Jesus' coming to serve (cf. Mark 10:45 and Luke 22:27). *In this,* Stott argues, Jesus is our model: "Now he sends us, he says, as the Father had sent him. Therefore our mission, like his, is to be one of service."[48]

Stott concludes, "To sum up, we are sent into the world, like Jesus, to serve. . . . 'Mission,' then, is not a word for everything. . . . 'Mission' describes rather *everything the church is sent into the world to do.*"[49] He expresses his underlying concern this way: "If we can accept this broader concept of mission as Christian service in the world comprising both evangelism and social action — a concept which is laid upon us by the model of our Saviour's mission in the world — then Christians could under God make a far greater impact on society, an impact commensurate with our numerical strength and with the radical demands of the commission of Christ."[50] Nevertheless, Stott affirms the priority of evangelism in the church's mission.[51]

In *The Contemporary Christian,* Stott essentially reiterates his earlier views. He states categorically, "[A]ll authentic mission is incarnational mission."[52] Stott refers to Paul, who, according to Stott, practiced the "principle of incarnation" (1 Cor. 9:19-22) as well as to Christ's model of humility (cf. Phil. 2:7-8).[53] Stott defines this "principle of incarnation" as an "identification without loss of identity."[54]

---

46. Stott, *Christian Mission,* 23.
47. Stott, *Christian Mission,* 24.
48. Stott, *Christian Mission,* 24.
49. Cf. Stott, *Christian Mission,* 30. Emphasis added. Cf. also *Contemporary Christian,* 341-42, where Stott, while acknowledging the criticism his definition has drawn, is quite unrepentant and essentially reiterates his earlier views.
50. Cf. Stott, *Christian Mission,* 34.
51. Cf. Stott, *Christian Mission,* 35.
52. Cf. Stott, *Contemporary Christian,* 358.
53. Stott, *Contemporary Christian,* 358.
54. Stott, *Contemporary Christian,* 373.

In the light of the findings of this present study, can Stott's views be judged to represent an accurate reflection of the Fourth Gospel's teaching on mission? The analysis of the missions of Jesus and of the disciples has shown that 17:18 and 20:21, while pointing to an analogous element in the missions of Jesus and of the disciples, do not equate these missions in every respect. The Fourth Gospel's portrayal of Jesus' mission centers on Jesus' provision of salvation (often called the "giving of life"; cf. 3:16-17; 6:53-58; 10:10; 17:2) and the forgiveness of sin (cf. 1:29, 36; cf. also 20:23). Even Jesus' signs transcend the actual works of Jesus, functioning as a revelation of the nature of Jesus' sender, the Father, and of the authenticity of Jesus' representation of his sender.[55]

Both 17:18 and 20:21-23 indicate that these dimensions of Jesus' mission are to continue in the disciples' mission. The disciples are to bear witness to Jesus in an evil, hostile world (cf. also 15:27) and to pronounce forgiveness or retain people's sins in continuation of Jesus' mission (cf. 20:23). The notion of the disciples' mission as a "service to humanity" founded on the model of Jesus' mission appears, contrary to Stott's assertions, to be inconsistent with the Fourth Gospel's teaching on mission.[56] A focus on human service and on human need, though often characteristic of contemporary mission practice, is not presented in the Fourth Gospel as the primary purpose of either Jesus' or the disciples' mission.

Another aspect of Stott's perspective that needs to be addressed is his use of the term "model." In what sense can Jesus be said to function as the "model" for his disciples? If Stott uses "model" in the sense of "example," his argument seems to be that Jesus is held up in the Fourth Gospel as the supreme paradigm of servanthood for his disciples. That is certainly true for chapter 13, but whether it is the thrust of the mission theme in the entire Gospel is doubtful. And even in chapter 13 Jesus is presented as a model of service of believers *to one another,* not to the unbelieving world, a fact that Stott fails to acknowledge.

It appears that Stott derives his "incarnational theology," at least in part, from the Lucan and Pauline writings. But even in Philippians 2:5-11, for example, it is not the incarnation itself but the humility reflected in it that Paul presents as an example for believers to imitate — again, the reference is to humility of believers toward *one another.*[57] And in 1 Corinthians 9:19-22, while

---

55. Cf. the discussion of Jesus' "signs" in Chapter 3 above.

56. Cf. the interchange between David Hesselgrave and John Stott: David J. Hesselgrave, "Holes in 'Holistic Mission,'" *Trinity World Forum* 19, no. 3 (1990): 1-5; John Stott, "An Open Letter to David Hesselgrave," *Trinity World Forum* 16, no. 3 (1991): 1-2; and David Hesselgrave, "To John Stott — A Surrejoinder," *Trinity World Forum* 16, no. 3 (1991): 3-4.

57. But note the objection to this traditional interpretation by Käsemann, who argues that Phil. 2:5-11 does not function as an ethical example but points to the salvation event. Cf. Ernst Käsemann, "A Critical Analysis of Philippians 2:5-11," in *God in Christ: Existence and Province,* ed. Robert W. Funk, *Journal for Theology and Church* 5 (New York: Harper & Row/Tübingen: J. C. B. Mohr [Paul Siebeck], 1968 [1950]), 45-88, especially p. 84. Cf. also Ralph P. Martin, *Carmen Christi: Philippians 2:5-11 in Recent Interpretation and in the Setting of Early Christian*

the context there is mission, there is no mention whatsoever of Christ's incarnation. It seems therefore precarious to refer to this passage as support for the "incarnational model" for mission.

Moreover, while Stott contends that the fourth evangelist portrays Jesus as a model of true servanthood, the context of 20:21 indicates that Jesus is a model for the disciples in his relationship to his sender, the Father: Jesus sought to bring glory to the one who sent him and to do his sender's will rather than his own. He represented his sender faithfully and maintained a close relationship with him. The thrust of this passage appears to be that the disciples are to relate to Jesus in the same way as Jesus related to his sender, the Father.

What is even more important, the Fourth Gospel consistently affirms that the purpose for Jesus' coming into the world was unique. Stott, by focusing on Jesus' *incarnation* as a model for the church's mission, seems to be at odds with the Fourth Gospel's presentation of Jesus' incarnation as thoroughly unique, unprecedented, and unrepeatable (cf. especially the designation μονογενής in 1:14, 18; 3:14, 18).[58] The incarnation is linked with Jesus' eternal preexistence (cf. 1:1, 14) and his unique relationship with God the Father (cf. 1:14, 18). Indeed, as the present study has indicated, mission terminology such as "coming into the world" or "descending" and "ascending" is in the Fourth Gospel reserved for Jesus.

Moreover, if Jesus' *incarnation* is to function as the model for the church's mission, why not Jesus' provision of *atonement*? It is unclear on what basis Stott chooses one and not the other. He repeatedly acknowledges the uniqueness of Jesus' person and work, but by linking the church's mission at every point with Jesus', Stott appears to jeopardize Jesus' salvation-historical uniqueness.[59] As the

---

Worship, rev. ed. (Grand Rapids: Wm. B. Eerdmans, 1983), xiii, who argues, "On any other interpretation than Käsemann's, verses 9-11 are left 'in the air' and must be treated as an excursus, because Christ's elevation to world rulership cannot be the theme of the Christian's imitation." But even if one grants the validity of Käsemann's syntactical observations and accepts that Phil. 2:5 refers to the Philippians' union with Christ and not to Christ's own attitude, there is no need to abandon an ethical interpretation of Phil. 2:6-11. And, as Silva rightly contends, Martin's objection inappropriately presents redemptive-historical events and ethical example as antithetical ideas. Cf. the refutation of Käsemann's and Martin's views by Moisés Silva, *Philippians*, BECNT (Grand Rapids: Baker, 1992), 107-11. Cf. also 128, where Silva approvingly refers to Gnilka: "Gnilka then is quite correct in pointing out . . . that we must restrict its [Phil 2:9] application in view of Jesus' uniqueness." It is therefore crucial to maintain both the value of Christ's example for believers' relationships with one another and Christ's uniqueness.

58. Note that in 1:14 the term μονογενής is used in the immediate context of Jesus' incarnation. Cf. the discussion of the person and of the uniqueness of Jesus in Chapter 3 above.

59. In this respect Stott's treatment in *The Contemporary Christian* takes his earlier work one step further by linking every phase in Christ's work to a stage in the church's mission: under the heading "The Christology of Mission," Stott lists the incarnation of Christ as the model of mission, the cross of Christ as indicative of the cost of mission, the resurrection as representing the mandate for mission, the exaltation of Christ as the incentive for mission, the Spirit-gift of Christ as the power for mission, and the parousia of Christ as pointing to the urgency of mission (cf. pp. 356-74).

Fourth Gospel makes clear, in the end it is Jesus who sends and the disciples who are sent. It is Jesus who calls others to follow, and his disciples who follow. It is Jesus who has done "the work," and the disciples who will have a part in the greater works the exalted Jesus will perform after his glorification. At every juncture a careful line seems to be drawn between the roles of Jesus and of the disciples.

The Fourth Gospel does therefore not appear to teach the kind of "incarnational model" advocated by Stott and others. Not the way in which Jesus came into the world (i.e., the incarnation), but *the nature of Jesus' relationship with his sender* (i.e., one of obedience and utter dependence), is presented in the Fourth Gospel as the model for the disciples' mission. Jesus' followers are called to imitate Jesus' selfless devotion in seeking his sender's glory, to submit to their sender's will, and to represent their sender accurately and know him intimately.

C. A Critique of Other Approaches

There are other kinds of approaches that consider Jesus' mission as the model for his disciples' mission. In these, Jesus is primarily viewed as a teacher who trained his disciples for their work. Certain principles for the training of disciples are identified in Jesus' ministry and then said to be permanently relevant, if not normative, for the training of disciples.[60]

However, while Jesus' training of his disciples as presented in the Fourth Gospel is certainly *part* of his mission — and the approaches focusing on this aspect of Jesus' mission have helpfully drawn our attention to this dimension — it is only *a part* of Jesus' mission and needs to be seen in the larger perspective of Jesus' salvation-historical role.[61] Moreover, by distilling supposedly timeless principles from Jesus' practice of training disciples that are subsequently applied to a contemporary setting, one runs the risk of emptying Jesus' mission of its salvation-historical particularity and specificity. This may be a reflection of the American penchant toward pragmatism rather than reflecting an accurate understanding of the overall mission of Jesus. Regrettably, such approaches have the effect of domesticating Jesus and his mission.

A focus on the "model aspect" of Jesus' mission and his role as a teacher training his disciples also tends to level the important areas of discontinuity and

---

60. Cf. especially the very influential works by Robert E. Coleman, *The Master Plan of Evangelism* (Old Tappan, N.J.: Fleming H. Revell, 1963); and *The Mind of the Master* (Old Tappan, N.J.: Fleming H. Revell, 1977). Cf. now also the sequel to *The Master Plan of Evangelism*, entitled *The Master Plan of Discipleship* (Old Tappan, N.J.: Fleming H. Revell, 1987). While some of the imbalances of Coleman's earlier study have been remedied by his more recent work, some of the weaknesses critiqued below remain.

61. Cf. the study of Jesus' mission according to the Fourth Gospel in Chapter 3.

distinction between Jesus — who everywhere in the Gospels, and especially in the Fourth Gospel, is represented as unique — and his followers. As the present study has shown, the Fourth Gospel portrays Jesus as the unique Son sent by the Father, the one who came from heaven and returned there. Even Jesus' role as a teacher, at least in the Fourth Gospel, has the added dimension of the eschatological Messianic shepherd who dies for his "sheep" and who calls his followers to help gather his eschatological Messianic harvest. One consequence of the pragmatic "flattening" of the biblical material in these approaches is therefore the loss of the eschatological dimension inherent in Jesus' salvation-historical role.[62]

What is perhaps most significant is that these approaches seem to be based on the underlying, but rarely explicitly stated, assumption that Jesus' principles of training his disciples have normative character. We may ask if this assumption is borne out by the teaching of Scripture itself. Is Jesus presented in the New Testament primarily as a teacher who models how disciples should be trained? Even if this were so, is it the intention of the biblical writers to establish a normative pattern in and through Jesus' training of his disciples? It may be charged that this kind of procedure fails to consider New Testament writings other than the Gospels such as the book of Acts or the Pauline epistles, which may provide alternative models for the church's mission.[63]

It is further cause for concern that these presuppositions inhibit the church's freedom to adapt methods of training disciples to the contemporary culture. The model of a Jewish rabbi who gathers around himself a group of disciples who leave their own surroundings to share their teacher's lifestyle, travel with him on his journeys, and depend on others' support for their sustenance should not be seen as paradigmatic for all times. There is no indication that the Scriptures present this model as normative.

The present study of the Fourth Gospel has indicated that a progression is made from a literal to a spiritual following of Jesus.[64] The latter kind of following, which is significant for believers today, is to result in lives that are characterized by spiritual self-denial and in loving, unified relationships (cf., e.g., 12:26; 13:12-15). This lifestyle, however, is not tied to a specific cultural model of the training of disciples. The characteristics are rather general, allowing for a variety of personal and cultural applications.

Moreover, as the study of the disciples' mission in the Fourth Gospel has shown, apart from general demands of discipleship there are also specific personal callings on individual disciples.[65] It appears that the approaches critiqued

---

62. Cf. Chapter 3 above.

63. Cf. Donald Senior and Carroll Stuhlmueller, *The Biblical Foundations for Mission* (Maryknoll, N.Y.: Orbis, 1983), 141-312; Johannes Verkuyl, *Contemporary Missiology* (Grand Rapids: Wm. B. Eerdmans, 1978 [1975]), 89-117.

64. Cf. the study of the disciples' mission according to the Fourth Gospel in Chapter 4.

65. Cf. especially the discussion of the missions of Peter and of the Beloved Disciple in Chapter 4 above.

here, by emphasizing "timeless principles" as a normative framework for training disciples, have the effect (doubtless unintended) of lessening this sphere of individual discipleship.

One wonders whether adequate room is given in these models for the work of the Spirit and of the exalted Lord in the disciples' mission. According to the Fourth Gospel, it is the Spirit and the exalted Jesus who are to direct the Messianic community and individual disciples (cf. chaps. 13–21). Therefore the Spirit and the exalted Jesus should be given liberty to lead the contemporary church in developing the kinds of approaches to training disciples that are culturally sensitive while remaining informed by Scripture.

The approaches that elevate Jesus' discipleship training model as normative thus should be replaced by a more accurate understanding of the missions of Jesus and of the disciples according to the biblical writings. Such an approach should respect the variety exemplified by the Scriptures and should allow the Spirit and the exalted Jesus to continue to lead believers today. This study has sought to make a contribution along these lines by exploring the missions of Jesus and of the disciples according to the Fourth Gospel. Ideally, other similar studies will be conducted in other New Testament writings in the future. Thus perhaps a truly biblical theology of mission could be developed that would give proper consideration to the biblical writers' intentions and make those the guide for biblical interpretation and contextualization.

IV. CONCLUSION

A church that is unsure of its mission will not be effective in carrying it out. In a day when the church at large has a confused understanding of its mission, a return to a thorough study of Scripture is necessary.[66] The church cannot afford to let urgent needs or pressing circumstances set its agenda. That agenda has already been set in its parameters by Jesus and needs to be defined and understood in relation to Jesus' mission.

Moreover, the church ought to be *focused* in the understanding of its mission. Its activities should be constrained by what helps others to come to believe that the Messiah, the Son of God, is Jesus. The church and individual believers should be set apart from the world in order to be effective in their mission to the world (cf. 17:17, 19). Unless believers are distinct from the world and rooted in Christ, they are too much "of" the world to be sent into the world (cf. 17:14, 16, 18).

---

66. All of Scripture, and especially the New Testament, needs to be studied regarding the Bible's message on mission. This study makes a contribution by exploring Johannine teaching of mission. This, of course, does not mean that John's teaching on mission exhausts all that Scripture says about mission.

Neither 17:18 nor 20:21 indicates that the missions of Jesus and of the disciples are equivalent in every respect. They rather present an analogy between two sender-sent relationships, between the Father and Jesus, and between Jesus and the disciples. The Fourth Gospel represents the Word's incarnation as unique (cf. especially 1:14), and the incarnate Jesus' work as complete (cf. 4:34; 17:4; 19:30). The disciples cannot and are not commanded to reproduce Jesus' incarnation or even model their own mission after it.

From the beginning to the end of the Fourth Gospel, the disciples are called to *follow Jesus*. Their role in Jesus' mission is one of entering into it (cf. 4:38), of "harvesting" and "bearing fruit" (cf. 4:38; 15:8, 16), and of witnessing to Jesus (cf. 15:27). This, too, is the role of the church of the ages.[67] The disciples' mission is to be characterized by an obedient relationship to their sender, Jesus, by a separation from the world, and by an inaugurated eschatological outlook. This perspective is to inspire the church's ingathering of believers into the Messianic community.

Care must be taken to balance the Fourth Gospel's assignment of primacy to Jesus' mission with the genuine responsibility given to the disciples and the church in making the word of "life in Jesus" available to a sinful world (cf. 15:20; 17:20; 20:21-23). The church has her Lord's appointment and command "to go and bear fruit" (15:16) and his promise of doing "greater works" (14:12). May she be faithful to her charge and unified in carrying out her mission.

---

67. For a discussion of the relationship between the Fourth Gospel's disciples and later believers, see Chapter 4 above.

Bibliography

Abbott, Edwin A. *Johannine Vocabulary: A Comparison of the Words of the Fourth Gospel with Those of the Three.* London: Adam and Charles Black, 1905.

———. *Johannine Grammar.* London: Adam and Charles Black, 1906.

Abreü, Jose M. "La misión cristiana en el pensamiento juanino." In *Hacia una teología de la evangelización,* edited by Orlando E. Costas, 55-66. Buenos Aires: Editorial La Aurora, 1973.

Agourides, Savas. "Peter and John in the Fourth Gospel." In *Studia Evangelica IV,* edited by Frank L. Cross, 3-7. Berlin: Akademie, 1968.

Ahr, Peter G. " 'He Loved Them to Completion': The Theology of John 13–14." In *Standing Before God: Studies on Prayer in Scriptures and in Tradition with Essays in Honor of John M. Oesterreicher,* edited by Asker Finkel and Lawrence Frizzell, 173-89. New York: Ktav, 1981.

Aragon, Jean-Louis. See D'Aragon.

Arens, Eduardo. *The ΕΛΘΟΝ-Sayings in the Synoptic Tradition: A Historico-Critical Investigation.* Orbis Biblicus et Orientalis 10. Freiburg/Schweiz: Universitätsverlag; Göttingen: Vandenhoeck & Ruprecht, 1976.

Arias, Mortimer and Alan Johnson. *The Great Commission: Biblical Models for Evangelism.* Nashville: Abingdon, 1992.

Ashton, John. *Understanding the Fourth Gospel.* Oxford: Oxford University Press, 1990.

Bammel, Ernst. "Die Abschiedsrede des Johannesevangeliums und ihr jüdischer Hintergrund." *Neotestamentica* 26 (1992): 1-12.

Bampfylde, Gillian. "More Light on John 12,34." *Journal for the Study of the New Testament* 17 (1983): 87-89.

Barr, James. *The Semantics of Biblical Language.* Oxford: Oxford University Press, 1961.

Barrett, C. K. *The Gospel according to St. John.* 2d ed. Philadelphia: Westminster, 1978.

Bassler, Jouette M. "Mixed Signals: Nicodemus in the Fourth Gospel." *Journal of Biblical Literature* 108 (1989): 635-46.

Bauder, Wolfgang. "Disciple." In *The New International Dictionary of New Testament Theology.* Edited by Colin Brown. Vol. 1:480-94. Grand Rapids: Zondervan, 1976.

Baumbach, Günther. "Gemeinde und Welt im Johannesevangelium." *Kairos* 14 (1972): 121-36.

Baumeister, Theofried. "Der Tod Jesu und die Leidensnachfolge des Jüngers nach dem

Johannesevangelium und dem ersten Johannesbrief." *Wissenschaft und Weisheit* 40 (1977): 81-99.

Beare, Francis W. "The Risen Jesus Bestows the Spirit: A Study of John 20:19-23." *Canadian Journal of Theology* 4 (1958): 95-100.

Beasley-Murray, George R. "John 12,31-34. The Eschatological Significance of the Lifting Up of the Son of Man." In *Studien zum Text und zur Ethik des Neuen Testaments: Festschrift zum 80. Geburtstag von Heinrich Greeven,* edited by Wolfgang Schrage, 70-81. Berlin/New York: de Gruyter, 1986.

————. *John.* Word Biblical Commentary 36. Waco, Tex.: Word, 1987.

————. "The Mission of the Logos-Son." In *The Four Gospels 1992: Festschrift Frans Neirynck.* Bibliotheca Ephemeridum Theologicarum Lovaniensium C, edited by F. van Segbroeck, C. M. Tuckett, G. van Belle, and J. Verheyden. Vol. 3, 1855-68. Leuven: University Press, 1992.

Beauvery, Robert. " 'Mon Père et votre Père.' " *Lumière et vie* 20 (1971): 75-87.

Becker, Jürgen. "Wunder und Christologie. Zum literarkritischen und christologischen Problem der Wunder im Johannesevangelium." *New Testament Studies* 16 (1969/70): 130-48.

Beekman, John, John Callow, and Michael Kopesec. *The Semantic Structure of Written Communication.* 5th ed. Dallas: Summer Institute of Linguistics, 1981.

Bernard, John H. *A Critical and Exegetical Commentary on the Gospel According to St. John.* 2 vols. Edinburgh: T & T Clark, 1928.

Betz, Hans-Dieter. *Nachfolge und Nachahmung Jesu Christi im Neuen Testament.* Beiträge zur historischen Theologie 37. Tübingen: J. C. B. Mohr (Paul Siebeck), 1967.

Betz, Otto. *Jesus. Der Messias Israels. Aufsätze zur biblischen Theologie.* Wissenschaftliche Untersuchungen zum Neuen Testament 42. Tübingen: J. C. B. Mohr (Paul Siebeck), 1987.

Beutler, Johannes. *Martyria: Traditionsgeschichtliche Untersuchungen zum Zeugnisthema bei Johannes.* Frankfurter Theologische Studien 10. Frankfurt am Main: Josef Knecht, 1972.

————. "Die Heilsbedeutung des Todes Jesu im Johannesevangelium nach Joh 13:1-20." In *Der Tod Jesu. Deutungen im Neuen Testament.* Quaestiones Disputatae 74, edited by Karl Kertelge, 188-205. Freiburg im Breisgau: Herder, 1976.

————. "Der alttestamentlich-jüdische Hintergrund der Hirtenrede in Johannes 10." In *The Shepherd Discourse of John 10 and Its Context,* edited by Johannes Beutler and Robert T. Fortna, 18-32. Society for New Testament Studies Monograph Series 67. Cambridge: Cambridge University Press, 1991.

————. "Greeks Come to See Jesus (John 12, 20f)." *Biblica* 71 (1990): 333-47.

Beyerhaus, Peter. *Allen Völkern zum Zeugnis. Biblisch-theologische Besinnung zum Wesen der Mission.* Wuppertal: Rolf Brockhaus, 1972.

Bieder, Werner. *Gottes Sendung und der missionarische Auftrag nach Matthäus, Lukas, Paulus, und Johannes.* Theologische Studien 82. Zürich: EVZ, 1965.

Billings, J. S. "Judas Iscariot in the Fourth Gospel." *Expository Times* 51 (1939-40): 156-57.

Bittner, Wolfgang J. *Jesu Zeichen im Johannesevangelium: Die Messias-Erkenntnis im Johannesevangelium vor ihrem jüdischen Hintergrund.* Wissenschaftliche Untersuchungen zum Neuen Testament 2/26. Tübingen: J. C. B. Mohr (Paul Siebeck), 1987.

Blank, Josef. *Krisis: Untersuchungen zur johanneischen Christologie und Eschatologie.* Freiburg im Breisgau: Lambertus, 1964.

————. "Die Sendung des Sohnes: Zur christologischen Bedeutung des Gleichnisses von den bösen Winzern Mk 12,1-12." In *Neues Testament und Kirche: Festschrift für Rudolf Schnackenburg*, edited by Joachim Gnilka, 11-41. Freiburg im Breisgau: Herder, 1974.

Bockmühl, Klaus. *Was heißt heute Mission? Entscheidungsfragen der neueren Missionstheologie*. Gießen-Basel: Brunnen, 1974.

Boismard, Marie-Émile. "Jésus, le Prophète par excellence, d'après Jean 10,24-39." In *Neues Testament und Kirche: Festschrift für Rudolf Schnackenburg*, edited by Joachim Gnilka, 160-71. Freiburg im Breisgau: Herder, 1974.

————. *Moses or Jesus: An Essay in Johannine Christology*. Translated by B. T. Viviano. Minneapolis: Fortress, 1993.

Borgen, Peder. *Bread from Heaven: An Exegetical Study of the Concept of Manna in the Gospel of John and the Writings of Philo*. Novum Testamentum Supplements 10. Leiden: E. J. Brill, 1965.

————. "God's Agent in the Fourth Gospel." In *Logos Was the True Light and Other Essays on the Gospel of John*, 121-32. Trondheim: Tapir, 1983.

Borig, Rainer. *Der wahre Weinstock: Untersuchungen zu Jo 15, 1-10*. Studien zum Alten und Neuen Testament 16. München: Kösel, 1967.

Bornhäuser, Karl. *Das Johannesevangelium: Eine Missionsschrift für Israel*. Beiträge zur Förderung christlicher Theologie 2/15. Gütersloh: Bertelsmann, 1928.

Bosch, David J. *Die Heidenmission in der Zukunftsschau Jesu*. Abhandlungen zur Theologie des Alten und Neuen Testaments 36. Zürich: Zwingli, 1959.

————. *Transforming Mission: Paradigm Shifts in Theology of Mission*. Maryknoll, N.Y.: Orbis, 1991.

Botha, J. Eugene. *Jesus and the Samaritan Woman: A Speech Act Reading of John 4:1-42*. Novum Testamentum Supplements 65. Leiden: E. J. Brill, 1991.

Bowker, J. W. "The Origin and Purpose of St John's Gospel." *New Testament Studies* 11 (1964/65): 398-408.

Bowman, John. "The Fourth Gospel and the Samaritans." *Bulletin of the John Rylands Library of Manchester* 40 (1958): 298-308.

Boyle, J. L. "The Last Discourse (Jn 13,31–16,33) and Prayer (Jn 17): Some Observations on their Unity and Development." *Biblica* 56 (1975): 210-22.

Braaten, Carl. *No Other Gospel: Christianity Among the World's Religions*. Minneapolis: Fortress, 1991.

Braun, François-Marie. *Jean le théologien et son évangile dans l'église ancienne*. Paris: J. Gabalda, 1959.

Brodie, Thomas L. *The Quest for the Origin of John's Gospel. A Source-oriented Approach*. Oxford: Oxford University Press, 1993.

Broomfield, Gerald Webb. *John, Peter, and the Fourth Gospel*. London: Society for Promoting Christian Knowledge, 1934.

Brown, Raymond E. *The Gospel According to John*. 2 vols. New York: Doubleday, 1966, 1970.

————. "'Other Sheep Not of This Fold': The Johannine Perspective on Christian Diversity in the Late First Century." *Journal of Biblical Literature* 97 (1978): 5-22.

————. *The Community of the Beloved Disciple*. New York: Paulist, 1979.

Brown, Raymond E., Karl P. Donfried, and John P. Reumann, eds. *Peter in the New Testament*. Minneapolis: Augsburg, 1973.

Bruce, F. F. "The Book of Zechariah and the Passion Narrative." *Bulletin of the John Rylands University Library of Manchester* 43 (1960/61): 336-53.

————. *The Gospel of John*. Grand Rapids: Wm. B. Eerdmans, 1983.

————. *The Hard Sayings of Jesus*. Downers Grove, Ill.: InterVarsity, 1983.

————. *The New Testament Development of Old Testament Themes*. Grand Rapids: Wm. B. Eerdmans, 1968.

Bühner, Jan Adolph. *Der Gesandte und sein Weg im 4. Evangelium: Die kultur- und religionsgeschichtliche Entwicklung*. Wissenschaftliche Untersuchungen zum Neuen Testament 2/2. Tübingen: J. C. B. Mohr (Paul Siebeck), 1977.

Bullinger, E. W. *Number in Scripture*. Grand Rapids: Kregel, 1967.

Bullock, Hassell. *An Introduction to the Old Testament Prophetic Books*. Chicago: Moody, 1986.

Bultmann, Rudolf. *Theology of the New Testament*. 2 vols. Translated by Kendrick Grobel. New York: Charles Scribner's Sons, 1951, 1955.

————. *The Gospel of John*. Translated by G. R. Beasley-Murray. Oxford: Basil Blackwell, 1971.

————. "Die Bedeutung der neuerschlossenen mandäischen und manichäischen Quellen für das Verständnis des Johannesevangeliums." In *Johannes und sein Evangelium*, Wege der Forschung 82, edited by Karl Heinrich Rengstorf, 402-64. Darmstadt: Wissenschaftliche Buchgesellschaft, 1973 [1925].

Burge, Gary M. *The Anointed Community: The Holy Spirit in the Johannine Tradition*. Grand Rapids: Wm. B. Eerdmans, 1987.

————. "The Literary Seams in the Fourth Gospel." *Covenant Quarterly* 48, no. 3 (1990): 15-23.

Burkett, Delbert. *The Son of Man in the Gospel of John*. Journal for the Study of the New Testament Supplement Series 56. Sheffield: JSOT, 1991.

Burnham, Frederic B., ed. *Postmodern Theology: Christian Faith in a Pluralistic World*. San Francisco: Harper, 1989.

Bussche, Henri van den. "Die Kirche im vierten Evangelium." In *Vom Christus zur Kirche: Charisma und Amt im Urchristentum*, edited by Jean Giblet, 79-107. Wien: Herder, 1966.

Busse, Ulrich. "Die 'Hellenen' Joh 12, 20ff. und der sogenannte 'Anhang' Joh 21." In *The Four Gospels 1992: Festschrift Frans Neirynck*. Bibliotheca Ephemeridum Theologicarum Lovaniensium, vol. 3, edited by F. van Segbroeck, C. M. Tuckett, G. van Belle, and J. Verheyden. 2083-2100. Leuven: University Press, 1992.

Caird, George Bradford. "The Glory of God in the Fourth Gospel." *New Testament Studies* 15 (1968/69): 265-77.

Cameron, Nigel M. de S., ed. *Universalism and the Doctrine of Hell*. Grand Rapids: Baker, 1992.

Caragounis, Chrys C. *The Son of Man*. Wissenschaftliche Untersuchungen zum Neuen Testament 38. Tübingen: J. C. B. Mohr (Paul Siebeck), 1986.

Carey, George L. "The Lamb of God and Atonement Theories." *Tyndale Bulletin* 32 (1981): 97-122.

Caroll, Kenneth L. "The Fourth Gospel and the Exclusion of Christians from the Synagogues." *Bulletin of the John Rylands University Library of Manchester* 40 (1957/58): 19-32.

Carson, D. A. *Divine Sovereignty and Human Responsibility: Biblical Perspectives in Tension*. Atlanta: John Knox, 1981.

————. *Exegetical Fallacies*. Grand Rapids: Baker, 1984.

————. "The Function of the Paraclete in John 16:7-11." *Journal of Biblical Literature* 98 (1979): 547-66.

————. *The Gagging of God: Christianity Confronts Pluralism*. Grand Rapids: Zondervan, 1996.

————. *The Gospel According to John*. Grand Rapids: Wm. B. Eerdmans, 1991.

————. "Historical Tradition in the Fourth Gospel: After Dodd, What?" In *Gospel Perspectives: Studies of History and Tradition in the Four Gospels*, edited by R. T. France and David Wenham, 2:83-145. Sheffield: JSOT, 1981.

————. "John and the Johannine Epistles." In *It Is Written: Scripture Citing Scripture*, edited by D. A. Carson and H. G. M. Williamson, 245-64. Cambridge: Cambridge University Press, 1988.

————. "The Purpose of the Fourth Gospel: Jn 20:31 Reconsidered." *Journal of Biblical Literature* 106 (1987): 639-51.

————. "The Purpose of Signs and Wonders in the New Testament." In *Power Religion*, edited by Michael S. Horton, 89-118. Chicago: Moody, 1992.

————. Review of *Overcoming the World: Politics and Community in the Gospel of John* by David Rensberger, *Themelios* 17 (1991): 27-28.

————. "Understanding Misunderstandings in the Fourth Gospel." *Tyndale Bulletin* 33 (1982): 59-89.

Cassem, Ned H. "A Grammatical and Contextual Inventory of the Use of κόσμος in the Johannine Cosmic Theology." *New Testament Studies* 19 (1972/73): 81-91.

Charles, J. Daryl. " 'Will the Court Please Call in the Prime Witness?' John 1:29-34 and the 'Witness'-Motif." *Trinity Journal* 10 NS (1989): 71-83.

Chilton, Bruce. "John xii 34 and the Targum Isaiah lii 13." *Novum Testamentum* 22 (1980): 176-78.

Clarke, Andrew D., and Bruce W. Winter, eds. *One God, One Lord: Christianity in a World of Religious Pluralism*. 2d ed. Grand Rapids: Baker, 1993.

Clowney, Edmund P. "Interpreting the Biblical Models of the Church: A Hermeneutical Deepening of Ecclesiology." In *Biblical Interpretation and the Church*, edited by D. A. Carson, 64-109. Exeter: Paternoster, 1984.

Cohn, M. "Die Stellvertretung im jüdischen Recht." *Zeitschrift für vergleichende Rechtswissenschaft* 36 (1920): 124-213, 354-460.

Coleman, Robert E. *The Master Plan of Discipleship*. Old Tappan, N.J.: Fleming H. Revell, 1987.

————. *The Master Plan of Evangelism*. Old Tappan, N.J.: Fleming H. Revell, 1963.

————. *The Mind of the Master*. Old Tappan, N.J.: Fleming H. Revell, 1977.

Collet, Giancarlo. *Das Missionsverständnis der Kirche in der gegenwärtigen Diskussion*. Tübinger Theologische Studien 24. Mainz: Matthias-Grünwald, 1984.

Collins, Raymond F. *These Things Have Been Written — Studies on the Fourth Gospel*. Louvain: Peeters; Grand Rapids: Wm. B. Eerdmans, 1990.

Colson, Jean. *L'énigme du disciple que Jésus aimait*. Théologie Historique 10. Paris: Beauchesne et ses fils, 1969.

Comblin, Jose. *Sent from the Father: Meditations on the Fourth Gospel*. Translated by Carl Kabat. Maryknoll, N.Y.: Orbis, 1974.

Conzelmann, Hans. *Grundriß der Theologie des Neuen Testaments*. München: Chr. Kaiser, 1967.

Cook, W. Robert. "The 'Glory' Motif in the Johannine Corpus." *Journal of the Evangelical Theological Society* 27 (1984): 291-97.

Coppens, Joseph. "Le fils de l'homme dans l'évangile johannique." *Ephemerides theologicae lovanienses* 52 (1976): 28-81.

Corell, Alf. *Consummatum Est: Eschatology and Church in the Gospel of St. John*. London: SPCK, 1958.

Cotterell, Peter, and Max Turner. *Linguistics and Biblical Interpretation*. Downers Grove, Ill.: InterVarsity, 1989.

Cribbs, F. Lamar. "A Reassessment of the Date of Origin and the Destination of the Gospel of John." *Journal of Biblical Literature* 89 (1970): 38-55.

Crockett, William V. and James G. Sigountos, eds. *Through No Fault of Their Own? The Fate of Those Who Have Never Heard*. Grand Rapids: Baker, 1991.

Cullmann, Oscar. "Der johanneische Gebrauch doppeldeutiger Ausdrücke als Schlüssel zum Verständnis des 4. Evangeliums." *Theologische Zeitschrift* 4 (1948): 360-72.

———. "Samaria and the Origins of the Christian Mission." In *The Early Church*, edited by A. J. B. Higgins, 185-92. London: SCM, 1956.

———. *The Johannine Circle*. London: SCM, 1976.

———. *Peter: Disciple, Apostle, Martyr*. London: SCM, 1976.

Culpepper, R. Alan. *The Anatomy of the Fourth Gospel: A Study in Literary Design*. Philadelphia: Fortress, 1983.

Dahl, Nils Alstrup. "The Johannine Church and History." In *Current Issues in New Testament Interpretation: Essays in Honor of Otto A. Piper*, edited by William Klassen and Graydon F. Snyder, 124-42 and 284-88. New York: Harper & Brothers, 1962.

Dahms, John V. "John's Use of μονογενής Reconsidered." *New Testament Studies* 29 (1983): 222-32.

D'Aragon, Jean-Louis. "Le caractère distinctif de l'Église johannique." In *L'Église dans la Bible. Communications présentées à la XVIIe réunion annuelle de l'Acébac*. Studia 13. Recherches de Philosophie et de Théologie, edited by C. Matura and A. M. Malo, 53-66. Montréal: Desclée de Brouwer, 1962.

Dautzenberg, Gerhard. *Sein Leben bewahren: ΨΥΧΗ in den Herrenworten der Evangelien*. SANT 14. München: Kösel, 1966.

Davies, W. D. "The Johannine 'Signs' of Jesus." In *A Companion to John: Readings in Johannine Theology*, edited by Michael J. Taylor, 91-115. New York: Alba, 1977.

Davis, John J. *Biblical Numerology*. Grand Rapids: Baker, 1968.

Davison, Leslie. *Sender and Sent: A Study in Mission*. London: Epworth, 1969.

Davy, Francis Noel. "The Gospel According to St. John and the Christian Mission." In *The Theology of the Christian Mission*, edited by Gerald H. Anderson, 85-93. Nashville/ New York: Abingdon, 1961.

de Jonge, Marinus. "Jesus as Prophet and King in the Fourth Gospel." *Ephemerides Theologicae Lovanienses* 49 (1973): 160-77.

———. *Jesus, Stranger from Heaven and Son of God: Jesus Christ and the Christians in Johannine Perspective*. SBL Sources for Biblical Study 11, edited and translated by John E. Steely. Missoula, Mont.: Scholars Press, 1977.

———. "Jewish Expectations about the 'Messiah' according to the Fourth Gospel." *New Testament Studies* 19 (1973): 246-70.

———. "Signs and Works in the Fourth Gospel." In *Miscellanea Neotestamentica*, vol. 2. Novum Testamentum Supplements 48, edited by T. Baarda, A. F. J. Klijn, and W. C. van Unnik, 107-25. Leiden: E. J. Brill, 1978.

Di Marco, Angelico-Salvatore. "Πέμπω: per una ricerca del 'campo semantico' nel NT." *Rivista biblica* 40 (1992): 385-419.

Dietzfelbinger, Christian. "Die größeren Werke (Joh 14.12f.)." *New Testament Studies* 35 (1989): 27-47.

Dodd, C. H. *The Interpretation of the Fourth Gospel*. Cambridge: Cambridge University Press, 1953.

————. *Historical Tradition in the Fourth Gospel.* Cambridge: Cambridge University Press, 1963.

Droge, Arthur J. "The Status of Peter in the Fourth Gospel (Jn 18:10-11)." *Journal of Biblical Literature* 109 (1990): 307-11.

DuBose, Francis M. *God Who Sends: A Fresh Quest for Biblical Mission.* Nashville: Broadman, 1983.

Dunn, James D. G. "Let John Be John." In *The Gospel and the Gospels,* edited by Peter Stuhlmacher, 293-322. Grand Rapids: Wm. B. Eerdmans, 1991.

————. *The Partings of the Ways Between Christianity and Judaism and Their Significance for the Character of Christianity.* London: SCM, 1991.

Dupuis, Jacques. *Jesus Christ at the Encounter of World Religions.* Translated by Robert R. Barr. Maryknoll, N.Y.: Orbis, 1989.

Edwards, Ruth B. "Χάριν ἀντί χάριτος (John 1,16): Grace and Law in the Johannine Prologue." *Journal for the Study of the New Testament* 32 (1988): 3-15.

Ellis, E. Earle. "Background and Christology of John's Gospel: Selected Motifs." *Southwestern Journal of Theology* 31 (1988): 24-31.

Enz, Jacob J. "The Book of Exodus as a Literary Type for the Gospel of John." *Journal of Biblical Literature* 76 (1957): 208-15.

Evans, Craig A. "The Voice from Heaven: A Note on John 12:28." *Catholic Biblical Quarterly* 43 (1981): 405-8.

————. "Obduracy and the Lord's Servant: Some Observations on the Use of the Old Testament in the Fourth Gospel." In *Early Jewish and Christian Exegesis: Studies in Memory of William Hugh Brownlee,* edited by Craig A. Evans and William F. Stinespring, 221-36. Atlanta: Scholars Press, 1987.

Fascher, Erich. "Theologische Betrachtungen zu δεῖ." In *Neutestamentliche Studien für Rudolf Bultmann zu seinem siebzigsten Geburtstag am 20. August 1954.* Beihefte zur Zeitschrift für die neutestamentliche Wissenschaft und die Kunde der älteren Kirche 21, edited by Walther Eltester, 228-54. 2d ed. Berlin: Alfred Töpelmann, 1957.

Faulhaber, Doris. "Das Johannes-Evangelium und die Kirche." Ph.D. diss., Heidelberg, 1935.

Fee, Gordon D. "On the Text and Meaning of John 20.30-31." In *The Four Gospels 1992: Festschrift Frans Neirynck.* Bibliotheca Ephemeridum Theologicarum Lovaniensium C, edited by F. van Segbroeck, C. M. Tuckett, G. van Belle, and J. Verheyden, vol. 3, 2193-2205. Leuven: University Press, 1992.

Fennema, David Allen. "Jesus and God According to John: An Analysis of the Fourth Gospel's Father/Son Christology." Ph.D. diss., Duke University, 1979.

Feuillet, André. "Deux références évangeliques cachées au Serviteur martyrisé (Is 52.13-53.12). Quelques aspects importants du mystère rédempteur." *La nouvelle revue théologique* 106 (1984): 549-65.

Forestell, J. Terence. *The Word of the Cross: Salvation as Revelation in the Fourth Gospel.* Analecta Biblica 57. Rome: Biblical Institute Press, 1974.

Fortna, Robert T. *The Gospel of Signs: A Reconstruction of the Narrative Source Underlying the Fourth Gospel.* Cambridge: Cambridge University Press, 1970.

————. "From Christology to Soteriology: A Redaction-Critical Study of Salvation in the Fourth Gospel." *Interpretation* 27 (1973): 31-47.

————. "Christology in the Fourth Gospel: Redaction-Critical Perspectives." *New Testament Studies* 21 (1975): 489-504.

————. *The Fourth Gospel and Its Predecessors: From Narrative Source to Present Gospel.* Philadelphia: Fortress, 1988.

France, R. T. *Jesus and the Old Testament: His Application of Old Testament Passages to Himself and His Mission*. London: Tyndale, 1971.

Freed, Edwin D. "Samaritan Influence in the Gospel of John." *Catholic Biblical Quarterly* 30 (1968): 580-87.

———. "Variations in the Language and Thought of John." *Zeitschrift für die neutestamentliche Wissenschaft* 55 (1964): 167-97.

———. "The Son of Man in the Fourth Gospel." *Journal of Biblical Literature* 86 (1967): 402-409.

———. "Did John Write His Gospel Partly to Win Samaritan Converts?" *Novum Testamentum* 12 (1970): 241-56.

———. "Ἐγώ εἰμι in John 8,24 in the Light of Its Context and Jewish Messianic Belief." *Journal of Theological Studies* 33 (1982): 163-67.

Fridrichsen, Anton. "La pensée missionnaire dans le Quatrième Évangile." In *Arbeiten und Mitteilungen aus dem neutestamentlichen Seminar zu Uppsala* VI, edited by Anton Fridrichsen, 39-45. Uppsala, 1935.

Friend, Helen S. "Like Father, Like Son: A Discussion of the Concept of Agency in Halakah and John." *Ashland Theological Journal* 21 (1990): 18-28.

Fuller, Reginald H. "John 20:19-23." *Interpretation* 32 (1978): 180-84.

Gaugler, Ernst. "Die Bedeutung der Kirche in den johanneischen Schriften." *Internationale Kirchliche Zeitschrift* 14 (1924): 97-117; *Internationale Kirchliche Zeitschrift* 14 (1924): 181-219; *Internationale Kirchliche Zeitschrift* 15 (1925): 27-42.

Gensichen, Hans-Werner. *Glaube für die Welt: Theologische Aspekte der Mission*. Gütersloh: Gütersloher Verlagshaus G. Mohn, 1971.

Gerhardsson, Birger. *The Good Samaritan — The Good Shepherd?* Coniectanea Neotestamentica 16. Lund: Gleerup, 1958.

Ghiberti, Giuseppe. "Missione di Gesù e di discepoli nel quarto Vangelo." *Ricerche Storico Bibliche* 2 (1990): 185-200.

Giblet, Jean. "Les promesses de l'Esprit et la mission des apôtres dans les Évangiles." *Irénikon* 30 (1957): 5-43.

Giesbrecht, Herbert. "The Evangelist John's Conception of the Church as Delineated in His Gospel." *Evangelical Quarterly* 58 (1986): 101-19.

Gillis, Chester. *Pluralism: A New Paradigm for Theology*. Louvain: Peeters; Grand Rapids: Wm. B. Eerdmans, 1993.

Glasson, T. Francis. *Moses in the Fourth Gospel*. Studies in Biblical Theology 40. London: SCM, 1963.

Goppelt, Leonhard. Typos: *The Typological Interpretation of the Old Testament in the New*. Grand Rapids: Wm B. Eerdmans, 1982 [1939].

Grayston, Kenneth. "Jesus and the Church in St. John's Gospel." *London Quarterly and Holborn Review* 36 (1967): 106-13.

Greeven, Heinrich. "Die missionierende Gemeinde nach den apostolischen Briefen." In *Sammlung und Sendung: Vom Auftrag der Kirche in der Welt: Eine Festgabe für Heinrich Rendtorff zu seinem 70. Geburtstag am 9. April 1958*, edited by Joachim Heubach and Heinrich-Hermann Ulrich, 59-71. Berlin: Christlicher Zeitschriftenverlag, 1958.

Grigsby, Bruce H. "The Cross as an Expiatory Sacrifice in the Fourth Gospel." *Journal for the Study of the New Testament* 15 (1982): 51-80.

Grossouw, Willem. "La glorification du Christ dans le quatrième évangile." In *L'Évangile de Jean, études et problèmes*, edited by Marie-Émile Boismard et al., 131-45. Recherches Bibliques 3. Bruges: Desclée de Brouwer, 1958.

Gruenler, Royce Gordon. *The Trinity in the Gospel of John: A Thematic Commentary on the Fourth Gospel.* Grand Rapids: Baker, 1986.

Gunther, John J. "The Relation of the Beloved Disciple to the Twelve." *Theologische Zeitschrift* 37 (1981): 129-48.

Guthrie, Donald. "The Importance of Signs in the Fourth Gospel." *Vox Evangelica* 5 (1967): 72-83.

————. *New Testament Theology.* Downers Grove, Ill.: InterVarsity, 1981.

Haacker, Klaus. *Die Stiftung des Heils: Untersuchungen zur Struktur der johanneischen Theologie.* Arbeiten zur Theologie 1/47. Stuttgart: Calwer, 1972.

————. "Jesus und die Kirche nach Johannes." *Theologische Zeitschrift* 29 (1973): 179-201.

Haenchen, Ernst. "Der Vater, der mich gesandt hat." *New Testament Studies* 9 (1963): 208-16.

————. *A Commentary on the Gospel of John.* 2 vols. Translated by R. W. Funk. Philadelphia: Fortress, 1984.

Hahn, Ferdinand. *Mission in the New Testament.* Studies in Biblical Theology 47. London: SCM, 1965.

————. "Die Jüngerberufung Joh 1,35-51." In *Neues Testament und Kirche: Festschrift für Rudolf Schnackenburg,* edited by Joachim Gnilka, 172-90. Freiburg im Breisgau: Herder, 1974.

————. "Sendung des Geistes — Sendung der Jünger: Die pneumatologische Dimension des Missionsauftrages nach dem Zeugnis des Neuen Testamentes." In *Universales Christentum angesichts einer pluralen Welt,* Beiträge zur Religionstheologie 1, edited by Andreas Bsteh, 87-106. Mödling bei Wien: St. Gabriel, 1976.

————. " 'Die Juden' im Johannesevangelium." In *Kontinuität und Einheit: Für Franz Mußner,* edited by Paul-Gerhard Müller and Werner Stenger, 430-38. Freiburg im Breisgau: Herder, 1981.

Hamerton-Kelly, Robert G. *Pre-Existence, Wisdom and the Son of Man.* Society for New Testament Studies Monograph Series 21. Cambridge: Cambridge University Press, 1973.

Hare, Douglas R. A. Review of *The Son of Man in the Gospel of John* by Delbert Burkett. *Journal of Biblical Literature* 112 (1993): 158-60.

Harnack, Adolf von. "κόπος (Κοπιᾶν, Οἱ Κοπιῶντες) im frühchristlichen Sprachgebrauch." *Zeitschrift für die neutestamentliche Wissenschaft* 27 (1928): 1-10.

Harner, Philip B. *The "I Am" of the Fourth Gospel.* Philadelphia: Fortress, 1970.

Harris, Murray J. *Jesus as God: The New Testament Use of Theos in Reference to Jesus.* Grand Rapids: Baker, 1992.

Hartin, Patrick J. "The Role of Peter in the Fourth Gospel." *Neotestamentica* 24 (1990): 49-61.

Harvey, Anthony E. "Christ as Agent." In *The Glory of Christ in the New Testament: Studies in Christology in Memory of George Bradford Caird,* edited by L. D. Hurst and N. T. Wright, 239-50. Oxford: Clarendon, 1987.

Hegermann, Harald. "Er kam in sein Eigentum: Zur Bedeutung des Erdenwirkens Jesu im vierten Evangelium." In *Der Ruf Jesu und die Antwort der Gemeinde: Exegetische Untersuchungen Joachim Jeremias zum 70. Geburtstag gewidmet von seinen Schülern,* edited by Eduard Lohse, Christoph Burchard, and Berndt Schaller, 112-31. Göttingen: Vandenhoeck & Ruprecht, 1970.

Hengel, Martin. "Jesus als messianischer Lehrer der Weisheit und die Anfänge der Christologie." In *Sagesse et Religion,* 148-88. Colloque de Strasbourg, October 1976. Paris, 1979.

————. "Maria Magdalena und die Frauen als Zeugen." In *Abraham unser Vater: Juden und Christen im Gespräch über die Bibel: Festschrift für Otto Michel zum 60. Geburtstag*, edited by Otto Betz, Martin Hengel, and Peter Schmidt, 243-56. Leiden: E. J. Brill, 1963.

————. "Die Ursprünge der christlichen Mission." *New Testament Studies* 18 (1971): 15-38.

————. *Der Sohn Gottes: Die Entstehung der Christologie und die jüdisch-hellenistische Religionsgeschichte.* Tübingen: J. C. B. Mohr (Paul Siebeck), 1975.

————. *The Johannine Question.* Translated by John Bowden. London: SCM, 1989.

————. *Die johanneische Frage.* Wissenschaftliche Untersuchungen zum Neuen Testament 67. Tübingen: J. C. B. Mohr (Paul Siebeck), 1993.

————. "Aufgaben der neutestamentlichen Wissenschaft." *New Testament Studies* 40 (1994): 321-57.

Hesselgrave, David J. "Holes in 'Holistic Mission.'" *Trinity World Forum* 19, no. 3 (1990): 1-5.

————. "To John Stott — A Surrejoinder." *Trinity World Forum* 16, no. 3 (1991): 3-4.

Hick, John H. *The Myth of God Incarnate.* London: SCM, 1977.

————. *God Has Many Names.* Philadelphia: Westminster, 1982.

————. "The Non-Absoluteness of Christianity." In *The Myth of Christian Uniqueness*, edited by John H. Hick and Paul F. Knitter, 16-36. Maryknoll, N.Y.: Orbis, 1987.

Hill, Harriet. "Incarnational Ministry: A Critical Examination," *Evangelical Missions Quarterly* 26 (1990): 196-201.

Hofius, Otto. "Die Sammlung der Heiden zur Herde Israels (Joh 10, 16; 11, 51f.)." *Zeitschrift für die neutestamentliche Wissenschaft* 58 (1967): 289-91.

————. "'Der in des Vaters Schoß ist.' Joh 1,18." *Zeitschrift für die neutestamentliche Wissenschaft* 80 (1989): 163-71.

Howton, Dom John. "'Son of God' in the Fourth Gospel." *New Testament Studies* 10 (1963/64): 227-37.

Hudry Clergeon, Charles. "Le quatrième évangile indique-t-il le nom de son auteur?" *Biblica* 56 (1975): 545-49.

Hurtado, Larry W. *One God, One Lord: Early Christian Devotion and Ancient Jewish Monotheism.* Philadelphia: Fortress, 1988.

————. "The Origins of the Worship of Christ." *Themelios* 19, no. 2 (1994): 4-8.

Ibuki, Yu. *Die Wahrheit im Johannesevangelium.* Bonner biblische Beiträge 39. Bonn: Peter Hanstein, 1972.

————. "Das Zeugnis Jesu im Johannesevangelium." In *Annual of the Japanese Bible Institute* 8, edited by Masao Sekine and Akira Satake, 123-61. Tokyo: Yamamoto Shoten, 1982.

————. "Die Doxa des Gesandten — Studie zur johanneischen Christologie." In *Annual of the Japanese Biblical Institute* 14, edited by Masao Sekine and Akira Satake, 38-81. Tokyo: Yamamoto Shoten, 1988.

Jeremias, Joachim. *Jesus' Promise to the Nations.* Studies in Biblical Theology 24. Translated by S. H. Hooke. London: SCM, 1958.

Johns, Loren L. and Douglas B. Miller. "The Signs as Witnesses in the Fourth Gospel: Reexamining the Evidence." *Catholic Biblical Quarterly* 56 (1994): 519-35.

Johnson, Nigel Edwin. "The Beloved Disciple in the Fourth Gospel." *Church Quarterly Review* 167 (1966): 278-91.

Jonge, Marinus de. See de Jonge

Judge, Peter J. "A Note on Jn 20,29." In *The Four Gospels 1992: Festschrift Frans Neirynck*.

Bibliotheca Ephemeridum Theologicarum Lovaniensium C, edited by F. van Seg-broeck, C. M. Tuckett, G. van Belle, and J. Verheyden, vol. 3, 2183-92. Leuven: University Press, 1992.

Käsemann, Ernst. *The Testament of Jesus: A Study of the Gospel of John in the Light of Chapter 17.* Translated by Gerhard Krodel. Philadelphia: Fortress, 1968.

————. "A Critical Analysis of Philippians 2:5-11." In *God in Christ: Existence and Province,* edited by Robert W. Funk, 45-88. *Journal for Theology and Church* 5. New York: Harper & Row/Tübingen: J. C. B. Mohr (Paul Siebeck), 1968 [1950].

Kato, Z. *Die Völkermission im Markusevangelium.* Europäische Hochschulschriften 23/252. Frankfurt am Main: Peter Lang, 1986.

Kertelge, Karl, ed. *Mission im Neuen Testament.* Quaestiones Disputatae 93. Freiburg: Herder, 1982.

Kiefer, Odo. *Die Hirtenrede: Analyse und Deutung von Johannes 10,1-18.* Stuttgart: Katholisches Bibelwerk, 1967.

Kiley, Mark. "The Exegesis of God: Jesus' Signs in John 1–11." In SBL Seminar Papers 27, 555-69. Atlanta, Ga.: Scholars Press, 1988.

Klauck, Hans-Josef. "Gemeinde ohne Amt? Erfahrungen mit der Kirche in den johanneischen Schriften." *Biblische Zeitschrift* 29 (1985): 193-220.

Klein, William W., Craig L. Blomberg, and Robert L. Hubbard, Jr. *Introduction to Biblical Interpretation.* Dallas: Word, 1993.

Knitter, Paul F. *No Other Name? A Critical Survey of Christian Attitudes Toward the World Religions.* Maryknoll, N.Y.: Orbis, 1985.

Köstenberger, Andreas J. "Jesus as Rabbi in the Fourth Gospel." *Bulletin of Biblical Research* 8 (1998): forthcoming.

Krafft, Eva. "Die Personen des Johannesevangeliums." *Evangelische Theologie* 16 (1956): 18-32.

Kraft, Charles H. *Communication Theory for Christian Witness.* Rev. ed. Maryknoll, N.Y.: Orbis, 1991.

Kragerud, Alv. *Der Lieblingsjünger im Johannesevangelium: Ein exegetischer Versuch.* Hamburg: Grosshaus Wegner, 1959.

Kuhl, Josef. *Die Sendung Jesu und der Kirche nach dem Johannes-Evangelium.* Studia Instituti Missiologica Societatis Verbi Domini 11. St. Augustin: Steyler, 1967.

Kümmel, Werner Georg. *Die Theologie des Neuen Testaments nach seinen Hauptzeugen.* 2d ed. Göttingen: Vandenhoeck & Ruprecht, 1972.

Kuhn, Karl Georg. "Das Problem der Mission in der Urchristenheit." *Evangelische Missions-Zeitschrift* 11 (1954): 161-68.

Kurz, William S. "The Beloved Disciple and Implied Readers: A Socio-Narratological Approach." *Biblical Theology Bulletin* 19 (1989): 100-107.

Kysar, Robert. *The Fourth Evangelist and His Gospel: An Examination of Contemporary Scholarship.* Minneapolis: Augsburg, 1975.

————. *John, the Maverick Gospel.* Atlanta: John Knox, 1975.

Lacomara, Aelred. "Deuteronomy and the Farewell Discourse (Jn 13:31–16:33)." *Catholic Biblical Quarterly* 36 (1974): 65-84.

Lamarche, Paul. *Zacharie IX–XIV: Structure Litteraire et Messianisme.* Paris: J. Gabalda, 1961.

Leidig, Edeltraud. *Jesu Gespräch mit der Samaritanerin und weitere Gespräche im Johannesevangelium.* Theologische Dissertationen 15. Basel: Friedrich Reinhardt, 1979.

Lemcio, Eugene E. "Father and Son in the Synoptics and John: A Canonical Reading." In Robert W. Wall and Eugene E. Lemcio, *The New Testament as Canon: A Reader in Canonical Criticism.* Journal for the Study of the New Testament Supplement Series 76, 78-108. Sheffield: JSOT, 1992.

Lemmer, Hermanus Richard. "A Possible Understanding by the Implied Reader, of Some of the *Coming-Going-Being Sent* Pronouncements, in the Johannine Farewell Discourses." *Neotestamentica* 25 (1992): 289-310.

Levinsohn, Stephen H. *Discourse Features of New Testament Greek.* Dallas, Tex.: Summer Institute of Linguistics, 1992.

Lindars, Barnabas. "The Son of Man in the Johannine Christology." In *Christ and Spirit: In Honour of C. F. D. Moule,* edited by Barnabas Lindars and Stephen S. Smalley, 43-60. London: SCM, 1973.

————. *The Gospel of John.* The New Century Bible Commentary. Grand Rapids: Wm. B. Eerdmans, 1981 [1972].

————. *Jesus Son of Man: A Fresh Examination of the Son of Man Sayings in the Gospels in the Light of Recent Research.* Grand Rapids: Wm. B. Eerdmans, 1983.

Lindemann, Andreas. "Gemeinde und Welt im Johannesevangelium." In *Kirche: Festschrift für Günther Bornkamm zum 75. Geburtstag,* edited by Dieter Lührmann and Georg Strecker, 133-61. Tübingen: J. C. B. Mohr (Paul Siebeck), 1980.

Loader, William. *The Christology of the Fourth Gospel.* Beiträge zur biblischen Exegese und Theologie 23. Frankfurt am Main: Peter Lang, 1992.

Lohmeyer, Ernst. "Über Aufbau und Gliederung des vierten Evangeliums." *Zeitschrift für die neutestamentliche Wissenschaft* 27 (1928): 11-36.

Lohse, Eduard. "Miracles in the Fourth Gospel." In *What about the New Testament? In Honour of Christopher Evans,* edited by Morna D. Hooker and Colin J. A. Hickling, 64-75. London: SCM, 1975.

Longenecker, Richard N. *The Christology of Early Jewish Christianity.* London: SCM, 1970.

Lorenzen, Thorwald. *Der Lieblingsjünger im Johannesevangelium: Eine redaktionsgeschichtliche Studie.* Stuttgarter Bibelstudien 55. Stuttgart: Katholisches Bibelwerk Verlag, 1971.

Louw, Johannes P. "Narrator of the Father — ἐξηγεῖσθαι and related terms in Johannine Christology." *Neotestamentica* 2 (1968): 32-40.

————. "On Johannine Style." *Neotestamentica* 20 (1986): 5-12.

Louw, Johannes P. and Eugene A. Nida. *Greek-English Lexicon of the New Testament Based on Semantic Domains.* 2d ed. 2 vols. New York: United Bible Societies, 1988, 1989.

Maddox, Randy L. "The Function of the Son of Man in the Gospel of John." In *Reconciliation and Hope: New Testament Essays on Atonement and Eschatology Presented to L. L. Morris on his 60th Birthday,* edited by Robert J. Banks, 186-204. Exeter: Paternoster; Grand Rapids: Wm. B. Eerdmans, 1974.

Mahoney, Robert K. *Two Disciples at the Tomb.* Frankfurt: Peter Lang, 1975.

Maier, Gerhard. "The Church in the Gospel of Matthew: Hermeneutical Analysis of the Current Debate." In *Biblical Interpretation and the Church: Text and Context,* edited by D. A. Carson, 45-63. Exeter: Paternoster, 1984.

Malatesta, Edward. *Interiority and Covenant. A Study of* εἶναι ἐν *and* μένειν ἐν *in the First Letter of Saint John.* Analecta Biblica 69. Rome: Biblical Institute Press, 1978.

Marshall, I. Howard. *Jesus the Saviour: Studies in New Testament Theology.* Downers Grove, Ill.: InterVarsity, 1990.

————. *The Origins of New Testament Christology.* Downers Grove, Ill.: InterVarsity, 1976.

Martin, P. J. "A Community in Crisis: The Christology of the Johannine Community as the Point at Issue." *Neotestamentica* 19 (1985): 37-49.

Martin, Ralph P. *Carmen Christi: Philippians 2:5-11 in Recent Interpretation and in the Setting of Early Christian Worship*. Rev. ed. Grand Rapids: Wm. B. Eerdmans, 1983.

Martyn, J. Louis. "Glimpses into the History of the Johannine Community." In *L'Évangile de Jean: Sources, Rédaction, Théologie. Bibliotheca ephemeridum theologicarum lovaniensium* 44, edited by Marinus de Jonge, 149-75. Leuven: University Press, 1977.

————. *The Gospel of John in Christian History: Essays for Interpreters*. New York: Paulist, 1978.

————. *History and Theology in the Fourth Gospel*. New York: Harper & Row, 1968. Rev. ed. Nashville: Abingdon, 1979.

Mastin, Brian. "A Neglected Feature of the Christology of the Fourth Gospel." *New Testament Studies* 22 (October 1975): 32-51.

Matera, Frank J. " 'On Behalf of Others,' 'Cleansing,' and 'Return': Johannine Images for Jesus' Death." *Louvain Studies* 13 (1988): 161-78.

Matsunaga, Kikuo. "The 'Theos' Christology as the Ultimate Confession of the Fourth Gospel." In *Annual of the Japanese Biblical Institute* 7, edited by Masao Sekine and Akira Satake, 124-45. Tokyo: Yamamoto Shoten, 1981.

Maynard, Arthur H. "The Role of Peter in the Fourth Gospel." *New Testament Studies* 30 (1984): 531-48.

McElhanon, Kenneth. "Don't Give Up on the Incarnational Model." *Evangelical Missions Quarterly* 27 (1991): 390-93.

McNamara, Martin. "The Ascension and Exaltation of Christ in the Fourth Gospel." *Scripture* 19 (1967): 65-73.

McNeil, Brian. "The Quotation at John XII 34." *Novum Testamentum* 19 (1977): 22-33.

McPolin, James. "Mission in the Fourth Gospel." *Irish Theological Quarterly* 36 (1969): 113-22.

Mealand, David L. "The Christology of the Fourth Gospel." *Scottish Journal of Theology* 31 (1978): 449-67.

Meeks, Wayne A. *The Prophet-King. Moses Traditions and the Johannine Christology*. Novum Testamentum Supplements 14. Leiden: E. J. Brill, 1967.

————. "The Man from Heaven in Johannine Sectarianism." *Journal of Biblical Literature* 91 (1972): 44-72.

————. " 'Am I a Jew?' — Johannine Christianity and Judaism." In *Christianity, Judaism, and Other Greco-Roman Cults*, edited by Jacob Neusner, 1:163-86. Leiden: E. J. Brill, 1975.

————. "The Divine Agent in the Fourth Gospel." In *Aspects of Religious Propaganda in Judaism and Early Christianity*, edited by Elisabeth Schüssler-Fiorenza, 43-67. Notre Dame: University of Notre Dame Press, 1976.

Meinertz, Max. "Zum Ursprung der Heidenmission." *Biblica* 40 (1959): 762-77.

Mercer, Calvin. "Ἀποστέλλειν and Πέμπειν in John." *New Testament Studies* 36 (1990): 619-24.

————. "Jesus the Apostle: 'Sending' and the Theology of John." *Journal of the Evangelical Theological Society* 35 (1992): 457-62.

Michel, Otto. "Die Botenlehre des vierten Evangeliums." *Theologische Beiträge* 7 (1976): 56-60.

————. "Der aufsteigende und herabsteigende Gesandte." In *The New Testament Age: Essays in Honor of Bo Reicke*, edited by W. C. Weinrich, 2:335-61. Mercer: Macon, 1984.

Milne, Bruce. " 'Even So Send I You': An Expository and Theological Reflection on John 20:21." In *Mission to the World: Essays to Celebrate the 50th Anniversary of George*

Raymond Beasley-Murray to the Christian Ministry, edited by Paul Beasley-Murray, 47-51. A supplement to the *Baptist Quarterly,* 1991.

Minear, Paul S. "The Original Functions of John 21." *Journal of Biblical Literature* 102 (1983): 85-98.

Miranda, José Porfirio. *Being and the Messiah: The Message of St. John.* Maryknoll, N.Y.: Orbis, 1977.

Miranda, Juan Peter. *Der Vater der mich gesandt hat: Religionsgeschichtliche Untersuchungen zu den johanneischen Sendungsformeln. Zugleich ein Beitrag zur johanneischen Christologie und Ekklesiologie.* Europäische Hochschulschriften 23/7. Frankfurt am Main: Lang, 1972; 2d rev. ed., 1976.

————. *Die Sendung Jesu im vierten Evangelium: Religions- und theologiegeschichtliche Untersuchungen zu den Sendungsformeln.* Stuttgarter Bibelstudien 87. Stuttgart: Katholisches Bibelwerk, 1977.

Mlakuzhyil, George. *The Christocentric Literary Structure of the Fourth Gospel.* Analecta Biblica 117. Rome: Pontifical Bible Institute, 1987.

Moloney, Francis J. "The Johannine Son of Man." *Biblical Theology Bulletin* 6 (1976): 177-89.

————. *The Johannine Son of Man.* Biblioteca di Scienze Religiose 14. 2d ed. Rome: Libreria Ateneo Salesiano, 1978.

Moo, Douglas J. *The Old Testament in the Gospel Passion Narratives.* Sheffield: Almond, 1983.

Mörchen, Roland. " 'Weggehen.' Beobachtungen zu Joh 12,36b." *Biblische Zeitschrift* 28 (1984): 240-42.

Moreno, Ramón. "El discípulo de Jesucristo, según el evangelio de S. Juan." *Estudios bíblicos* 30 (1971): 269-311.

Moreton, M. B. "The Beloved Disciple Again." In *Studia Biblica 1978. II. Papers on the Gospels.* Journal for the Study of the New Testament Supplement Series 2, edited by E. A. Livingstone, 215-18. Sheffield: JSOT, 1980.

Morgan-Wynne, J. E. "The Cross and the Revelation of Jesus as ἐγώ εἰμι in the Fourth Gospel (John 8.28)." In *Studia Biblica 1978. II. Papers on the Gospels.* Journal for the Study of the New Testament Supplement Series 2, edited by E. A. Livingstone, 219-26. Sheffield: JSOT, 1980.

Morris, Leon L. *Studies in the Fourth Gospel.* Grand Rapids: Wm. B. Eerdmans, 1969.

————. *The Gospel According to John.* New International Commentary on the New Testament. Grand Rapids: Wm. B. Eerdmans, 1971.

————. "The Composition of the Fourth Gospel." In *Scripture, Tradition and Interpretation,* edited by W. Ward Gasque and William Sanford LaSor, 157-75. Grand Rapids: Wm. B. Eerdmans, 1973.

————. "The Atonement in John's Gospel." *Criswell Theological Review* 3 (1988): 49-64.

————. *Jesus Is the Christ: Studies in the Theology of John.* Grand Rapids: Wm. B. Eerdmans, 1989.

————. "The Jesus of Saint John." In *Unity and Diversity in New Testament Theology: Essays in Honor of George E. Ladd,* ed. Robert A. Guelich, 37-53. Grand Rapids: Wm. B. Eerdmans, 1978.

Morrison, Clifton D. "Mission and Ethic: An Interpretation of Jn 17." *Interpretation* 19 (1965): 259-73.

Moule, Charles Francis Digby. "The Individualism of the Fourth Gospel." In *Essays in New Testament Interpretation,* 91-109. Cambridge: Cambridge University Press, 1982.

————. "Neglected Features in the Problem of 'the Son of Man.' " In *Neues Testament und Kirche: Festschrift für Rudolf Schnackenburg,* edited by Joachim Gnilka, 413-28. Freiburg im Breisgau: Herder, 1974.

————. *The Origin of Christology.* Cambridge: Cambridge University Press, 1977.

Mowvley, Henry. "John 1,14-18 in the Light of Exodus 33,7–34,35." *Expository Times* 95, no. 5 (1984): 135-37.

Müller, Karlheinz. "Joh 9,7 und das jüdische Verständnis des Siloh-Spruches." *Biblische Zeitschrift* 13 (1969): 251-56.

Müller, Theophil. *Das Heilsgeschehen im Johannesevangelium: Eine exegetische Studie, zugleich der Versuch einer Antwort an Rudolf Bultmann.* Zürich/Frankfurt am Main: Gotthelf, 1961.

Müller, Ulrich B. "Die Bedeutung des Kreuzestodes Jesu im Johannesevangelium: Erwägungen zur Kreuzestheologie im Neuen Testament." *Kerygma und Dogma* 21 (1975): 49-71.

————. *Die Geschichte der Christologie in der johanneischen Gemeinde.* Stuttgarter Bibelstudien 77. Stuttgart: Katholisches Bibelwerk, 1975.

Mußner, Franz. ΖΩΗ. *Die Anschauung vom "Leben" im vierten Evangelium unter Berücksichtigung der Johannesbriefe.* Münchener Theologische Studien I/5. München: Karl Zink, 1952.

————. *The Historical Jesus in the Gospel of St John.* Quaestiones Disputatae 19. Translated by W. J. O'Hara. New York: Herder and Herder, 1967.

————. "Ursprünge und Entfaltung der neutestamentlichen Sohneschristologie: Versuch einer Rekonstruktion." In *Grundfragen der Christologie heute.* Quaestiones Disputatae 72, edited by Leo Scheffczyk, 77-113. Freiburg im Breisgau: Herder, 1975.

————. "Die 'semantische Achse' des Johannesevangeliums. Ein Versuch." In *Vom Urchristentum zu Jesus: Für Joachim Gnilka,* edited by Hubert Frankemölle and Karl Kertelge, 246-55. Freiburg im Breisgau: Herder, 1989.

Napole, Gabriel M. "Pedro y el discípulo amado en Juan 21,1-25." *Revista bíblica* 52, NS 39 (1990): 153-77.

Neill, Stephen. *Christian Faith and Other Faiths.* London: Oxford University Press, 1961.

Neirynck, Frans. "The 'Other Disciple' in Jn 18,15-16." *Ephemerides Theologicae Lovanienses* 51 (1975): 113-41.

Nereparampil, Lucius. *Destroy This Temple: An Exegetico-Theological Study on the Meaning of Jesus' Temple-Logion in Jn 2:19.* Bangalore: Dharmaram Publications, 1978.

Netland, Harold A. *Dissonant Voices: Religious Pluralism and the Question of Truth.* Grand Rapids: Wm. B. Eerdmans, 1991.

Neusner, Jacob, William Scott Green, and Ernest S. Frerichs, eds. *Judaisms and Their Messiahs at the Turn of the Christian Era.* Cambridge: Cambridge University Press, 1987.

Nicholson, Godfrey Carruthers. *Death as Departure: The Johannine Descent-Ascent Schema.* SBL Dissertation Series 63. Chico, Calif.: Scholars Press, 1983.

Nicol, Willem. *The Semeia in the Fourth Gospel: Tradition and Redaction.* Novum Testamentum Supplements 32. Leiden: E. J. Brill, 1972.

Nida, Eugene A. "The Implications of Contemporary Linguistics for Biblical Scholarship." *Journal of Biblical Literature* 91 (1972): 73-89.

O'Day, Gail. *Revelation in the Fourth Gospel: Narrative Mode and Theological Claim.* Philadelphia: Fortress, 1986.

Oehler, Wilhelm. *Das Johannesevangelium, eine Missionsschrift für die Welt, der Gemeinde ausgelegt.* Gütersloh: Bertelsmann, 1936.

————. *Das Johannesevangelium, eine Missionsschrift für die Welt*. 3 vols. Württemberg: Buchhandlung der Evangelischen Missionsschule Unterweissach, 1957.

————. *Zum Missionscharakter des Johannesevangeliums*. Gütersloh: Bertelsmann, 1941.

Oepke, Albrecht. "Das missionarische Christuszeugnis des Johannesevangeliums." *Evangelische Missions-Zeitschrift* 2 (1941): 4-26.

Okure, Teresa. *The Johannine Approach to Mission: A Contextual Study of John 4:1-42*. Wissenschaftliche Untersuchungen zum Neuen Testament 2/31. Tübingen: J. C. B. Mohr (Paul Siebeck), 1988.

Oliveira, J.-C. Pinto de. "Le verbe ΔΙΔΟΝΑΙ comme expression des rapports du Père et du Fils dans le IVe Évangile." *Revue des sciences philosophiques et théologiques* 49 (1965): 81-104.

Olsson, Birger. *Structure and Meaning in the Fourth Gospel: A Text-Linguistic Analysis of John 2:1-11 and 4:1-42*. Coniectanea Biblica, New Testament 6. Lund: Gleerup, 1974.

Onuki, Takashi. *Gemeinde und Welt im Johannesevangelium: Ein Beitrag zur Frage nach der theologischen und pragmatischen Funktion des johanneischen "Dualismus."* Wissenschaftliche Monographien zum Alten und Neuen Testament 56. Neukirchen-Vluyn: Neukirchener, 1984.

Osborne, Grant R. *The Hermeneutical Spiral: A Comprehensive Introduction to Biblical Interpretation*. Downers Grove, Ill.: InterVarsity, 1991.

————. "Redactional Trajectories in the Crucifixion Narrative." *Evangelical Quarterly* 51 (1979): 80-96.

Osten-Sacken, Peter von der. "Leistung und Grenze der johanneischen Kreuzestheologie." *Evangelische Theologie* 36 (1976): 154-76.

Painter, John. *John: Witness and Theologian*. London: SPCK, 1975.

————. "The Farewell Discourses and the History of Johannine Christianity." *New Testament Studies* 27 (1981): 525-43.

————. "Christology and the History of the Johannine Community in the Prologue of the Fourth Gospel." *New Testament Studies* 30 (1984): 460-74.

————. "The Enigmatic Johannine Son of Man." In *The Four Gospels 1992: Festschrift Frans Neirynck*. Bibliotheca Ephemeridum Theologicarum Lovaniensium C, edited by F. van Segbroeck, C. M. Tuckett, G. van Belle, and J. Verheyden, vol. 3, 1869-87. Leuven: University Press, 1992.

————. "Tradition, History and Interpretation in John 10." In *The Shepherd Discourse of John 10 and Its Context*, edited by Johannes Beutler and Robert T. Fortna, 53-74. Society for New Testament Studies Monograph Series 67. Cambridge: Cambridge University Press, 1991.

Pamment, Margaret. "The Fourth Gospel's Beloved Disciple." *Expository Times* 94 (1983): 363-67.

————. "The Son of Man in the Fourth Gospel." *Journal of Theological Studies* 36 (1985): 56-66.

————. "Path and Residence Metaphors in the Fourth Gospel." *Theology* 88 (1985): 118-24.

Pancaro, Severino. "'People of God' in St John's Gospel?" *New Testament Studies* 16 (1970): 114-29.

————. *The Law in the Fourth Gospel: The Torah and the Gospel, Moses and Jesus, Judaism and Christianity According to John*. Supplements to Novum Testamentum 42. Leiden: E. J. Brill, 1975.

————. "The Relationship of the Church to Israel in the Gospel of St. John." *New Testament Studies* 21 (1975): 396-405.

Parker, James. "The Incarnational Christology of John." *Criswell Theological Review* 3 (1988): 31-48.

Paschal, R. Wade. "Farewell Discourse." In *Dictionary of Jesus and the Gospels*, edited by Joel B. Green, Scot McKnight, and I. Howard Marshall, 229-33. Downers Grove, Ill.: InterVarsity, 1992.

Peters, George W. *A Biblical Theology of Missions*. Chicago: Moody, 1972.

Peterson, Peter M. *Andrew, Brother of Simon Peter: His History and His Legends*. Supplements to Novum Testamentum 1. Leiden: E. J. Brill, 1963.

Pietrantonio, Ricardo. "'El Mesías permanece para siempre' (Juan 12:12-36)." *Revista bíblica* 47 (1985): 121-42.

————. "Los 'Judaioi' en el evangelio de Juan." *Revista bíblica* 47 (1985): 27-41.

Pinnock, Clark. "The Finality of Jesus Christ in a World of Religions." In *Christian Faith and Practice in the Modern World*, edited by Mark A. Noll and David F. Wells, 152-68. Grand Rapids: Wm. B. Eerdmans, 1988.

————. *A Wideness in God's Mercy*. Grand Rapids: Zondervan, 1992.

Pollard, T. E. *Johannine Christology and the Early Church*. Cambridge: Cambridge University Press, 1970.

Popkes, Wiard. "Zum Verständnis der Mission bei Johannes." *Zeitschrift für Mission* 4 (1978): 63-69.

Porsch, Felix. *Pneuma und Wort: Ein exegetischer Beitrag zur Pneumatologie des Johannesevangeliums*. Frankfurter Theologische Studien 16. Frankfurt am Main: Josef Knecht, 1974.

Porter, Stanley E. *Verbal Aspect in the Greek of the New Testament, with Reference to Tense and Mood*. New York: Peter Lang, 1989.

Potterie, Ignace de la. "La notion de témoignage chez Saint Jean." In *Sacra Pagina II*, 193-208. Paris: J. Gabalda, 1959.

Prescott-Ezickson, Robert. "The Sending Motif in the Gospel of John: Implications for Theology of Mission." Ph.D. diss., Southern Baptist Theological Seminary, 1986.

Pritchard, Gregory D., ed. *Hermeneutics, Religious Pluralism, and Truth*. Winston-Salem, N.C.: Wake Forest University, 1989.

Pryor, John W. "Covenant and Community in John's Gospel." *Reformed Theological Review* 47 (1988): 44-51.

————. "Jesus and Israel in the Fourth Gospel — John 1:11." *Novum Testamentum* 32 (1990): 201-18.

————. *John: Evangelist of the Covenant People: The Narrative and Themes of the Fourth Gospel*. Downers Grove, Ill.: InterVarsity, 1992.

Quast, Kevin. *Peter and the Beloved Disciple: Figures for a Community in Crisis*. Journal for the Study of the New Testament Supplement Series 32. Sheffield: JSOT, 1989.

Radermakers, Jean. "Mission et Apostolat dans l'Évangile Johannique." In *Studia Evangelica II/1*, edited by Frank L. Cross, 100-121. Texte und Untersuchungen 87. Berlin: Akademie, 1964.

Reim, Günter. *Studien zum alttestamentlichen Hintergrund des Johannesevangeliums*. Society for New Testament Studies Monograph Series 22. Cambridge: Cambridge University Press, 1974.

————. "Jesus as God in the Fourth Gospel: The Old Testament Background." *New Testament Studies* 30 (1984): 158-60.

Rengstorf, Karl-Heinz. "ἀποστέλλω, et al." In *Theological Dictionary of the New Testament*, edited by Gerhard Kittel, 1:398-446. Translated by Geoffrey W. Bromiley. Grand Rapids: Wm. B. Eerdmans, 1964.

———. "μανθάνω, et al." In *Theological Dictionary of the New Testament*, edited by Gerhard Kittel, 4:390-461. Translated by Geoffrey W. Bromiley. Grand Rapids: Wm. B. Eerdmans, 1967.

———. "σημεῖον, et al." In *Theological Dictionary of the New Testament*, edited by Gerhard Friedrich, 7:200-269. Translated by Geoffrey W. Bromiley. Grand Rapids: Wm. B. Eerdmans, 1971.

Rensberger, David. Review of *Gemeinde und Welt im Johannesevangelium: Ein Beitrag zur Frage nach der theologischen und pragmatischen Funktion des johanneischen "Dualismus,"* by Takashi Onuki. *Journal of Biblical Literature* 105 (1986): 728-31.

———. *Overcoming the World: Politics and Community in the Gospel of John.* London: SPCK, 1989.

———. *Johannine Faith and Liberating Community.* Philadelphia: Westminster, 1988.

Rhea, Robert. *The Johannine Son of Man.* Abhandlungen zur Theologie des Alten und Neuen Testaments 76. Zürich: Theologischer, 1990.

Richard, Earl. "Expressions of Double Meaning and Their Function in the Gospel of John." *New Testament Studies* 31 (1985): 96-112.

Richter, Georg. "Die Deutung des Kreuzestodes Jesu in der Leidensgeschichte des Johannesevangeliums (Jo 13–19)." *Bibel und Leben* 9 (1968): 21-36.

———. "Zum gemeindebildenden Element in den johanneischen Schriften." In *Studien zum Johannesevangelium,* 383-414. Biblische Untersuchungen 13. Regensburg: Friedrich Pustet, 1977.

Riedl, Johannes. "Die Funktion der Kirche nach Johannes: 'Vater, wie du mich in die Welt gesandt hast, so habe ich auch sie in die Welt gesandt' (Joh 17, 18)." *Bibel und Kirche* 28 (1973): 12-14.

———. *Das Heilswerk Jesu nach Johannes.* Freiburger Theologische Studien 93. Freiburg im Breisgau: Herder, 1973.

Riesner, Rainer. *Jesus als Lehrer.* Wissenschaftliche Untersuchungen zum Neuen Testament 2/7. 3d ed. Tübingen: J. C. B. Mohr (Paul Siebeck), 1988.

Riga, Peter J. "Signs of Glory: The Use of Semeion in John's Gospel." *Interpretation* 17 (1963): 402-10.

Rissi, Mathias. "Der Aufbau des vierten Evangeliums." *New Testament Studies* 29 (1983): 48-54.

Ritt, Hubert. "Die Frau als Glaubensbotin: Zum Verständnis der Samaritanerin von Joh 4,1-42." In *Vom Urchristentum zu Jesus: Für Joachim Gnilka,* edited by Hubert Frankemölle and Karl Kertelge, 287-306. Freiburg im Breisgau: Herder, 1989.

Robertson, Archibald Thomas. *The Divinity of Christ in the Gospel of John.* New York: Fleming H. Revell, 1916.

Robinson, John Arthur Thomas. "The 'Others' of John 4.38. A Test of Exegetical Method." In *Studia Evangelica I,* edited by Kurt Aland et al., 510-15. Texte und Untersuchungen 73. Berlin: Akademie, 1959.

———. "The Destination and Purpose of St John's Gospel." *New Testament Studies* 6 (1959-60): 117-31.

———. "The Use of the Fourth Gospel for Christology Today." In *Christ and Spirit in the New Testament: Essays in Honor of Charles Francis Digby Moule,* edited by Barnabas Lindars and Stephen S. Smalley, 61-78. Cambridge: Cambridge University Press, 1973.

————. *Redating the New Testament.* London: SCM, 1976.

————. *The Priority of John.* London: SCM, 1985.

————. *Twelve New Testament Studies.* Studies in Biblical Theology 34. London: SCM, 1962.

Roloff, Jürgen. "Der johanneische 'Lieblingsjünger' und der Lehrer der Gerechtigkeit." *New Testament Studies* 15 (1968-69): 129-51.

Rosenkranz, Gerhard. *Die christliche Mission: Geschichte und Theologie.* München: Chr. Kaiser, 1977.

Ruckstuhl, Eugen. "Die johanneische Menschensohnforschung 1957-1969." In *Theologische Berichte 1,* edited by Josef Pfammatter and Franz Furger, 171-284. Zürich: Benziger, 1972.

————. "Abstieg und Erhöhung des johanneischen Menschensohnes." In *Jesus und der Menschensohn: Für Anton Vögtle,* edited by Rudolf Pesch and Rudolf Schnackenburg, 314-41. Freiburg im Breisgau: Herder, 1975.

————. "Johannine Language and Style." In *L'Évangile de Jean. Sources, Rédaction, Théologie.* Bibliotheca Ephemeridum Theologicarum Lovaniensium 44, edited by Marinus de Jonge, 125-47. Leuven: Gembleux, 1977.

————. *Die literarische Einheit des Johannesevangeliums. Der gegenwärtige Stand der einschlägigen Forschung.* Novum Testamentum et Orbis Antiquus 5. Göttingen: Vandenhoeck & Ruprecht, 1987 [1951].

Ruckstuhl, Eugen and Peter Dschulnigg. *Stilkritik und Verfasserfrage im Johannesevangelium: Die johanneischen Sprachmerkmale auf dem Hintergrund des Neuen Testaments und des zeitgenössischen hellenistischen Schrifttums.* Novum Testamentum et Orbis Antiquus 17. Göttingen: Vandenhoeck & Ruprecht, 1991.

Ruiz, Miguel Rodriguez. *Der Missionsgedanke des Johannesevangeliums: Ein Beitrag zur johanneischen Soteriologie und Ekklesiologie.* Forschung zur Bibel 55. Würzburg: Echter, 1986.

Sanders, E. P. *Jesus and Judaism.* Philadelphia: Fortress, 1985.

Sanders, John N. *A Commentary on the Gospel According to St. John.* London: Adam & Charles Black, 1968.

Sanders, John. *No Other Name: An Investigation into the Destiny of the Unevangelized.* Grand Rapids: Wm. B. Eerdmans, 1992.

Schlatter, Adolf. *Der Evangelist Johannes: Wie er spricht, denkt und glaubt.* 2d ed. Stuttgart: Calwer, 1948.

Schnackenburg, Rudolf. "Das Brot des Lebens," in *Das Johannesevangelium,* vol. 4, *Ergänzende Auslegungen und Exkurse.* Herders theologischer Kommentar zum Neuen Testament, 119-31. Freiburg im Breisgau: Herder, 1984.

————. "Die Erwartung des 'Propheten' nach dem Neuen Testament und den Qumran-Texten." In *Studia Evangelica I,* edited by Frank L. Cross, 622-39. Texte und Untersuchungen 73. Berlin: Akademie, 1959.

————. "Die Messiasfrage im Johannesevangelium." In *Neutestamentliche Aufsätze. Festschrift für Josef Schmid,* edited by Josef Blinzler, Otto Kuss, and Franz Mußner, 240-64. Regensburg: Friedrich Pustet, 1963.

————. "Der Menschensohn im Johannesevangelium." *New Testament Studies* 11 (1964/65): 123-37.

————. *The Gospel According to St. John.* Herder's Theological Commentary on the New Testament. 3 vols. New York: Crossroad, 1990 [1965, 1971, 1975].

————. "Der Jünger, den Jesus liebte." In *Evangelisch-Katholischer Kommentar zum Neuen Testament: Vorarbeiten.* 2:105-7. Zürich: Neukirchener, 1970.

————. "Is There a Johannine Ecclesiology?" In *A Companion to John: Readings in Johannine Theology,* edited by Michael J. Taylor, 247-56. New York: Alba, 1977.

————. "Ist der Gedanke des Sühnetodes Jesu der einzige Zugang zum Verständnis unserer Erlösung durch Jesus Christus?" In *Der Tod Jesu: Deutungen im Neuen Testament.* Quaestiones Disputatae 74, edited by Karl Kartelge, 205-30. Freiburg im Breisgau: Herder, 1978.

————. "Der Missionsgedanke des Johannesevangeliums im heutigen Horizont." In *Das Johannesevangelium,* vol. 4, *Ergänzende Auslegungen und Exkurse.* Herders theologischer Kommentar zum Neuen Testament, 58-72. Freiburg im Breisgau: Herder, 1984.

————. "The Disciples, the Community and the Church in the Gospel of John." In *The Gospel According to St. John,* vol. 3. Herder's Theological Commentary on the New Testament. New York: Crossroad, 1990 [1975].

————. " 'Der Vater, der mich gesandt hat': Zur johanneischen Christologie." In *Anfänge der Christologie: Festschrift für Ferdinand Hahn zum 65. Geburtstag,* edited by Cilliers Breytenbach and Henning Paulsen, 275-91. Göttingen: Vandenhoeck & Ruprecht, 1991.

Schneider, Gerhard. "Präexistenz Christi: Der Ursprung einer neutestamentlichen Vorstellung und das Problem ihrer Auslegung." In *Neues Testament und Kirche: Festschrift für Rudolf Schnackenburg,* edited by Joachim Gnilka, 399-412. Freiburg im Breisgau: Herder, 1974.

————. "Der Missionsauftrag Jesu in der Darstellung der Evangelien." In *Mission im Neuen Testament.* Quaestiones Disputatae 93, ed. Karl Kertelge, 71-92. Freiburg im Breisgau: Herder, 1982.

Schnelle, Udo. *Antidocetic Christology in the Gospel of John: An Investigation of the Place of the Fourth Gospel in the Johannine School.* Translated by Linda M. Maloney. Minneapolis: Fortress, 1992.

————. "Die Abschiedsreden im Johannesevangelium." *Zeitschrift für die neutestamentliche Wissenschaft* 80 (1989): 64-79.

————. "Johanneische Ekklesiologie." *New Testament Studies* 37 (1991): 37-50.

Schottroff, Luise. *Der Glaubende und die feindliche Welt: Beobachtungen zum gnostischen Dualismus und seine Bedeutung für Paulus und das Johannesevangelium.* Wissenschaftliche Monographien zum Alten und Neuen Testament 37. Neukirchen-Vluyn: Neukirchener, 1970.

Schulz, Anselm. *Nachfolgen und Nachahmen: Studien über das Verhältnis der neutestamentlichen Jüngerschaft zur urchristlichen Vorbildethik.* Studien zum Alten und Neuen Testament 6. München: Kösel, 1962.

Schulz, Siegfried. *Das Evangelium nach Johannes.* 13th ed. Göttingen: Vandenhoeck & Ruprecht, 1975.

————. *Untersuchungen zur Menschensohn-Christologie im Johannesevangelium: Zugleich ein Beitrag zur Methodengeschichte der Auslegung des 4. Evangeliums.* Göttingen: Vandenhoeck & Ruprecht, 1957.

Schweizer, Eduard. *Ego Eimi: Die religionsgeschichtliche Herkunft und theologische Bedeutung der johanneischen Bildreden, zugleich ein Beitrag zur Quellenfrage des vierten Evangeliums.* Forschungen zur Religion und Literatur des Alten und Neuen Testaments 56, NF 38. Göttingen: Vandenhoeck & Ruprecht, 1939.

————. "Der Kirchenbegriff im Evangelium und den Briefen des Johannes." In *Studia Evangelica I,* edited by Kurt Aland et al., 363-81. Texte und Untersuchungen 73. Berlin: Akademie, 1959.

————. "Jesus as the One Obedient in Suffering and Therefore Exalted to the Father." In *Lordship and Discipleship*, 68-76. Studies in Biblical Theology 28. Naperville, Ill.: Alec R. Allenson, 1960 [1955].

————. "Discipleship after Easter." In *Lordship and Discipleship*, 77-92. Studies in Biblical Theology 28. Naperville, Ill.: Alec R. Allenson, 1960 [1955].

————. "Zum religionsgeschichtlichen Hintergrund der 'Sendungsformel' Gal 4,4f, Röm 8,3f, Joh 3,16f, 1 Joh 4,9." *Zeitschrift für die neutestamentliche Wissenschaft* 57 (1966): 199-210.

————. "Was meinen wir eigentlich, wenn wir sagen 'Gott sandte seinen Sohn . . .'?" *New Testament Studies* 37 (1991): 204-24.

Segovia, Fernando. "The Love and Hatred of Jesus and Johannine Sectarianism." *Catholic Biblical Quarterly* 43 (1981): 258-72.

Seidensticker, Philip. *Die Auferstehung Jesu in der Botschaft der Evangelisten*. Stuttgarter Bibelstudien 26. Stuttgart: Katholisches Bibelwerk, 1968.

Senior, Donald, and Carroll Stuhlmueller. *The Biblical Foundations for Mission*. Maryknoll, N.Y.: Orbis, 1983.

Seynaeve, Jaak. "Les verbes ἀποστέλλω et πέμπω dans le vocabulaire théologique de Saint Jean." In *L'Évangile de Jean. Sources, Rédaction, Théologie*, Bibliotheca Ephemeridum Theologicarum Lovaniensium 44, edited by Marinus de Jonge, 385-89. Leuven: Gembleux, 1977.

Shepherd, M. H. "The Twelve." In *The Interpreter's Dictionary of the Bible*. Vol. 4:719. New York: Abingdon, 1962.

Sidebottom, Ernest M. "The Ascent and Descent of the Son of Man in the Gospel of St. John." *Anglican Theological Review* 39 (1957): 115-22.

————. *The Christ of the Fourth Gospel in the Light of First-Century Thought*. London: SPCK, 1961.

Siker-Gieseler, Jeffrey S. "Disciples and Discipleship in the Fourth Gospel: A Canonical Approach." *Studia Biblica et Theologica* 10 (1980): 199-227.

Silva, Moisés. *Biblical Words and Their Meanings: An Introduction to Lexical Semantics*. Grand Rapids: Zondervan, 1983.

————. *God, Language, and Scripture: Reading the Bible in the Light of General Linguistics*. Grand Rapids: Zondervan, 1990.

————. *Philippians*. Baker Exegetical Commentary on the New Testament. Grand Rapids: Baker, 1992.

————. Review of *Greek-English Lexicon Based on Semantic Domains* by Johannes P. Louw and Eugene A. Nida. *Westminster Theological Journal* 51 (1989): 163-67.

Simon, U. E. "Eternal Life in the Fourth Gospel." *Studies in the Fourth Gospel*, edited by Frank L. Cross, 97-109. London: A. R. Mowbray, 1957.

Smalley, Stephen S. "The Sign in John XXI." *New Testament Studies* 20 (1974): 275-88.

————. *John: Evangelist and Interpreter: History and Interpretation in the Fourth Gospel*. Greenwood, S.C.: Attic, 1978.

————. "The Johannine Son of Man Sayings." *New Testament Studies* 15 (1979): 278-301.

Smith, D. Moody. *The Composition and Order of the Fourth Gospel: Bultmann's Literary Theory*. New Haven: Yale University Press, 1965.

————. "The Presentation of Jesus in the Fourth Gospel." In *Johannine Christianity — Essays on Its Setting, Sources, and Theology*, 175-89. Columbia, S.C.: University of South Carolina, 1984.

————. "Johannine Studies." In *The New Testament and Its Modern Interpreters*, edited by Eldon Jay Epp and George W. MacRae, 271-96. Atlanta: Scholars Press, 1989.

————. "The Contribution of J. Louis Martyn to the Understanding of the Gospel of John." In *The Conversation Continues: Studies in Paul and John in Honor of J. Louis Martyn,* edited by Robert T. Fortna and Beverly R. Gaventa, 275-94. Nashville: Abingdon, 1990.

Smith, Robert Houston. "Exodus Typology in the Fourth Gospel." *Journal of Biblical Literature* 81 (1962): 329-42.

Smith, Taylor Clarence. "The Christology of the Fourth Gospel." *Review and Expositor* 71 (1974): 19-30.

Snyder, Graydon F. "John 13.16 and the Anti-Petrinism of the Johannine Tradition." *Biblical Research* 16 (1971): 5-15.

Stählin, Gustav Wilhelm. "Κατὰ τὸ θέλημα τοῦ θεοῦ: Von der Dynamik der urchristlichen Mission." In *Wort und Geist: Studien zur christlichen Erkenntnis von Gott, Welt und Mensch: Festgabe für Karl Heim,* edited by Adolf Köberle and Otto Schmitz, 99-119. Berlin: Furche, 1934.

Stibbe, Mark W. G. *John as Storyteller: Narrative Criticism and the Fourth Gospel.* Society for New Testament Studies Monograph Series 73. Cambridge: Cambridge University Press, 1992.

————. " 'Return to Sender': A Structuralist Approach to John's Gospel." *Biblical Interpretation* 1 (1993): 189-206.

Stolz, Fritz. "Zeichen und Wunder: Die prophetische Legitimation und ihre Geschichte." *Zeitschrift für Theologie und Kirche* 69 (1972): 125-44.

Stott, John R. W. *Christian Mission in the Modern World.* London: Church Pastoral Aid Society, 1975.

————. *The Contemporary Christian: Applying God's Word to Today's World.* Downers Grove, Ill.: InterVarsity, 1992.

————. "An Open Letter to David Hesselgrave." *Trinity World Forum* 16, no. 3 (1991): 1-2.

Suggit, J. N. "Nicodemus — The True Jew." *Neotestamentica* 14 (1981): 90-110.

Sullivan, Barry F. "Ego Te Absolvo: The Forgiveness of Sins in the Context of the Pneumatic Community." Th.M. thesis, Grand Rapids Baptist Theological Seminary, 1988.

Sundberg, Albert C., Jr. "Christology in the Fourth Gospel." *Biblical Research* 21 (1976): 29-37.

Talbert, Charles H. "The Myth of a Descending-Ascending Redeemer in Mediterranean Antiquity." *New Testament Studies* 22 (1976): 418-40.

————. "Appendix: Descending-Ascending Redeemer Figures in Mediterranean Antiquity." In *Reading John: A Literary and Theological Commentary on the Fourth Gospel and the Johannine Epistles,* 265-84. New York: Crossroad, 1992.

Tarelli, C. C. "Johannine Synonyms." *Journal of Theological Studies* 47 (1946): 175-77.

Tenney, Merrill C. *John.* Expositor's Bible Commentary, vol. 9. Grand Rapids: Zondervan, 1981.

Theron, S. W. " Ἵνα ὦσιν ἕν: A Multi-Faceted Approach to an Important Thrust in the Prayer of Jesus in John 17." *Neotestamentica* 21 (1987): 77-94.

Thiselton, Anthony C. *New Horizons in Hermeneutics.* Grand Rapids: Zondervan, 1992.

————. "Semantics and New Testament Interpretation." In *New Testament Interpretation,* edited by I. Howard Marshall, 75-104. Grand Rapids: Wm. B. Eerdmans, 1977.

————. *The Two Horizons: New Testament Hermeneutics and Philosophical Description.* Grand Rapids: Wm. B. Eerdmans, 1980.

Thompson, Marianne Meye. "The Historical Jesus and the Johannine Christ," in *Explor-*

ing the Gospel of John: In Honor of D. Moody Smith, edited by R. Alan Culpepper and C. Clifton Black, 21-42. Louisville, Ky.: Westminster John Knox, 1996.

————. *The Humanity of Jesus in the Fourth Gospel.* Philadelphia: Fortress, 1988.

————. "Signs and Faith in the Fourth Gospel." *Bulletin for Biblical Research* 1 (1991): 89-108.

Thüsing, Wilhelm. *Die Erhöhung und Verherrlichung Jesu im Johannesevangelium.* Neutestamentliche Abhandlungen 21, 1/2. Münster: W. Aschendorff, 1979.

Tröger, Karl-Wolfgang. "Ja oder Nein zur Welt: War der Evangelist Johannes Christ oder Gnostiker?" *Theologische Versuche* 7 (1976): 61-80.

Trudinger, L. Paul. "An Israelite in Whom There Is No Guile: An Interpretative Note on John 1,45-51." *Evangelical Quarterly* 54 (1982): 117-20.

Turner, Max. "Atonement and the Death of Jesus in John: Some Questions to Bultmann and Forestell." *Evangelical Quarterly* 62 (1990): 99-122.

Turner, Nigel. Volume 4, *Style.* In *A Grammar of New Testament Greek,* edited by James Hope Moulton. Edinburgh: T & T Clark, 1976.

Uro, R. *Sheep Among the Wolves: A Study on the Mission Instruction of Q.* Helsinki: Soumalainen Tiedeakatemia, 1987.

Vanhoye, Albert. "Témoignage et vie en Dieu selon le IV Évangile." *Christus* 16 (1951): 155-71.

————. "L'œuvre du Christ, don du Père (Jn. 5,36 et 17,4)." *Recherches de science religieuse* 48 (1960): 377-419.

van Unnik, W. C. "The Purpose of St. John's Gospel." In *Studia Evangelica I,* edited by Kurt Aland et al., 382-411. Texte und Untersuchungen 73. Berlin: Akademie, 1959.

————. "The Quotation from the Old Testament in John 12:34." *Novum Testamentum* 3 (1959): 174-79.

Vellanickal, Matthew. "Evangelization in the Johannine Writings." In *Good News and Witness,* edited by Lucien Legrand, J. Pathrapankal, and Matthew Vellanickal, 121-68. Bangalore: Theological Publications in India, 1973.

Veloso, Mario. "Sentido misional de la santificación en el evangelio de Juan." *Revista Bíblica* 35 (1973): 314-18.

————. *El Compromiso Cristiano: Un Estudio Sobre la Actualidad Misionera en el Evangelio de San Juan.* Buenos Aires: Zunino Ediciones, 1975.

————. "La vocación de los creyentes en Cristo según el evangelio de Juan." *Revista Bíblica* 38 (1976): 223-32.

Vergote, Antoine. "L'Exaltation du Christ en Croix selon le Quatrième Évangile." *Ephemerides theologicae lovanienses* 28 (1952): 5-23.

Verkuyl, Johannes. *Contemporary Missiology.* Grand Rapids: Wm B. Eerdmans, 1978 [1975].

Via, Dan O. "Darkness, Christ and Church in the Fourth Gospel." *Scottish Journal of Theology* 14 (1961): 172-93.

Viviano, Benedict T. "The Missionary Program of John's Gospel." *Bible Today* 22 (1984): 387-93.

Vorster, Willem S. "The Growth and Making of John 21." In *The Four Gospels 1992: Festschrift Frans Neirynck.* Bibliotheca Ephemeridum Theologicarum Lovaniensium C, edited by F. van Segbroeck, C. M. Tuckett, G. van Belle, and J. Verheyden, 3:2207-21. Leuven: University Press, 1992.

Wahlde, Urban C. von. "The Johannine 'Jews': A Critical Survey." *New Testament Studies* 28 (1982): 33-60.

Wall, Robert W., and Eugene E. Lemcio. *The New Testament as Canon: A Reader in*

Canonical Criticism. Journal for the Study of the New Testament Supplement Series 76. Sheffield: JSOT, 1992.

Watty, William W. "The Significance of Anonymity in the Fourth Gospel." *Expository Times* 90 (1979): 209-12.

Wengst, Klaus. *Bedrängte Gemeinde und verherrlichter Christus: Der historische Ort des Johannesevangeliums als Schlüssel zu seiner Interpretation.* Biblisch-theologische Studien 5. 2d ed. Neukirchen-Vluyn: Neukirchener, 1983.

Westcott, Brooke Foss. *The Gospel according to St. John.* Grand Rapids: Wm. B. Eerdmans, 1975 [1881].

Wilkens, Wilhelm. *Zeichen und Werke: Ein Beitrag zur Theologie des 4. Evangeliums in Erzählungs- und Redestoff.* Abhandlungen zur Theologie des Alten und Neuen Testaments 55. Zürich: Zwingli, 1969.

Wilkins, Michael J. *The Concept of Disciple in Matthew's Gospel as Reflected in the Use of the Term* Μαθητής. Supplements to Novum Testamentum 59. Leiden: E. J. Brill, 1988.

Wilson, S. G. *The Gentiles and the Gentile Mission in Luke-Acts.* Society for New Testament Studies Monograph Series 23. Cambridge: Cambridge University Press, 1973.

Wind, A. "Destination and Purpose of the Gospel of John." *Novum Testamentum* 14 (1972): 26-69.

Windisch, Hans. "Der johanneische Erzählungsstil." In ΕΥΧΑΡΙΣΤΗΡΙΟΝ. *Forschungen zur Religion und Literatur des Alten und Neuen Testaments* NS 19, edited by H. Schmidt, 2:174-213. Göttingen: Vandenhoeck & Ruprecht, 1923.

Winn, Albert Curry. *A Sense of Mission: Guidance from the Gospel of John.* Philadelphia: Westminster, 1981.

Winter, Paul. "Μονογενὴς παρὰ πατρός." *Zeitschrift für Religions- und Geistesgeschichte* 5 (1953): 335-65.

Wright, Charles J. H. "Jesus: The Revelation of God." In *The Mission and Message of Jesus — An Exposition of the Gospels in the Light of Modern Research,* edited by Henry D. A. Major, Thomas W. Manson, and Charles J. Wright, 643-956. New York: E. P. Dutton, 1938.

Yarbro-Collins, Adela. "Crisis and Community in John's Gospel." *Currents in Theology and Mission* 7 (1980): 196-204.

Young, Franklin W. "A Study of the Relation of Isaiah to the Fourth Gospel." *Zeitschrift für die neutestamentliche Wissenschaft* 46 (1955): 215-33.

Zimmermann, Heinrich. "Das absolute ἐγώ εἰμι als neutestamentliche Offenbarungs-formel." *Biblische Zeitschrift* 4 (1960): 54-69, 266-76.

Zumstein, Jean. "L'interprétation johannique de la mort du Christ." In *The Four Gospels 1992: Festschrift Frans Neirynck.* Bibliotheca Ephemeridum Theologicarum Lovaniensium C, edited by F. van Segbroeck, C. M. Tuckett, G. van Belle, and J. Verheyden, 3:2119-38. Leuven: University Press, 1992.

Index of Subjects

Index of Names

252

Index of Scripture References

257

Index of Greek Words